Hands-On Data Visualization

Interactive Storytelling from Spreadsheets to Code

Jack Dougherty and Ilya Ilyankou

Beijing · Boston · Farnham · Sebastopol · Tokyo

Hands-On Data Visualization

by Jack Dougherty and Ilya Ilyankou

Printed in the United States of America.

Published by O'Reilly Media, Inc., 1005 Gravenstein Highway North, Sebastopol, CA 95472.

O'Reilly books may be purchased for educational, business, or sales promotional use. Online editions are also available for most titles (*https://oreilly.com*). For more information, contact our corporate/institutional sales department: 800-998-9938 or *corporate@oreilly.com*.

Acquisitions Editor: Andy Kwan
Development Editor: Amelia Blevins
Production Editor: Katherine Tozer
Copyeditor: Stephanie English
Proofreader: Piper Editorial Consulting, LLC

Indexer: Sue Klefstad
Interior Designer: David Futato
Cover Designer: Karen Montgomery
Illustrator: O'Reilly Media

Revision History for the First Edition
2021-03-11:   First Release

See *https://oreilly.com/catalog/errata.csp?isbn=9781492086000* for release details.

978-1-492-08600-0

[LSC]

Table of Contents

Part II.   Building Visualizations

Preface

This introductory book teaches you how to tell your story and show it with data using free and easy-to-learn tools on the web. You'll discover how to design interactive charts and customized maps for your website, beginning with easy drag-and-drop tools, such as Google Sheets, Datawrapper, and Tableau Public. You'll also gradually learn how to edit open source code templates like Chart.js, Highcharts, and Leaflet on GitHub. Follow along with the step-by-step tutorials, real-world examples, and online resources. This book is ideal for students, educators, community activists, nonprofit organizations, small business owners, local governments, journalists, researchers, or anyone who wants to tell their story and show the data. No coding experience is required.

Audience and Overview

As educators, we designed this book to be accessible for new learners, to introduce key concepts in data visualization and reinforce them with hands-on examples. We assume no prior knowledge other than a basic familiarity with computers and some vague memories of secondary school mathematics. Based on feedback we received from an earlier draft, many readers across the globe have taught themselves with this book, and others educators are already using it as a textbook to teach their students.

Our subtitle, "Interactive Storytelling from Spreadsheets to Code," reflects how the scope of the book progresses from strengthening basic skills to editing open source code templates, while continually maintaining our focus on telling true and meaningful data stories. We explain both the *why* and the *how* of visualization, and encourage critical thinking about how data is socially constructed and whose interests are served or ignored.

Unlike many computer books that focus on selling you a specific software application, this book introduces you to more than 20 different visualization tools, all of them free and easy to learn. We also offer guiding principles on how to make wise choices among digital tools as they continue to evolve in the future. By working through the sample datasets and tutorials, you will create more than a dozen different interactive charts, maps, and tables, and share these data stories with other readers on the public web.

Although our introductory book is comprehensive, we do not address certain advanced topics. For example, while we discuss ways to make meaningful data comparisons, we do not delve into the field of statistical data analysis. Also, we focus primarily on software tools with a friendly graphical user interface (GUI), rather than those that require you to memorize and enter command-line instructions, such as the powerful R statistics packages (*https://www.r-project.org*). Finally, while we teach readers how to modify HTML-CSS-JavaScript code templates with the Chart.js, Highcharts, and Leaflet libraries, we do not explore more advanced visualization code libraries, such as D3 (*https://d3js.org*). Nevertheless, we believe that nearly everyone who reads this book will discover something new and valuable.

Advice for Hands-On Learning

Learn by following our step-by-step tutorials on a laptop or desktop computer with an internet connection. Most of the tools introduced in the book are web-based, and we recommend you use an up-to-date version of Firefox, Chrome, Safari, or Edge browsers. We advise against using Internet Explorer as this older browser is no longer correctly supported by many web services. A Mac or a Windows computer will allow you to complete all tutorials, but if you use a Chromebook or Linux computer, you still should be able to complete most of them, and we'll point out any limitations in specific sections. While it may be possible to complete some tutorials on a tablet or smartphone, we don't recommend it because these smaller devices will prevent you from completing several key steps.

If you're working on a laptop, consider buying or borrowing an external mouse that plugs into your computer. We've met several people who find it much easier to click, hover, and scroll with an external mouse than a laptop's built-in trackpad. If you're new to working with computers—or teaching newer users with this book—consider starting with basic computer and mouse tutorial skills from the Goodwill Community Foundation (*https://oreil.ly/8VLJb*). Also, if you're reading a digital version of this book on a laptop, consider connecting a second computer monitor or working with a tablet or second computer alongside you. This allows you to read the book on one screen and build data visualizations in the other screen.

Chapter Outline

The chapters in this book build up toward our central goal: telling true and meaningful stories with data.

The Introduction asks why data visualization matters and shows how charts, maps, and words can draw us farther into a story or deceive us from the truth.

Part I: Foundational Skills

Chapter 1 helps you navigate the process of sketching out your story and selecting which visualization tools you need to tell it effectively.

Chapter 2 starts with basics and moves on to ways of organizing and analyzing data with pivot tables and lookup formulas, as well as geocoding add-on tools and collecting data with online forms.

Chapter 3 offers concrete strategies for locating reliable information, while raising deeper questions about what data truly represents and whose interests it serves.

Chapter 4 introduces ways to spot and fix inconsistencies and duplicates with spreadsheets and more advanced tools, and also how to create extra tables from digital documents.

Chapter 5 provides common-sense strategies to begin analyzing and normalizing your data, while watching out for biased methods.

Part II: Building Visualizations

Chapter 6 teaches how to create visualizations with easy-to-learn drag-and-drop tools, and which ones work best with different data stories.

Chapter 7 focuses on building different types of visualizations that include a spatial element, and the challenges of designing true and meaningful maps.

Chapter 8 explains how to create interactive tables that include thumbnail visualizations called sparklines.

Chapter 9 connects prior chapters by demonstrating how to copy and modify embed codes to publish your visualizations online and share your work with wider audiences.

Part III: Code Templates and Advanced Tools

Chapter 10 walks through the web interface for this popular platform for modifying and sharing open source visualization code templates.

Chapter 11 brings together open source code templates to create charts you can customize and host anywhere on the web.

Chapter 12 gathers open source code templates to build a wider variety of maps to communicate your data story.

Chapter 13 takes a deeper look into geospatial data and easy-to-learn tools to customize data for your maps.

Part IV: Tell True, Meaningful Stories

Chapter 14 explores how to lie with charts and maps, to teach you how to do a better job of telling the truth.

Chapter 15 brings together all of the prior chapters to emphasize how data visualization is not simply about numbers, but truthful narratives that persuade readers how and why your interpretation matters.

The Appendix: Fix Common Problems serves as a guide for when your visualization tool or code doesn't work, which is also a great way to learn how it works.

Conventions Used in This Book

The following typographical conventions are used in this book:

Italic
> Indicates new terms, URLs, email addresses, filenames, column names, and file extensions.

`Constant width`
> Used for program listings, as well as within paragraphs to refer to program elements such as variable or function names, databases, data types, environment variables, statements, and keywords.

`Constant width bold`
> Shows commands or other text that should be typed literally by the user.

`Constant width italic`
> Shows text that should be replaced with user-supplied values or by values determined by context.

 This element signifies a tip or suggestion.

 This element signifies a general note.

 This element indicates a warning or caution.

O'Reilly Online Learning

O'REILLY® For more than 40 years, *O'Reilly Media* has provided technology and business training, knowledge, and insight to help companies succeed.

Our unique network of experts and innovators share their knowledge and expertise through books, articles, and our online learning platform. O'Reilly's online learning platform gives you on-demand access to live training courses, in-depth learning paths, interactive coding environments, and a vast collection of text and video from O'Reilly and 200+ other publishers. For more information, visit *http://oreilly.com*.

How to Contact Us

Please address comments and questions concerning this book to the publisher:

O'Reilly Media, Inc.
1005 Gravenstein Highway North
Sebastopol, CA 95472
800-998-9938 (in the United States or Canada)
707-829-0515 (international or local)
707-829-0104 (fax)

We have a web page for this book, where we list errata, examples, and any additional information. You can access this page at *https://learning.oreilly.com/library/view/~/9781492085997*.

Email *bookquestions@oreilly.com* to comment or ask technical questions about this book.

For news and information about our books and courses, visit *http://oreilly.com*.

Find us on Facebook: *http://facebook.com/oreilly*

Follow us on Twitter: *http://twitter.com/oreillymedia*

Watch us on YouTube: *http://www.youtube.com/oreillymedia*

Acknowledgments

In 2016, we launched an earlier draft of this book under a different title, *Data Visualization for All*, as part of an introductory course for Trinity College students and their community partners in Hartford, Connecticut to tell their organization's data stories through interactive charts and maps. Veronica X. Armendariz (Trinity Class of 2016) served as an outstanding teaching assistant and provided initial tutorials. The draft expanded in 2017 when we launched a free online Trinity edX course (*https://oreil.ly/-lq7k*) by the same name with our wonderful co-instructors Stacy Lam (Trinity Class of 2019) and David Tatem (Instructional Technologist), who contributed rich ideas and countless hours.

To date, more than 23,000 students have started the edX course, though only a small fraction actually complete the six-week curriculum (*https://oreil.ly/6QbUq*). Thanks also to the Trinity Information Technology Services staff and friends who produced edX course videos: Angie Wolf, Sean Donnelly, Ron Perkins, Samuel Oyebefun, Phil Duffy, and Christopher Brown. Funding for students who worked on the earlier draft was generously provided by the Office of Community Learning and Information Technology Services at Trinity College.

We thank the many individuals and organizations who helped us learn several of the skills that we teach in this book, especially Alvin Chang and Andrew Ba Tran, who were previously data journalists at *The Connecticut Mirror*; Michael Howser, Steve Batt, and their colleagues at the University of Connecticut Library Map and Geographic Information Center (MAGIC); and Jean-Pierre Haeberly, Director of Web Development at Trinity College. Also, thank you to everyone who inspired Jack to be *code-curious* at The Humanities and Technology Camp (THATCamp) events, sponsored by the Roy Rosenzweig Center for History and New Media at George Mason University and The Andrew W. Mellon Foundation, and encouraged him and his students to explore civic technology for the public good at the Transparency Camp sponsored by the Sunlight Foundation.

We also appreciated opportunities to share our work in progress at data workshops hosted by Scott Gaul and Doug Shipman, formerly at the Hartford Foundation for Public Giving, and Michelle Riordan-Nold at the Connecticut Data Collaborative.

Guided by feedback from readers, educators, and our editors, we rewrote the entire draft in 2020 to reorganize the structure, deepen the concepts, and enhance the tutorials. We thank everyone at O'Reilly Media who worked with us to bring you this finished product, especially our outstanding developmental editor, Amelia Blevins, our meticulous copy editor, Stephanie English, our well-organized production editor, Katie Tozer, and other members of their team: Nick Adams, Jonathan Hassel, and Andy Kwan. We also appreciate O'Reilly's support for three technical reviewers who provided excellent commentary that helped us to improve the manuscript: Carl Allchin, Derek Eder, and Erica Hayes.

Thanks also to readers who kindly shared feedback on the draft text or code templates: Jen Andrella, Gared Bard, Alberto Cairo, Fionnuala Darby-Hudgens, Nick Klagge, Federico Marini, Elizabeth Rose, Lisa Charlotte Rost, Xavier Ruiz, Laura Tateosian, Elizabeth von Briesen, and Colleen Wheeler.

Introduction

Why Data Visualization?

In this book, you'll learn how to create true and meaningful data visualizations through chapters that blend design principles and step-by-step tutorials to make your information-based analysis and arguments more insightful and compelling. Just as sentences become more persuasive with supporting evidence and source notes, your data-driven writing becomes more powerful when paired with appropriate tables, charts, or maps. Words tell us stories, but visualizations show us *data stories* by transforming quantitative, relational, or spatial patterns into images. When visualizations are well-designed, they draw our attention to what is most important in the data in ways that would be difficult to communicate through text alone.

Our book features a growing number of free and easy-to-learn digital tools for creating *data visualizations*. We broadly define this term primarily as *charts*, which encode data as images, and *maps*, which add a spatial dimension. While *tables* do not illustrate data in the same way, we include them in this book because of our pragmatic need to direct new learners through a decision-making process that often results in building one of these three products. Furthermore, in this digital era we define data visualizations as images that can be easily reused by modifying the underlying information, typically stored in a data file, in contrast to *infographics* that are generally designed as single-use artwork.[1]

---

1 Note that other data visualization books may use these terms differently. For example, all visualizations are defined as "charts" in Alberto Cairo, *How Charts Lie: Getting Smarter About Visual Information* (W.W. Norton & Company, 2019), *https://oreil.ly/wXcBX*, p. 23.

As educators, we designed *Hands-On Data Visualization* to introduce key concepts and provide step-by-step tutorials for new learners. You can teach yourself, or use the book to teach others. Also, unlike many technical books that focus solely on one tool, our book guides you on how to choose among more than 20 free and easy-to-use visualization tools that we recommend. Finally, while some other books focus on only *static* visualizations that can be distributed only on paper or PDF documents, we demonstrate how to design *interactive* tables, charts, and maps, and embed them on the web. Interactive visualizations engage wider audiences on the internet by inviting them to interact with the data, explore patterns that interest them, download files if desired, and easily share your work on social media.

Data visualizations have spread widely on the internet over the last decade. Today in our web browsers, we encounter more digital charts and maps than we previously saw in the print-only past. But rapid growth also raises serious problems. The "information age" now overlaps with the "age of disinformation." Now that nearly anyone can post online, how do you make wise decisions about whom to trust? When presented with conflicting data stories about divisive policy issues such as social inequality or climate change, which one do you believe? In the next section, we'll delve into this thorny topic by exploring what types of evidence persuades you, and why. And we'll share this dirty little secret about data visualization: it illuminates our path in pursuit of the truth, but it also empowers us to deceive and lie.

What Can You Believe?

To begin, how do you know whether to believe us, the authors of this book? Could we be lying to you? How do you determine what information is truthful? Let's start with a simple one-sentence statement.

Example I-1.

> *Economic inequality has sharply risen in the United States since the 1970s.*

Do you believe this claim—or not? Perhaps you've never thought about the topic in this particular way before now (and if so, there's a lot of information out there to help). It's possible your response depends on whether this statement blends in with your prior beliefs, or pushes against them. Or perhaps you've been taught to be skeptical of claims lacking supporting evidence (and if so, thank your teachers). So let's move on to a more complex two-sentence statement, one that cites a source.

Example I-2.

> *In 1970, the top 10% of US adults received an average income of about $135,000 in today's dollars, compared to the bottom 50% who earned around $16,500. This inequality gap grew sharply over the next five decades, as the top tier income climbed to about $350,000, while the bottom half barely moved to about $19,000, according to the World Inequality Database.*[2]

Is Example I-2 more believable than Example I-1? It makes a more precise claim by defining economic inequality in terms of average income for the upper 10% versus the bottom 50% over time. Also, Example I-2 pins its claims to a specific source, and invites us to read further by following the footnote. But how do these factors influence its persuasiveness? Does Example I-2 lead you to ask about the trustworthiness of the source and how it defines "income?" Does the wording make you wonder about the other 40% of the population between the two extremes?

To answer some of those questions, let's supplement Example I-2 with a bit more information, as shown in Table I-1.

Table I-1. Average US adult income, 1970–2019[a]

US Income Tier	1970	2019
Top 10%	$136,308	$352,815
Middle 40%	$44,353	$76,462
Bottom 50%	$16,515	$19,177

[a] Shown in constant 2019 US dollars. National income for individuals aged 20 and over, prior to taxes and transfers, but includes pension contributions and distributions. Source: World Inequality Database 2020 (*https://oreil.ly/eUYZn*).

Does Table I-1 make Example I-2 more persuasive? Since the table contains essentially the same information as the two sentences about top and bottom income levels, it shouldn't make any difference. But the table communicates the evidence more effectively, and makes a more compelling case.

For many people, it's easier to read and grasp the relationship between numbers when they're organized in a grid, rather than complex sentences. As your eyes skim down the columns, you automatically notice the huge jump in income for the top 10%, which nearly tripled over time, while the bottom 50% barely budged. In addition, the table fills in more information that was missing from the text about the middle 40%, whose income grew over time, but not nearly as much as the top tier. Furthermore, the note at the bottom of the table adds a bit more context about how the data is shown in constant 2019 US dollars, which means that the 1970s numbers were adjusted to account for changes to the cost of living and purchasing power of

---

2 World Inequality Database, "Income Inequality, USA, 1913–2019," accessed 2020, *https://oreil.ly/eUYZn*.

dollars over a half-century. The note also briefly mentions other terms used by the World Inequality Database to calculate income (such as taxes, transfers, and pensions), though you would need to consult the source for clearer definitions. Social scientists use different methods to measure income inequality, but generally report findings similar to those shown here.[3]

Some Pictures Are More Persuasive

Now let's substitute a data visualization—specifically the line chart in Figure I-1—in place of the table, to compare which one is more persuasive.

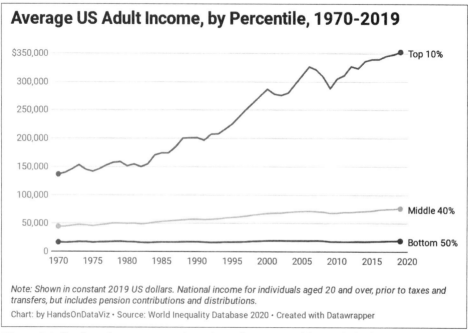

Figure I-1. Explore the interactive line chart (https://oreil.ly/x0Phg) of US adult income inequality over time.

---

3 The World Inequality Database builds on the work of economists Thomas Piketty, Emmanuel Saez, and their colleagues, who have constructed US historical income data based not only on self-reported surveys, but also large samples of tax returns submitted to the Internal Revenue Service. See WID methods at World Inequality Database, "Methodology," 2020, *https://oreil.ly/F4SNk*. See the overview of methodological approaches in Chad Stone et al., "A Guide to Statistics on Historical Trends in Income Inequality" (Center on Budget and Policy Priorities, January 13, 2020), *https://oreil.ly/uqAzm*. See comparable findings on US income inequality by the Pew Charitable Trust in "Trends in US Income and Wealth Inequality" by Julia Menasce Horowitz, Ruth Igielnik, and Rakesh Kochhar (Pew Research Center's Social & Demographic Trends Project, January 9, 2020), *https://oreil.ly/W5nPq*.

Is Figure I-1 more persuasive than Table I-1? Since the line chart contains the same historical start and stop points as the table, it should not make any difference. But the line chart also communicates a powerful, visualized data story about income gaps that grabs your attention more effectively than the table.

As your eyes follow the colored lines horizontally across the page, the widening inequality between the top versus the middle and bottom tiers is striking. The chart also packs so much granular information into one image. Looking closely, you also notice how the top-tier income level was relatively stable during the 1970s, then spiked upward from the 1980s to the present, and grew more distant from other lines. Meanwhile, as the middle-tier income rose slightly over time, the fate of the lowest-tier remained relatively flat, reached its peak in 2007, and then dipped back downward for much of the past decade. The rich got richer, and the poor got poorer, as the saying goes. But the chart reveals how rapidly those riches grew, while poverty remained recalcitrant in recent years.

Now let's insert Figure I-2, which contains the same data as Figure I-1, but presented in a different format. Which chart should you believe? Remember, we warned you to watch out for people who use data visualizations to tell lies.

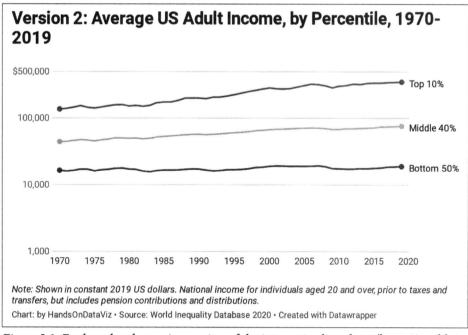

Figure I-2. Explore the alternative version of the interactive line chart (https://oreil.ly/vECje) of US adult income inequality over time, using the same data as the first version.

What's going on? If Figure I-2 contains the same data as Figure I-1, why do they look so different? What happened to the striking growth in inequality gaps, which now seem to be smoothed away? Did the crisis suddenly disappear? Was it a hoax?

Although the chart in Figure I-2 is technically accurate, we intentionally designed it to mislead readers. Look closely at the labels in the vertical axis. The distance between the first and second figures ($1,000 to $10,000) is the same as the distance between the second and the third ($10,000 to $100,000), but those jumps represent very different amounts of money ($9,000 versus $90,000). That's because this chart was constructed with a logarithmic scale (*https://oreil.ly/Hr4dL*), which is most appropriate for showing exponential growth.

You may recall seeing logarithmic scales during the COVID-19 pandemic, when they were appropriately used to illustrate very high growth rates, which are difficult to display with a traditional linear scale. This second chart is technically accurate, because the data points and scale labels match up, but it's misleading because there is no good reason to interpret this income data using a logarithmic scale, other than to deceive us about this crisis. People can use charts to illuminate the truth, but also can use them to disguise it.

Different Shades of the Truth

Let's expand our analysis of income inequality beyond the borders of one nation. Example I-3 introduces comparative evidence and its source. Unlike the prior US examples that showed historical data for three income tiers, this global example focuses on the most current year of data available for the top 1% in each nation. Also, instead of measuring income in US dollars, this international comparison measures the percentage share of the national income held by the top 1%. In other words, it indicates how large the slice of the pie is that's eaten by the richest 1% in each nation.

Example I-3.

> *Income inequality is more severe in the US, where the richest 1% of the population currently receives 20% of the national income. By contrast, in most European nations the richest 1% receives a smaller share, ranging between 6% to 15% of the national income.[4]*

Continuing on the same train of thought, let's supplement Example I-3 with a visualization to evaluate its persuasiveness. While we could create a table or a chart, those would not be the most effective ways to quickly display information for more than 120 nations in our dataset. Because this is spatial data, let's transform it into an

---

4 World Inequality Database, "Top 1% National Income Share," 2020, accessed 2020, *https://oreil.ly/fwQQV*.

interactive map to help us identify any geographic patterns and to encourage readers to explore income levels around the globe, as shown in Figure I-3.

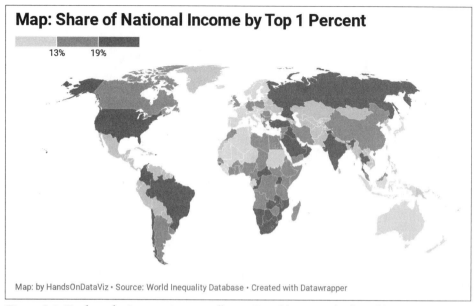

Figure I-3. Explore the interactive map (https://oreil.ly/6CUz-) of world income inequality, measured by the share of national income held by the top 1% of the population, based on the most recent data available. Source: World Inequality Database 2020 (https://oreil.ly/fwQQV).

Is Figure I-3 more persuasive than Example I-3? While the map and the text present the same data about income inequality in the US versus Europe, there should be no difference. But the map pulls you into a powerful story that vividly illustrates gaps between the rich and poor, similar to the chart example above. Colors in the map signal a crisis because red expresses urgency in many cultures. Income inequality in the US (along with several other countries, including Russia and Brazil) stands out in dark red at the highest level of the legend, where the top 1% holds 19% or more of the national income. By contrast, as your eye floats across the Atlantic, nearly all of the European nations appear in lighter beige and orange colors, indicating no urgent crisis as their top tier holds a smaller share of the national income.

Now let's introduce the alternative map in Figure I-4, which contains the same data as shown in Figure I-3, but is displayed in a different format. Which map should you believe?

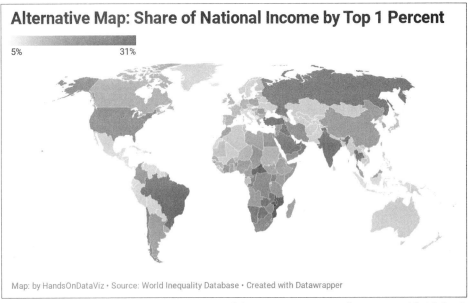

Figure I-4. Explore an alternative version of the interactive map (https://oreil.ly/-l9bM) of world income inequality, using the same data as the preceding map.

Why does the second map in Figure I-4 look different than the first map in Figure I-3? Instead of dark red, the US is now colored medium blue, closer on the spectrum to Canada and most European nations. Did the inequality crisis simply fade away from the US, and move to dark-blue Brazil? Which map tells the truth?

This time, neither map is misleading. Both make truthful interpretations of the data with reasonable design choices, even though they create very different impressions in our eyes. To understand why, look closely at the map legends. The first map sorts nations into three categories (less than 13%, 13–19%, and 19% and above), while the second map displays the entire range in a green-blue color gradient. Since the US share is 20.5%, in the first map it falls into the top bucket with the darkest red color, but in the second map it falls somewhere closer to the middle as medium blue. Yet both maps are equally valid because neither violates a definitive rule in map design, nor are we intentionally disguising data. People can mislead with maps, but it's also possible to make more than one portrait of the truth.

The interpretive nature of data visualization poses a serious challenge. As the authors of this book, our goal is to guide you in creating truthful and meaningful charts and maps. We'll point you toward the principles of good design, encourage thoughtful habits of mind, and try to teach by example. Occasionally, we'll even tell you what *not* to do. But data visualization is a slippery subject to teach—sometimes more art than science. We know that charts and maps can be manipulated—just like words—to mislead your audience, and we'll demonstrate common deception techniques to help you spot them in other people's work, and consciously avoid them in your own. But newcomers may be frustrated by the somewhat fuzzy rules of data visualization. Often there is no *single* correct answer to a problem, but rather *several* plausible solutions, each with their own strengths and weaknesses.

As a learner, your job is to continually search for *better answers* without necessarily expecting to find the *one right answer*, especially as visualization methods and tools continue to evolve, and people invent new ways to show the truth.

Organization of the Book

We've organized the chapters of this book to serve as an introductory, hands-on guide to data visualization, from spreadsheets to code. Also, we assume no prior skills other than general familiarity with operating a computer and a vague memory of secondary school mathematics, along with an innate curiosity about telling stories with data. Imagine the book in four parts.

In Part I, you'll develop foundational skills about envisioning your data story, along with the tools and data you'll need to tell it. We'll gradually move from Chapters 1, 2, 3, 4, and 5. These chapters feature hands-on tutorials to enrich learning by doing.

In Part II, you'll build lots of visualizations with easy-to-learn drag-and-drop tools, and find out which types work best with different data stories. We'll start with Chapters 6, 7, and 8, and develop your understanding of the interpretive style that each one emphasizes. In Chapter 9, you'll learn how to insert all of these interactive visualizations on common web platforms, to invite readers to explore your data and share your work more widely.

In Part III, you'll advance to working with more powerful tools, specifically code templates that give you more control over customizing the appearance of your visualizations and where you host them online. We'll start with Chapter 10, and walk you through the easy web interface for a popular open source coding platform. Then you'll build using Chapters 11 and 12, and discover more advanced spatial tools in Chapter 13. At the end of the book, we include the Appendix: Fix Common Problems for you to consult when you accidentally break your code, which is also a great way to learn how the code works.

In Part IV, we'll wrap up all of the visualization skills you've developed by returning to the central theme of this introduction: telling true and meaningful stories with data. In Chapter 14, you'll learn how to lie with charts and maps in order to do a better job of telling the truth. Finally, Chapter 15 emphasizes how the goal of data visualization is not simply to make pictures about numbers, but to craft a truthful narrative that convinces readers how and why your interpretation matters.

Summary

Now you have a clearer sense of our primary goal for this book. We aim for you to learn how to tell true and meaningful stories with interactive data visualizations, while being mindful of the ways that people can use them to mislead. In the next chapter, let's get started on clarifying the data story you wish to tell and the factors to consider when choosing tools to do the job.

PART I

Foundational Skills

CHAPTER 1

Choose Tools to Tell Your Story

If you feel overwhelmed by the avalanche of digital tools available today, you're not alone. When you're simply trying to do your regular work, keeping up with the latest software developments can feel like an additional part-time job you didn't sign up for. Digital tools are constantly changing and evolving. That's good news if you like to experiment and choose among different options, but not-so-good news if you lack the time to make complex decisions.

In this chapter, we'll help you navigate the decision-making process. We'll begin with the most important step—sketching out your data story—to help identify the types of tools you need to tell it effectively. Next, we'll review "Ten Factors When Considering Tools" on page 4. Finally, we'll present "Our Recommended Tools" on page 9, plus one extra to help you get organized: "Use a Password Manager" on page 11. All of these tools are free to use, and the book introduces them gradually, from easy-to-learn beginner tools to more advanced power tools that grant you more control over where your work is hosted and how it looks.

Start Sketching Your Data Story

Before we dive into digital tools, let's focus on what's most important: our *data story*. We build visualizations to help us tell a story about the information we've gathered— a narrative that draws the audience's attention to meaningful patterns and key insights amid all of the pieces of data. In your data story, help them to see the forest, rather than listing every single tree.

But in the early stage of a data visualization project, a common problem is that we don't yet have a clear sense of the key pieces of our data story, or how they fit together. That's perfectly normal. One of the best ways to address that problem is a quick exercise that's designed to move partially-formed ideas from inside our heads out onto pieces of paper, to help you and any coworkers see them more clearly.

For this exercise, push away your computer and pick up some of our favorite old-school tools:

- Several blank sheets of paper
- Colored pencils, pens, or markers
- Your imagination

Get ready to sketch out your data story in words and pictures (no artistic skills are required):

1. On the first sheet of paper, *write down the problem* that motivates your data project. If you prefer a prompt, try filling in these blanks: *We need to find out _____ in order to _____.*

   In many cases, people come to data visualization with an information-driven problem, which they hope will lead them to achieve a broader goal. For example, when working on the first draft of this book, our problem statement was: *We need to find out our readers' backgrounds and interests about data visualization, in order to write a better introductory guide that meets their needs.*

2. On the second sheet of paper, *rewrite your problem statement as a question.* Write a question for which you genuinely do not yet know the answer—and punctuate it with a question mark.

   If your brain is tempted to jump ahead and try to answer the question, fight that urge. Instead, focus on framing the question by using more precise wording than you wrote initially, without limiting the range of possible results. For example, when working on the first draft, our question was: *How do readers of our book describe their prior experience with data visualization, their education level, and their learning goals?* While we had some preliminary guesses, we honestly didn't know the answer at that stage, which made it an authentic question.

3. On the third sheet of paper, *draw pictures and arrows to show how you'll find data* to answer your question.

   Are you conducting door-to-door interviews with neighborhood residents, or sending an online survey to customers, or downloading family income and county maps from the US Census? Sketch a picture of your data collection process, to show how you plan to bring together different pieces of information. For example, when writing the first draft of our book, we asked readers to fill out a quick online survey form, and reminded them not to insert any private data, because we shared back their collected responses in a public spreadsheet.

4. On the fourth sheet of paper, *sketch at least one type of visualization you plan to create* after you obtain your data.

Do you envision some type of chart, like a bar, line, or scatter chart? Or do you imagine some type of map, maybe with points or polygons? If your visualizations will be interactive, try to show the concept using buttons and more than one sheet of paper. You can add *imaginary data* at this stage because it's just a preliminary sketch. Have fun!

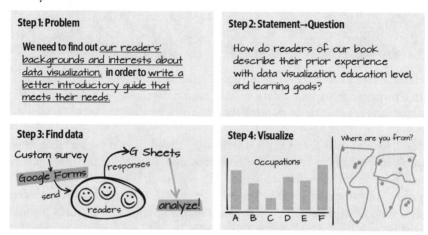

This exercise can help you in multiple ways, whether you do it by yourself, or even better, with a team of coworkers, as shown in Figure 1-1. First, by migrating ideas from your mind to paper, you'll make your thinking clearer not only for you, but also more visible for others. When ideas are sketched out, you can reflect on them, listen to feedback, cross-out not-so-good ones, and replace them with better ones on new sheets of paper. If your initial sketches are too complicated or confusing, break down those ideas into separate pages to make them more coherent.

Figure 1-1. The data-story-sketching exercise can be done solo, but works even better with a team of people. In our data visualization course, college students and community partners collaborate on framing the data story for their projects.

Second, look at your sheets like a storyboard. Spread them out on a table, move them around to potentially reorder the sequence, and start to define the three essential stages of your story: the beginning, middle, and end. Also, these pages can help you organize your thinking about how you'll communicate your data story to larger audiences, such as a presentation slide deck, or paragraphs and pictures for your next report or web page. Don't throw them away, because we'll return to this exercise at the end of the book in Chapter 15.

Finally, this sketching exercise can help you identify which chapters you should focus on in the body of this book. If you're puzzled about where to search for data, check out Chapter 3. If you're thinking about building a chart or map, but need examples of different types, look at the beginning of Chapters 6 and 7.

Now that you have a clearer sense of the story you wish to tell, and some initial ideas about the visualizations you wish to create, in the next two sections we'll discuss tools to do the job, and factors you should consider when deciding among them.

Ten Factors When Considering Tools

Making decisions between the seemingly endless number of digital tools can feel overwhelming. To help you decide, we list 10 key factors that we consider when evaluating new visualization tools or online services. When comparing options, many decisions involve some type of trade-off, a balance between competing wants and needs, such as ease-of-use versus extensive features. By identifying key factors, we believe that each reader can make a more informed decision about which tools offer the best trade-off for you, since all of us are different. Furthermore, we worded our categories broadly, because the concepts can be applied to other areas of your digital life, but followed up with more context about data visualization in particular.

1. Easy to Learn

How much time will be required to learn a new tool? In our busy lives, this is often the most important factor, but also one that varies widely, as your personal investment of time and energy depends on your prior experience in using related tools and grasping key concepts.

In this book, we use the label *easy tools* to identify those tools best suited for beginners (and even some advanced users prefer them too). They usually feature a GUI, meaning you operate them with pull-down menus or drag-and-drop steps, rather than memorizing commands to be typed into a blank screen. The better ones also offer user-friendly error messages that guide you in the right direction after a wrong turn.

Later in the book, we'll introduce *power tools* that provide more control and customization of your visualizations, such as code templates that you can copy and edit, which is easier than writing them from scratch. Overall, when deciding which tools to include in this book, we placed easy to learn at the top of our list. In fact, we removed a popular free drag-and-drop tool from an earlier draft of this book because even *we* had difficulty following our own instructions in how to use it. When faced with several good options, choose simplicity.

2. Free or Affordable

Is the tool free to use? Or is it based on a *freemium* model that offers basic functions for free, with premium features at a price? Or does it require paying a one-time purchase or monthly subscription fee? Of course, the answer to what is affordable will vary for each reader.

We fully understand that the business model for many software developers requires steady revenue, and both of us willingly pay to use specific tools necessary for our work. If you regularly rely on a tool to do your job, with no clear alternative, it's in your best interest to financially support their continued existence. But when creating this book, we were impressed by the wide array of high-quality data visualization tools that are available at no cost to users. To increase access to data visualization for all readers, every tool we recommend is free, or its core features are freely available.

3. Powerful

Does the tool offer all of the features you anticipate needing? For example, does it support building sufficient types of data visualizations for your project? Although more is usually better, some types of charts are obscure and rarely used, such as radar charts (*https://oreil.ly/B-LVF*) and waterfall charts (*https://oreil.ly/7f6AF*). Also, look out for limits on the amount of data you can upload, or restrictions on visualizations you create. For example, we previously removed a freemium tool from an earlier version of this book when the company began to require a paid license if your map was viewed more than one hundred times on the web. Furthermore, to what extent does the tool allow you to customize the appearance of your visualizations? Since drag-and-drop and freemium tools commonly limit your display options, you may need to make trade-offs between them and more powerful and customizable tools. In this book, we begin with easy tools and gradually introduce more advanced ones in each chapter, to help you identify your ideal combination of simplicity and power.

4. Supported

Does the developer regularly maintain and update the tool, and respond to questions or issues? Is there an active user community that supports the tool and shares its knowledge about using it? If you've worked with digital tools as long as we have, you'll recognize our pain in losing several whose developers pulled the plug. For example, Killed By Google (*https://killedbygoogle.com*) lists nearly two hundred applications and online services that this multibillion dollar corporation closed down. One of these was a popular data visualization tool, Google Fusion Tables (*https://oreil.ly/ eZVYF*), which once occupied a full chapter in an earlier version of this book, which we removed when Google shut down the tool after a 10-year run in 2019.

Although none of us can predict which online tools will persist, we looked for signs of active support before including them in this book, such as regular updates, stars earned on a GitHub (*https://github.com*) developer's site, and questions answered in the Stack Overflow (*https://stackoverflow.com*) user forum. But never assume that the future will resemble the past. The continuous evolution of digital tools means that some become extinct.

5. Portable

How easily can you migrate your data *into* and *out* of a tool? For example, we stopped recommending an online story map tool created by a well-known software company when we discovered that while users could easily upload locations, text, and photos, there was no way to export all of their work!

As digital technology inevitably changes, all data will need to migrate to another platform, and it's your job to be prepared for this eventual transition. Think about the issue as historical preservation, to increase the likelihood that your projects will continue to function on some unknown platform in the future. If your current tool developer announced that it was shutting down next month, could you easily extract all of the underlying data in a commonly used file format to upload to a different tool? A key step to future-proof your visualizations is to ensure that your data files are easily separated from the presentation software that generates the charts or maps. When recommending tools for this book, we favored those that support portable data downloads for future migrations.

6. Secure and Private

This category combines related questions about security and privacy. First, does the online tool or service take reasonable precautions to protect your personal information from malicious hackers and malware? Review a list of major data breaches on Wikipedia (*https://oreil.ly/8LJj0*) to help you make informed decisions. If your tool developer recently experienced a malicious data hack, find out how they responded.

Second, when you access tools through your browser, do they track your web activity across different sites? Also be aware of internet censorship by different governments around the globe (*https://oreil.ly/D6NmK*), as compiled by Wikipedia, unless you happen to be reading this book in China, which has blocked access to all of Wikipedia since April 2019 (*https://oreil.ly/6nAL_*).

Finally, does the tool clearly explain whether the data you enter or the products you create will stay private or become public? For example, some companies offer free access to their visualization tools, but in exchange require you to make your data, charts, and maps publicly accessible. That trade-off may be acceptable if you're working with open access data and already plan to freely share your visualizations, as many journalists and scholars do. In any case, make sure the terms of service are clearly defined before you start using a tool.

7. Collaborative

Does the tool allow people to work together and co-create a data visualization? If so, does the tool allow different levels of access or version control to help prevent team members from accidentally overwriting each other's contributions? Prior generations of digital tools were designed primarily for solo users, in part to address security and privacy issues raised previously. But today, many data visualization projects require access and input from multiple team members. Collaboration is essential for success. As co-authors of this book, who jointly wrote the text and co-created many of the visualizations, we favor a newer generation of tools designed for team work environments.

8. Cross-Platform

This category refers to both creating and consuming digital content. First, does the tool work across different computer operating systems? In this book, we highlight several tools that run inside any modern web browser, which usually (but not always) means they will operate on all major desktop and laptop computer platforms, such as Windows, Mac, Chromebook, and Linux. When necessary, we specify when a tool will run only on specific computer operating systems, and this often reduces access for people using lower-cost computers.

Second, does the tool create visualizations that are responsive to different screen sizes? In other words, does it produce charts and maps that display satisfactorily on smaller devices, such as smartphones and tablets? In this book, we favor cross-platform tools that also display content responsively on smaller devices, but we do not necessarily expect that tools can be operated on small devices to create visualizations. In other words, when we say that a tool runs inside any modern web browser, we don't necessarily mean phone and tablet browsers, but sometimes they work there too.

9. Open Source

Is the tool's software code publicly viewable? Can the code be modified and redistributed, so that other developers can suggest improvements, or build new features or extensions? We recognize that many developers rely on nonpublic proprietary code to sell their tools at a profit, and several of those tools appear in the book. But we also have been impressed with the number of high-quality data visualization tools offered under different types of open source licensing arrangements, by sustainable communities of volunteer developers, nonprofit organizations, and also for-profit companies who recognize some economic benefits of open source code development. When recommending tools for this book, we highlight open source options when available.

10. Accessible for Visually Impaired Readers

Does the tool create visualizations that are accessible for visually impaired readers? Although disability advocacy laws were passed decades ago, digital technology still lags behind and is slowly catching up, especially in the field of data visualization. But some tools include a built-in check for colorblindness (*https://oreil.ly/Z231v*) and offer chart types designed for people with low vision using screen readers (*https://oreil.ly/4XzXO*), as shown in Figure 1-2.

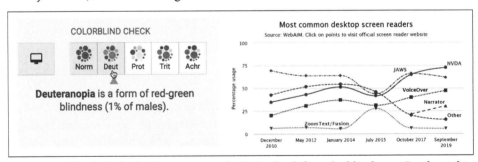

Figure 1-2. On the left, the Datawrapper built-in check for colorblindness. On the right, a Highcharts line chart designed for low-vision accessibility.

Those are 10 factors we consider when deciding whether to add another item into our digital toolkit. Often we need to make compromises, as you'll read in the next section. Of course, your list of factors may vary, and might include other values that are vitally important yet sometimes harder to judge, such as a software developer's ethical business practices or contribution to the public good. Whatever criteria you value, make them explicit in your decision-making process, and inform others about what influences your choices.

Also consider other people's perspectives on making tool decisions. When visualization designer Lisa Charlotte Rost wrote about her fascinating experiment in re-creating one chart with 24 different tools (*https://oreil.ly/qIVcx*), she concluded that "there are no perfect tools, just good tools for people with certain goals." On a related note, when digital historian Lincoln Mullen offered advice on making prudent choices about digital tools (*https://oreil.ly/YsqCs*), his first recommendation was: "The best possible tool is the one you're already using to get work done." Don't fall into the familiar trap of believing that your productivity will increase if only you began to use yet another new tool. Mullen's second piece of advice was: "Prefer the tool that your local coworkers use." Even if a different tool is objectively better, it may be outweighed by the benefits of mutual support and collaboration with people using a less-awesome application in your local setting.[1]

Now that you've considered different factors behind tool decisions, in the next section you'll see an overview of our recommendations for readers of this book, with a quick description and link to the chapter where we introduce each of them.

Our Recommended Tools

When creating this book, we aimed to identify the most essential data visualization tasks that beginners are likely to face, and the digital toolkit needed to complete those tasks. In the prior section, we listed 10 factors that influenced our tool recommendations, such as being easy to learn, free or affordable, and with powerful capacity. In this section, we have listed all of the tools featured in this book, with recommended uses and references to chapters where they appear, as shown in Table 1-1. Your data visualization projects may require you to use only a small number of these, or perhaps even just one tool. But it's important to be aware of the different types of tools, because you may not realize how they can help you if don't know that they exist.

---

[1] Lisa Charlotte Rost, "What I Learned Recreating One Chart Using 24 Tools" (Source, December 8, 2016), *https://oreil.ly/qIVcx;* Lincoln Mullen, "How to Make Prudent Choices About Your Tools" (ProfHacker, August 14, 2013), *https://oreil.ly/YsqCs.* See also criteria for educational tools by Audrey Watters, "*The Audrey Test*: Or, What Should Every Techie Know About Education?" (Hack Education, March 17, 2012), *https:// oreil.ly/cD9-Q.*

Table 1-1. Recommended tools and uses, with chapter references

Tool	Collect	Clean	Chart	Geocode	Map	Table	Code	Transform
Google Sheets spreadsheet/charts	Chapter 2	Chapter 4	Chapter 6	Chapter 2		Chapter 8		
LibreOffice Calc spreadsheet/charts	Chapter 2							
Airtable relational database	Chapter 2							
Tabula PDF table extractor		Chapter 4						
OpenRefine data cleaner		Chapter 4						
Datawrapper charts/maps/tables			Chapter 6	Chapter 7	Chapter 7	Chapter 8		
Tableau Public charts/maps/tables			Chapter 6		Chapter 7	Chapter 7		
Chart.js code templates			Chapter 11					
Highcharts code templates			Chapter 11					
Google My Maps simple map maker				Chapter 7	Chapter 7			
Leaflet map code templates					Chapter 12			
GitHub edit & host code							Chapter 10	
GitHub Desktop & Atom code editor							Chapter 10	
GeoJson.io edit & draw geodata								Chapter 13
Mapshaper edit & join geodata								Chapter 13
Map Warper georeference images								Chapter 13

If this list initially looks overwhelming, don't worry! Newer users can complete most of the 12 introductory-level chapters in this book with only two easy-to-learn tools. Begin with "Select Your Spreadsheet Tools" on page 15, then move up to "Datawrapper Charts" on page 131. You can create amazing data visualizations with just these two tools. Also, they play nicely together, as Datawrapper allows you to directly import and update data from Google Sheets.

In addition to the tools featured in Table 1-1, you'll also see many more useful add-ons and assistants mentioned in the text, including ColorBrewer to select map colors ("Map Design Principles" on page 160), the Geocoding by SmartMonkey add-on for Google Sheets ("Geocode Addresses in Google Sheets" on page 23), and the

W3Schools TryIt iframe page (*https://oreil.ly/xgWyc*). Also, consider enhancing your web security by installing the free Privacy Badger browser extension from the Electronic Frontier Foundation (*https://privacybadger.org*) to view and exercise some control over who's tracking you, and also review the EFF's Surveillance Self-Defense Guide (*https://ssd.eff.org*).

We often make compromises about tools that excel in some criteria but not others. For example, the tool most frequently featured in our book's tutorials is Google Sheets (*https://oreil.ly/d7iYi*), because it's easy to learn, free, and powerful. But Google Sheets is not open source, and some people express concerns about giving Google too much access to their information. To address the latter point, one way to make this compromise more palatable is to create a specific Google account for your data visualization work distinct from the one you use for your private life.

Finally, we recognize that digital tools are continually changing and evolving. Some tools we discovered only because someone mentioned or tweeted about it while we were writing this book. As time goes by, we expect that some tools will no longer be available, and we also anticipate discovering newer ones that do a better job of telling our data stories.

Use a Password Manager

Finally, we highly recommend a password manager: think of it as one tool to rule them all! Password managers help you keep track of all of the accounts you will create when using several of the online tools mentioned. We recommend installing Bitwarden (*https://bitwarden.com*), an open source password manager that offers its core features for free for Windows, Mac, and Linux computers, all major web browsers, and iOS and Android mobile devices. When you install Bitwarden, you create one universal password (be careful not to forget it) that grants you access to all of the account usernames and passwords you catalog. You also install the Bitwarden extension in your preferred web browsers. When you register for a new account in your browser, the password manager typically asks if you wish to store that information in your vault with end-to-end encryption. Also, when you visit that site in the future, the password manager usually recognizes it and enters your login credentials with one click, as shown in Figure 1-3.

We recommend storing your passwords inside a tool like Bitwarden, rather than in a specific web browser (such as Chrome or Firefox) for two reasons. First, you can set up Bitwarden to sync and access your passwords across *different* browsers and *multiple* devices, including your laptop and smartphone. Second, if your primary browser or computer crashes, you still have online access to your secure Bitwarden vault, which means you can continue to work on a different computer.

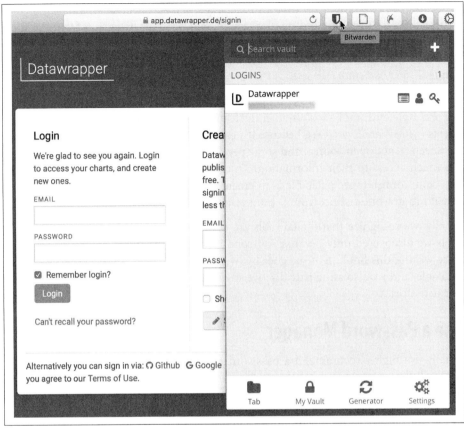

Figure 1-3. The Bitwarden browser extension recognizes sites for which you have stored login and password information and enters your credentials with one click.

Summary

Now you have a better sense of the wide range of data visualization tools we recommend in this book, and how to make wise decisions when choosing among tools in general. Always keep the data story in the forefront of your mind, since the tools are simply means by which to achieve that end. The next chapter is designed to strengthen your skills regarding the most common tool in our data visualization toolkit: spreadsheets.

Strengthen Your Spreadsheet Skills

Before we begin to design data visualizations, it's important to make sure our spreadsheet skills are up to speed. While teaching this topic, we've heard many people describe how they "never really learned" how to use spreadsheet tools as part of their official schooling or workplace training. But spreadsheet skills are vital to learn, not only as incredible time-savers for tedious tasks, but more importantly, to help us discover the stories buried inside our data.

The interactive charts and maps that we'll construct later in this book are built on data tables, which we typically open with spreadsheet tools, such as Google Sheets, LibreOffice, or Microsoft Excel. Spreadsheets typically contain columns and rows of numerical or textual data, as shown in Figure 2-1. The first row often contains headers, meaning labels describing the data in each column. Also, columns are automatically labeled with letters, and rows with numbers, so that every cell or box in the grid can be referenced, such as C2. When you click on a cell, it may display a formula that automatically runs a calculation that references other cells. Formulas always begin with an equal sign, and may simply add up other cells (such as =C2+C3+C4), or may contain a function that performs a specific operation (such as calculating the average of a range of cells: =average(C2:C7)). Some spreadsheet files contain multiple sheets (sometimes called workbooks), where each tab across the bottom opens a specific sheet.

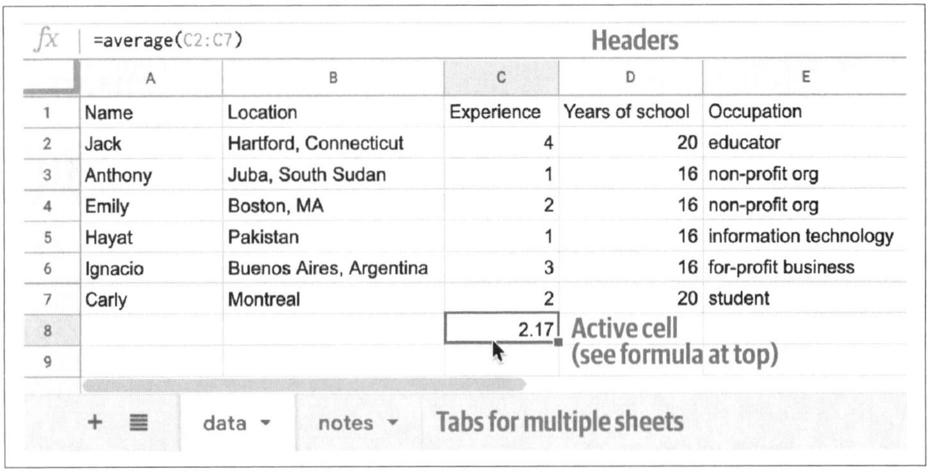

fx	=average(C2:C7)			Headers	
	A	B	C	D	E
1	Name	Location	Experience	Years of school	Occupation
2	Jack	Hartford, Connecticut	4	20	educator
3	Anthony	Juba, South Sudan	1	16	non-profit org
4	Emily	Boston, MA	2	16	non-profit org
5	Hayat	Pakistan	1	16	information technology
6	Ignacio	Buenos Aires, Argentina	3	16	for-profit business
7	Carly	Montreal	2	20	student
8			2.17		Active cell
9					(see formula at top)

+ ≡   data ▾   notes ▾   **Tabs for multiple sheets**

Figure 2-1. A typical spreadsheet, with headers, tabs, and the active cell displaying a formula.

In this chapter, we'll start by reviewing basic steps in "Share Your Google Sheets" on page 20, "Upload and Convert to Google Sheets" on page 21, "Geocode Addresses in Google Sheets" on page 23, and "Collect Data with Google Forms" on page 26. Then we'll move on to ways of organizing and analyzing your data, such as "Sort and Filter Data" on page 28, "Calculate with Formulas" on page 31, and "Summarize Data with Pivot Tables" on page 33. Finally, we'll examine ways to connect different sheets in "Match Columns with VLOOKUP" on page 38 and "Spreadsheet Versus Relational Database" on page 42. We illustrate all of these methods with beginner-level users in mind, meaning they do not require any prior background.

We'll practice several of these skills using sample data that may interest you, because it includes people like you. So far, more than three thousand readers of this book have responded to a short public survey about their general location, prior level of experience and education, and goals for learning data visualization. If you haven't already done so, fill out the survey (*https://oreil.ly/GXTUT*) to contribute your own response, and also to give you a better sense of how the questions were posed, then see the results in the public sample dataset (*https://oreil.ly/_Lpm8*).

If you want to learn ways to make your computer do more of the tedious data preparation work for you, this chapter is definitely for you. Or if you already feel very familiar with spreadsheets, you should at least skim this chapter, and perhaps you'll learn a trick or two that will help you to create charts and maps more efficiently later in the book.

Select Your Spreadsheet Tools

Which spreadsheet tools should you use? As we described in more detail in Chapter 1, the answer depends on how you respond to different questions about your work.

First, is your data public or private? If private, consider using a downloadable spreadsheet tool that runs on your computer, to reduce the risk of an accidental data breach that might happen when using an online spreadsheet tool that automatically stores your data in the cloud. Second, will you be working solo or with other people? For collaborative projects, consider using an online spreadsheet tool that's designed to allow other team members to simultaneously view or edit data. Third, do you need to import or export data in any specific format (which we'll describe in the next section), such as comma-separated values (CSV)? If yes, then choose a spreadsheet tool that supports that format. Finally, do you prefer a free tool, or are you willing to pay for it, or donate funds to support open source development?

Here's how three common spreadsheet tools compare on these questions:

Google Sheets (https://oreil.ly/d7iYi)
> A free online spreadsheet tool that works in any modern web browser, and automatically stores your data in the cloud. While data you upload is private by default, you can choose to share it with specific individuals or anyone on the internet, and allow them to view or edit for real-time collaboration, similar to Google Documents. Google Sheets also imports and exports data in CSV, OpenDocument Spreadsheet (ODS), Excel, and other formats.

> You can sign up for a free personal Google Drive (*https://drive.google.com*) account with the same username as your Google Mail account, or create a separate account under a new username to reduce Google's invasion into your private life. Another option is to pay for a Google Workspace (*https://workspace.google.com*) business account subscription (formerly known as G Suite), which offers nearly identical tools, but with sharing settings designed for larger organizations or educational institutions.

LibreOffice (https://www.libreoffice.org)
> A free downloadable suite of tools, including its Calc spreadsheet, available for Mac, Windows, and Linux computers, and an increasingly popular alternative to Microsoft Office. When you download LibreOffice, its sponsor organization, The Document Foundation, requests a donation to continue its open source software development. The Calc spreadsheet tool imports and exports data in its native ODS format, as well as CSV, Excel, and others. While an online collaborative platform is under development, it's not yet available for broad use.

Microsoft Excel (https://oreil.ly/3NWyx)

> The spreadsheet tool in the Microsoft Office suite, which is available in different versions, though commonly confused because the company has changed its product names over time. A paid subscription to Microsoft 365 (*https://oreil.ly/Ca8sH*) provides you with two versions: the full-featured downloadable version of Excel (which is what most people mean when they simply say "Excel") for Windows or Mac computers and other devices, and access to a simpler online Excel through your browser, including file sharing with collaborators through Microsoft's online hosting service.

> If you do not wish to pay for a subscription, anyone can sign up for a free version of online Excel at Microsoft's Office on the Web (*https://office.com*), but this does *not* include the full-featured downloadable version. The online Excel tool has limitations. For example, neither the paid nor the free version of online Excel allows you to save files in the single-sheet generic CSV format, an important feature required by some data visualization tools in later chapters. You can export to CSV format only using the downloadable Excel tool, which is available only with a paid Microsoft 365 subscription.

Deciding which spreadsheet tools to use is not a simple choice. Sometimes our decisions change from project to project, depending on costs, data formats, privacy concerns, and the personal preferences of any collaborators. Occasionally we've also had coworkers or clients specifically request that we send them nonsensitive spreadsheet data attached to an email, rather than sharing it through a spreadsheet tool platform that was designed for collaboration. So it's best to be familiar with all three commonly used spreadsheet tools mentioned, and to understand their respective strengths and weaknesses.

In this book, we primarily use Google Sheets for most of our examples. All of the data we distribute through this book is public. Also, we wanted a spreadsheet tool designed for collaboration, so that we can share links to data files with readers like you, so that you can view our original version, and either make a copy to edit in your own Google Drive, or download in a different format to use in LibreOffice or Excel. Most of the spreadsheet methods we teach look the same across all spreadsheet tools, and we point out exceptions when relevant.

Common Data Formats

Spreadsheet tools organize data in different formats. When you download spreadsheet data to your computer, you typically see its filename, followed by a period and an abbreviated extension, which represents the data format. The most common data formats we use in this book are:

.csv
> CSVs, a generic format for a single sheet of simple data, which saves neither formulas nor styling.

.ods
> ODS, a standardized open format that saves multitabbed sheets, formulas, styling, etc.

.xlsx (or the older .xls)
> Excel, a Microsoft format that supports multitabbed sheets, formulas, styling, etc.

.gsheet
> Google Sheets, which also supports multitabbed sheets, formulas, styling, etc., but you don't normally see these on your computer because they are primarily designed to exist online.

The Mac computer hides filename extensions by default, meaning you may not be able to see the abbreviated file format after the period, such as *data.csv* or *map.geojson*. We recommend that you change this setting by going to Finder > Preferences > Advanced, and check the box to "Show all filename extensions."

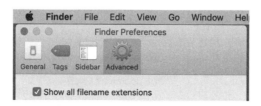

Download to CSV or ODS Format

In Chapter 1, you learned why we recommend software that supports portability, so you can migrate data to other platforms as technology evolves. Never upload important data into a tool that doesn't allow you to easily get it back out. Ideally, spreadsheet tools should allow you to export your work in generic or open data file formats, such as CSV and ODS, to maximize your options to migrate to other platforms.

If you're working in any spreadsheet with multiple tabs and formulas, a CSV export will save only the *active* sheet (meaning the one you're currently viewing), and only the *data* in that sheet (meaning that if you inserted formulas to run calculations, only the results would appear, not the formulas). Later in this book you may need to create a CSV file to import into a data visualization tool, so if the source was a multitabbed spreadsheet with formulas, keep a copy of the original.

One reason we feature Google Sheets in this book is because it exports data in several common formats. To try it, open this Google Sheets sample data file (*https://oreil.ly/jCZg6*) in a new tab, and go to File > Download to export in CSV format (for only the data in the active sheet) or ODS format (which keeps data and most formulas in multitab spreadsheets), or other formats such as Excel, as shown in Figure 2-2. Similarly, in the downloadable LibreOffice and its Calc spreadsheet tool, select File > Save As to save data in its native ODS format, or to export to CSV, Excel, or other formats.

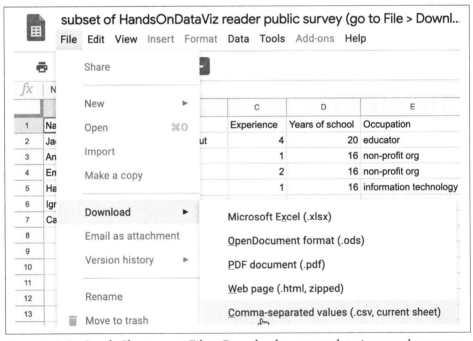

Figure 2-2. In Google Sheets, go to File > Download to export data in several common formats.

But exporting data can be trickier in Microsoft Excel. Using the online Excel tool in your browser (either the free or paid version), you *cannot* save files in the generic single-sheet CSV format, a step required by some data visualization tools in later chapters of this book. Only the downloadable Excel tool (which now requires a paid subscription) will export in CSV format. And when using the downloadable Excel tool to save in CSV format, the steps sometimes confuse people.

First, if you see multiple CSV options, choose *CSV UTF-8*, which should work best across different computer platforms. Second, if your Excel workbook contains multiple sheets or formulas, you may see a warning that it cannot be saved in CSV format, which saves only data (not formulas) contained in the active sheet (not all sheets). If you understand this, click OK to continue. Third, on the next screen, Excel may warn you about "Possible data loss" when saving an Excel file in CSV format, for reasons described previously. Overall, when working with the downloadable Excel tool, first save the full version of your Excel file in XLSX format before exporting a single sheet in CSV format.

Once you've learned how to export your spreadsheet data into an open format, you're ready to migrate it into other data visualization tools or platforms that we'll introduce in later chapters. Data portability is key for ensuring that your charts and maps will last well into the future.

Make a Copy of a Google Sheet

In this book we provide several data files using Google Sheets. Our links point to the online files, and we set the sharing settings to allow anyone to view—but not edit—the original version. This allows everyone to have access to the data, but no one can accidentally modify the contents. To complete several exercises in this chapter, you need to learn how to make your own copies of our Google Sheets—which you can edit—without changing our originals.

1. Open this Google Sheet of Hands-On Data Visualization reader public survey responses (*https://oreil.ly/SOuTl*) in a new tab in your browser. We set it to "View only" so that anyone on the internet can see the contents, but not edit the original file. Learn more about the survey at the top of the chapter.

2. Sign in to your Google account by clicking the blue button in the upper-right corner.

3. Go to File > "Make a copy" to create a duplicate of this Google Sheet in your Google Drive. You can rename the file to remove "Copy of..."

4. To keep your Google Drive files organized, save them in folders with relevant names to make them easier to find. For example, you can click My Drive and New Folder ( ) to create a folder for your data, before clicking OK.

Your copy of the Google Sheet will be private to you only, by default. In the next section we'll learn about different options for sharing your Google Sheet data with others.

Share Your Google Sheets

If you're working on a collaborative project with other people, Google Sheets offers several ways to share your data online, even with people who do not own a Google account. When you create a new Sheet, its default setting is private, meaning only you can view or edit its contents. In this section, you'll learn how to expand those options using the Share button:

1. Log into your Google Drive account, click New, select Google Sheets, and create a blank spreadsheet. You will need to name your file to proceed with next steps.

2. Click Share in the upper-right corner, and your options will appear on the "Share with people and groups" screen.

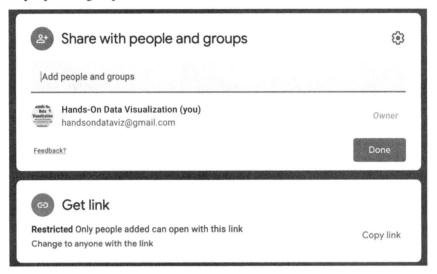

3. In the top half of the screen, you can share access with specific individuals by typing their Google usernames into the "Add people and groups" field. For each person or group you add, on the next screen, select the drop-down menu to assign them as a Viewer, Commenter, or Editor of the file. Decide if you wish to notify them with a link to the file and optional message.

4. In the lower half of the screen, you can share access more widely by clicking "Change to anyone with the link." On the next screen, the default option is to allow anyone who has the link to View the file, but you can change this to allow anyone to Comment on or Edit it. Also, you can click "Copy link" to paste the web address to your data in an email or public website.

If you don't want to send people a really long and ugly Google Sheet web address, such as:

https://docs.google.com/spreadsheets/d/
1egX_akJccnCSzdk1aaDdtrEGe5HcaTrlOW-
Yf6mJ3Uo

use a free link-shortening service. For example, by using our free Bitly.com (*https://bitly.com*) account and its handy Chrome browser extension (*https://oreil.ly/fCTCN*) or Firefox browser extension (*https://oreil.ly/JtNVP*), we can paste in a long URL and customize the latter half to something shorter, such as *bit.ly/reader-responses*. If someone else has already claimed your preferred custom name, you'll need to think up a different one. Beware that bit.ly links are case-sensitive, so we prefer to customize the latter half in all lowercase to match the front half.

Now that you have different options for sharing a Google Sheet, let's learn how to upload and convert data from different formats.

Upload and Convert to Google Sheets

We feature Google Sheets in this book partly because it supports data migration, meaning the ability to import and export files in many common formats. But imports work best when you check the "Convert uploads" box, which is hidden inside the Google Drive Settings gear symbol. Checking this box automatically transforms Microsoft Excel sheets into Google Sheets format (and also Microsoft Word and PowerPoint files into Google Documents and Slides formats), which allows easier editing. If you don't check this box, then Google will keep your files in their original format, which makes them harder to edit. Google turns off this conversion setting by default on new accounts, but we'll teach you how to turn it on, and the benefits of doing so:

1. Find a sample Excel file you can use on your computer. If you don't have one, open and save to download to your computer this Excel file of a subset of the *Hands-On Data Visualization* reader public survey responses (*https://oreil.ly/ pu8cr*).

2. Log into your Google Drive account, and click the gear symbol in the upper-right corner to open the Settings screen (⚙). Note that this global gear symbol > Settings appears at Google Drive level, *not* inside each Google Sheet.

3. On the Settings screen, check the box to "Convert uploaded files to Google Docs editor format," and click Done. This turns on the conversion setting globally,

meaning it will convert all possible files that you upload in the future—including Microsoft Excel, Word, PowerPoint, and more—unless you turn it off.

4. Upload a sample Excel file from your computer to your Google Drive. Either drag and drop it to the desired folder or use the New button and select "File upload."

If you forget to check "Convert uploads," Google Drive will keep uploaded files in their original format, and display their icons and filename extensions such as *.xlsx* or *.csv*.

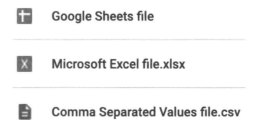

 Google Drive now allows you to edit Microsoft Office file formats, but not all features are guaranteed to work across platforms. Also, Google Drive now allows you to convert a specific uploaded Excel file into its Google format by using the File > "Save as Google Sheets" menu. Finally, to convert individual files to your Google Drive, while keeping the global conversion setting off, from inside any Google Sheet you can select File > Import > Upload. But we recommend that most people turn on the global conversion setting as described previously, except in cases where you intentionally use Google Drive to edit an Excel-formatted file, and understand that some features may not work.

Now that you know how to upload and convert an existing dataset, in the next section you'll learn how to install and use a Google Sheets add-on tool to geocode address data into latitude and longitude coordinates.

Geocode Addresses in Google Sheets

In this section, you'll learn how to geocode data by installing a free Google Sheets add-on tool. This allows you to geocode addresses directly inside your spreadsheet, which will be very useful when using Leaflet map code templates in Chapter 12.

Geocoding means converting addresses or location names into geographic coordinates (or x and y coordinates) that can be plotted on a map, as shown in Figure 2-3. For example, the Statue of Liberty in the New York City area is located at *40.69, –74.04*. The first number is the latitude and the second is the longitude. Since the equator is 0 degrees latitude, positive latitude is the northern hemisphere, and negative latitude is in the southern hemisphere. Similarly, the prime meridian is 0 degrees longitude, which passes through Greenwich, England. So positive longitude is east of the meridian, and negative longitude is west, until you reach the opposite side of the globe, roughly near the International Date Line in the Pacific Ocean.

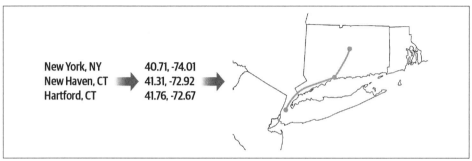

Figure 2-3. To map addresses, you first need to geocode them.

If you have just one or two addresses, you can quickly geocode them with Google Maps (*https://www.google.com/maps*). Search for an address, right-click that point, and select "What's here?" to reveal a pop-up window with its latitude and longitude, as shown in Figure 2-4.

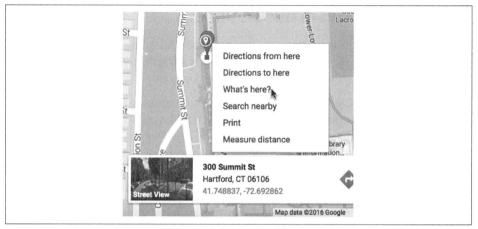

Figure 2-4. To geocode one address, search in Google Maps and right-click "What's here?" to show coordinates.

But what if you need to geocode a dozen or a hundred addresses? To geocode multiple addresses inside your spreadsheet, install a free Google Sheets add-on called Geocoding by SmartMonkey (*https://oreil.ly/KUHsE*), created by Xavier Ruiz, the CEO of SmartMonkey (*https://www.smartmonkey.io*), a geographic route-planning company in Barcelona, Spain. Add-ons are created by third-party companies to expand features for Google Sheets, Google Docs, and related tools. Add-ons are verified to meet Google's requirements and distributed through its Google Workspace Marketplace (*https://oreil.ly/DYchU*).

To install this Google Sheets add-on to geocode your addresses, follow these steps:

1. Sign into your Google Drive account, go to the Geocoding by SmartMonkey add-on page (*https://oreil.ly/QTgJ7*), and click the blue button to install it in your Google Sheets. The add-on will ask for your permission before installing, and if you agree, press Continue. In the next window, choose your Google Drive account, and if you agree with the terms, click Allow to complete the installation. Google will email you to confirm that you have installed this third-party app with access to your account. You can always review permissions and revoke access (*https://oreil.ly/JmBor*) in the future, if desired.

2. Go to your Google Drive and create a new Google Sheet. Select the Add-ons menu to see the new "Geocoding by SmartMonkey" options, and select "Geocode details." The add-on will create a new sheet with sample data and display results for three new columns: Latitude, Longitude, and "Address found." Always review the quality of geocoded results by comparing the *Address found* column to the original *Address* entered.

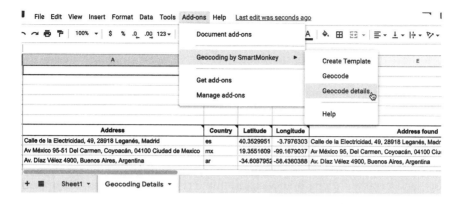

3. Paste your own address data to replace the sample data in the sheet, and geocode it as you did in step 2. Follow these guidelines to improve the quality of your results:

- Do not skip any rows in the Address column.

- Insert the full address using the format of the national postal service of the country where it is located. Separate terms with spaces.

- You can leave the Country column blank, but its default value is the US. To specify other nations, use their top-level internet domain code (*https://oreil.ly/ BObCf*), such as es for Spain.

- If your original data splits street, city, state, and zip code into different columns, see "Combine Data into One Column" on page 75.

- Give the tool time to work. For example, if you enter 50 addresses, expect to wait at least 15 seconds for your geocoded results.

- Always inspect the quality of your results, and never assume that geocoding services from any provider are accurate.

If you need a faster geocoding service for US addresses, one that can handle up to 10,000 requests in one upload, see "Bulk Geocode with US Census" on page 361 in Chapter 13.

Now that you know how to use a Google Sheets add-on to geocode addresses, in the next section you will learn how to collect data using an online form, and access it as a spreadsheet.

Collect Data with Google Forms

At the beginning of this chapter, we invited you and other readers of this book to fill out a short online survey (*https://oreil.ly/GXTUT*), which publicly shares all of the responses in a sample dataset (*https://oreil.ly/SOuTl*), so that we can learn more about people like you, and to continue to make revisions to match your expectations. In this section, you'll learn how to create your own online form and link the results to a live Google Sheet.

Inside your Google Drive account, click New and select Google Forms. The Google Forms Questions tab allows you to design questions with different types of responses: short- and paragraph-length answers, multiple choice, checkboxes, file uploads, etc., as shown in Figure 2-5. Furthermore, Google Forms attempts to interpret questions you enter to predictively assign them to a type.

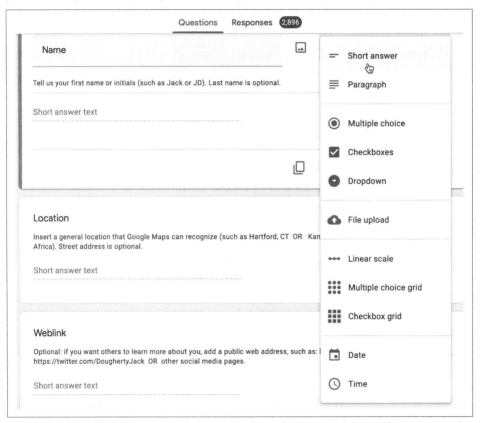

Figure 2-5. The Google Forms Questions tab allows you to designate different types of responses.

Give each question a very short title, since these will appear as column headers in the linked spreadsheet you'll create later. If a question needs more explanation or examples, click the three-dot kebab menu in the bottom-right corner to Show > Description, which opens a text box where you can type in more details, as shown in Figure 2-6. Also, you can Show > "Response validation," which requires users to follow a particular format, such as an email address or phone number. Furthermore, you can select the Required field to require users to respond to a question before proceeding. See additional options on the Google Forms support page (*https://oreil.ly/ CX77G*).

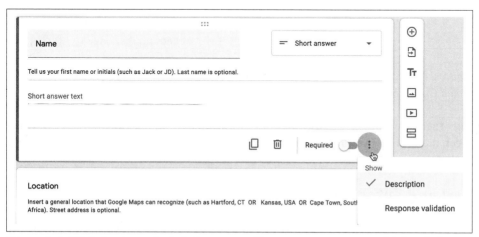

Figure 2-6. Click the three-dot kebab menu to Show > Description to add details for any question.

 Another name for the three-dot menu symbol is the *kebab menu* because it resembles Middle Eastern food cooked on a skewer, in contrast to the three-line *hamburger menu* on many mobile devices. Software developers must be hungry.

To preview how your online form will appear to recipients, click the Eyeball symbol near the top of the page (◉). When your form is complete, click Send to distribute it via email, a link, or to embed the live form as an iframe on a web page. Learn more about the latter option in Chapter 9.

The Google Forms Responses tab will show individual results you receive, and also includes a powerful button to open the data in a linked Google Sheet, as shown in Figure 2-7.

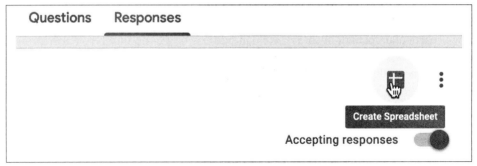

Figure 2-7. The Google Forms Responses tab includes a button to open results in a linked Google Sheet.

Now that you've learned how to collect data with an online form and linked spreadsheet, the next two sections will teach you how to sort, filter, and pivot tables to begin analyzing their contents and the stories they reveal.

Sort and Filter Data

Spreadsheet tools help you dig deeper into your data and raise the stories you find to the surface. A basic step in organizing your data is to *sort* a table by a particular column, to quickly view its minimum and maximum values and the range that lies in between. A related method is to *filter* an entire table to display only rows that contain certain values, to help them stand out for further study among all of the other entries. Both of these methods become more powerful when your spreadsheets contain hundreds or thousands of rows of data. To learn how to sort and filter, let's explore the reader survey sample dataset we described at the top of the chapter:

1. Open this Google Sheet of *Hands-On Data Visualization* reader public survey responses (*https://oreil.ly/SOuTl*) in a new tab in your browser.

2. Log in to your Google Sheets account, and go to File > "Make a copy" to create your own version that you can edit.

3. Before sorting, click the upper-left corner of the sheet to select all cells. When the entire sheet becomes light blue, and all of the alphabetical column and numerical row headers become dark gray, this confirms you've selected all cells.

	A	B	
1	Timestamp	Name	Location
2	1/14/2017 11:49:02	Jack	Hartford, C
3	2/4/2017 9:02:39	Ania	Needham,
4	2/8/2017 14:35:56	Devan Suggs	Hartford, C
5	2/8/2017 17:42:02	Alex	Chicago, IL
6	2/8/2017 21:49:00	Nhat Pham	Hanoi, Viet

 If you forget to select all cells, you might accidentally sort one column independently of the others, which will scramble your dataset and make it meaningless. Always select all cells before sorting!

4. In the top menu, go to Data > "Sort range" to review all of your sort options. In the next screen, check the "Data has header row box" to view the column headers in your data. Let's sort the "Experience with data visualization" column in ascending order (from A to Z), to display the minimum at the top, the maximum at the bottom, and the range in between.

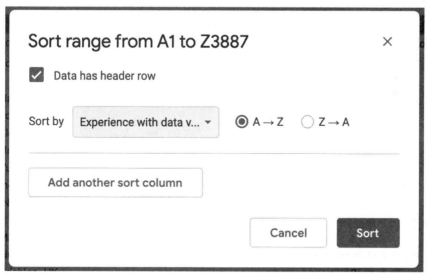

Scroll through your sorted data and you'll see that more than one thousand readers rated themselves as beginners (level 1) with data visualization.

When working with large spreadsheets, you can "freeze" the first row so that column headers will still appear as you scroll downward. In Google Sheets, go to View > Freeze and select one row. You can also freeze one or more columns to continuously display when scrolling sideways. LibreOffice has the same option to View > "Freeze Rows and Columns," but Excel has a different option, called Window > Split.

5. Now let's try filtering your sheet. Go to Data > "Create a filter," which inserts downward arrows in each column header. Click on the downward arrow-shaped toggle in the *Occupation* column and see options to display or hide rows of data. For example, look under "Filter by values," then click Clear to undo all options, then click "educator" to display only rows with that response. Click OK.

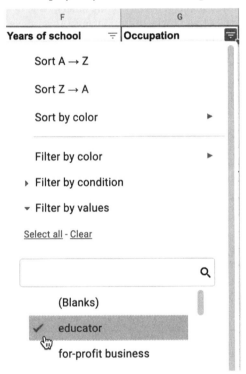

Now your view of reader responses is sorted by experience and filtered to show only educators. Scroll through their one-sentence goals for learning about data visualization. How do they compare to your own goals? In the next section, we'll learn how to start analyzing your data with simple formulas and functions.

Calculate with Formulas

Spreadsheet tools can save you lots of time when you insert simple formulas and functions to automatically perform calculations across entire rows and columns of data. Formulas always begin with an equal sign, and may simply add up other cells (such as =C2+C3+C4), or may contain a function that performs a specific operation (such as calculating the sum of a range of cells: =SUM(C2:C100)). In this section, you'll learn how to write two formulas with functions: one to calculate an average numeric value, and another to count the frequency of a specific text response. Once again, let's learn this skill using the reader survey sample dataset we described at the top of the chapter:

1. Open this Google Sheet of *Hands-On Data Visualization* reader public survey responses (*https://oreil.ly/SOuTl*) in a new tab in your browser.

2. Log into your Google Drive account, and go to File > "Make a copy" to edit your own version.

3. Add a blank row immediately below the header to make space for our calculations. Right-click on row number 1 and select "Insert 1 below" to add a new row.

4. Let's calculate the average level of reader experience with data visualization. Click on cell E2 in the new blank row you just created, and type an equal symbol (=) to start a formula. Google Sheets will automatically suggest possible formulas based on the context, and you can select one that displays the average for current values in the column, such as =AVERAGE(E3:E2894), then press Return or Enter on your keyboard.

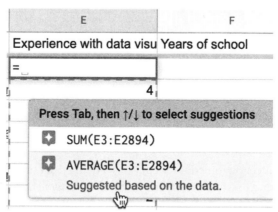

Since our live spreadsheet has a growing number of survey responses, you'll have a larger number in the last cell reference to include all of the entries in your version. Currently, the average level of reader experience with data visualization is around 2 on a scale from 1 (beginner) to 5 (professional), but this may change as more readers fill out the survey. Note that if any readers leave this question blank, spreadsheet tools ignore empty cells when performing calculations.

 In Google Sheets, =AVERAGE(E3:E) is another way to write the formula, which averages *all* values in column E, beginning with cell E3, without specifying the last cell reference. Using this syntax will keep your calculations up to date if more rows are added, but it does *not* work with LibreOffice or Excel.

5. Part of the magic of spreadsheets is that you can use the built-in hold-and-drag feature to copy and paste a formula across other columns or rows, and it will automatically update its cell references. Click in cell E2, then press and hold down the blue dot in the bottom-right corner of that cell, which transforms your cursor into a crosshair symbol. Drag your cursor to cell F2 and let go. The formula =AVERAGE(F3:F2894) or AVERAGE(F3:F) will be automatically pasted and updated for the new column, depending on which way you entered it to begin with. Once again, since this is a live spreadsheet with a growing number of responses, your sheet will have a larger number in the last cell reference.

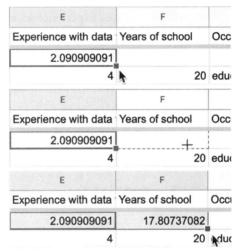

6. Because the Occupation column contains a defined set of text responses, let's use a different function to count them using an *if statement*, such as the number of responses if a reader listed "educator." Click in cell G2 and type the equal symbol (=) to start a new formula. Google Sheets will automatically suggest possible formulas based on the context, and you can select one that displays the count if the response is "educator" for current values in the entire column. You can directly type in the formula =COUNTIF(G3:G2894,"=educator"), where your last cell reference will be a larger number to reflect all of the rows in your version, or type in

the Google Sheets syntax **=COUNTIF(G3:G,"=educator")** that runs the calculation on the entire column without naming a specific endpoint.

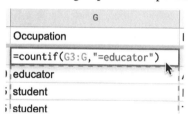

Spreadsheet tools contain many more functions to perform numerical calculations and also to modify text. Read more about functions in the support pages for Google Sheets (*https://oreil.ly/GJUJm*), LibreOffice (*https://oreil.ly/XMWDM*), or Microsoft Excel (*https://oreil.ly/sIH7m*).

See additional spreadsheet skills in later chapters of the book, such as "Find and Replace with Blank" on page 69, "Split Data into Separate Columns" on page 72, and "Combine Data into One Column" on page 75 in Chapter 4. See also "Pivot Points into Polygon Data" on page 363 and "Normalize Your Data" on page 90.

Now that you've learned how to count one type of survey response, the next section will teach you how to regroup data with pivot tables that summarize all responses by different categories.

Summarize Data with Pivot Tables

Pivot tables are another powerful feature built into spreadsheet tools to help you reorganize your data and summarize it in a new way, hence the name "pivot." Yet pivot tables are often overlooked by people who were never taught about them or have not yet discovered how to use them. Let's learn this skill using the reader survey sample dataset we described at the top of the chapter. Each row represents an individual reader, including their occupation and prior level of experience with data visualization. You'll learn how to "pivot" this individual-level data into a new table that displays the total number of reader responses by two categories: occupation and experience level.

1. Open this Google Sheet of *Hands-On Data Visualization* reader public survey responses (*https://oreil.ly/SOuTl*) in a new tab in your browser. Log into your Google Drive account, and go to File > "Make a copy" to edit your own version.

2. Or, if you have already created your own copy for the prior section on Formulas and Functions, delete row 2 that contains our calculations, because we don't want those getting mixed into our pivot table.

3. Go to Data > "Pivot table," and on the next screen, select Create in a new sheet. The new sheet will include a pivot table tab at the bottom.

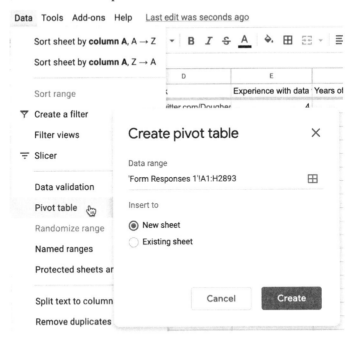

4. In the "Pivot table editor" screen, you can regroup data from the first sheet by adding rows, columns, and values. First, click the Rows Add button and select Occupation, which displays the unique entries in that column.

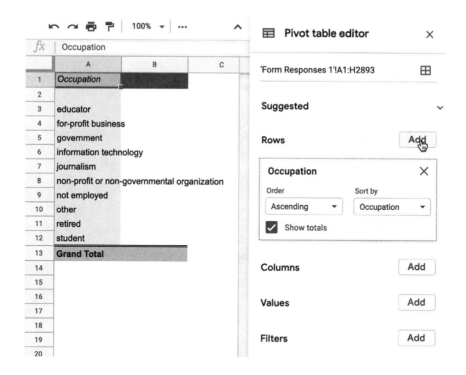

5. Next, to count the number of responses for each entry, click the Values Add button and select Occupation again. Google Sheets will automatically summarize the values by *COUNTA*, meaning it displays the frequency of each textual response.

Currently, the top three occupations listed by readers are information technology, for-profit business, and student. This is a live spreadsheet, so these rankings may change as more readers respond to the survey.

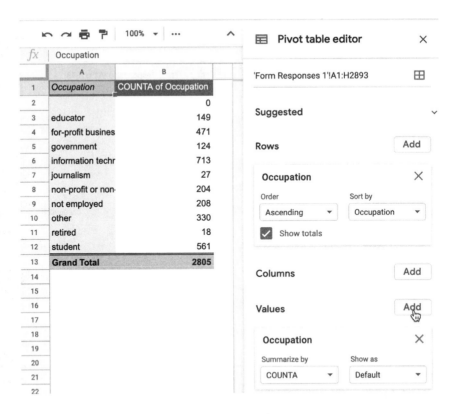

6. Furthermore, you can create a more advanced pivot cross-tabulation of occupation and experience among reader responses. Click the Columns button to add "Experience with data visualization."

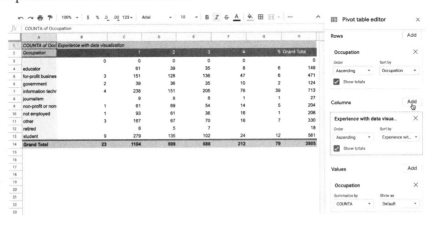

To go one step further, Filter the data to limit the pivot table results by another category. For example, in the drop-down menu, you can click the Filters Add button, select "Years of school," then under "Filter by values" select Clear, then check 20 to display only readers who listed 20 or more years.

Deciding how to add Values in the "Pivot table editor" can be challenging because there are multiple options to summarize the data, as shown in Figure 2-8. Google Sheets will offer its automated guess based on the context, but you may need to manually select the best option to represent your data as desired. Three of the most common options to summarize values are:

SUM
   The total value of numeric responses. (What is the total years of schooling for readers?)

COUNT
   Frequency of numeric responses. (How many readers listed 20 years of schooling?)

COUNTA
   Frequency of text responses. (How many readers listed their occupation as "educator"?)

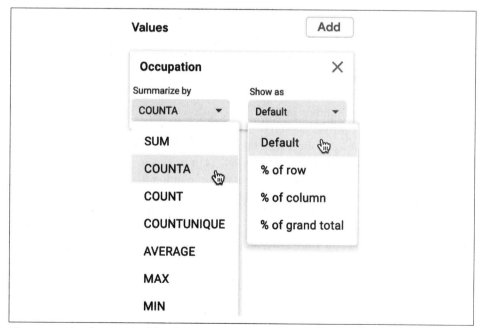

Figure 2-8. In the Pivot table editor, see multiple options to summarize Values.

Although Google Sheets pivot tables display raw numbers by default, under the *Show as* drop-down menu you can choose to display them as percentages of the row, of the column, or of the grand total.

While designing pivot tables may look different across other spreadsheet tools, the concept is the same. Learn more about how pivot tables work in the support pages for Google Sheets (*https://oreil.ly/GJUJm*) or LibreOffice (*https://oreil.ly/utHh1*) or Microsoft Excel (*https://oreil.ly/XP26v*). Remember that you can download the Google Sheets data and export to ODS or Excel format to experiment with pivot tables in other tools.

Now that you've learned how to regroup and summarize data with pivot tables, in the next section you'll learn a related method to connect matching data columns across different spreadsheets using VLOOKUP.

Match Columns with VLOOKUP

Spreadsheet tools also allow you to "look up" data in one sheet and automatically find and paste matching data from another sheet. This section introduces the VLOOKUP function, where the *V* stands for "vertical," meaning matches across columns, which is the most common way to look up data. You'll learn how to write a function in one sheet that looks for matching cells in select columns in a second sheet, and pastes the relevant data into a new column in the first sheet. If you've ever faced the tedious task of manually looking up and matching data between two different spreadsheets, this automated method will save you lots of time.

Here's a scenario that illustrates why and how to use the VLOOKUP function. Figure 2-9 shows two different sheets with sample data about food banks that help feed hungry people in different parts of the US, drawn from Feeding America: Find Your Local Food Bank (*https://oreil.ly/yliMu*). The first sheet lists individual people at each food bank, the second sheet lists the address for each food bank, and the two share a common column named *organization*. Your goal is to produce one sheet that serves as a mailing list, where each row contains one individual's name, organization, and full mailing address. Since we're using a small data sample to simplify this tutorial, it may be tempting to manually copy and paste in the data. However, imagine an actual case that includes more than two hundred US food banks and many more individuals, where using an automated method to match and paste data is essential.

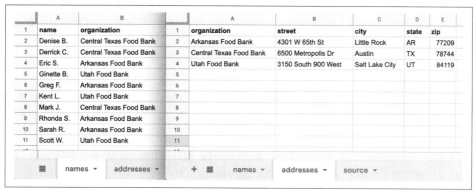

Figure 2-9. Your goal is to create one mailing list that matches individual names and organizations on the left sheet with their addresses on the right sheet.

Here are the steps to match your data with VLOOKUP:

1. Open this Google Sheet of Food Bank sample names and addresses (*https:// oreil.ly/YRicv*) in a new browser tab. Log into your Google Drive, and go to File > "Make a copy" to create your own version that you can edit.

   We simplified this two-sheet problem by placing both tables in the same Google Sheet. Click on the first tab, called *names*, and the second tab, called *addresses*. In the future, if you need to move two separate Google Sheets into the same file, go to the tab of one sheet, right-click the tab to "Copy to" > "Existing spreadsheet," and select the name of the other sheet.

2. In your editable copy of the Google Sheet, the *names* tab will be our destination for the mailing list we will create. Go to the *addresses* sheet, copy the column headers for *street, city, state, zip,* and paste them into cells C1 through F1 on the *names* sheet. This creates new column headers where our lookup results will be automatically pasted.

3. In the *names* sheet, click in cell C2 and type **=VLOOKUP**, and Google Sheets will suggest that you complete the full formula in this format:

   ```
   VLOOKUP(search_key, range, index, [is_sorted])
   ```

Here's what each part means:

search_key

The cell in the first sheet you wish to match.

range

At least two columns in the second sheet to search for your match and desired result.

index

The column in the second sheet range that contains your desired result, where 1 = first column, 2 = second column, etc.

[is_sorted]

Enter false to find exact matches only, which makes sense in this case. Otherwise, enter true if the first column of the second sheet range is sorted and you will accept the closest match, even if not an exact one.

4. One option is to directly type this formula into cell C2, using comma separators: **=VLOOKUP(B2,'addresses'!A:E,2,false)**. Another option is to click on the "VLOOKUP Vertical lookup" gray box that Google Sheets suggests, and click on the relevant cells, columns, and sheets for the formula to be automatically entered for you. What's new here is that this formula in the *names* sheet refers to a range of columns A to E in the *addresses* sheet. Press Return or Enter on your keyboard.

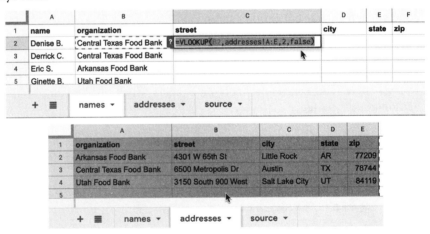

Let's break down each part of the formula you entered in cell C2 of the *names* sheet:

`B2`

The search_key: the cell in the *organization* column you wish to match in the *names* sheet

`'addresses'!A:E`

The range where you are searching for your match and results across columns A to E in the *addresses* sheet.

`2`

The index, meaning your desired result appears in the second column (*street*) of the range.

`false`

Find exact matches only.

5. After you enter the full VLOOKUP formula, it will display the exact match for the first organization, the Central Texas Food Bank, whose address is 6500 Metropolis Drive. Click and hold down on the blue dot in the bottom-right corner of cell C2, drag your crosshair cursor across columns D to F, and let go, which will automatically paste and update the formula for the city, state, and zip columns.

	A	B	C	D	E	F
1	name	organization	street	city	state	zip
2	Denise B.	Central Texas Food Bank	6500 Metropolis Dr	Austin	TX	78744
3	Derrick C.	Central Texas Food Bank				

6. Finally, use the same hold-and-drag method to paste and update the formula downward to fill in all rows.

	A	B	C	D	E	F
1	name	organization	street	city	state	zip
2	Denise B.	Central Texas Food Bank	6500 Metropolis Dr	Austin	TX	78744
3	Derrick C.	Central Texas Food Bank	6500 Metropolis Dr	Austin	TX	78744
4	Eric S.	Arkansas Food Bank	4301 W 65th St	Little Rock	AR	77209
5	Ginette B.	Utah Food Bank	3150 South 900 West	Salt Lake Cit	UT	84119
6	Greg F.	Arkansas Food Bank	4301 W 65th St	Little Rock	AR	77209
7	Kent L.	Utah Food Bank	3150 South 900 West	Salt Lake Cit	UT	84119
8	Mark J.	Central Texas Food Bank	6500 Metropolis Dr	Austin	TX	78744
9	Rhonda S.	Arkansas Food Bank	4301 W 65th St	Little Rock	AR	77209
10	Sarah R.	Arkansas Food Bank	4301 W 65th St	Little Rock	AR	77209
11	Scott W.	Utah Food Bank	3150 South 900 West	Salt Lake Cit	UT	84119
12						

+ ≡   names ▾   addresses ▾   source ▾

If you save this spreadsheet in CSV format, your calculated results will appear in the CSV sheet, but any formulas you created to produce those results will disappear. Always keep track of your original spreadsheet to remind yourself how you constructed the formulas.

You've successfully created a mailing list—including each person's name, organization, and full mailing address—using the VLOOKUP function to match and paste data from two sheets. Now that you understand how to use formulas to connect different spreadsheets, the next section will teach you how to manage multiple relationships between spreadsheets with the help of a relational database.

Spreadsheet Versus Relational Database

In the previous section, you learned how the VLOOKUP function can search for matching data in columns across spreadsheets and automatically paste results. Building on that concept, let's distinguish between a spreadsheet and a relational database, and under what circumstances it might be wiser to use the latter.

A spreadsheet is sometimes called a *flat-file database* because all of the records are stored in rows and columns in a single table. For example, if you kept a single spreadsheet of US food bank staff, every row would list an individual person, organization, and address, just like the mailing list we created in step 6 in the prior section on VLOOKUP.

Keeping all of your data in a single spreadsheet can raise problems, however. For example, if it contains lots of duplicated entries. For people who all work at the same food bank, each row contains a duplicate of that organization's address. If an organization moves to a new location, you need to update all of the rows that contain those addresses. Or if two organizations merge under a new name, you need to update all of the rows for individuals affected by that change. While keeping all of your information organized in a single spreadsheet initially sounds like a good idea, when your dataset grows in size and internal relationships (such as tracking people who are connected to organizations, etc.), continually updating every row becomes a lot of extra work.

Instead of a single spreadsheet, consider using a relational database, which organizes information into separate sheets (also known as tables), but continually maintains the relevant connections between them. Look back at the two-sheet problem we presented in Figure 2-9 at the beginning of the VLOOKUP section. The first sheet lists individual people at each food bank, the second sheet lists the address for each food bank, and the two sheets share a column named *organization* that shows how they are related. Relational databases can save you time. For example, if you update an organization's address in one sheet, the linked sheet will automatically reflect this change in every row for staff who work at that organization.

Although Google Sheets is a great spreadsheet, it's not a relational database. Instead, consider a better tool such as Airtable (*https://airtable.com*), which allows you to create relational databases in your web browser with up to 1,200 free records (or more with the paid version), using existing templates or your own designs. Airtable enables data migration by importing or exporting all records in CSV format, and it also supports real-time editor collaboration with coworkers.

To demonstrate, we imported both of the Google Sheets into this live Airtable database called Food Banks sample (*https://oreil.ly/mielX*), which anyone with the link can view, but only we can edit. At the top are tabs to view each sheet, named *people* and *food banks*. To transform this into a relational database, we used Airtable settings to link the *organization* column in the *people* sheet to the *food banks* sheet, where the addresses are stored, as shown in Figure 2-10. In our editable version, we double-clicked on the column name, then selected "Link to another record" in the dropdown menu, to connect it to another tab.

Figure 2-10. In this Airtable sample, we linked the organization column in the people sheet to the food banks sheet.

In our Airtable sample, click on a linked row to expand it and view related data. For example, if you click and expand on the first row in the *people* sheet, their organization's full address appears from the *food banks* sheet, as shown in Figure 2-11. In our editable version, if we update the address for one organization in the *food banks* sheet, it's automatically changed for all employees linked to that organization in the *people* sheet. In addition, Airtable allows you to sort, filter, and create different views of your data that you can share with others, a topic we'll cover in Chapter 9. See more about its features in the Airtable support page (*https://support.airtable.com*).

It's important to understand the conceptual differences between a "flat-file" spreadsheet and a relational database to help you determine when to use one tool versus another. As you've learned in the previous sections, spreadsheets are your best choice to begin organizing and analyzing your data, using methods such as sorting, filtering, pivoting, and lookup, to help reveal the underlying stories that you may wish to visualize. But relational databases are your best choice when maintaining large amounts of data with internal links, like one-to-many relationships, such as an organization with several employees.

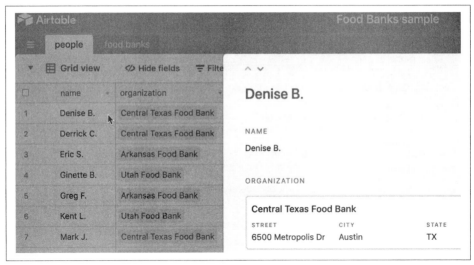

Figure 2-11. In this Airtable demo (https://airtable.com/shrOlb4XT11Xy2LP2), click on a row in one sheet to expand and view its linked data in another sheet.

Summary

If you're one of the many people who "never really learned" about spreadsheets in school or on the job, or if you've taught yourself bits and pieces along the way, we hope that this chapter has successfully strengthened your skills. All of the subsequent chapters in this book, especially those on designing interactive charts in Chapter 6 and interactive maps in Chapter 7, require a basic level of familiarity with spreadsheets. In addition to serving as incredible time-savers when it comes to tedious data tasks, the spreadsheet tools and methods featured are designed to help you share, sort, calculate, pivot, and look up matching data, with the broader goal of visualizing your data stories.

The next chapter describes strategies for finding and questioning your data, particularly on open data sites operated by governmental and nonprofit organizations, where you'll also need spreadsheet skills to download and organize public information.

CHAPTER 3

Find and Question Your Data

In the early stages of a visualization project, we often start with two interrelated issues: *Where can I find reliable data?* And after you find something, *What does this data truly represent?* If you leap too quickly into constructing charts and maps without thinking deeply about these dual issues, you run the risk of creating meaningless, or perhaps worse, misleading visualizations.

This chapter breaks down both of these broad issues in "Guiding Questions for Your Search" on page 48, "Public and Private Data" on page 52, "Mask or Aggregate Sensitive Data" on page 56, "Open Data Repositories" on page 57, "Source Your Data" on page 59, "Recognize Bad Data" on page 61. Finally, once you've found some files, we propose some ways to question and acknowledge the limitations of your data in "Question Your Data" on page 64.

Information does not magically appear out of thin air. Instead, people collect and publish data, with explicit or implicit purposes, within the social contexts and power structures of their times. As data visualization advocates, we strongly favor evidence-based reasoning over less-informed alternatives. We caution against embracing so-called data objectivity, however, since numbers and other forms of data are *not* neutral. Therefore, when working with data, pause to inquire more deeply about *Whose stories are told?* and *Whose perspectives remain unspoken?* Only by asking these types of questions, according to *Data Feminism* (*https://oreil.ly/YvupZ*) authors Catherine D'Ignazio and Lauren Klein, will we "start to see how privilege is baked into our data practices and our data products."[1]

---

1 Catherine D'Ignazio and Lauren F. Klein, *Data Feminism* (MIT Press, 2020), *https://oreil.ly/YvupZ*.

Guiding Questions for Your Search

For many people, a data search is simply googling some keywords on the web. Sometimes that works, sometimes not. When that approach flounders, we reflect on the many lessons we've learned about data-hunting while working alongside talented librarians, journalists, and researchers. Collectively, they taught us a set of guiding questions that outline a more thoughtful process about *how to search* for data.

What Exactly Is the Question You're Seeking to Answer With Data?

Literally write it down—in the form of a question, punctuated with a question mark at the end—to clarify your own thinking, and also so that you can clearly communicate it to others who can assist you. All too often, our brains automatically leap ahead to try to identify the *answer*, without reflecting on the best way frame the *question* in a way that does not limit the range of possible outcomes.

Look back at data visualization projects that made a lasting impression on you to identify the underlying question that motivated them. In their coverage of the US opioid epidemic, the *Washington Post* and the West Virginia *Charleston Gazette-Mail* successfully fought a legal battle to obtain a US Drug Enforcement Agency database that the federal government and the drug industry sought to keep secret. In 2019, a team of data journalists published the database with interactive maps to answer one of their central questions: *How many prescription opioid pills were sent to each US county, per capita, and which companies and distributors were responsible?* Their maps revealed (*https://oreil.ly/Xx7dh*) high clusters in several rural Appalachian counties that received more than 150 opioid pills per resident, on average, each year from 2006 to 2014. Moreover, only six companies distributed more than three-quarters of the 100 billion oxycodone and hydrocodone pills across the US during this period: McKesson Corp., Walgreens, Cardinal Health, AmerisourceBergen, CVS, and Walmart.[2] Even if you're not working with data as large or as controversial as this, the broader lesson is to clearly identify the question you're seeking to answer.

Also, it's perfectly normal to revise your question as your research evolves. For example, Jack and his students once began a data project by naively asking, *What were Connecticut public school test scores in the 1960s?* Soon we discovered that standardized state-level school testing as we know it today did not appear in states like Connecticut until the mid-1980s school accountability movement. Even then, results weren't widely visible to the public until newspapers began to publish them once a year in print in the 1990s. Later, real estate firms, school-ratings companies, and government agencies began to publish data continuously on the web as the internet expanded in the late 1990s and early 2000s. Based on what we learned, we revised our

---

2 "Drilling into the DEA's Pain Pill Database" (*Washington Post*, July 16, 2019), *https://oreil.ly/Xx7dh*.

research question to, *When and how did Connecticut homebuyers start to become aware of school test scores, and how did these influence the prices they were willing to pay for access to selected public school attendance areas?*[3] Be prepared to refine your question when the evidence leads you in a better direction.

What Types of Organizations May Have Collected or Published the Data You Seek?

If a governmental organization may have been involved, then at what level: local, regional, state/provincial, national, or international? Which branch of government: executive, legislative, or judicial? Or which particular governmental agency might have been responsible for compiling or distributing this information? Since all of these different structures can be overwhelming, reach out to librarians who are trained to work with government documents and databases, often at state government libraries (*https://oreil.ly/vEGoJ*) or at local institutions participating in the US Federal Depository Library Program (*https://oreil.ly/Au6SG*). Or might the data you seek have been compiled by a nongovernmental organization, such as academic institutions, journalists, nonprofit groups, or for-profit corporations? Figuring out *which organizations* might have collected and published the data can help point you to the digital or print materials they typically publish and the most appropriate tools to focus your search in that particular area.

What Level(s) of Data Are Available?

Is information disaggregated into individual cases or aggregated into larger groups? Smaller units of data allow you to make more granular interpretations, while larger units can help you to identify broader patterns. Librarians can help us decipher how and why organizations publish data at different levels. For example, the US Census collects data every 10 years about each person residing in the nation. Under law, individual-level data about each person is confidential for 72 years, then released to the public. Currently, you can search for specific individuals in the 1940 Census and earlier decades at the US National Archives (*https://oreil.ly/BkCal*) and other websites, as shown in Figure 3-1.

---

3 Jack Dougherty et al., "School Choice in Suburbia: Test Scores, Race, and Housing Markets," *American Journal of Education* 115, no. 4 (August 2009): 523–48, *https://oreil.ly/T2I81*.

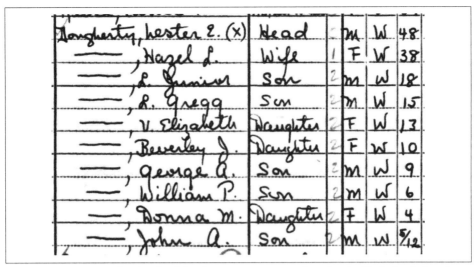

Figure 3-1. Excerpt of individual-level 1940 US Census data for Jack's father's family.

Meanwhile, the US Census publishes data for current years by aggregating individual records into larger geographic areas to protect people's privacy. Using the Standard Hierarchy of US Census Geographic Entities (*https://oreil.ly/pkY2n*), we created a simplified map in Figure 3-2 to show the relationships between some of the most common geographic areas for Hartford, Connecticut:

- State
- County
- County subdivisions (equivalent to Connecticut towns and cities)
- Census tracts (designated areas, roughly 1,200–8,000 people)
- Block groups (subunit of tracts, roughly 600–3,000 people)
- Census blocks (subunit of block groups, but not always a city block)[4]

---

4 Katy Rossiter, "What Are Census Blocks?" US Census Bureau, July 11, 2011, *https://oreil.ly/UTxpk*.

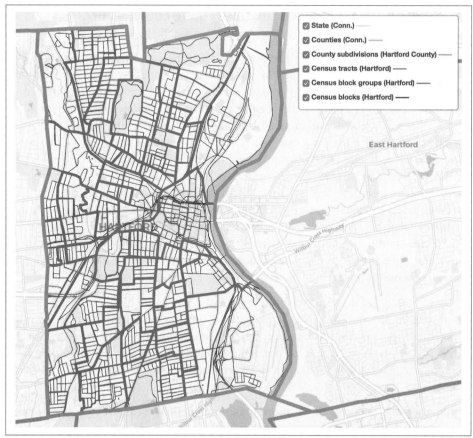

Figure 3-2. Common US Census geographies around Hartford, Connecticut, 2019. Zoom out in the interactive version (https://oreil.ly/JaQUN) for county and state boundaries.

Have Prior Publications Drawn on Similar Data, and, if so, How Can We Trace Their Sources?

Some of our best ideas began when reading an article or book that described its source of evidence, and we imagined new ways to visualize that data. Several times, we have stumbled across a data table in a print publication, or perhaps an old web page, which sparked our interest in tracking down a newer version to explore. Even *outdated* data helps by demonstrating how someone previously collected it at one point in time. Follow the footnotes to track down its origins. Use Google Scholar (*https://google.com/scholar*) and more specialized research databases (ask librarians for assistance if needed) to track down the source of previously published data. One bonus is that if you can locate more current data, you may be able to design a visualization that compares change over time.

What if No One Has Collected the Data You're Looking For?

Sometimes this happens due to more than a simple oversight. In *Data Feminism*, Catherine D'Ignazio and Lauren Klein underscore how issues of data collection "are directly connected to larger issues of power and privilege" by recounting a story about tennis star Serena Williams. When Williams experienced life-threatening complications while giving birth to her daughter in 2017, she called public attention to the way that she, a Black woman, needed to advocate for herself in the hospital. After her experience, she wrote on social media that "Black women are over 3 times more likely than white women to die from pregnancy- or childbirth-related causes," citing the US Centers for Disease Control and Prevention (CDC). When journalists followed up to investigate further, they discovered the absence of detailed data on maternal mortality, and what a 2014 United Nations report described as a "particularly weak" aspect of data collection in the US healthcare system. Journalists reported that "there was still no national system for tracking complications sustained in pregnancy and childbirth," despite comparable systems for other health issues such as heart attacks or hip replacements.

Power structures are designed to count people whose lives are highly valued, or under a high degree of surveillance. D'Ignazio and Klein call on us to critically examine these power systems, collect data to counter their effects, and make everyone's labor in this process more visible.[5] If no one has collected the data you're looking for, perhaps you can take valuable steps to publicly recognize the issue, and possibly gather it yourself.

Hunting for data involves much more than googling keywords. Deepen your search by reflecting on the types of questions that librarians, journalists, and other researchers have taught us to ask: What types of organizations might—or might not—have collected the data? At what levels? At any prior point in time? And under what social and political contexts? In the next section, you'll learn more about related issues to consider over public and private data.

Public and Private Data

When searching for data, you also need to be informed about debates regarding public and private data. Not only do these debates influence the kinds of data you might be able to legally use in your visualizations, but they also raise deeper ethical issues about the extent to which anyone should be able to collect or circulate private information about individuals. This section offers our general observations on these debates, based primarily on our context in the US. Since we are not lawyers (thank

---

5 D'Ignazio and Klein, *Data Feminism*.

goodness!), please consult with legal experts for advice about your specific case if needed.

The first debate asks: *To what extent should anyone be allowed to collect data about private individuals?*

Several critics of "big data" worry that governments are becoming more like a totalitarian "Big Brother" as they collect more data about individual citizens in the digital age. In the US, concerns mounted in 2013 when whistleblower Edward Snowden disclosed how the National Security Agency conducted global surveillance using US citizen email and phone records provided by telecommunications companies. Shoshana Zuboff, a Harvard Business School professor and author of *The Age of Surveillance Capitalism*, warns of an equal threat posed by corporations that collect and commodify massive amounts of individually identifiable data for profit.[6] Due to the rise of digital commerce, powerful technology companies own data that you and others consider to be private:

- Google knows what words you typed into their search engine, as shown in aggregated form in Google Trends (*https://oreil.ly/zxYZC*). Also, Google's Chrome browser tracks your web activity through cookies, as described by *Washington Post* technology reporter Geoffrey Fowler.[7]

- Amazon eavesdrops and records your conversations with its Alexa home assistants, as Fowler also documents.[8]

- Facebook follows which friends and political causes you favor, and Fowler also reports how it tracks your off-Facebook activity, such as purchases made at other businesses, to improve its targeted advertising.[9]

Some point out that "big data" collected by large corporations can offer public benefits. For example, Apple shared its aggregated mobility data (*https://oreil.ly/QRdkB*) collected from iPhone users to help public health officials compare which populations stayed home rather than travel during the COVID-19 pandemic. Others point out that corporations are largely setting their own terms for how they collect data and what they can do with it. Although California began to implement its Consumer

---

6 Shoshana Zuboff, *The Age of Surveillance Capitalism: The Fight for a Human Future at the New Frontier of Power* (PublicAffairs, 2019).

7 Geoffrey A. Fowler, "Goodbye, Chrome: Google's Web Browser Has Become Spy Software," *The Washington Post*, June 21, 2019, *https://oreil.ly/_ef8H*.

8 Geoffrey A. Fowler, "Alexa Has Been Eavesdropping on You This Whole Time," *The Washington Post*, May 6, 2019, *https://oreil.ly/eR6RG*.

9 Geoffrey A. Fowler, "Facebook Will Now Show You Exactly How It Stalks You — Even When You're Not Using Facebook," *The Washington Post*, January 28, 2020, *https://oreil.ly/rmV9T*.

Privacy Act in 2020 (*https://oreil.ly/9swiI*), which promises to allow individuals the right to review and delete the data that companies collect about them, US state and federal government has not fully entered this policy arena. If you work with data that was collected from individuals by public or private organizations, learn about these controversies to help you make wise and ethical choices about what to include in your visualizations.

The second question is: *When our government collects data, to what extent should it be publicly available?*

In the US, the 1966 Freedom of Information Act (*https://oreil.ly/By-zV*) and its subsequent amendments have sought to open access to information in the federal government, with the view that increased transparency would promote public scrutiny and pressure officials to make positive changes. In addition, state governments operate under their own freedom of information laws, sometimes called "open records" or "sunshine laws." When people say they've submitted an "FOI," it means they've sent a written request to a government agency for information that they believe should be public under the law. But federal and state FOIA laws are complex, and courts have interpreted cases in different ways over time, as summarized in the Open Government Guide (*https://oreil.ly/zFVmg*) by the Reporters Committee for Freedom of the Press, and also by the National Freedom of Information Coalition (*https://www.nfoic.org*). Sometimes government agencies quickly agree and comply with an FOI request, while other times they may delay or reject it, which may pressure the requester to attempt to resolve the issue through time-consuming litigation. Around the world, more than one hundred nations have their own version of freedom of information laws (*https://oreil.ly/aAPZ0*), with the oldest being Sweden's 1766 Freedom of the Press Act, but these laws vary widely.

In most cases, individual-level data collected by US federal and state governments is considered private, except in cases where our governmental process has determined that a broader interest is served by making it public. To illustrate this distinction, let's begin with two cases where US federal law protects the privacy of individual-level data:

- Patient-level health data is generally protected under the Privacy Rule of the Health Insurance Portability and Accountability Act (*https://oreil.ly/IlSRk*), commonly known as HIPAA. In order for public health officials to track broad trends about illness in the population, individual patient data must be aggregated into larger anonymized datasets in ways that protect specific people's confidentiality.

- Similarly, student-level education data is generally protected under the Family Educational Rights and Privacy Act (*https://oreil.ly/DpRBa*), commonly known as FERPA. Public education officials regularly aggregate individual student records into larger anonymized public datasets to track the broad progress of schools, districts, and states, without revealing individually identifiable data.

On the other hand, here are three cases where government has ruled that the public interest is served by making individual-level data widely available:

- Individual contributions to political candidates are public information in the US Federal Election Commission database (*https://oreil.ly/n-nfB*), and related databases by nonprofit organizations, such as Follow The Money (*https://www.follow themoney.org*) by the National Institute on Money in Politics and Open Secrets (*https://www.opensecrets.org*) by the Center for Responsive Politics. The latter two sites describe more details about donations submitted through political action committees and controversial exceptions to campaign finance laws. Across the US, state-level political contribution laws vary widely, and these public records are stored in separate databases. For example, anyone can search the Connecticut Campaign Reporting Information System (*https://oreil.ly/ycsTB*) to find donations Jack made to state-level political campaigns.

- Individual property ownership records are public, and increasingly hosted online by many local governments. A privately funded company compiled this US public records directory (*https://oreil.ly/OD7MO*) with links to county and municipal property records, where available. For example, anyone can search the property assessment database for the Town of West Hartford, Connecticut (*https://oreil.ly/ jQigl*) to find property Jack owns, its square footage, and purchase price.

- Individual salaries for officers of tax-exempt organizations are public, which these organizations are required to file on Internal Revenue Service (IRS) 990 forms each year. For example, anyone can search 990 forms on ProPublica's Nonprofit Explorer (*https://oreil.ly/SbNVi*), and view the salary and other compensation of the top officers of Jack's employer and Ilya's alma mater, Trinity College in Hartford, Connecticut.

Social and political pressures are continually changing the boundary over what types of individual-level data collected by government should be made publicly available. For example, the Black Lives Matter movement has gradually made more individual-level data about violence by police officers more widely available. For example, in 2001, the State of New Jersey required local police departments to document any "use of force" by officers, whether minor or major, such as firing their gun. But no one could easily search these paper forms until a team of journalists from NJ Advance Media submitted more than five hundred public records requests and compiled The Force Report digital database (*https://force.nj.com*), where anyone can look up individual officers and investigate patterns of violent behavior. Similarly, a team of ProPublica journalists created The NYPD Files database (*https://oreil.ly/cCS_m*), which allows anyone to search closed cases of civilian complaints against New York City police officers, by name or precinct, for patterns of substantiated allegations.

Everyone who works with data needs to get informed about key debates over what should be public or private, become active in policy discussions about whose interests are being served, and contribute to making positive change. In the next section, you'll learn about ethical choices you'll need to make when working with sensitive individual-level data.

Mask or Aggregate Sensitive Data

Even if individual-level data is legally and publicly accessible, each of us is responsible for making ethical decisions about if and how to use it when creating data visualizations. When working with sensitive data, some ethical questions to ask are: *What are the risks that publicly sharing individual-level data might cause more harm than good?* and *Is there a way to tell the same data story without publicly sharing details that may intrude on individual privacy?*

There are no simple answers to these ethical questions, since every situation is different and requires weighing the risks of individual harm against the benefits of broader knowledge about vital public issues. This section clarifies some of the alternatives to blindly redistributing sensitive information, such as masking and aggregating individual-level data.

Imagine that you're exploring crime data and wish to create an interactive map about the frequency of different types of 911 police calls across several neighborhoods. If you search for public data about police calls (*https://oreil.ly/_EX06*), as described in "Open Data Repositories" on page 57, you'll see different policies and practices for sharing individual-level data published by police call centers. In many US states, information about victims of sexual crimes or child abuse (such as the address where police were sent) is considered confidential and exempt from public release, so it's not included in the open data. But some police departments publish open data about calls with the full address for other types of crimes, in a format like this:

```
| Date  | Full Address | Category          |
| Jan 1 | 1234 Main St | Aggravated Assault |
```

While this information is publicly available, it's possible that you could cause some type of physical or emotional harm to the victims by redistributing detailed information about a violent crime with their full address in your data visualization.

One alternative is to *mask* details in sensitive data. For example, some police departments hide the last few digits of street addresses in their open data reports to protect individual privacy, while still showing the general location, in a format like this:

```
| Date  | Masked Address | Category          |
| Jan 1 | 1XXX Main St   | Aggravated Assault |
```

You can also mask individual-level data when appropriate, using methods similar to the Find and Replace method with your spreadsheet tool as discussed in Chapter 4.

Another strategy is to *aggregate* individual-level data into larger groups, which can protect privacy while showing broader patterns. In the preceding example, if you're exploring crime data across different neighborhoods, group individual 911 calls into larger geographic areas, such as census tracts or area names, in a format like this:

```
| Neighborhood | Crime Category     | Frequency |
| East Side    | Aggravated Assault | 13        |
| West Side    | Aggravated Assault | 21        |
```

Aggregating individual-level details into larger, yet meaningful categories, is also a better way to tell data stories about the bigger picture. To aggregate simple spreadsheet data, see "Summarize Data with Pivot Tables" on page 33; to normalize data for more meaningful maps, see "Normalize Your Data" on page 90. See also "Bulk Geocode with US Census" on page 361, and "Pivot Points into Polygon Data" on page 363.

Next you'll learn how to explore datasets that governments and nongovernmental organizations have intentionally shared with the public.

Open Data Repositories

Over the past decade, an increasing number of governmental and nongovernmental organizations around the globe have begun to proactively share public data through open data repositories. While some of these datasets were previously available as individual files on isolated websites, these growing networks have made open data easier to find, enabled more frequent agency updates, and sometimes support live interaction with other computers. Open data repositories often include these features:

View and export
At minimum, open data repositories allow users to view and export data in common spreadsheet formats, such as CSV, ODS, and XLSX. Some repositories also provide geographical boundary files for creating maps.

Built-in visualization tools
Several repositories offer built-in tools for users to create interactive charts or maps on the platform site. Some also provide code snippets for users to embed these built-in visualizations into their own websites, which you'll learn more about in Chapter 9.

Application programming interface (APIs)
Some repositories provide endpoints with code instructions that allow other computers to pull data directly from the platform into an external site or online visualization. When repositories continuously update data and publish an API

endpoint, it can be an ideal way to display live or "almost live" data in your visualization, which you'll learn more about in Chapter 12.

Due to the recent growth of open data repositories, especially in governmental policy and scientific research, there is no single website that lists all of them. Instead, here are just a few sites from the US and around the globe to spark readers' curiosity and encourage you to dig deeper:

Data.gov (https://www.data.gov)
    The official repository for US federal government agencies.

Data.census.gov (https://data.census.gov)
    The main platform to access US Census Bureau data. The Decennial Census is a full count of the population every ten years, while the American Community Survey (ACS) is an annual sample count that produces one-year and five-year estimates for different census geographies, with margins of error.

Eurostat (https://ec.europa.eu/eurostat)
    The statistical office of the European Union.

Federal Reserve Economic Research (https://fred.stlouisfed.org)
    For US and international data.

Global Open Data Index (https://index.okfn.org/dataset)
    By the Open Knowledge Foundation.

Google Dataset Search (https://datasetsearch.research.google.com)
    A search engine for datasets developed by Google.

Harvard Dataverse (https://dataverse.harvard.edu)
    Open to all researchers from any discipline.

Humanitarian Data Exchange (https://data.humdata.org)
    By the United Nations Office for the Coordination of Humanitarian Affairs.

IPUMS (https://www.ipums.org)
    Integrated Public Use Microdata Series, the world's largest individual-level population database, with microdata samples from US and international census records and surveys, hosted by the University of Minnesota.

openAfrica (https://africaopendata.org)
    By Code for Africa.

Open Data Inception (https://opendatainception.io)
    A map-oriented global directory.

Open Data Network (https://www.opendatanetwork.com)
   A directory by Socrata, primarily of US state and municipal open data platforms. United Nations data (*https://data.un.org*).

World Bank Open Data (https://data.worldbank.org)
   A global collection of economic-development data.

World Inequality Database (https://wid.world)
   A global data on income and wealth inequality.

For more options, see *Open Data* listings that have been organized and maintained by staff at several libraries, including the University of Rochester (*https://oreil.ly/G4zJn*), State University of New York (SUNY) College at Geneseo (*https://oreil.ly/Sgs_0*), Brown University (*https://oreil.ly/K8tJ8*), and many others.

In addition, better-resourced higher-education libraries and other organizations may pay subscription fees that allow their students and staff to access "closed" data repositories. For example, Social Explorer (*https://www.socialexplorer.com*) offers decades of demographic, economic, health, education, religion, and crime data for local and national geographies, primarily for the US, Canada, and Europe. Previously, Social Explorer made many files available to the public, but it now requires a paid subscription or 14-day free trial. Also, Policy Map (*https://www.policymap.com*) provides demographic, economic, housing, and quality-of-life data for US areas, and makes some publicly visible in its Open Map view (*https://www.policymap.com/maps*), but you need a subscription to download them.

See also "Find GeoJSON Boundary Files" on page 340, an open data standard used for creating maps in this book.

Now that you've learned more about navigating open data repositories, the next section will teach you ways to properly source the data that you discover.

Source Your Data

When you find data, write the source information inside the downloaded file or a new file you create. Add key details about its origins, so that you—or someone else in the future—can replicate your steps. We recommend doing this in two places: the spreadsheet filename and a source notes tab. As a third step, make a backup sheet of your data. The first step is to label every data file that you download or create. All of us have experienced "bad filenames" like the following, which you should avoid:

- *data.csv*
- *file.ods*
- *download.xlsx*

Write a short but meaningful filename. While there's no perfect system, a good strategy is to abbreviate the source (such as census or worldbank or eurostat), add topic keywords, and a date or range. If you or coworkers will be working on different versions of a downloaded file, include the current date in YYYY-MM-DD (year-month-date) format. If you plan to upload files to the web, type names in all lowercase and replace blank spaces with dashes (-) or underscores (_). Better filenames look like this:

- *town-demographics-2019-12-02.csv*
- *census2010_population_by_county.ods*
- *eurostat-1999-2019-co2-emissions.xlsx*

The second step is to save more detailed source notes about the data on a separate tab inside the spreadsheet, which works for multitab spreadsheet tools such as Google Sheets, LibreOffice, and Excel. Add a new tab named *notes* that describes the origins of the data, a longer description for any abbreviated labels, and when it was last updated, as shown in Figure 3-3. Add your own name and give credit to collaborators who worked with you. If you need to create a CSV file from this data, give it a parallel name to your multitabbed spreadsheet file so that you can easily find your original source notes again in the future.

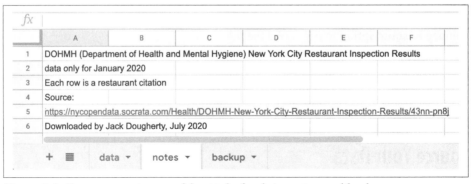

Figure 3-3. Create separate spreadsheet tabs for data, notes, and backup.

A third step is to make a backup of the original data before cleaning or editing it. For a simple one-sheet file in a multitab spreadsheet tool, right-click the tab containing the data to make a duplicate copy in another tab, also shown in Figure 3-3. Clearly label the new tab as a backup and leave it alone! For CSV files, or more complex spreadsheets, create a separate backup file. To be clear, these simple backup strategies only help you avoid making nonfixable edits to your original data. Make sure you have a broader strategy to back up your files from your computer or cloud account in case either of those are deleted or those systems crash.

Make a habit of using these three sourcing strategies—filenames, notes, and backups—to increase the credibility and replicability of your data visualizations. In the next section, we'll explore more ways to reduce your chances of making "bad data" errors.

Recognize Bad Data

When your data search produces some results, another key step is to open the file, quickly scroll through the content, and look for any warning signs that it might contain "bad data." If you fail to catch a problem in your data at an early stage, it could lead to false conclusions and diminish the credibility of all of your work. Fortunately, members of the data visualization community have shared multiple examples of problems we've previously encountered, to help save newer members from making the same embarrassing mistakes. One popular crowdsourced compilation by data journalists was The Quartz Guide to Bad Data (*https://oreil.ly/9YTFX*). Watch out for spreadsheets containing these "bad data" warning signs:

Missing values
> If you see blank or "null" entries, does that mean data was not collected? Or maybe a respondent did not answer? If you're unsure, find out from the data creator. Also beware when humans enter a 0 or -1 to represent a missing value without thinking about its consequences on running spreadsheet calculations, such as SUM or AVERAGE.

Missing leading zeros
> One of the zip codes for Hartford, Connecticut is 06106. If someone converts a column of zip codes to numerical data, it will strip out the leading zero and appear as 6106. Similarly, the US Census Bureau lists every place using a Federal Information Processing Standards (FIPS) code, and some of these also begin with a meaningful zero character. For example, the FIPS code for Los Angeles County, California is 037, but if someone accidentally converts a column of text to numbers, it will strip out the leading zero and convert that FIPS code to 37, which may break some functions that rely on this code being a three-digit number, or may make some people interpret it as a two-digit state code for North Carolina instead.

65536 rows or 255 columns
> These are the maximum number of rows supported by older-style Excel spreadsheets, or columns supported by Apple Numbers spreadsheet, respectively. If your spreadsheet stops exactly at either of these limits, you probably have only partial data. As we wrote this, the BBC reported that Public Health England lost thousands of COVID-19 test results (*https://oreil.ly/kUyEi*) due to this row limit in older Excel spreadsheets.

Inconsistent date formats

For example, November 3, 2020, is commonly entered in spreadsheets in the US as 11/3/2020 (month-day-year), while people in other locations around the globe commonly type it as 3/11/2020 (day-month-year). Check your source.

Dates such as January 1st 1900, 1904, or 1970

These are default timestamps in Excel spreadsheets and Unix operating systems, which may indicate the actual date was blank or overwritten.

Dates similar to 43891

When you type March 1 during the year 2020 into Microsoft Excel, it automatically displays as 1-Mar, but is saved using Excel's internal date system as 43891. If someone converts this column from date to text format, you'll see Excel's five-digit number, not the dates you're expecting.

Other ways to review the quality of data entry in any spreadsheet column are discussed in "Sort and Filter Data" on page 28 and "Summarize Data with Pivot Tables" on page 33, as well as in Chapter 6, where you will learn to create a histogram. These methods enable you to quickly inspect the range of values that appear in a column and to help you identify bad data.

Also beware of bad data due to poor geocoding, when locations have been translated into latitude and longitude coordinates that cannot be trusted (see "Geocode Addresses in Google Sheets" on page 23). For example, visualization expert Alberto Cairo describes how data *appeared* to show that Kansas residents viewed more online pornography than other US states. On closer examination, the internet protocol (IP) addresses of many viewers couldn't be accurately geocoded, perhaps because they sought to maintain their privacy by using virtual private networks (VPN) to disguise their location. As a result, the geocoding tool automatically placed large numbers of users in the geographic center of the contiguous US, which happens to be in Kansas.[10] Similarly, when global data is poorly geocoded, the population booms on imaginary "Null Island" (*https://oreil.ly/ZuwAx*), which is actually a weather buoy located in the Atlantic Ocean at the intersection of the prime meridian and the equator, where the latitude and longitude coordinates are 0,0. For these reasons, carefully inspect geocoded data for errors caused by tools that mistakenly place results in the exact center of your geography, as shown in Figure 3-4.

---

10 Cairo, *How Charts Lie*, 2019, pp. 99–102

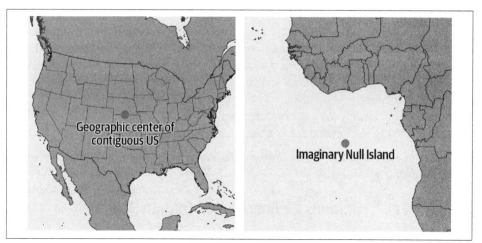

Figure 3-4. Beware of bad geocoding that automatically places data in the geographic center of the contiguous US (in northern Kansas), or on imaginary Null Island in the Atlantic Ocean (the location of coordinates 0,0).

What should you do when you discover bad data in your project? Sometimes small issues are relatively straightforward and do not call into question the integrity of the entire dataset. Sometimes you can fix these using methods we describe in Chapter 4. Larger issues can be more problematic. Follow the source of your data stream to try to identify where the issue began. If you cannot find and fix the issue on your own, contact the data provider to ask for their input, since they should have a strong interest in improving the quality of the data. If they cannot resolve an important data issue, then you need to pause and think carefully. In this case, is it wiser to continue working with problematic data and add a cautionary note to readers, or should you stop using the dataset entirely and call attention to its underlying problem? These are not easy decisions, and you should ask for opinions from colleagues. In any case, never ignore the warning signs of bad data.

Finally, you can help prevent bad data from occurring by following key steps we've outlined. Give meaningful names to your data files and add source notes in a separate tab about when and where you obtained it, along with any definitions or details about what it claims to measure and how it was recorded. Explain what any blanks or null values mean, and avoid replacing those with zeros or other symbols. Always watch out for formatting issues when entering data or running calculations in spreadsheets.

In the next section, you'll learn more questions to help you understand your data at a deeper level.

Question Your Data

Now that you've found, sourced, and inspected some files, the next step is to *question your data* by looking more deeply than the surface level. Read the *metadata*, which are the notes that describe the data and its sources. Examine the contents to reflect on what is explicitly stated—or unstated—to better understand its origin, context, and limitations. You cannot program a computer to do this step for you, as it requires critical thinking to see beyond the characters and numbers appearing on your screen.

One place to start is to ask: *What do the data labels really mean?* and to consider the following potential issues.

What Are Full Definitions for Abbreviated Column Headers?

Spreadsheets often contain abbreviated column headers, such as *Elevation* or *Income*. Sometimes the original software limited the number of characters that could be entered, or the people who created the header names preferred to keep them short. But was *Elevation* entered in meters or feet? An abbreviated data label does not answer that key question, so you'll need to check the source notes, or if that's not available, compare elevation data for a specific point in the dataset to a known source that includes the measurement unit. Similarly, if you're working with US Census data, does the *Income* abbreviation refer to per person, per family, or per household? Also, does the value reflect the *median* (the midpoint in a range of numbers) or the *mean* (the average, calculated by adding up the sum and dividing by the number of values). Check definitions in the source notes.

How Exactly Was the Data Collected?

For example, was *Elevation* for a specific location measured by a GPS unit on the ground? Or was the location geocoded on a digital map that contains elevation data? In most cases, the two methods will yield different results, and whether that matters depends on the degree of precision required in your work. Similarly, when the US Census reports data from its annual American Community Survey (ACS) estimates for *Income* and other variables, these are drawn from small samples of respondents for lower levels of geography, such as a census tract with roughly four thousand residents, which can generate very high margins of error. For example, it's not uncommon to see ACS estimates (*https://oreil.ly/GNKUY*) for a census tract with a mean family income of $50,000—but also with a $25,000 margin of error—which tells you that the actual value is somewhere between $25,000 and $75,000. As a result, some ACS estimates for small geographic units are effectively meaningless. Check how data was recorded, and note any reported margins of error, in the source notes. See also how to create error bars in Chapter 6.

To What Extent Is the Data Socially Constructed?

What do the data labels reveal or hide about how people defined categories in different social and political contexts, which differ across place and time? For example, we designed an interactive historical map of racial change (*https://oreil.ly/cEu9W*) for Hartford County, Connecticut using more than one hundred years of US Census data. But census categories for race and ethnicity shifted dramatically during those decades because people in power redefined these contested terms and reassigned people to different groups.[11] Into the 1930s, US Census officials separated "Native White" and "Foreign-born White" in reports, then combined and generally reported these as "White" in later decades. Also, US Census officials classified "Mexican" as "Other races" in 1930, then moved this group back to "White" in 1940, then reported "Puerto Rican or Spanish surname" data in 1960, followed by "Hispanic or Latino" as an ethnic category distinct from race in later decades. Finally, the Census replaced "Negro" with "Black" in 1980, and finally dropped mutually-exclusive racial categories in 2000, so that people could choose more than one. As a result, these historical changes in the social construction of race and ethnicity influenced how we designed our map to display "White" or "White alone" over time, with additional Census categories relevant to each decade shown in the pop-up window, with our explanation about these decisions in the caption and source notes.

There is no single definitive way to visualize socially constructed data when definitions change across decades. When you make choices about data, describe your thought process in the notes or companion text.

What Aspects of the Data Remain Unclear or Uncertain?

Here's a paradox about working with data: some of these deep questions may not be fully answerable if the data was collected by someone other than yourself, especially if that person came from a distant place or time period, or a different position in a social hierarchy. Even if you can't fully answer these questions, don't let that stop you from asking good questions about the origins, context, and underlying meaning of your data. Our job is to tell true and meaningful stories with data, but that process begins by clarifying what we know—and what we don't know—about the information we've gathered. Sometimes we can visually depict its limitations through error bars, as you'll learn in "Chart Design Principles" on page 103, and sometimes we need to acknowledge uncertainty in our data stories, as we'll discuss in "Acknowledge Sources and Uncertainty" on page 405.

---

11 For a deeper analysis, see Margo J. Anderson, *The American Census: A Social History*, 2nd edition (Yale University Press, 2015).

Summary

This chapter reviewed two broad questions that everyone should ask during the early stages of their visualization project: *Where can I find data?* and *What do I really know about it?* We broke down both questions into more specific parts to develop your knowledge and skills in guiding questions for your search, engaging with debates over public and private data, masking and aggregating sensitive data, navigating open data repositories, sourcing data origins, recognizing bad data, and questioning your data more deeply than its surface level. Remember these lessons as you leap into the next few chapters on cleaning data and creating interactive charts and maps. We'll come back to related issues on this topic in Chapter 14.

CHAPTER 4

Clean Up Messy Data

More often than not, datasets will be messy and hard to visualize right away. They will have missing values, dates in different formats, text in numeric-only columns, multiple items in the same columns, various spellings of the same name, and other unexpected things. See Figure 4-1 for inspiration. Don't be surprised if you find yourself spending more time cleaning up data than you do analyzing and visualizing it.

Year	City	Amount
1990	New York City	$1,123,456.00
1995-96		2.2 mil
2000's	NYC	No data
2020	New_York	5000000+

Figure 4-1. More often than not, raw data looks messy.

In this chapter, you'll learn about different tools to help you make decisions about which one to use to clean up your data efficiently. We'll start with basic cleanup methods using Google Sheets in "Smart Cleanup with Google Sheets" on page 68, "Find and Replace with Blank" on page 69, "Transpose Rows and Columns" on page 71, "Split Data into Separate Columns" on page 72, and "Combine Data into One Column" on page 75. While we feature Google Sheets in our examples, many of these principles (and in some cases, the same formulas) apply to Microsoft Excel, LibreOffice Calc, Mac's Numbers, or other spreadsheet packages. Next, you'll learn how to extract table data from text-based PDF documents with Tabula, a free tool used by data journalists and researchers worldwide to analyze spending data, health reports, and all sorts of other datasets that get trapped in PDFs (see "Extract Tables from PDFs with Tabula" on page 76). Finally, we will introduce OpenRefine in "Clean Data with OpenRefine" on page 79, a powerful and versatile tool to clean up the messiest spreadsheets, such as those containing dozens of different spellings of the same name.

Smart Cleanup with Google Sheets

One of the newest reasons to work with your data in Google Sheets is to use its Smart Cleanup feature, which helps identify and suggest corrections for inaccurate data. The tool opens a sidebar menu that spots potential problems, and you decide whether to accept its suggestion.

Learn what types of issues Smart Cleanup catches, and which ones it misses, using our sample data on the 10 most populated nations in the world, which contains some problems that we intentionally added:

1. Open the Smart Cleanup sample data file in Google Sheets (*https://oreil.ly/ NxGPN*), sign in with your account, and go to File > "Make a copy" to create a version you can edit in your Google Drive.

2. Go to Data > "Cleanup suggestions" and view items that appear in the sidebar.

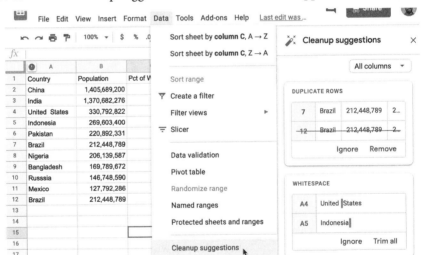

The Smart Cleanup feature successfully caught a duplicate entry (row 12), and white spaces in cells A4 and A5. Click the green Remove and "Trim all" buttons to confirm that Google Sheets should clean them up.

Can you spot these other errors that Smart Cleanup missed?

- In cell A10, *Russsia* is misspelled with an extra *s*.
- In cell C6, Pakistan's share of the world population appears in decimal form, not percentage.
- In cell D4, the US date appears in a format unlike the other entries. If you're familiar with different international date formats, you'll also wonder if 12/10/2020 is meant to be MM/DD/YYYY format that's commonly used in the US, or the DD/MM/YYYY format that's commonly used elsewhere. Smart Cleanup cannot answer this for you.

The Google Sheets Smart Cleanup feature is a good place to start. If your data is really messy, you may need to turn to more sophisticated tools described later in this chapter, such as "Clean Data with OpenRefine" on page 79. In the next section, you'll learn another cleanup method that works in any spreadsheet: find and replace with a blank entry.

Find and Replace with Blank

One of the simplest and most powerful cleanup tools inside every spreadsheet is the "Find and Replace" command. You can also use it to bulk-change different spellings of the same name, such as shortening a country's name (from *Republic of India* to *India*), expanding a name (from *US* to *United States*), or translating names (from *Italy* to *Italia*). Also, you can use find and replace with a blank entry to remove units of measurement that sometimes reside in the same cells as the numbers (such as changing *321 kg* to *321*).

Let's look at "Find and Replace" in practice. A common problem with US Census data is that geographic names contain unnecessary words. For example, when you download data on the population of Connecticut towns, the location column will contain the word "town" after every name:

```
Hartford town
New Haven town
Stamford town
```

Usually you want a clean list of towns, either to display in a chart or to merge with another dataset, like this:

```
Hartford
New Haven
Stamford
```

Let's use "Find and Replace" on a sample US Census file we downloaded with 169 Connecticut town names and their populations to remove the unwanted "town" label after each place-name:

1. Open the CT Town Geonames file in Google Sheets (*https://oreil.ly/OQ5Tu*), sign in with your account, and go to File > "Make a copy" to create a version you can edit in your Google Drive.

2. Select the column you want to modify by clicking its header. If you don't select a column, you will be searching and replacing in the entire spreadsheet.

3. In the Edit menu, choose "Find and replace." You'll see the following.

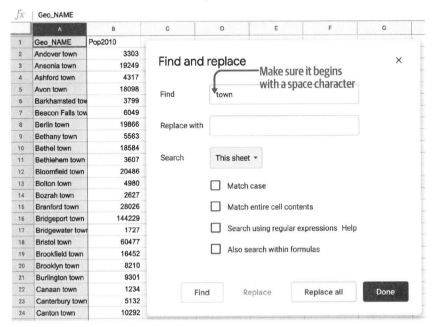

4. In the Find field, type **town**, and be sure to *insert a blank space* before the word. If you do not insert a space, you'll accidentally remove *town* from places such as *Middletown*. Also, you'll accidentally create trailing spaces, or whitespace at the end of a line without any other characters following it, which can cause trouble in the future.

5. Leave the "Replace with" field blank. Don't insert a space. Just leave it empty.

6. The Search field should be set to the range you selected in step 2, or "All sheets" if you didn't select anything.

7. You have the option to "Match case." If checked, town and Town and tOwN will be treated differently. For our purpose, you can leave "Match case" unchecked.

8. Press "Replace all." Because this sample file contains 169 towns, the window will state that 169 instances of "town" have been replaced.

9. Inspect the resulting sheet. Make sure that places that include *town* in their name, such as *Middletown*, remained untouched.

Transpose Rows and Columns

Sometimes you download good data, but your visualization tool requires you to transpose, or swap, the rows and the columns to create the chart or map you desire. This problem often arises when working with time-series or historical data because they are treated in opposite ways in tables and charts. When designing a table, the proper method is to place dates horizontally as column headers, so that we read them from left to right, like this:[1]

```
| Year     | 2000 | 2010 | 2020 |
|----------|------|------|------|
| Series1  | 333  | 444  | 555  |
| Series2  | 777  | 888  | 999  |
```

When designing a line chart in Google Sheets and similar tools, which you'll learn about in Chapter 6, we need to transpose the data so that dates run vertically down the first column, so the software reads them as labels for a data series, like this:

```
| Year | Series1 | Series2 |
|------|---------|---------|
| 2000 |     333 |     777 |
| 2010 |     444 |     888 |
| 2020 |     555 |     999 |
```

Learn how to transpose rows and columns in our sample data:

1. Open the Transpose sample data file in Google Sheets (*https://oreil.ly/lD0G-*), sign in with your account, and go to File > "Make a copy" to create a version you can edit in your Google Drive.

2. Select all of the rows and columns you wish to transpose, and go to Edit > Copy.

3. Scroll farther down the spreadsheet and click on a cell, or open a new spreadsheet tab, and go to Edit > "Paste special" > "Paste transposed."

---

1 Stephen Few, *Show Me the Numbers: Designing Tables and Graphs to Enlighten*, 2nd edition (Burlingame, CA: Analytics Press, 2012), p. 166.

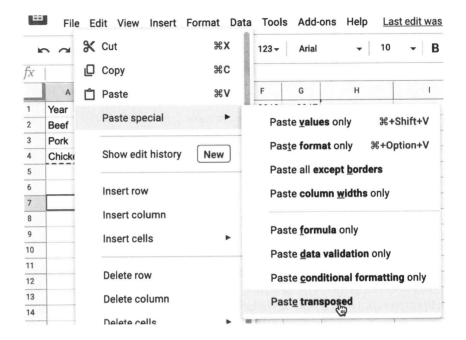

Now that you know how to clean up data by transposing rows and columns, in the next section you'll learn how to split data into separate columns.

Split Data into Separate Columns

Sometimes multiple pieces of data appear in a single cell, such as first and last names (John Doe), geographic coordinates (40.12,-72.12), or addresses (300 Summit St, Hartford, CT, 06106). For your analysis, you might want to split them into separate entities, so that your *FullName* column (with John Doe in it) becomes *FirstName* (John) and *LastName* (Doe) columns, coordinates become *Latitude* and *Longitude* columns, and your *FullAddress* column becomes four columns: *Street*, *City*, *State*, and *Zip* (postcode).

Example 1: Simple Splitting

Let's begin with a simple example of splitting pairs of geographic coordinates, separated by commas, into separate columns:

1. Open the Split Coordinate Pairs sample data in Google Sheets (*https://oreil.ly/t6MZt*), sign in with your account, and go to File > "Make a copy" to create a version you can edit in your Google Drive.

2. Select the data you wish to split, either the full column or just several rows. Note that you can split data only from one column at a time.

3. Make sure there is no data in the column to the right of the one you're splitting, because all the data there will be written over.

4. Go to Data and select "Split text to columns."

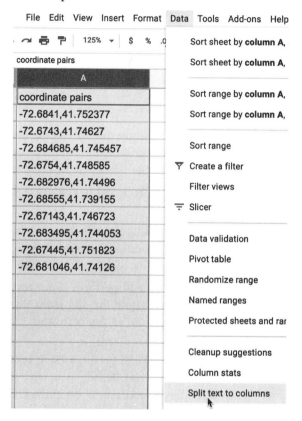

5. Google Sheets will automatically try to guess your separator. You'll see that your coordinates are now split with the comma, and the Separator is set to *Detect automatically* in the drop-down. You can manually change it to a comma (,), a semicolon (;), a period (.), a space character, or any other custom character (or even a sequence of characters, which we'll discuss in Example 2 of this section).

6. You can rename the new columns into *Longitude* (first number) and *Latitude* (second number).

Example 2: Complex Splitting

Now, let's look at a slightly more complicated example. Each cell contains a full address, which you want to split into four columns: street, city, state, and zip code (postcode). But notice how the separators differ: a comma between street and city, a space between city and state, and two dashes between state and the zip code. In this case, you'll need to manually add some instructions to properly split the text into four columns:

```
| Location                        |
| ------------------------------- |
| 300 Summit St, Hartford CT--06106 |
| 1012 Broad St, Hartford CT--06106 |
| 37 Alden St, Hartford CT--06114   |
```

1. Open the Split Complex Address sample file in Google Sheets (*https://oreil.ly/ F6v6P*), sign in to your account, and go to File > "Make a copy" to save a version in your Google Drive that you can edit.

2. Select the column and go to Data > "Split text to columns" to start splitting from left to right.

3. Google Sheets will automatically split your cell into two parts, `300 Summit St` and `Hartford CT--06106`, using a comma as a separator. (If it didn't, just select *Comma* from the drop-down menu that appeared).

4. Now select only the second column and perform "Split text to columns" again. Google Sheets will automatically separate the city from the state and zip code, because it automatically chose a space as the separator. (If it did not, choose *Space* from the drop-down menu.)

5. Finally, select only the third column and perform "Split text to columns" again. Google Sheets won't recognize the two dashes as a separator, so you need to manually select *Custom*, type those two dashes (`--`) in the *Custom separator* field, and press Enter. Now you have successfully split the full address into four columns.

A	B	C	D	E	F
Complex Address					
300 Summit St	Hartford	CT--06106			
1012 Broad St	Hartford	CT--06106			
37 Alden St	Hartford	CT--06114			
			Separator: Custom ⬍	Custom separator	

Google Sheets will treat zip codes as numbers and will delete leading zeros (so 06106 will become 6106). To fix that, select the column, and go to Format > Number > "Plain text." Now you can manually re-add zeros. If your dataset is large, consider adding zeros using the formula introduced in the following section.

Combine Data into One Column

Let's perform the reverse action by combining data into one column with a spreadsheet formula, also called concatenation, using the ampersand symbol (&). Imagine you receive address data in four separate columns: street address, city, state, and zip code:

```
| Street        | City       | State | Zip   |
| ------------- | ---------- | ----- | ----- |
| 300 Summit St | Hartford   | CT    | 06106 |
```

But imagine you need to geocode the addresses using a tool like the one we introduced in "Geocode Addresses in Google Sheets" on page 23, which requires all of the data to be combined into one column like this:

```
| Location                      |
| ----------------------------- |
| 300 Summit St, Hartford, CT 06106 |
```

Using any spreadsheet, you can write a simple formula to combine (or concatenate) terms using the ampersand (&) symbol. Also, you can add separators into your formula, such as quoted space (" "), or spaces with commas (", "), or any combination of characters. Let's try it with some sample data:

1. Open the Combine Separate Columns sample data in Google Sheets (*https://oreil.ly/-BxHA*), sign in with your account, and go to File > "Make a copy" to create a version you can edit in your Google Drive. The sheet contains addresses that are separated into four columns: street, city, state, and zip.

2. In column E, type a new header named *location*.

3. In cell E2, type **=A2 & ", " & B2 & ", " & C2 & " " & D2**. This formula combines the four items using ampersands, and separates them with quoted commas and spaces. Then press Enter.

4. Click cell E2 and drag the bottom-right corner crosshair downward to fill in the rest of the column.

fx	=A2 & ", " & B2 & ", " & C2 & " " & D2						
	A	B	C	D	E	F	G
1	street	city	state	zip	location		
2	300 Summit St	Hartford	CT	06106	?=A2 & ", " & B2 & ", " & C2 & " " & D2		
3	950 Main St	Hartford	CT	06103			
4	77 Forest St	Hartford	CT	06105			

Now that you have successfully combined the terms into one location column, you can use the Geocoding by SmartMonkey Google Sheets add-on we described in "Geocode Addresses in Google Sheets" on page 23 to find the latitude and longitude coordinates in order to map your data, as we'll discuss in Chapter 7.

For further reading, we recommend Lisa Charlotte Rost's brilliant Datawrapper blog post about cleaning and preparing spreadsheet data for analysis and visualization.[2]

Spreadsheets are great tools to find and replace data, split data into separate columns, or combine data into one column. But what if your data table is trapped inside a PDF? In the next section, we will introduce Tabula and show you how to convert tables from text-based PDF documents into tables that you can analyze in spreadsheets.

Extract Tables from PDFs with Tabula

It sometimes happens that the dataset you're interested in is available only as a PDF document. Don't despair—you can *likely* use Tabula to extract tables and save them as CSV files. Keep in mind that PDFs generally come in two flavors: text-based and image-based. If you can use the cursor to select and copy and paste text in your PDF, then it's text-based, which is great because you can process it with Tabula; if you can't, then it's image-based, meaning it was probably created as a scanned version of the original document. You need to use optical character recognition (OCR) software, such as Adobe Acrobat Pro or another OCR tool, to convert an image-based PDF into a text-based PDF. Furthermore, Tabula can extract only data from tables, not charts or other types of visualizations.

Tabula is a free tool that runs on Java in your browser, and is available for Mac, Windows, and Linux computers. It runs on your local machine and doesn't send your data to the cloud, so you can also use it for sensitive documents.

To get started, download the newest version of Tabula (*https://tabula.technology*). You can use download buttons on the left-hand side or scroll down to the "Download

---

2 Lisa Charlotte Rost, "How to Prepare Your Data for Analysis and Charting in Excel & Google Sheets," Datawrapper (blog), accessed August 28, 2020, *https://oreil.ly/emSQz*.

& Install Tabula" section to download a copy for your platform. Unlike most other programs, Tabula doesn't require installation. Just unzip the downloaded archive, and double-click the icon.

 On a Mac, you may see this warning when launching Tabula for the first time: "Tabula is an app downloaded from the internet. Are you sure you want to open it?" If so, click Open.

When you start up Tabula, it opens your default browser as a localhost with a URL similar to `http://127.0.0.1/`, with or without an additional port number, such as `:8080`, as shown in Figure 4-2. Tabula runs on your local computer, not the internet. If your default browser (such as Safari or Edge) doesn't play nicely with Tabula, you can copy and paste the URL into a different browser (such as Firefox or Chrome).

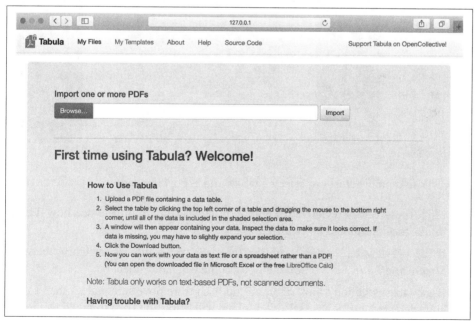

Figure 4-2. The Tabula welcome page.

Now let's upload a sample text-based PDF and detect any tables we wish to extract. In the beginning of the COVID-19 pandemic, the Department of Public Health in Connecticut issued data on cases and deaths only in PDF document format. For this demonstration, you can use our sample text-based PDF (*https://oreil.ly/9Iue4*) from May 31, 2020, or provide your own:

1. Select the PDF you want to extract data from by clicking the blue Browse… button.

2. Click Import. Tabula will begin analyzing the file.

3. As soon as Tabula finishes loading the PDF, you will see a PDF viewer with individual pages. The interface is fairly clean, with only four buttons in the header.

4. Click Autodetect Tables to let Tabula look for relevant data. The tool highlights each table it detects in red.

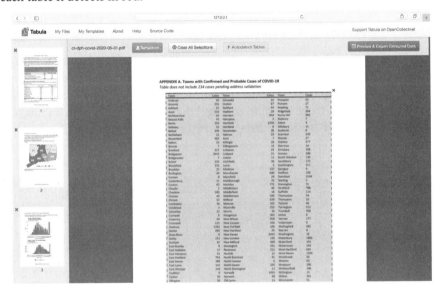

Now let's manually adjust our selected tables and export the data:

5. Click the green "Preview & Export Extracted Data" button to see how Tabula thinks the data should be exported.

6. If the preview tables don't contain the data you want, try switching between *Stream* and *Lattice* extraction methods in the left-hand sidebar.

7. If the tables still don't look right, or you wish to remove some tables that Tabula auto-detected, hit "Revise selection." That will bring you back to the PDF viewer.

8. Now you can Clear All Selections and manually select tables of interest. Use drag-and-drop movements to select tables of interest (or parts of tables).

9. If you want to "copy" the selection to some or all pages, you can use "Repeat this Selection" drop-down, which appears in the lower-right corner of your selections, to propagate changes. This is extremely useful if your PDF consists of many similarly formatted pages.

10. Once you are happy with the result, you can export it. If you have only one table, we recommend using CSV as export format. If you have more than one table, consider switching export format in the drop-down menu to "zip of CSVs." This way, each table will be saved as an individual file, rather than all tables inside one CSV file.

After you have exported your data to your computer, navigate to the file and open it with a spreadsheet tool to analyze and visualize.

Now that you have extracted a table from a PDF document, the results may be messy. In the next section, we will clean up messy datasets with a very powerful tool called OpenRefine.

Clean Data with OpenRefine

Open the US Foreign Aid sample dataset in Google Sheets format (*https://oreil.ly/RsBGt*) as shown in Figure 4-3. Can you spot any problems with it? This data excerpt is from US Overseas Loans and Grants (Greenbook) dataset (*https://oreil.ly/WDs4j*), which shows US economic and military assistance to various countries. We chose to include only assistance to South Korea and North Korea for the years between 2000 and 2018. We added deliberate misspellings and formatting issues for demonstration purposes, but we didn't alter values.

Notice how the *Country* column has various spellings of North and South Korea. Also note how the *FundingAmount* column is not standardized. Some amounts use commas to separate thousands, while some uses spaces. Some amounts start with a dollar sign, and some do not. Datasets like this can be an absolute nightmare to analyze. Luckily, OpenRefine provides powerful tools to clean up and standardize data.

	A	B	C	D
1	Year	Country	FundingAgency	FundingAmount
2	2000	Korea, N	Dept of Agriculture	$32 242 376
3	2000	Korea–North	Dept of Agriculture	$86,151,301
4	2000	Korea North	department of State	166855
5	2000	SouthKorea	U.S. Agency for International Development	282,805a
6	2000	south Korea	Trade and Development Agency	735718
7	2001	North Korea	US Agency for International Development	345,399
8	2001	N Korea	Department of Argic	117715223
9	2001	So Korea	Department of agriculture	2260293
10	2001	Korea, North	State Department	183,752
11	2001	Korea, South	Trade and Development Agency	329,953
12	2002	Korea, N	Department of Agriculture	37,322,244.00
13	2002	Korea, South	U.S. Agency for International Development	67,990.00
14	2002	Korea, South	Trade and Development Agency	$294,340
15	2003	Korea, North	U.S. Agency for International Development	$333 823
16	2003	Korea, North	Department - Agriculture	$26,766,828
17	2003	Korea, North	Department - Agriculture	$19,337,695
18	2003	Korea, No	Department of State	220,323
19	2003	Korea, South	U.S. Agency for International Development	66,765
20	2003	Korea, South	Trade and Development Agency	19,899

Figure 4-3. Can you spot any problems with this sample data?

Set Up OpenRefine

Let's use OpenRefine to clean up this messy data. Download OpenRefine (*https://oreil.ly/Q2QgL*) for Windows, Mac, or Linux. Just like Tabula, it runs in your browser and no data leaves your local machine, which is great for confidentiality.

To launch OpenRefine in Windows, unzip the downloaded file, double-click the *.exe* file, and the tool should open in your default browser.

To launch OpenRefine on a Mac, double-click the downloaded *.dmg* file to install it. You'll likely see a security warning that prevents OpenRefine from automatically launching because Apple doesn't recognize the developer for this open source project. To resolve the problem, go to System Preferences > "Security & Privacy" > General tab, and click Open Anyway in the lower half of the window, as shown in Figure 4-4. If prompted with another window, click Open.

Figure 4-4. If your Mac displays a warning about launching OpenRefine, adjust your "Security & Privacy" settings to open the program.

When you start up OpenRefine, it will open your default browser with the localhost 127.0.0.1 address, with or without the additional port number :3333, as shown in Figure 4-5. If your regular browser (such as Safari) does not behave nicely with Open‐Refine, copy and paste the localhost address into a different browser (such as Firefox or Chrome).

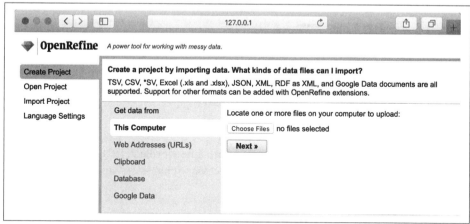

Figure 4-5. The OpenRefine welcome page.

Load Data and Start a New Project

To start cleaning up a messy dataset, we need to load it into a new project. Open Refine lets you upload a dataset from your local machine or a remote web address (such as a Google Sheet). OpenRefine also can extract data directly from SQL databases, but that's beyond the scope of this book:

1. Open the US Foreign Aid sample dataset in Google Sheets (*https://oreil.ly/ RsBGt*), sign in with your account, and go to File > Download to save a version in CSV format to your computer.

2. In OpenRefine, under "Get data from: This computer," click Browse... and select the CSV file you downloaded. Click Next.

3. Before you can start cleaning up data, OpenRefine allows you to make sure data is *parsed* properly. In our case, parsing means the way the data is split into columns. Make sure OpenRefine assigned values to the right columns, or change the setting in the "Parse data as" block at the bottom of the page until it starts looking meaningful. Then press Create Project in the upper-right corner.

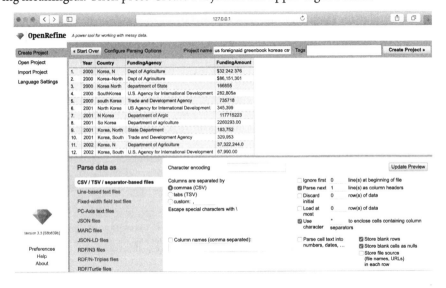

Now when you've successfully read the data into a new project, let's start the fun part: converting text into numbers, removing unnecessary characters, and fixing the spellings for North and South Koreas.

Convert Dollar Amounts from Text to Numbers

Once your project is created, you will see the first 10 rows of the dataset. You can change it to 5, 10, 25, or 50 by clicking the appropriate number in the header.

Each column header has its own menu, which you can select by clicking its arrow-down button. Left-aligned numbers in a column are likely represented as text, as is our case with the *FundingAmount* column, and they need to be transformed into numeric format:

1. To transform text into numbers, select the *FundingAmount* column menu, and go to "Edit cells" > "Common transforms" > "To number."

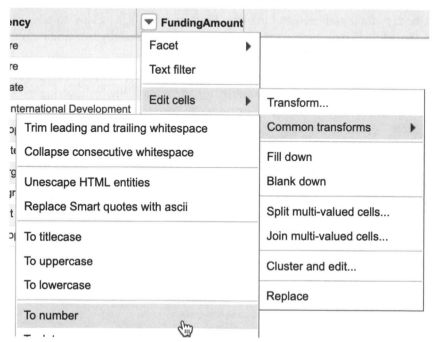

You'll see that *some* numbers became green and right-aligned, which signals partial success, but most did not change. That's because dollar sign ($) and commas (,) confuse OpenRefine and prevent values being converted into numbers.

2. Let's remove $ and , from the *FundingAmount* column. In the column menu, this time select "Edit cells" > Transform..., because we need to manually enter the edit we wish to make. In the Expression window, type **value.replace(',', '')** and notice how commas disappear in the preview window. When you confirm your formula has no syntax errors, click OK.

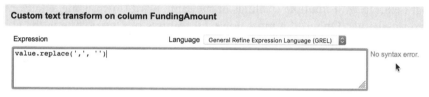

3. Now, repeat the previous step, but instead of a comma, remove the $ character by typing a different expression: **value.replace('$', '')**, confirm the formula, and click OK.

4. In steps 2 and 3, we replaced text (or string) values with other text values, making OpenRefine think this column is no longer numeric. As a result, all values are once again left-aligned and in black. Perform step 1 again. This time, nearly all of the cells will have turned green, meaning they successfully converted to numeric. However, a few nonnumeric black cells remain.

5. To fix the remaining nonnumeric black cells, we need to remove spaces and an a character at the end of one number. Fix these manually by hovering over a cell, click Edit, and in the new pop-up window, change "Data type" to "number," and press Apply.

At this point, all funding amounts should be clean numbers, right-aligned, and colored in green. We're ready to move on to the *Country* column and fix different spellings of Koreas.

Cluster Similar Spellings

When you combine different data sources or process survey data where respondents wrote down their answers as opposed to selecting them from a drop-down menu, you might end up with multiple spellings of the same word (town name, education level —you name it!). One of the most powerful features of OpenRefine is the ability to cluster similar responses.

If you use our original sample file, take a look at the *Country* column and all spellings variations of North and South Korea. From the *Country* column's drop-down menu, go to Facet > "Text facet." This will open up a window in the left-hand side with all spellings (and counts) of column values—26 choices for a column that should have just two distinct values, North Korea and South Korea!

1. To begin standardizing spellings, click on the arrow-down button of the *Country* column header and choose "Edit cells" > "Cluster and edit…" You'll see a window like this.

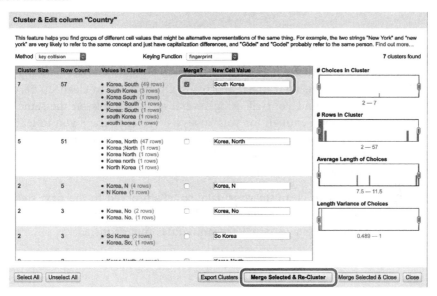

You'll have a choice of two clustering methods, *key collision* or *nearest neighbor*. Key collision clustering is a much faster technique that is appropriate for larger datasets, but it's less flexible. Nearest neighbor is a more computationally expensive approach and will be slow on larger datasets, but it allows for greater fine-tuning and precision. Both methods can be powered by different functions, which you can read about on the project's Wiki page (*https://oreil.ly/LhSI7*). For the purpose of this exercise, let's leave the default *key collision* method with *fingerprint* function.

OpenRefine will calculate a list of clusters. The *Values in Cluster* column contains grouped spellings that OpenRefine considers the same.

2. If you agree with a grouping, check the "Merge?" box and assign the *true* value to the New Cell Value input box, as shown in the first cluster in step 1. In our example, this would be either `North Korea` or `South Korea`.

3. You can go through all groupings, or stop after one or two and click the "Merge Selected & Re-Cluster" button. The clusters you selected will be merged, and grouping will be recalculated. (Don't worry, the window won't go anywhere.) Keep regrouping until you are happy with the result.

Spend some time playing with *Keying function* parameters, and notice how they produce clusters of different sizes and accuracy.

4. After you finish cleaning up and clustering data, save the clean dataset by clicking Export in the upper-right corner of OpenRefine window. You can choose your format (we recommend CSV). Now you have a clean dataset that's ready to be analyzed and visualized.

Summary

In this chapter, we looked at cleaning up tables in Google Sheets, liberating tabular data trapped in PDFs using Tabula, and using OpenRefine to clean up very messy datasets. You'll often find yourself using several of these tools on the same dataset before it becomes good enough for your analysis. We encourage you to learn more formulas in Google Sheets, and explore extra functionality of OpenRefine in your spare time. The more cleanup tools and techniques you know, the more able and adaptable you become to tackle more complex cases.

You now know how to clean up your data, so let's proceed to the next step before visualizing it. In the following chapter, we'll talk about why you should normalize data and use precise language to make meaningful comparisons.

CHAPTER 5

Make Meaningful Comparisons

Now that you've refined your data story, improved your spreadsheet skills, found and questioned your data, and cleaned up any messy parts in Chapters 1, 2, 3, and 4, this chapter focuses on the key question to ask while analyzing your evidence: "Compared to what?" That's how statistician Edward Tufte defined the "heart of quantitative reasoning."[1] We search for insightful findings in our data by judging their significance against each other, to identify those that truly stand out. Sometimes we need to adjust our scales to ensure that we're weighing data fairly, or as the saying goes, comparing apples to apples, not apples to oranges. Before you communicate your findings in any format—text, tables, charts, or maps—be sure that you're making meaningful comparisons, because without this, your work may become meaningless.

This book does not intend to cover statistical data analysis because many excellent resources already address this expansive field of study.[2] Instead, this chapter offers several common-sense strategies to make meaningful comparisons while you analyze your data to help you design true and insightful visualizations that tell your story in "Precisely Describe Comparisons" on page 87, "Normalize Your Data" on page 90, and "Beware of Biased Comparisons" on page 93.

Precisely Describe Comparisons

Sometimes we make poor comparisons because we fail to clarify the meaning of commonly used words that can have different definitions. Three troublesome words are

---

1 Edward R. Tufte, *Envisioning Information* (Cheshire, CT: Graphics Press, 1990), p. 67.

2 For a reader-friendly introduction to statistical logic and its limits, see Charles Wheelan, *Naked Statistics: Stripping the Dread from the Data* (W.W. Norton & Company, 2013); David Spiegelhalter, *The Art of Statistics: How to Learn from Data* (Basic Books, 2019).

average, *percent*, and *causes*. We use them loosely in everyday conversation, but their definitions require more precision when working with data.

Imagine a series of numbers: 1, 2, 3, 4, 5. When calculating the *average*, by hand or with a built-in spreadsheet formula as described in "Calculate with Formulas" on page 31, we add up the sum and divide by the count of numbers. A more precise term is the *mean*, which in this case equals 3. A different term is the *median*, which refers to the number in the middle of the ordered series, also known as the *50th percentile*, which in this case is also 3.

When working with data, it's useful to use the terms *median* and *percentile* to make comparisons because they resist the influence of *outliers* at the extreme ends of the series. For example, imagine the same numbers as before, but replace the 5 with 100 to serve as an outlier. Suddenly the mean jumps up to 22, but the median remains the same at 3, as shown in Figure 5-1. There's an old joke that when a billionaire walks into a room, everyone becomes a millionaire—on average—but the median barely changes. Since we ordinary people don't actually become richer by the presence of the billionaire outlier among us, the median is a better term to make meaningful comparisons about the overall distribution of the data.

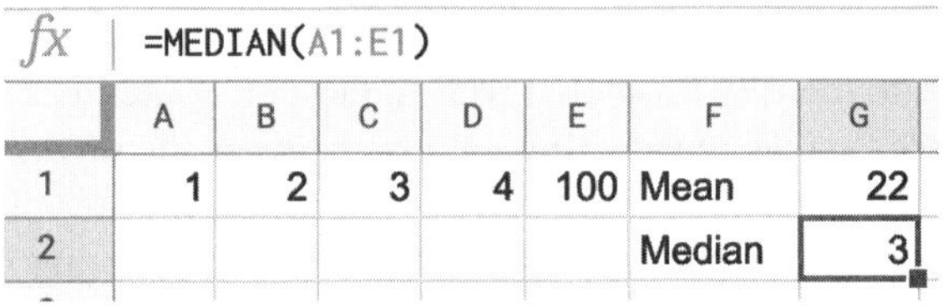

fx | =MEDIAN(A1:E1)

	A	B	C	D	E	F	G
1	1	2	3	4	100	Mean	22
2						Median	3

Figure 5-1. The median is a more useful comparative term than average or mean because it resists the influence of outliers.

Percentage is another common term, which nearly everyone intuitively grasps as a *ratio* of parts per hundred. For example, a 1970s commercial for Trident gum (*https://oreil.ly/7FsBC*) claimed that "4 out of 5 dentists surveyed recommend sugarless gum for their patients who chew gum."[3] Even if you're too young to remember that slogan, or wonder how that survey was actually conducted, or are puzzling over how the fifth dentist resisted such intense peer pressure, we all understand that four out of five dentists is equivalent to 4/5 = 0.8 = 80%.

Confusion arises sometimes when people hastily compare percentages, so we need to carefully choose our words. One term is *percent change* (also called relative change), which works best when comparing *old versus new values*. Percent change is calculated

---

3 Andrew Adam Newman, "Selling Gum with Health Claims," *The New York Times*: Business, July 27, 2009, *https://oreil.ly/BN9HT*.

by the difference between new and old values, divided by the absolute value of the old value, or (New value - Old value) / |Old value|. For example, if four dentists recommended sugarless gum in 1970, but peer pressure finally prevailed and five dentists recommend it in 2020, we calculate the percent change as (5 - 4)/4 = 1/4 = 0.25 = 25%.

Another term is *percentage point difference* (sometimes abbreviated p.p. difference), which works best when comparing *old versus new percentages* and is calculated by subtracting one from the other. For example, if 80% of dentists recommended sugarless gum in 1970, but 100% recommended it in 2020, we could calculate the difference as New percentage - Old percentage = 100% - 80% = 20 percentage point difference.

When we precisely use each term, there are two correct ways to compare these figures. One way is to state that, "The number of dentists who recommended sugarless gum increased 25% over time." Another way is to state that, "The percentage of dentists who recommended sugarless gum increased 20 percentage points over time." Both statements are accurate. Even if someone confuses the two terms, there's not a big gap between a "25% change" and a "20% point increase" in this particular example.

Consider a different example where someone intentionally misleads you with imprecise wording about percentages. Imagine a politician who proposes to raise the sales tax on products and services you purchase from 5% to 6%. If that politician says, "It's only a 1% increase," they're wrong. Instead, there are two truthful ways to describe this change. One way is to state that the tax "will increase 20%" because (6 - 5)/5 = 0.20. Another way is to state that the tax "will increase by 1 percentage point" because 6% - 5% = 1 percentage point difference. See why the politician preferred to say it in their misleading way, rather than either of the two correct ways? Don't let anyone fool you by describing how percentages change with very loose wording, and be precise about its meaning in your own work to avoid confusing other people.

A final recommendation about using more precise language is to be cautious with words that suggest a *cause-and-effect relationship* in your data. In everyday conversation, there are many ways that we loosely imply a causal relationship, where an action directly results in a reaction. For example, when we say one thing "leads to" another, "promotes growth," or "sparks" change, those words suggest causality. While that's fine in daily conversation, we need to choose our words more carefully when discussing data, using three steps. The first step is to describe any *correlation* between two variables, which means to show how they are associated or related interdependently. But statisticians always warn us that correlation does not imply causation (*https:// oreil.ly/oQ2m2*). The fact that two things are related does not necessarily mean that one causes the other to happen. To show causation, we must take the second step of proving both correlation and demonstrating a *persuasive theory* for how one factor (sometimes called the independent variable) creates a change in another factor (called the dependent variable). Third, we need to identify and isolate any *confounding variables* that we haven't considered that may also influence the cause-and-effect relationship. While the details are beyond the scope of this book, be mindful of the steps—and choose your words carefully—when working with data.

See also "Table Design Principles" on page 216 for showing data correlations and possible causal relationships in Chapter 8.

Now that you have a clearer understanding of how to use key words to describe data relationships more precisely, in the next section you'll build on this knowledge and adjust data to create more meaningful comparisons.

Normalize Your Data

When we work with data expressed in *counts*, such as 3,133 motor vehicle crash deaths in Florida in 2018, it usually makes no sense to compare these numbers until we *normalize* them. This means to adjust data that has been collected using different scales into a common reference scale, or in other words, to convert *raw data* into *rates* to make more meaningful comparisons. Even if you've never heard the term, perhaps you're already normalizing data without realizing it.

Here's an example about motor vehicle safety that was inspired by visualization expert Alberto Cairo, with updated 2018 data (*https://oreil.ly/fGD8N*) from the Insurance Institute for Highway Safety (IIHS) and the US Department of Transportation.[4] More than 36,000 people died in motor vehicle crashes in 2018, including car and truck drivers and occupants, motorcyclists, pedestrians, and bicyclists. Although only a small fraction of this data appears in the tables that follow, you can view all of the data in Google Sheets format (*https://oreil.ly/1zZHO*), and save an editable copy to your Google Drive to follow along in this exercise.

Let's start with what appears to be a simple question, and see where our search for more meaningful comparisons takes us:

1. *Which US states had the lowest number of motor vehicle crash deaths?*

   When we sort the data by the numbers of deaths, the District of Columbia *appears* to be the safest state with only 31 deaths, as shown in Table 5-1, even though Washington, DC, is not legally recognized as a state.

---

4 Alberto Cairo, *The Truthful Art: Data, Charts, and Maps for Communication* (Pearson Education, 2016), pp. 71-74.

Table 5-1. US states with lowest number of motor vehicle crash deaths, 2018

State	Deaths
District of Columbia	31
Rhode Island	59
Vermont	68
Alaska	80
North Dakota	105

But wait—this isn't a fair comparison. Take another look at the five states listed and you'll may notice that all of them have smaller populations than larger states, such as California and Texas, which appear at the very bottom of the full dataset. To paint a more accurate picture, let's rephrase the question to adjust for population differences.

2. *Which US states had the lowest number of motor vehicle crash deaths when adjusted for population?*

Now let's *normalize* the death data by taking into account the total population of each state. In our spreadsheet, we calculate it as `Deaths / Population × 100,000`. While it's also accurate to divide deaths by population to find a *per capita* rate, those very small decimals would be difficult for most people to compare, so we multiply by 100,000 to present the results more clearly. When we sort the data, Washington, DC, *appears* to be the safest once again, with only 4.4 motor vehicle crash deaths per 100,000 residents, as shown in Table 5-2.

Table 5-2. US states with lowest number of motor vehicle crash deaths per population, 2018

State	Deaths	Population	Deaths per 100,000 population
District of Columbia	31	702,455	4.4
New York	943	19,542,209	4.8
Massachusetts	360	6,902,149	5.2
Rhode Island	59	1,057,315	5.6
New Jersey	564	8,908,520	6.3

But wait—this still isn't a fair comparison. Look at the five states on the list and you'll notice that all of them are located along the Northeastern US corridor, which has a high concentration of public transit, such as trains and subways. If people in urban areas like New York and Boston are less likely to drive motor vehicles, or take shorter trips than people in rural states where homes are more distantly spread out, that might affect our data. Let's strive for a better comparison and rephrase the question again, this time to adjust for differences in mileage, not population.

3. *Which US states had the lowest number of motor vehicle crash deaths when adjusted for vehicle mileage?*

Once again, we *normalize* the death data by adjusting it to account for a different factor: vehicle miles traveled (VMT), the estimated total number of miles (in millions) traveled by cars, vans, trucks, and motorcycles, on all roads and highways in the state, in 2018. In our spreadsheet, we calculate it as `Deaths / Vehicle Miles × 100`, with the multiplier to present the results more clearly. This time Massachusetts *appears* to be the safest state, with only 0.54 motor vehicle crash deaths per 100 million miles traveled, as shown in Table 5-3. Also, note that the District of Columbia has fallen further down the list and been replaced by Minnesota.

Table 5-3. US states with lowest number of motor vehicle crash deaths per miles traveled, 2018

State	Deaths	Vehicle miles traveled (millions)	Deaths per 100 million vehicle miles traveled
Massachusetts	360	66,772	0.54
Minnesota	381	60,438	0.63
New Jersey	564	77,539	0.73
Rhode Island	59	8,009	0.74
New York	943	123,510	0.76

Have we finally found the *safest* state as judged by motor vehicle crash deaths? Not necessarily. While we normalized the raw data relative to the population and amount of driving, the IIHS reminds us that several other factors may influence these numbers, such as vehicle types, average speed, traffic laws, weather, and so forth. As Alberto Cairo reminds us, every time we refine our calculations to make a more meaningful comparison, our interpretation becomes a closer representation of the truth. "It's unrealistic to pretend that we can create a *perfect* model," Cairo said. "But we can certainly come up with a *good enough* one."[5]

As we demonstrated, the most common way to normalize data is to adjust raw counts into relative rates, such as percentages or per capita. But there are many other ways to normalize data, so make sure you're familiar with different methods when you find and question your data, as described in Chapter 3.

When working with historical data (also called time-series or longitudinal data), you may need to *adjust for change over time*. For example, it's not fair to directly compare median household income in 1970 to those in 2020, because $10,000 US dollars had far more purchasing power a half-century ago than it does today, due to inflation and

---

5 Cairo, p. 95

related factors. Similarly, economists distinguish between *nominal data* (unadjusted) versus *real data* (adjusted over time), typically by converting figures into "constant dollars" for a particular year that allow better comparisons by accounting for purchasing power.[6] Also, economic data is often *seasonally adjusted* to improve comparisons for data that regularly varies across the year, such as employment or revenue during the summer tourism season versus the winter holiday shopping season. Another normalization method is to create an *index* to measure how values have risen or fallen in relation to a given reference point over time. Furthermore, statisticians often normalize data collected using different scales by calculating its *standard score*, also known as its *z-score*, to make better comparisons. While these methods are beyond the scope of this book, it's important to be familiar with the broader concept: everyone agrees that it's better to compare apples to apples, rather than apples to oranges.

Finally, you do *not* always need to normalize your data, because sometimes its format already does this for you. Unlike raw numbers or simple counts, most *measured variables* do not need normalization because they already appear on a common scale. One example of a measured variable is *median age*, the age of the "middle" person in a population, when sorted from youngest to oldest. Since we know that humans live anywhere between 0 and 120 years or so, we can directly compare the median age among different populations. Similarly, another measured variable is *median income*, if measured in the same currency and in the same time period, because this offers a common scale that allows direct comparisons across different populations.

Now that you have a better sense of why, when, and how to normalize data, the next section will warn you to watch out for biased comparisons in data sampling methods.

Beware of Biased Comparisons

You've likely heard not to *cherry-pick* your data, which means to select only the evidence that supports a predetermined conclusion, while ignoring the remainder. When we make a commitment to tell true and meaningful data stories, we agree to keep an open mind, examine all of the relevant evidence, and weigh the merits of competing interpretations. If you agree to these principles, then also watch out for biased data comparisons, especially *sampling biases*, which refers to data collection procedures that may appear legitimate on the surface, but actually include partially-hidden factors that skew the results. While we may believe we're operating with an open mind, we might overlook methods that effectively cherry-pick our evidence without our knowledge.

---

6 "What's Real About Wages?" Federal Reserve Bank of St. Louis (The FRED Blog, February 8, 2018), *https://oreil.ly/yljnI*.

First, look out for *selection bias*, which means that the sample chosen for your study differs systematically from the larger population. "What you see depends on where you look," cautions professors Carl Bergstrom and Jevin West, authors of a book with an unforgettable title, *Calling Bullshit*.[7] If you randomly measured the height of people who happened to be leaving the gym after basketball practice, selection bias would cause artificially taller results, and that would be due to selection bias, as shown in Figure 5-2.

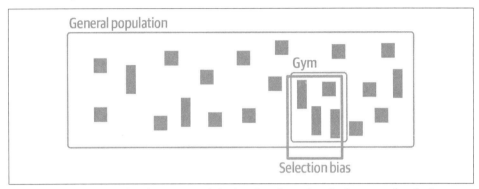

Figure 5-2. If you randomly measured the height of people who happened to be leaving the gym after basketball practice, you would get artificially taller results due to selection bias.

Second, beware of *nonresponse bias*. If you send a survey to a broad population, but not everyone responds, you need to be aware that those who chose to participate may possess certain qualities that make them less representative of the whole population. For example, US Census researchers discovered that the nonresponse rate for lower-income people was significantly higher than usual for the 2020 Current Population Survey supplement, which they determined by comparing individual survey results to prior years. Because richer people were more likely to respond, this artificially raised the reported median income level, which researchers needed to correct.[8] See also the US Census Bureau Hard to Count 2020 map (*https://oreil.ly/lTEoq*) that visualizes self-response rates by states, counties, and tracts. If you conduct a survey that doesn't correct for nonresponse bias, you may have biased results.

Third, watch out for *self-selection bias*, which often arises when attempting to evaluate the effectiveness of a particular program or treatment where people applied or volunteered to participate, as shown in Figure 5-3. If your job is to judge whether a

---

7 Carl T. Bergstrom and Jevin D. West, *Calling Bullshit: The Art of Skepticism in a Data-Driven World* (Random House, 2020), *https://oreil.ly/kpD_S*, pp. 79, 104–133.

8 Jonathan Rothbaum and Adam Bee, "Coronavirus Infects Surveys, Too: Nonresponse Bias During the Pandemic in the CPS ASEC" (US Census Bureau), accessed December 8, 2020, *https://oreil.ly/auhUm*.

weight-loss program actually works, this requires a deep understanding of how data samples were chosen, because self-selection bias can secretly shape the composition of both groups, and result in a meaningless comparison. For example, it would be a mistake to compare the progress of nonparticipants (group A) versus participants who signed up for this program (group B), because those two groups were *not* randomly chosen. Participants differ because they took the initiative to join a weight-loss program, and most likely have higher motivation to improve their diet and exercise more often than nonparticipants. It's surprising how often we fool ourselves and forget to consider how voluntary participation skews program effectiveness, whether the subject is weight-loss clinics, social services, or school choice programs.[9]

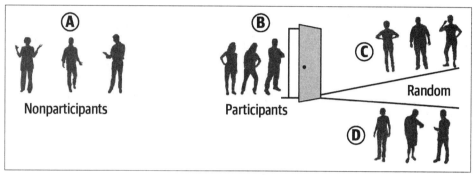

Figure 5-3. To evaluate program effectiveness, don't compare program nonparticipants (A) with those who apply or volunteer to participate (B). Instead, randomly split all participants into two subgroups (C and D).

How can we reduce self-selection bias in program evaluation data? As you learned in "Question Your Data" on page 64, it's important to look below the surface level to fully comprehend how terms have been defined, and how data was collected and recorded. By contrast, a well-designed program evaluation will reduce self-selection bias by *randomly dividing* all volunteer participants (group B) into two subgroups: half will be assigned to participate in one weight-loss program (group C) and the other half will be assigned to a different weight-loss program (group D), as shown in Figure 5-3. Because subgroups C and D were selected by chance from the same larger group of volunteers, we can be more confident when comparing their progress because there's no reason to suspect any difference in motivation or other hard-to-see factors. Of course, there are many more research design details that are beyond the scope of this book, such as ensuring that sample sizes are sufficiently large, comparing participants before, during, and after the weight-loss activity, and so forth. But the logic of avoiding selection bias is simple: randomly divide the people who apply or volunteer to

9 If you're interested in more on self-selection bias in school choice programs, Richard D. Kahlenberg and Halley Potter's *A Smarter Charter* (Teachers College Press), 54 is a good place to start.

participate into subgroups, to better compare program effectiveness among people with similar motivations and other hard-to-see characteristics.

Bias warnings appear in several chapters of this book because we continually need to be aware of different types that negatively influence our work at various stages of the data visualization process. In "Recognize and Reduce Data Bias" on page 388, you'll learn how to recognize and reduce other types of biases when working with data, such as cognitive biases, algorithmic biases, intergroup biases, and mapping biases.

Summary

Although we don't claim to teach you statistical data analysis in this book, in this chapter we discussed several common-sense strategies to make meaningful comparisons while analyzing your data. You learned how to use words more precisely for comparing data, why and how to normalize data, and we gave you advice on watching out for biased comparisons. In Part I, you built up your skills on refining your data story, working with spreadsheets, finding and questioning data, and cleaning up messy data. Now you can combine all of this knowledge and begin to create interactive charts and maps in Part II.

PART II

Building Visualizations

CHAPTER 6

Chart Your Data

Charts pull readers deeper into your story. Images such as the slope of a line chart, or clusterings of dots on a scatter chart, can communicate your evidence to readers' eyes more effectively than text or tables. But creating meaningful charts that draw our attention to key insights in your data requires clear thinking about design choices.

In this chapter, we'll learn to identify good charts from bad ones in "Chart Design Principles" on page 103. You'll review important rules that apply to all charts, and also some aesthetic guidelines to follow when customizing your own designs. While many tools allow you to download charts as *static* images, our book also demonstrates how to construct *interactive* charts that invite readers to explore the data in their web browsers. Later you'll learn how to embed interactive charts on your website in Chapter 9.

Learn about different types of charts you can create in this book in Table 6-1. Decisions about chart types are based on two main factors: the format of your data and the kind of story you wish to tell. For example, line charts work best to show a series of continuous data points (such as change over time), while range charts are better suited to emphasize the distance between data categories (such as inequality gaps). After selecting your chart type, follow our tool recommendations and step-by-step tutorials. This chapter features *easy tools* with drag-and-drop menus in "Google Sheets Charts" on page 113, "Datawrapper Charts" on page 131, and "Tableau Public Charts" on page 146. But the table also points you to *power tools* that give you more control to customize and host your visualizations, such as Chart.js and Highcharts code templates in Chapter 11. These advanced tools require prior knowledge of how to edit and host code templates with GitHub, which is in Chapter 10.

We jointly refer to *bar and column charts* because they're essentially the same, except that bars are oriented horizontally and columns vertically. The main difference is the length of your data labels. Use bar charts to display longer labels (such as "Mocha Frappuccino 24-ounce" and "Double Quarter Pounder with Cheese") because they require more horizontal reading space. You can use either bar or column charts for shorter labels that do not require as much room (such as "Starbucks" and "McDonald's"). You'll also notice that all of the examples in this chapter focus on food (because we were really hungry when writing it) and healthy eating (because we also need to lose weight).

Table 6-1. Basic chart types, best uses, and tutorials[a]

Chart	Best use and tutorials in this book
Grouped bar or column chart	Best to compare categories side-by-side. If labels are long, use horizontal bars instead of vertical columns. • Easy tool: "Bar and Column Charts" on page 114 or "Datawrapper Charts" on page 131 • Power tool: Chart.js and Highcharts templates in Chapter 11
Split bar or column chart	Best to compare categories in separate clusters. If labels are long, use horizontal bars instead of vertical columns. • Easy tool: "Bar and Column Charts" on page 114 or "Datawrapper Charts" on page 131 • Power tool: Chart.js and Highcharts templates in Chapter 11
Stacked bar or column chart	Best to compare subcategories, or parts of a whole. If labels are long, use horizontal bars instead of vertical columns. • Easy tool: "Bar and Column Charts" on page 114 or "Datawrapper Charts" on page 131 • Power tool: Chart.js and Highcharts templates in Chapter 11

Error bars in bar or column chart

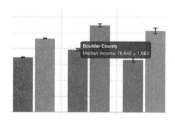

Best to show margin of error bars when comparing categories side by side. If labels are long, use horizontal bars instead of vertical columns.

- Easy tool: Google Sheets Charts has limited support for error bars ("Bar and Column Charts" on page 114)
- Power tool: Chart.js and Highcharts templates in Chapter 11

Histogram

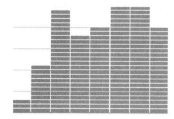

Best to show distribution of raw data, with number of values in each bucket.

- Easy tool: "Histograms" on page 121
- Power tool: Chart.js and Highcharts templates in Chapter 11

Pie chart

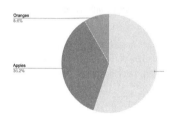

Best to show parts of a whole, but hard to estimate size of slices.

- Easy tools: "Pie, Line, and Area Charts" on page 126 or "Datawrapper Charts" on page 131
- Power tool: Chart.js and Highcharts templates in Chapter 11

Line chart

Best to show continuous data, such as change over time.

- Easy tools: Line Chart (see "Pie, Line, and Area Charts" on page 126) or "Datawrapper Charts" on page 131
- Power tool: Chart.js and Highcharts templates in Chapter 11

Annotated line chart

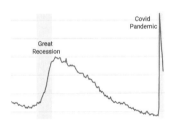

Best to add notes or highlight data inside a chart, such as historical context in a line chart.

- Easy tools: "Annotated Charts" on page 132
- Power tool: Chart.js and Highcharts templates in Chapter 11

Filtered line chart

Best to show multiple lines of continuous data, which users can toggle on and off.

- Easy tool: "Filtered Line Chart" on page 152

Stacked area chart

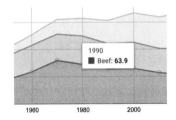

Best to show parts of a whole, with continuous data such as change over time.

- Easy tools: Stacked Area Chart (see "Pie, Line, and Area Charts" on page 126) or "Datawrapper Charts" on page 131
- Power tool: Chart.js and Highcharts templates in Chapter 11

Range chart

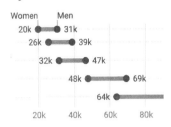

Best to show gaps between data points, such as inequalities.

- Easy tool and power tool: "Range Charts" on page 137

Scatter chart

Best to show the relationship between two variables, with each dot representing its *x* and *y* coordinates.

- Easy tool: "Scatter and Bubble Charts" on page 139 or "Scatter Charts with Tableau Public" on page 147
- Power tool: Chart.js and Highcharts templates in Chapter 11

Bubble chart

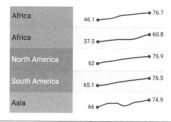

Best to show the relationship between three or four sets of data, with *x* and *y* coordinates, bubble size, and color.

- Easy tool: "Scatter and Bubble Charts" on page 139
- Power tool: Chart.js and Highcharts templates in Chapter 11

Sparklines

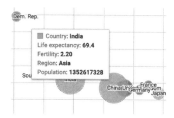

Best to compare data trends with tiny line or bar charts, aligned in a table column.

- Easy tool: "Datawrapper Table with Sparklines" on page 218

---

a For a more extensive collection of chart types and use cases, see the Financial Times Visual Vocabulary (*https://ft.com/vocabulary*).

Chart Design Principles

There are *so* many different types of charts. However, just because data *can* be made into a chart doesn't necessarily mean that it *should* be turned into one. Before creating a chart, stop and ask: *Does a visualized data pattern really matter to your story?* Sometimes a simple table, or even text alone, can communicate the idea more effectively to your audience. Creating a well-designed chart requires time and effort, so make sure it enhances your data story.

Although not a science, data visualization comes with a set of principles and best practices that serve as a foundation for creating truthful and eloquent charts. In this section, we'll identify some important rules about chart design. You may be surprised to learn that some rules are less rigid than others and can be "broken" when necessary to emphasize a point, as long as you honestly interpret the data.

To better understand this tension between following and breaking rules in data visualization, see Lisa Charlotte Rost's thoughtful reflection on "What To Consider When Considering Data Vis Rules." By articulating the unspoken rules behind good chart design, Rost argues that we all benefit by moving them into the public realm, where we can openly discuss and improve on them, as she had done in many Datawrapper Academy posts (*https://oreil.ly/heYLn*), which also beautifully visualize each rule. But Rost reminds us that rules also have a downside. First, following rules too closely can block creativity and innovation, especially when we look for ways to overcome challenges in design work. Second, since rules have emerged from different "theories of data visualization," they sometimes contradict one another. One example of colliding rules is the tension between creating easy-to-grasp data stories and those that reveal the complexity of the data, as it often feels impossible to do both. Rost concludes that the rules we follow reflect our values, and each of us needs to ask, "What do you want your data visualizations to be judged for?"—for how good the designs look, how truthful they are, or how they evoke emotions, or inform and change minds?[1]

To delve further into chart design, let's start by establishing a common vocabulary about charts.

Deconstruct a Chart

Let's take a look at Figure 6-1. It shows basic chart components that are shared among most chart types.

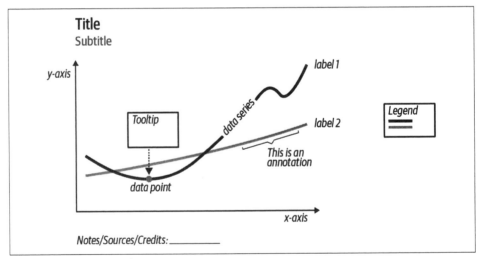

Figure 6-1. Common chart components.

---

1 Lisa Charlotte Rost, "What to Consider When Considering Data Vis Rules" (Lisa Charlotte Rost, November 27, 2020), *https://oreil.ly/e4uBM*.

A *title* is perhaps the most important element of any chart. A good title is short, clear, and tells a story on its own. For example, "Pandemic Hits Black and Latino Population Hardest" or "Millions of Tons of Plastic Enter the Ocean Every Year" are both clear titles that quickly convey a larger story.

Sometimes your editor or audience will prefer a more technical title for your chart. If so, the two titles could be changed, respectively, to "COVID-19 Deaths by Race in New York City, Spring 2020" and "Tons of Plastic Entering the Ocean, 1950–2020."

A hybrid strategy is to combine a story-oriented title with a more technical subtitle, such as: "Pandemic Hits Black and Latino Population Hardest: COVID-19 Deaths by Race in New York City, Spring 2020." If you follow this model, make your subtitle less prominent than your title by decreasing its font size, changing its font style or color, or both.

Horizontal (x) and vertical (y) *axes* define the scale and units of measure.

A *data series* is a collection of observations, which is usually a row or a column of numbers, or *data points*, in your dataset.

Labels and *annotations* are often used across the chart to give more context. For example, a line chart showing US unemployment levels between 1900 and 2020 can have a "Great Depression" annotation around the 1930s, and a "COVID-19 Impact" annotation for 2020, both representing spikes in unemployment. You might also choose to label items directly instead of relying on axes, which is common with bar charts. In that case, a relevant axis can be hidden and the chart will look less cluttered.

A *legend* shows symbology, such as the colors and shapes used in the chart and their meaning (usually values that they represent).

You should add *Notes*, *Data Sources*, and *Credits* underneath the chart to give more context about where the data came from, how it was processed and analyzed, and who created the visualization. Remember that being open about these things helps build credibility and accountability.

If your data comes with uncertainty (or margins of error), use *error bars* to show it, if possible. If not, accompany your chart with a statement like, "the data comes with uncertainty of up to 20% of the value" or "for geographies X and Y, margins of error exceed 10%." This will help readers assess the reliability of the data source.

In interactive charts, a *tool tip* is often used to provide more data or context once a user clicks or hovers over a data point or a data series. Tool tips are great for complex visualizations with multiple layers of data because they declutter the chart. Because tool tips are harder to interact with on smaller screens, such as phones and tablets, and are invisible when the chart is printed, you should rely on them only to convey additional, nice-to-have information. Make sure all essential information is visible without any user interaction.

Some Rules Are More Important Than Others

Although the majority of rules in data visualization are open to interpretation, as long as you honestly interpret the data, here are two rules that cannot be bent: zero-baselines for bar and column charts, and 100% baselines for pie charts.

Bar and column charts must begin at zero

Bar and column charts use *length* and *height* to represent value, therefore their value axis *must start at the zero baseline*. This ensures that a bar twice the length of another bar represents twice its value. Figure 6-2 contrasts a good and a bad example. The same rule applies to area charts, which display filled-in area underneath the line to represent value. Starting the baseline at a number other than zero is a trick commonly used to exaggerate differences in opinion polls and election results, as we describe later in Chapter 14.

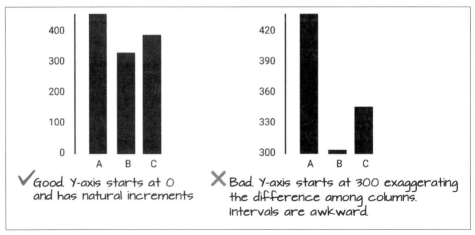

Figure 6-2. Start your bar chart at zero.

The zero-baseline rule does *not* apply to line charts. According to visualization expert Alberto Cairo, line charts represent values through the *position* and *angle* of the line, rather than its height or length. Starting a line chart at a number other than zero does *not* necessarily distort its encoded information because our eyes rely on its shape to determine its meaning, rather than its proximity to the baseline.[2] For example, compare both the right and left sides of Figure 6-3, where both are correct.

---

2 Cairo, *How Charts Lie*, 2019, p. 61.

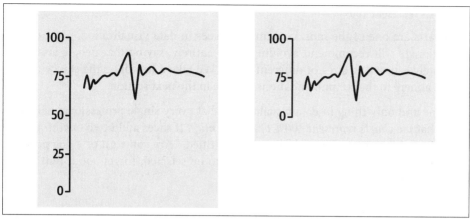

Figure 6-3. Since line charts do not require a zero baseline, both sides are correct.

Furthermore, while forcing a line chart to begin at the zero baseline is acceptable, it may not produce the best visualization for your data story. In Figure 6-4, the left side shows a line chart that starts the vertical axis at zero, but as a result, the line appears very flat at the top of the chart and hides changes in values. The right side shows a line chart where the vertical axis was reduced to match the range of values, which results in a clearer depiction of change. Both sides are technically correct, and in this case, the right side is a better fit for the data story. Still, you need to be cautious, because, as you'll learn in "How to Lie with Charts" on page 371, people can mislead us by modifying the vertical axis, and there is no uniform rule about where it belongs on a line chart.

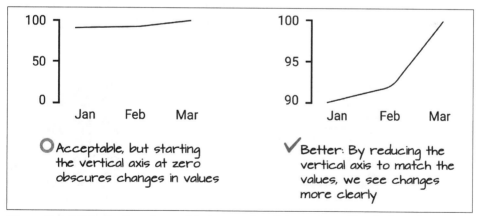

Figure 6-4. While the line chart with the zero baseline is acceptable, the line chart with a modified baseline more clearly tells a data story about change.

Pie charts represent 100%

Pie charts are one of the most contentious issues in data visualization. Most dataviz practitioners will recommend avoiding them entirely, saying that people are bad at accurately estimating sizes of different slices. We take a less dramatic stance as long as you adhere to the recommendations we give in the next section.

The one and only thing in data visualization that every single professional will agree on is that *pie charts represent 100% of the quantity.* If slices add up to anything other than 100%, it's a crime. If you design a survey titled, "Are you a cat or a dog person?" and allow both "cat" and "dog" checkboxes to be selected, forget about putting the results into a pie chart.

Chart Aesthetics

Remember that you create a chart to help the reader understand the story, not to confuse them. Decide if you want to show raw counts, percentages, or percent changes, and do the math for your readers.

Avoid chart junk

Start with a white background and add elements as you see appropriate. You should be able to justify each element you add. To do so, ask yourself: Does this element improve the chart, or can I drop it without decreasing readability? This way you won't end up with so-called "chart junk" as shown in Figure 6-5, which includes 3D perspectives, shadows, and unnecessary elements. They might have looked cool in early versions of Microsoft Office, but let's stay away from them today. Chart junk distracts the viewer and reduces chart readability and comprehension. It also looks unprofessional and doesn't add credibility to you as a storyteller.

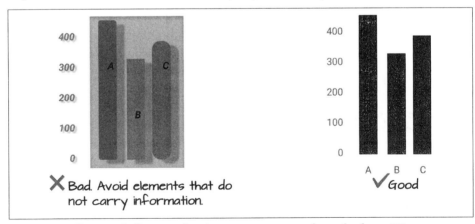

Figure 6-5. Chart junk distracts the viewer, so stay away from shadows, 3D perspectives, unnecessary colors and other fancy elements.

Don't use shadows or thick outlines with bar charts, because the reader might think that decorative elements are part of the chart, and thus misread the values that bars represent.

The only justification for using three dimensions is to plot three-dimensional data, which has x, y, and z values. For example, you can build a three-dimensional map of population density (*https://oreil.ly/rWmEg*), where x and y values represent latitude and longitude. In most cases, however, three dimensions are best represented in a bubble chart, or a scatterplot with varying shapes and/or colors.

Beware of pie charts

Remember that pie charts show only part-to-whole relationship, so all slices need to add up to 100%. Generally, the fewer slices, the better. Arrange slices from largest to smallest, clockwise, and put the largest slice at 12 o'clock, as shown in Figure 6-6.

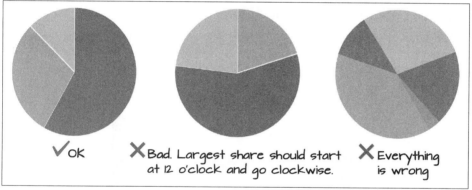

Figure 6-6. Sort slices in pie charts from largest to smallest, and start at 12 o'clock.

If your pie chart has more than five slices, consider showing your data in a bar chart, either stacked or split, like Figure 6-7 shows.

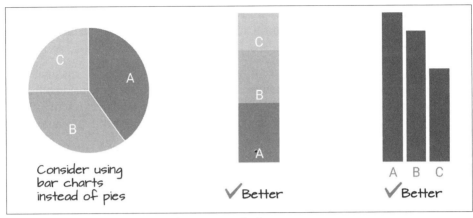

Figure 6-7. Consider using bar charts instead of pies.

Don't make people turn their heads to read labels

When your column chart has long x-axis labels that have to be rotated (often 90 degrees) to fit, consider turning the chart 90 degrees so that it becomes a horizontal bar chart. Take a look at Figure 6-8 to see how much easier it is to read horizontally-oriented labels.

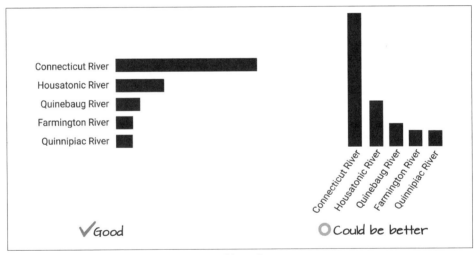

Figure 6-8. For long labels, use horizontal bar charts.

Arrange elements logically

If your bar chart shows different categories, consider ordering them, as shown in Figure 6-9. You might want to sort them alphabetically, which can be useful if you want the reader to be able to quickly look up an item, such as their town. Ordering categories by value is another common technique that makes comparisons possible.

If your columns represent a value of something at a particular time, they have to be ordered sequentially, of course.

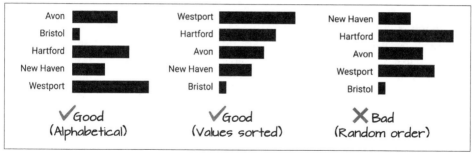

Figure 6-9. For long labels, use horizontal bar charts.

Do not overload your chart

When labeling axes, choose natural increments that space equally, such as [0, 20, 40, 60, 80, 100], or [1, 10, 100, 1000] for a logarithmic scale. Don't overload your scales. Keep your typography simple, and use (but do not overuse) **bold type** to highlight major insights. Consider using commas as thousands separators for readability (1,000,000 is much easier to read than 1000000).

Be careful with colors

In this section, we would like to briefly introduce three important rules about colors. First, remember that in most cases monochromatic (single-hue) charts suffice, and there may be no need to introduce the extra dimension of color at all.

Second, refer to the color wheel and standard harmony rules (*https://oreil.ly/1sIzk*) when choosing your palette. Consider the rule of complementary colors—opposites in the color wheel—to find color pairs, such as blue and orange or yellow and purple. Analogous colors, or neighbors in the color wheel, make good palettes, such as orange, red, and pink.

Third, stay away from pure saturated colors and instead choose their "earthier" versions, such as olive green instead of bright green, or navy instead of neon blue.

Once you have chosen the color palette for your visualization, ask yourself:

- Is there a conflict of meaning between colors and the phenomenon they represent? Am I using red to represent profit or green to represent death rate? This question is complex as colors carry different associations for different social groups and cultures, but try to exercise your best sensitivity.

- Can people with color blindness interpret your chart? Palettes that contain reds and greens or yellows and blues can be challenging. Consider using Color Oracle (*https://www.colororacle.org*) or another simulator to make sure your visualization is accessible.

- Will the colors be distinguishable in black and white? Even if you don't expect viewers to print your chart, they may. You can use Color Oracle or another simulator to check that your colors have different brightness levels and look distinguishable in grayscale. Figure 6-10 shows some good and bad examples of color use.

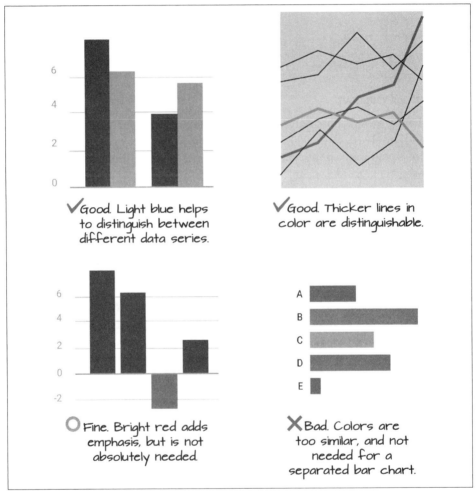

Figure 6-10. Don't use colors just for the sake of it.

The use of color is a complex topic, and there is plenty of research devoted to it. For an excellent overview, see Lisa Charlotte Rost's "Your Friendly Guide to Colors in

Data Visualization" and "How to Pick More Beautiful Colors for Your Data Visualizations," both on the Datawrapper blog.[3]

If you follow our advice, you should end up with a decluttered chart, as shown in Figure 6-11. Notice how your eyes are drawn to the bars and their corresponding values, not bright colors or secondary components like the axes lines.

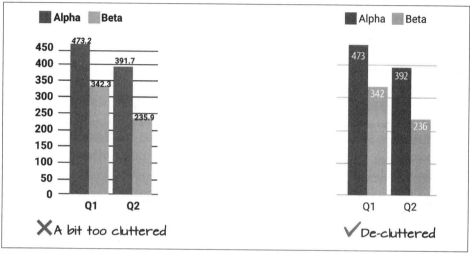

Figure 6-11. Make sure important things catch the eye first.

In summary, good chart design requires training your eyes and your brain to understand what works and what fails when telling data stories. Build up your data visualization muscles by looking at lots of different charts, both bad and good ones. For example, browse through both the Data Is Beautiful (*https://oreil.ly/HryZv*) and Data Is Ugly (*https://oreil.ly/wo9yd*) pages on Reddit. Read comments by other readers, but develop your own opinions, which may not necessarily match those expressed by others. Also, it's a fun way to learn!

Google Sheets Charts

In this section, you'll learn about the pros and cons of creating interactive charts in Google Sheets (*https://sheets.google.com*), the powerful spreadsheet tool we introduced in Chapter 2. Google Sheets has many advantages for newcomers to data visualization. First, Google Sheets allows you to clean, analyze, share, and publish charts, all in the same platform. One tool does it all, which makes it easier to organize your

---

3 Lisa Charlotte Rost, "Your Friendly Guide to Colors in Data Visualization," Datawrapper (blog), July 31, 2018, *https://oreil.ly/ndITD*; Lisa Charlotte Rost, "How to Pick More Beautiful Colors for Your Data Visualizations," Datawrapper (blog), accessed October 21, 2020, *https://oreil.ly/dRCBy*.

work by keeping it all together in one place. Second, Google Sheets is familiar and easy to learn for many users, so it will help you *quickly* create good-looking interactive charts. See all of the types of charts you can create with Google Sheets (*https:// oreil.ly/bE5ng*). Although some people export charts as static images in *JPG* or *PNG* format, this chapter focuses on creating interactive charts that display more info about your data when you hover over them in your browser. Later, you'll learn how to embed an interactive chart on your website in Chapter 9.

But Google Sheets also has limitations. First, while you can enter textual source notes in a chart subtitle, there's no easy way to place a clickable link to your source data inside a Google Sheets chart, so you will need to add source details or links in a web page that contains your embedded interactive chart. Second, you cannot add text annotations or highlight specific items inside your charts. Finally, you are limited in customizing your chart design, especially tool tips when hovering over data visualizations. (If Google Sheets doesn't meet your needs, refer back to Table 6-1 for other tools and tutorials in "Datawrapper Charts" on page 131, "Tableau Public Charts" on page 146, and Chapter 11.)

In the next two sections, we'll review the most appropriate cases to use bar, column, pie, line, and area charts. Each section features hands-on examples and step-by-step instructions with sample datasets to help you learn.

Bar and Column Charts

Before you begin, be sure to review the pros and cons of designing charts with Google Sheets in the prior section. In this section, you'll learn how to create bar and column charts, the most common visualization methods to compare values across categories. We'll focus on why and how to create three different types: grouped, split, and stacked. For all of these, we blend the instructions for bar and column charts because they're essentially the same, though oriented in different directions. If your data contains long labels, create a horizontal bar chart, instead of a vertical column chart, to give them more space for readability.

Grouped Bar and Column Charts

A grouped bar or column chart is best to compare categories side-by-side. For example, if you wish to emphasize gender differences in obesity across age brackets, then format the male and female data series together in vertical columns in your Google Sheet, as shown in Figure 6-12. Now you can easily create a grouped column chart to display these data series side by side, as shown in Figure 6-13.

	A	B	C
1	Age Range	Men	Women
2	20 - 39	40.3	39.7
3	40 - 59	46.4	43.3
4	60 and over	42.2	43.3
5			

Figure 6-12. To create a grouped bar or column chart, format each data series vertically in Google Sheets.

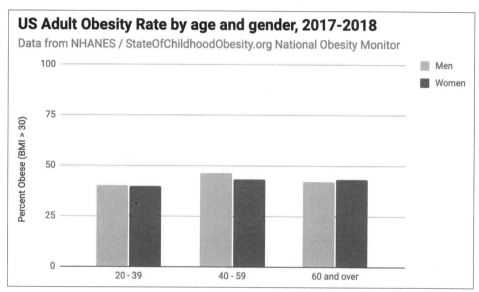

Figure 6-13. Grouped column chart: explore the interactive version (https://oreil.ly/ cPfLn). Data from NHANES/State of Childhood Obesity, 2017–18 (https://oreil.ly/8- OES).

To create your own interactive grouped column (or bar) chart, use our template and follow these steps:

1. Open our Grouped Column chart template in Google Sheets (*https://oreil.ly/ bY2zh*) with US obesity data by gender and age. Sign in to your account, and go to File > "Make a copy" to save a version you can edit to your own Google Drive.

2. To remove the current chart from your copy of the spreadsheet, float your cursor to the top-right corner of the chart to make the three-dot kebab menu appear, and select Delete.

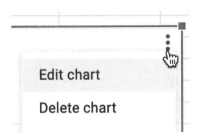

3. Format your data to make each column a data series (such as male and female), as shown in Figure 6-12, which means it will display as a separate color in the chart. Feel free to add more than two columns.

4. Use your cursor to select only the data you wish to chart, then go to the Insert menu and select Chart.

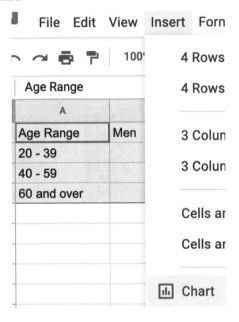

5. In "Chart editor," change the default selection to "Column chart," with "Stacking none," to display Grouped Columns. Or select "Horizontal bar chart" if you have longer labels.

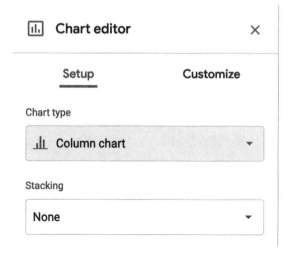

6. To customize title, labels, and more in "Chart editor" select Customize. Also, you can select the chart and axis titles to edit them.

7. To make your data public, go to the upper-right corner of your sheet to click the Share button, and in the next screen, click the words "Change to anyone with the link." This means your sheet is no longer restricted to only you, but can be viewed by anyone with the link (see "Share Your Google Sheets" on page 20).

8. To embed an interactive version of your chart in another web page, click the kebab menu in the upper-right corner of your chart, and select Publish chart. In the next screen, select Embed and press the Publish button. See Chapter 9 to learn what to do with the iframe code.

Unfortunately, Google Sheets functionality is very limited when it comes to displaying error bars or uncertainty. You can only assign either constant numbers or percent values as error bar values to an individual series, not to specific data points. If you wish to display error bars in Google Sheets, in "Chart editor," select Customize tab, scroll down to Series, and select a series from the drop-down menu. Check "Error bars," and customize its value as either percent or a constant value. This setting will be applied to all data points in that series.

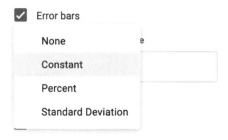

9. Finally, remember that providing your data source adds credibility to your work. You can briefly describe the source in a chart subtitle in Google Sheets. But there is no easy way to insert a clickable link in your chart, so you would need to add more details or links in the separate web page that contains your embedded interactive chart.

Split Bar and Column Charts

A split column (or bar) chart is best to compare categories in separate clusters. For example, imagine you wish to emphasize calorie counts for selected foods offered at two different restaurants, Starbucks and McDonalds. Format the restaurant data in vertical columns in your Google Sheet, as shown in Figure 6-14.

	A	B	C
1	Fast Food items	Starbucks	McDonalds
2	Mocha Frappuccino (24-ounce, 2% milk, whip cream)	500	
3	White Hot Chocolate (20-ounce, 2% milk, whip cream)	710	
4	Big Mac		540
5	Double Quarter Pounder with cheese		770

Figure 6-14. To create a split bar (or column) chart, format each data series vertically, and leave cells blank where appropriate.

Because food items are unique to each restaurant, enter only calorie data in the appropriate column, and leave other cells blank. Now you can easily create a split bar (or column) chart that displays the restaurant data in different clusters, as shown in Figure 6-15. Unlike the grouped column chart previously shown in Figure 6-13, here the bars are separated from each other because we do not wish to draw comparisons between food items that are unique to each restaurant. Also, our chart displays horizontal bars (not columns) because some data labels are long.

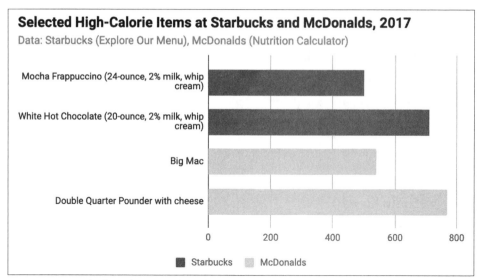

Figure 6-15. Split bar chart: explore the full-screen interactive version (https://oreil.ly/ NUHiq). Data from Starbucks and McDonalds (https://oreil.ly/jXnER).

Create your own version using our Split Bar Chart in Google Sheets template (*https:// oreil.ly/uWOeA*) with Starbucks and McDonalds data. Organize each data series vertically so that it becomes its own color in the chart. Leave cells blank when no direct comparisons are appropriate. The remainder of the steps are similar to the grouped column chart tutorial.

Stacked Bar and Column Charts

Stacked column (or bar) charts are best to compare subcategories, or parts of a whole. For example, if you wish to compare the percentage of overweight residents across nations, format each weight-level data series in vertical columns in your Google Sheet, as shown in Figure 6-16. Now you can easily create a stacked column (or bar) chart that displays comparisons of weight-level subcategories across nations, as shown in Figure 6-17. Often it's better to use a stacked chart instead of multiple pie charts because people can see differences more precisely in rectangular stacks than in circular pie slices.

	A	B	C	D
1	Nation	Underweight	Normal weight	Overweight
2	United States	2	35.2	62.8
3	South Africa	8.6	46.2	45.1
4	Italy	3.4	52.6	44
5	Iran	5.7	51.5	42.8
6	Brazil	4	55.4	40.6
7	South Korea	4.7	63.2	32.1
8	India	32.9	62.5	4.5

Figure 6-16. To create a stacked column (or bar) chart, format each data series vertically in Google Sheets.

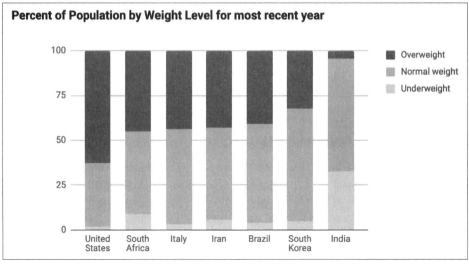

Figure 6-17. Stacked column chart: explore the interactive version (https://oreil.ly/VQPIy). Data from WHO and CDC (https://oreil.ly/E72Jg).

Create your own version using our Stacked Column Chart in Google Sheets template (*https://oreil.ly/6E3ti*) with international weight-level data. Organize each data series vertically so that it becomes its own color in the chart. In the "Chart editor" window, choose Chart Type > "Stacked column chart" (or choose "Stacked bar chart" if you have long data labels). The rest of the steps are similar to the previous ones.

To change the color of a data series (for example, to show the Overweight category in red), click the kebab menu in the top-right corner of the chart, then go to "Edit chart" > Customize > Series. Choose the appropriate series from the drop-down menu, and set its color in the drop-down menu, as shown in Figure 6-18.

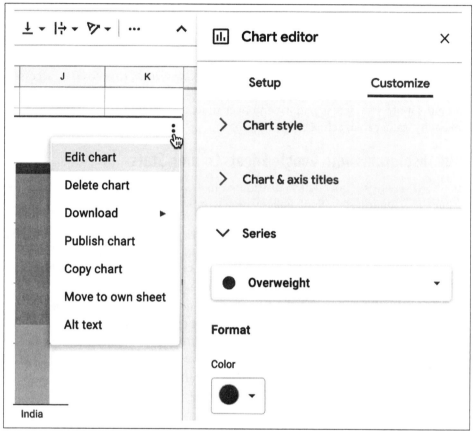

Figure 6-18. To edit a column color, select "Edit chart" > Customize > Series.

Histograms

Histograms are best to show the distribution of raw data by displaying the number of values that fall within defined ranges, often called *buckets* or *bins*. Creating a histogram can be a great way to better understand what your data looks like to inform your decision making when designing more advanced visualizations, such as choropleth maps, as you'll learn in "Design Choropleth Colors and Intervals" on page 167. Although histograms may look similar to column charts, the two are different. First, histograms show *continuous* data, and usually you can adjust the bucket ranges to explore frequency patterns. For example, you can shift histogram buckets from 0–1,

1–2, 2–3, etc., to 0–2, 2–4, etc. By contrast, column charts show *categorical* data, such as the number of apples, bananas, carrots, etc. Second, histograms don't usually show spaces between buckets because these are continuous values, while column charts show spaces to separate each category.

In this section, you'll create two types of histograms in Google Sheets: quick histograms using the "Column stats" menu and regular histograms using the Chart menu, and learn the advantages of each method. For both tutorials we'll use the same data: the average calorie supply per capita for 174 countries in 2017, compiled by the United Nations Food and Agriculture Organization (*https://oreil.ly/GVZWO*), accessed through Our World In Data (*https://oreil.ly/7kEd4*). Note that methods for measuring food supply vary across nations and over time, and estimate the amount of food availability, rather than actual consumption.

Quick Histograms with Google Sheets Column Stats

The fastest way to see how data is distributed in a column in Google Sheets is to use the built-in "Column stats" tool. Follow these steps to try it:

1. Open the sample data on Average Daily Calorie Supply per Capita by Country, 2017, in Google Sheets (*https://oreil.ly/xCXAR*), log in with your account, and go to File > "Make a copy" to create a version you can edit in your Google Drive.

2. To create a quick histogram in Google Sheets, select any column, then go to Data > "Column stats," and click the Distribution button in the sidebar to view a histogram for that column. The advantage is that this method is very fast, and you can quickly create histograms for other columns in the same sheet using the arrows near the top of the sidebar (< >). However, you cannot manually adjust the bucket ranges or make other edits to these quick histograms, and you cannot embed them on the web as you can with regular charts in Google Sheets.

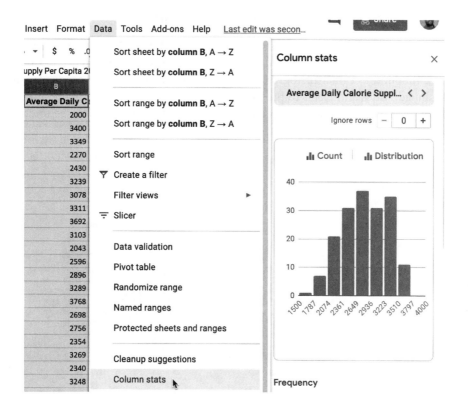

Histograms are designed to show broad patterns of data distribution, not individual values. The preceding histogram shows that while most nations have an average daily supply around 2,800 calories per capita, 8 nations have fewer than 2,000, and 11 nations have more than 3,500. Without annotations, histograms don't tell us the names of those outlier countries. But they do offer a better sense of the shape of the data distribution.

Regular Histograms with Google Sheets Charts

Compare the histogram from "Quick Histograms with Google Sheets Column Stats" on page 122 with the regular histogram created with Charts in Figure 6-19. You'll notice that in the regular histogram, you can define the bucket ranges, display dividers, and add titles and labels to provide more context to readers. Also, the interactive version of the regular histogram allows users to float their cursor to see underlying data on the count for each column.

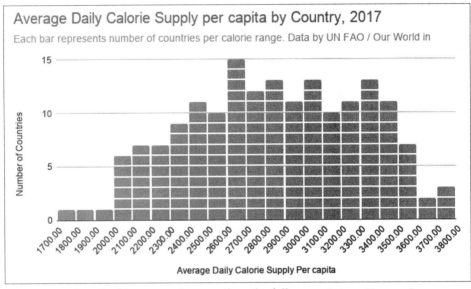

Figure 6-19. Regular histogram chart: explore the full-screen interactive version (https://oreil.ly/YRcLs).

To create a regular histogram in Google Sheets:

1. Select a column with values and go to Insert > Chart. If Google Sheets does not automatically select "Histogram chart" as the "Chart type" in "Chart editor," use the drop-down menu and select it manually, near the bottom of the list in the Other category.

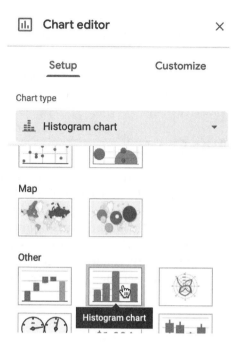

2. You can manually set the range of each bucket and round the breakpoints to whole numbers (such as multiple of 1, 5, or 100), if this makes sense for the distribution of your data. In "Chart editor," go to Customize > Histogram > "Bucket size." Larger intervals will contain more data points and will appear wider, while smaller intervals will contain fewer points and appear narrower.

 Currently, Google Sheets does not allow users to remove decimal points in the x-axis label of a histogram, even when all of the breakpoints are integers.

3. Optionally, you can break down the column into individual items (in our case, countries), which will appear as blocks with white boundaries. To do this, go to Customize > Histogram > "Show item dividers."

4. In the Chart editor, customize further to add a *Chart title*, a *subtitle* to describe the source, and also vertical and horizontal axis titles to help readers interpret the chart.

Since the regular histogram is created using the Charts feature, you can choose to Publish it and copy the embed code for the interactive version, as you'll learn in Chapter 9.

Now that you've learned how to create histograms to show the distribution of raw data, in the next section we'll move on to other types of Google Sheets chart types, such as pie, line, and area charts.

Pie, Line, and Area Charts

Before starting this section, be sure to review the pros and cons of designing charts in "Google Sheets Charts" on page 113, as well as beginner-level step-by-step instructions in "Bar and Column Charts" on page 114. In this section, you'll learn why and how to use Google Sheets to build three more types of interactive visualizations: pie charts (to show parts of a whole), line charts (to show change over time), and stacked area charts (to combine showing parts of a whole, with change over time). If Google Sheets or these chart types do not meet your needs, refer back to Table 6-1 for other tools and tutorials.

Pie Charts

Some people use pie charts to show parts of a whole, but we urge caution with this type of chart. For example, if you wish to show the number of different fruits sold by a store in one day, as a proportion of total fruit sold, then format the labels and values in vertical columns in your Google Sheet, as shown in Figure 6-20. Values can be expressed as either raw numbers or percentages. Now you can easily create a pie chart that displays these values as colored slices of a circle, as shown in Figure 6-21. Viewers can see that bananas made up slightly over half of the fruit sold, followed by apples and oranges.

	A	B
1	Bananas	32
2	Apples	21
3	Oranges	5

Figure 6-20. To create a pie chart, format the data values vertically in Google Sheets.

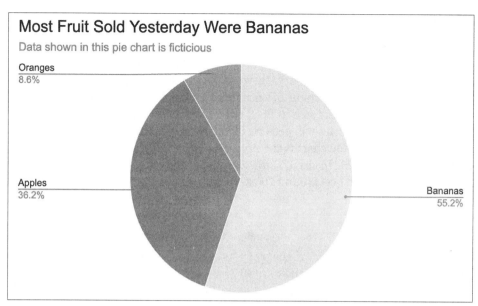

Most Fruit Sold Yesterday Were Bananas

Data shown in this pie chart is ficticious

Oranges
8.6%

Apples
36.2%

Bananas
55.2%

Figure 6-21. Pie chart: explore the interactive version (https://oreil.ly/24X3m). Data is fictitious.

But you need to be careful when using pie charts, as we described in "Chart Design Principles" on page 103. First, make sure your data adds up to 100%. If you created a pie chart that displayed *some* but *not all* of the fruits sold, it wouldn't make sense. Second, avoid creating too many slices, since people cannot easily distinguish smaller ones. Ideally, use no more than five slices in a pie chart. Finally, start the pie at the top of the circle (12 o'clock) and arrange the slices clockwise, from largest to smallest.

Create your own version using our Pie Chart in Google Sheets template (*https://oreil.ly/PGhmJ*). The steps are similar to those in prior Google Sheets chart tutorials in this chapter. Go to File > "Make a copy" to create a version you can edit in your Google Drive. Select all of the cells and go to Insert > Chart. If Google Sheets does not correctly guess that you wish to create a pie chart, then in the "Chart editor" window, in the Setup tab, select "Pie chart" from the "Chart type" drop-down list.

Note that slices are ordered the same way they appear in the spreadsheet. Select the entire sheet and *Sort* the values column from largest to smallest, or from Z to A. In the *Customize* tab of "Chart editor," you can change colors and add borders to slices. Then add a meaningful title and labels as desired.

Line Charts

A line chart is the best way to represent continuous data, such as change over time. For example, imagine you wish to compare the availability of different meats per capita in the US over the past century. In your Google Sheet, organize the time units (such as years) into the first column, since these will appear on the horizontal x-axis. Also, place each data series (such as beef, pork, chicken) alongside the vertical time-unit column, and each series will become its own line, as shown in Figure 6-22. Now you can easily create a line chart that emphasizes each data series changed over time, as shown in Figure 6-23. In the US, the amount of chicken per capita steadily rose and surpassed pork and beef around 2000.

	A	B	C	D
1	Year	Beef	Pork	Chicken
2	1910	48.5	38.2	11
3	1920	40.7	39	9.7
4	1930	33.7	41.1	11.1
5	1940	37.8	45.1	10
6	1950	44.6	43	14.3
7	1960	59.1	48.6	19.1
8	1970	79.6	48.1	27.4
9	1980	72.1	52.1	32.7
10	1990	63.9	46.4	42.4
11	2000	64.5	47.8	54.2
12	2010	56.7	44.3	58
13	2017	54	47	64

Figure 6-22. To create a line chart, format the time units and each data series in vertical columns.

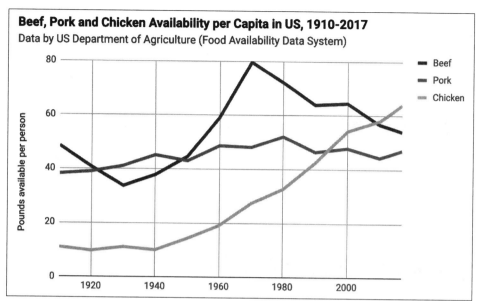

Figure 6-23. Line chart: explore the interactive version (https://oreil.ly/9_XUo). Data from US Department of Agriculture (https://oreil.ly/ADEwa).

Create your own version using our Line Chart in Google Sheets template (*https://oreil.ly/hbZD-*). The steps are similar to those in prior Google Sheets chart tutorials in this chapter. Go to File > "Make a copy" to create a version you can edit in your Google Drive. Select the data, and choose Insert > Chart. If Google Sheets does not correctly guess that you wish to create a line chart, in "Chart editor," Setup tab, select "Line chart" from the Chart type drop-down list.

Rows Versus Columns in Time-Series Data

Tables and charts approach time-series data from opposite directions. When designing a table, the proper method is to place dates horizontally as column headers, so that we read them from left to right, like this:[4]

Year	2000	2010	2020
Series1	...	...	...
Series2	...	...	...

When designing a line chart in Google Sheets and several other tools, we organize the spreadsheet by placing the dates vertically down the first column, so that the tool reads them as labels for a data series, like this:

Year	Series1	Series2
2000	...	...
2010	...	...
2020	...	...

Learn how to convert data from tables to charts in "Transpose Rows and Columns" on page 71.

Stacked Area Charts

Area charts resemble line charts with filled space underneath. The most useful type is a stacked area chart, which is best for combining two previously mentioned concepts: showing parts of the whole (like a pie chart) and continuous data over time (like a line chart). For example, the line chart shows how the availability of three different meats changed over time. However, if you also wish to show how the total availability of these combined meats went up or down over time, it's hard to see this in a line chart. Instead, use a stacked line chart to visualize the availability of each meat *and* the total combined availability per capita over time. Stacked line charts show both aspects of your data simultaneously.

To create a stacked area chart, organize the data in the same way as you did for the line chart in Figure 6-22. Now you can easily create a stacked line chart that displays the availability of each meat—and their combined total—over time, as shown in Figure 6-24. Overall, we can see that total available meat per capita increased after the

4 Few, *Show Me the Numbers*, p. 166

1930s Great Depression, and chicken steadily became a larger portion of the total after 1970.

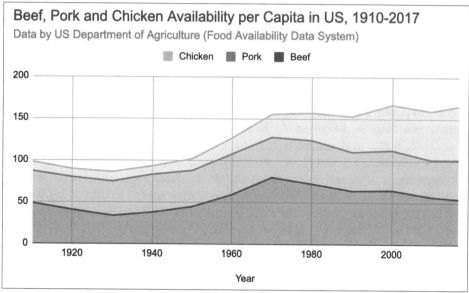

Figure 6-24. Stacked area chart: explore the interactive version (https://oreil.ly/mdZlY). Data from US Department of Agriculture (https://oreil.ly/PXFbI).

Create your own version using our Stacked Area Chart in Google Sheets template (*https://oreil.ly/PXFbI*). The steps are similar to those in prior Google Sheets chart tutorials in this chapter. Go to File > "Make a copy" to create a version you can edit in your Google Drive. Set up the data exactly as you would for a line chart, with the first column for time units in the x-axis, and place each data series in its own column. Select the data, and choose Insert > Chart. In "Chart editor," in tab Setup, select "Stacked area chart" from the Chart type drop-down list.

Now that you've built several basic charts in Google Sheets, in the next section we'll build some slightly more advanced charts in a different tool, Datawrapper.

Datawrapper Charts

Another free and collaborative tool for creating interactive charts is Datawrapper (*https://www.datawrapper.de*), which has several advantages over Google Sheets. First, you can start creating in Datawrapper right away in your browser, even without creating an account, and its four-step process is intuitive for many new users. Second, you can add credit bylines, links to data sources, and even allow visitors to download the data from a button inside your Datawrapper visualizations that you publish online, which makes your work more credible and accessible. Third, Datawrapper supports a wider array of interactive chart types than Google Sheets, as well as maps, which we'll discuss in Chapter 7, and tables, in Chapter 8. With Datawrapper, you can build all of the basic charts we've constructed so far in this chapter, as well as three new types we'll cover in "Annotated Charts" on page 132, "Range Charts" on page 137, and "Scatter and Bubble Charts" on page 139. Later, you'll learn how to embed interactive Datawrapper charts on your website in Chapter 9.

While no single tool does everything, we recommend that you consider using both Google Sheets and Datawrapper, which turns this pair of easy-to-use tools into a visualization powerhouse. First, use Google Sheets as your spreadsheet to organize and analyze your data as described in Chapter 2, record your detailed source notes and save raw data files as described in Chapter 3, and clean up your data as described in Chapter 4. Although Datawrapper can transpose data (swap the rows and columns), it cannot create pivot tables or look up and merge data as spreadsheets can do. Second, import your data from Google Sheets to Datawrapper to create visualizations, because the latter tool offers you more control over their appearance, annotations, and additional features, as we'll describe. You'll discover that Datawrapper plays nicely with Google Sheets by accepting a direct link to data stored there. Together, Google Sheets and Datawrapper are a powerful combination.

In addition, we strongly recommend the high-quality Datawrapper Academy support pages, the extensive gallery of examples (*https://oreil.ly/mIdeT*), and well-designed training materials (*https://oreil.ly/LbCo_*). Reading these will not only teach you which buttons to press, but more importantly, how to design better visualizations that tell true and meaningful stories about your data. While writing this book, we learned a great deal from Datawrapper Academy, and we give credit and specific links in sections that follow. Finally, one more plus is that Datawrapper Core is open source code (*https://oreil.ly/xQjHJ*), though that does not apply to most of the platform's plug-ins to create charts and maps.

Now you're ready to use Datawrapper to create new types of charts that step beyond the basics. But if Datawrapper or the chart types in this section do not meet your needs, refer back to Table 6-1 for other tools and tutorials, or prior chapters on spreadsheets, sourcing, and cleaning up data.

Annotated Charts

An annotated chart is best to highlight specific data or add contextual notes inside the visualization. Well-designed annotations can help answer the "So what?" question by briefly noting the significance of data in the chart, with greater detail in the sentences or paragraphs that follow. Be cautious with annotations, because it's important to avoid adding unnecessary "chart junk," as described in "Chart Design Principles" on page 103.

You can add annotations to any chart created with Datawrapper, and we'll illustrate how with a line chart about US unemployment data from 2000 through 2020, since adding a bit of historical context often helps readers to better understand data stories about change over time. To create a line chart in Datawrapper, organize your data the same way you did in "Pie, Line, and Area Charts" on page 126. Place units of time (such as months/years) in the first column, and numerical data values (such as the unemployment rate) in the second column. Now you're ready to create an interactive line chart with annotations, as shown in Figure 6-25. Since 2000, the unemployment rate has peaked three times, but the tallest peak occurred during the 2020 economic crisis sparked by the COVID-19 pandemic.

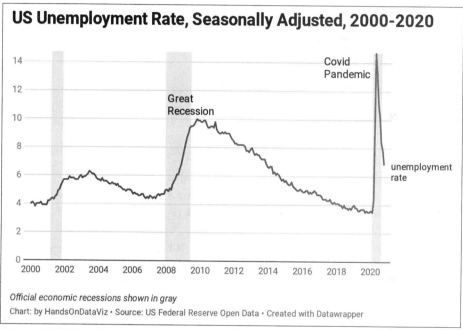

Figure 6-25. Line chart with annotation: explore the interactive version (https://oreil.ly/ 4stDc). Data from US Federal Reserve Open Data (https://oreil.ly/ky4m_).

Create your own annotated line chart in Datawrapper by following this tutorial:

1. Open the US Unemployment Seasonally Adjusted 2000-2020 sample data in Google Sheets (*https://oreil.ly/ipFZ-*) and go to File > "Make a copy" to create your own version in your Google Drive. Or go to File > Download to export a CSV or Excel version to your computer.

2. Open Datawrapper in your browser and click Start Creating. We recommend that you create a free account to better manage your visualizations, but it's not required.

3. In the Upload Data screen, click Import Google Spreadsheet and paste the link to the data in the shared Google Sheet, then click Proceed. To upload a Google Sheet, the Share setting must be changed from Private, the default setting, to "Anyone with the link can view" at minimum. Also, if you update cells in your Google Sheet, they will be updated automatically in a linked Datawrapper chart, but not after your chart is published online. Alternatively, you can upload data by copying and pasting it into the data table window, or uploading an Excel or CSV file.

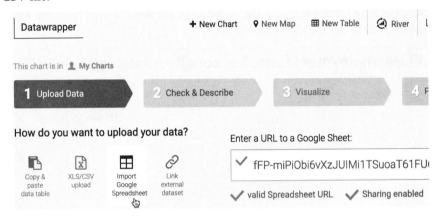

4. In the "Check & Describe" screen, inspect your data to make sure that numbers appear in blue, dates in green, and text in black type, and click Proceed.

 If needed, at the bottom of the "Check & Describe" screen there's a button that will transpose your data (swap rows and columns), which is useful in cases where the data you receive is organized in the opposite direction from what Datawrapper expects. But our sample data does not need to be transposed because it's organized correctly.

5. In the Visualize screen, Datawrapper will attempt to guess the chart type you desire, based on the data format. If you entered our sample data correctly, it will correctly display a line chart. If not, you can select a different chart type.

6. Click the Annotate tab near the top left of the Visualize screen. Type in a meaningful title, such as "US Unemployment Rate, Seasonally Adjusted, 2000–2020." Also, add a data source, such as "US Federal Reserve Open Data," and a link to the source, such as the shared Google Sheet (*https://oreil.ly/ipFZ-*) or the Federal Reserve Open Data web page (*https://oreil.ly/I1IhJ*). Finally, in the byline line, add your name or organization to credit the people who created this chart. You'll

see all of these details and links appear automatically at the bottom of your chart, to add credibility to your work.

7. Scroll down further in the Annotate tab to the "Text annotations" section, and click the button to add one. Draw a pink rectangle to place your annotation on the chart, where unemployment rose sharply from 2008 to 2010, and type **Great Recession** into the text field. This helps readers place the Great Recession (*https://oreil.ly/ZhQG_*) in historical context. Click the button a second time to add another text annotation, place it around the second unemployment peak in 2020, and type **COVID-19 Pandemic** into the text field to offer readers a comparison. You can fine-tune the style and position of annotations with additional options further down on the screen.

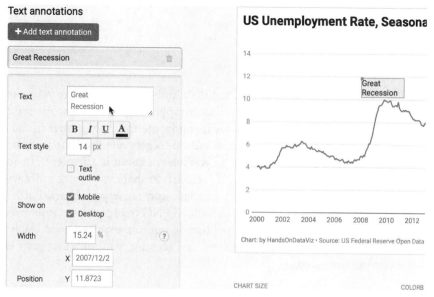

8. Scroll down further in the Annotate tab to the "Highlight range" section, and click the button to add one to the chart. Click inside the chart to draw pink lines from December 2007 to June 2009, which will highlight that portion of the chart in gray. This period represents the official beginning and ending of the US Great Recession in the eyes of economists, although unemployment continued to grow for the population at large. To highlight other official recession periods, draw two more ranges: March through November 2001 and February through October 2020 (the most current data as we write this). Once again, you can fine-tune the style and positioning of a highlighted range with additional options further down the screen.

Highlight range

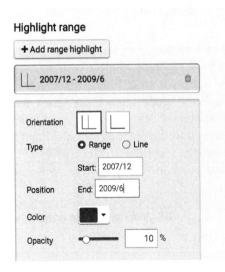

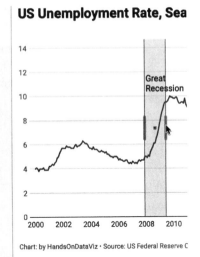

9. Click Proceed or advance to the Publish & Embed screen to share your work with others. If you logged into your free Datawrapper account, your work is automatically saved online in the My Charts menu in the top-right corner of the screen. Also, you can click the blue Publish button to generate the code to embed your interactive chart on your website, as you'll learn about in Chapter 9. In addition, you can "add your chart to River" if you wish to share your work more widely by allowing other Datawrapper users to adapt and reuse your chart. Furthermore, scroll all the way down and click Download PNG to export a static image of your chart. Additional exporting and publishing options require a paid Datawrapper account. Or, if you prefer not to create an account, you can enter your email to receive the embed code.

See this Datawrapper Academy article to learn how to create a line chart with confidence intervals (*https://oreil.ly/vROCU*), which are similar to error bars.

Congratulations on creating your first interactive Datawrapper chart! Now let's use Datawrapper to create a new type of chart, called a range chart.

Range Charts

A range chart, which can be classed as a specific type of a dot chart, emphasizes gaps between data points, and is often used to highlight inequalities. In this tutorial, we will use Datawrapper to build a range chart about the US gender pay gap. The chart compares the median earnings of American men and women by education level, according to the 2019 American Community Survey, which treated gender as binary, as shown in Figure 6-26. We were inspired by the Datawrapper Academy range plot tutorial (*https://oreil.ly/jzw0L*) and created our version using more recent data. Overall, the range chart shows how men, on average, earn more than women at all education levels. In fact, an average US man with a bachelor's degree earns more than an average US woman with a graduate degree.

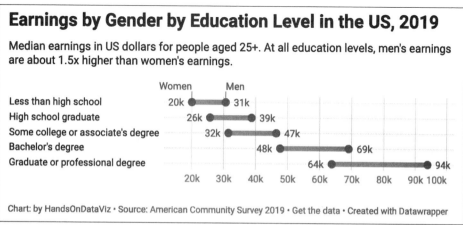

Figure 6-26. Range chart: explore the interactive version (https://oreil.ly/JP02b). Data from US Census 2019 American Community Survey (https://oreil.ly/k2UDS).

To build this range chart, we organized the data as shown in Figure 6-27. The first column contains five educational attainment levels, from lowest (*less than high school*) to highest (*graduate or professional degree*). The second and third columns contain numeric values of median earnings for *Men* and *Women*, respectively.

	A	B	C
1	**Educational Attainment**	**Men**	**Women**
2	Less than high school	30725	20046
3	High school graduate	38906	25829
4	Some college or associate's degree	46610	31644
5	Bachelor's degree	69201	47895
6	Graduate or professional degree	93998	63912

Figure 6-27. Organize your range chart data into three columns: labels and values for both subgroups.

By now you should be familiar with Datawrapper, so the steps to create a range chart are less detailed than in the previous tutorial on annotated line charts. If you get lost, see more detailed steps about Datawrapper charts in the previous section.

1. Open the US Earnings by Gender by Education Level data in Google Sheets (*https://oreil.ly/ol2CP*) and go to File > "Make a copy" to create your own version in your Google Drive.

2. Open Datawrapper in your browser and click Start Creating. We recommend that you create a free account to better manage your visualizations, but it's not required.

3. In the Upload Data screen, click Import Google Spreadsheet and paste the link to the data in the shared Google Sheet, then click Proceed. Alternatively, you can upload data by copying and pasting it into the data table window, or uploading an Excel or CSV file.

4. In the "Check & Describe" screen, inspect your data, then click Proceed.

5. In the Visualize screen, Datawrapper will attempt to guess the chart type you desire, based on the data format, but you will need to select Range Plot.

6. Click the Annotate tab near the top left of the Visualize screen to add a meaningful title, data source, and byline credits.

7. Click the Refine tab of the Visualize screen to modify the range chart appearance. You have several options, but here are the most important ones in this case. First, in the Labels section, change the visibility of the values from *start* to *both*, which places numbers at both ends of each range. Second, push the slider to *Label first range*, which places the words *Men* and *Women* above the first range. Third, change "Number format" to *123k*, which will round dollar amounts to the nearest thousand, and replace thousands with a *k*.

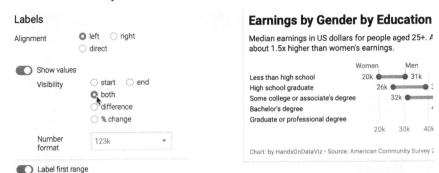

8. Still in the Refine tab, scroll down to the Appearance section to improve the colors. Select the "Range end" drop-down menu to select a better color, such as red. Change the "Range color" setting to "gradient" to emphasize the range.

The Refine tab includes options to re-sort or group data rows, change the chart size for different devices, and check visibility for colorblind readers.

9. After modifying your visualization, proceed to the "Publish & Embed" screen, and follow the prompts to share your work, or refer to the previous detailed Datawrapper tutorial.

Now that you've completed a range chart, let's see how we can use Datawrapper to build scatter and bubble charts to show relationships between two or more variables.

Scatter and Bubble Charts

Scatter charts (also known as scatter plots) are best to show the relationship between two datasets by displaying their *x* and *y* coordinates as dots to reveal possible correlations. In the upcoming scatter chart example, each dot represents a nation, with its life expectancy on the horizontal x-axis and its fertility rate (births per woman) on the vertical y-axis. The overall dot pattern illustrates a correlation between these two datasets: life expectancy tends to increase as fertility decreases.

Bubble charts go farther than scatter charts by adding two more visual elements—dot size and color—to represent a third or fourth dataset. Our bubble chart example begins with the same life expectancy and fertility data for each nation that we previously saw in the scatter chart, but the size of each circular dot represents a third dataset (population) and its color indicates a fourth dataset (region of the world). As a result, bubble charts are scatter charts on steroids because they pack even more information into the visualization.

Fancier bubble charts introduce one more visual element—animation—to represent a fifth dataset, such as change over time. Although creating an animated bubble chart is beyond the scope of this book, watch a famous TED talk by Hans Rosling (*https://oreil.ly/jyHQ2*), a renowned Swedish professor of global health, to see animated bubble charts in action, and learn more about his work at the Gapminder Foundation (*https://www.gapminder.org*).

In this section, you'll learn why and how to create a scatter chart and a bubble chart in Datawrapper. Be sure to read about the pros and cons of designing charts with Datawrapper in the prior section ("Datawrapper Charts" on page 131).

Scatter Charts with Google Sheets

A scatter chart is best to show the relationship between two sets of data as x and y coordinates on a grid. Imagine you wish to compare life expectancy and fertility data for different nations. Organize your data in three columns, as shown in Figure 6-28. The first column contains the *Country* labels, and the second column, *Life Expectancy*, will appear on the horizontal x-axis, while the third column, *Fertility*, will appear on the vertical y-axis. Now you can easily create a scatter chart that displays a relationship between these datasets, as shown in Figure 6-29. One way to summarize the chart is that nations with lower fertility rates (or fewer births per woman) tend to have high life-expectancy rates. Another way to phrase it is that nations with higher life expectancy at birth have lower fertility. Remember that correlation is not causation, so you cannot use this chart to argue that fewer births produce longer lives, or that longer-living females create fewer children.

	A	B	C
1	Life Expectancy	Fertility	Country
2	76.7	1.7	China
3	69.4	2.2	India
4	78.5	1.7	United States
5	71.5	2.3	Indonesia
6	75.7	1.7	Brazil
7	67.1	3.5	Pakistan
8	54.3	5.4	Nigeria
9	72.3	2	Bangladesh

Figure 6-28. To create a scatter chart in Datawrapper, format data in three columns: labels, x values, and y values.

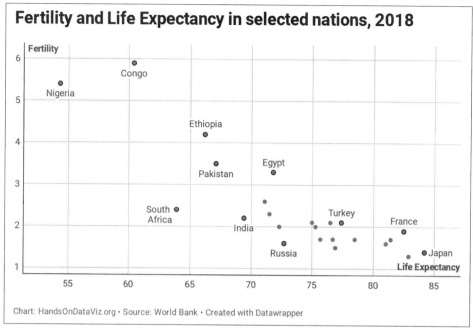

Fertility and Life Expectancy in selected nations, 2018

Chart: HandsOnDataViz.org • Source: World Bank • Created with Datawrapper

Figure 6-29. Scatter chart: explore the interactive version (https://oreil.ly/KBchE). Data from the World Bank (https://oreil.ly/VmYst).

Create your own interactive scatter chart in Datawrapper, and edit the tool tips to properly display your data:

1. Open our Scatter Chart sample data in Google Sheets (*https://oreil.ly/gU1bE*), or use your own data in a similar format.

2. Open Datawrapper and click to start a new chart.

3. In the Datawrapper Upload Data screen, either copy and paste the link to the data tab of the Google Sheet, or copy and directly paste in the data. Click Proceed.

4. In the "Check & Describe" screen, inspect your data and make sure that the Life Expectancy and Fertility columns are blue, which indicates numeric data. Click Proceed.

5. In the Visualize screen, under the "Chart type" tab, select Scatter Plot. Float your cursor over the scatter chart that appears in the right-hand window, and you'll notice that we still need to edit the tool tips to properly display data for each point.

6. In the Visualize screen, under the Annotate tab, scroll down to the "Customize tooltip" section, select "Show tooltips," and click the "Customize tooltips" button to open its window. Click inside the first field, which represents the tool tip Title,

then click further down on the blue Country button to add {{ Country }} there. This means that the proper country name will appear in the tool tip title when you hover over each point. In addition, click inside the second field, which represents the tool tip Body, type **Life expectancy:** and click the blue button with the same name to add it, so that {{ Life_expectancy }} appears after it. Press Return twice on your keyboard, then type **Fertility:** and click on the blue button with the same name to add it, so that {{ Fertility }} appears right after it. Press Save to close the tool tip editor window.

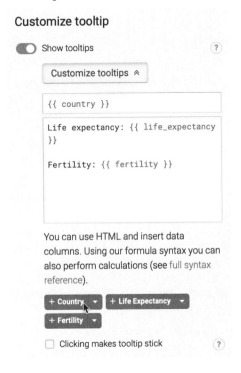

7. Back in the Visualize screen, when you hover your cursor over a point, the tool tip will properly display its data according to your editor settings.

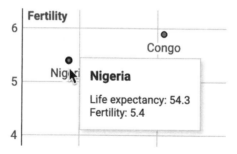

8. Finish the annotations to add your title and data source, then proceed to publish and embed your chart by following the prompts or reading the more detailed Datawrapper tutorial. Learn about your next steps in Chapter 9.

Bubble Charts

In your scatter chart, you learned how to visualize the relationship between two datasets: life expectancy (the x-axis coordinate) and fertility (the y-axis coordinate). Now let's expand on this concept by creating a bubble chart that adds two more datasets: population (shown by the size of each point, or bubble) and region of the world (shown by the color of each bubble). We'll use similar World Bank data as before, with two additional columns, as shown in Figure 6-30. Note that we're using numeric data (population) for bubble size, but categorical data (regions) for color. Now you can easily create a bubble chart that displays a relationship between these four datasets, as shown in Figure 6-31.

	A	B	C	D	E
1	Country	Life expectancy	Fertility	Population	Region
2	United States	78.5	1.70	326687501	North America
3	United Kingdom	81.4	1.70	66460344	Europe
4	China	76.7	1.70	1392730000	Asia
5	India	69.4	2.20	1352617328	Asia
6	Japan	84.2	1.40	126529100	Asia

Figure 6-30. To create a bubble chart in Datawrapper, organize the data into five columns: labels, x-axis, y-axis, bubble size, and bubble color.

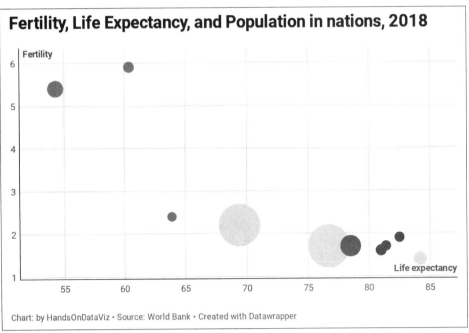

Fertility, Life Expectancy, and Population in nations, 2018

Chart: by HandsOnDataViz • Source: World Bank • Created with Datawrapper

Figure 6-31. Bubble chart: explore the interactive version (https://oreil.ly/7xqM-). Data from the World Bank (https://oreil.ly/JfAFp).

Create your own interactive bubble chart in Datawrapper, and edit the tool tips, bubble sizes, and colors to display your data:

1. Open our Scatter Chart sample data in Google Sheets (*https://oreil.ly/1aUkj*), or use your own data in a similar format.

2. Open Datawrapper and click to start a new chart.

3. Follow steps 3 through 5 from "Scatter Charts with Google Sheets" on page 140 to upload, check, and visualize the data as a Scatter Plot chart type.

4. In the Visualize screen, under the Annotate tab, scroll down to "Customize tooltip," and click "edit tooltip template." In the "Customize tooltip HTML" window, type in the fields and click on the blue column names to customize your tool tips to display country, life expectancy, fertility, and population. Press Save to close the tool tip editor window.

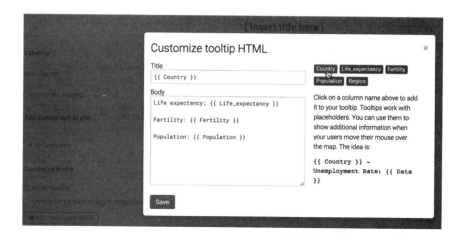

5. Back in the Visualize screen, under the Refine tab, scroll down to *Color*, select column for Region, and click the "Customize colors" button to assign a unique color to each. Then scroll down to Size, check the box to change size to "variable," select column for Population and increase the max size slider. Click Proceed.

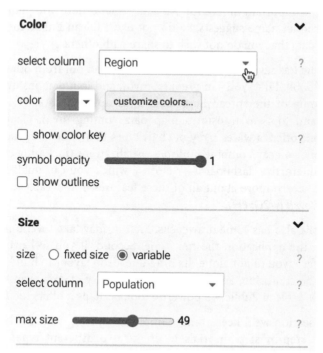

6. Test your visualization tool tips. Then finish the annotations to add your title and data source, and proceed to publish and embed your chart, by following the prompts or reading the more detailed Datawrapper tutorial. See your next steps in Chapter 9.

For more information about creating scatter and bubble charts, see the Datawrapper Academy support site (*https://oreil.ly/q112s*).

Now that you've learned how to create a scatter chart in Datawrapper, in the next section you'll learn how to create the same chart type with a different tool, Tableau Public, to build up your skills so that you can make more complex charts with this powerful tool.

Tableau Public Charts

Tableau is a powerful data visualization tool used by many professionals and organizations to analyze and present data. Our book focuses on the free version, Tableau Public (*https://public.tableau.com*), a desktop application for Mac or Windows computers that you can download at no cost by providing an email address. The free Tableau Public tool is very similar to the pricier Tableau versions sold by the company, with one important difference. All data visualizations you publish become public, as the product name suggests, so do not use Tableau Public for any sensitive or confidential data that you do not wish to share with others.

Tableau Public has several features that make it stand out from other drag-and-drop tools in this book. First, you can prepare, pivot, and join data inside Tableau Public, similar to some of the spreadsheet skills in Chapter 2, data cleaning methods in Chapter 4, and tools to transform map data coming up in Chapter 13. Second, Tableau Public offers a wider array of chart types than other free tools. Finally, with Tableau Public you can combine multiple visualizations (including tables, charts, and maps) into interactive dashboards or stories, which you can publish and embed on your website. Learn more about all of these features in the Tableau Public resources page (*https://oreil.ly/2QxcH*).

Tableau Public also has some drawbacks. First, it may take several minutes to install and start up the application the first time. Second, if you feel overwhelmed by its design interface, you're not alone. Its drag-and-drop layout to build charts and maps initially can be confusing, and its internal vocabulary of data terms may seem unfamiliar. While Tableau Public is a powerful tool, perhaps it offers too many options.

In the next section we'll keep things simple by starting with the basics of Tableau Public, with step-by-step tutorials to create two different types of charts. First, you'll build on skills you already learned in the previous section by building a scatter chart in Tableau Public. Then in "Filtered Line Chart" on page 152, you'll learn how to create a filtered line chart, which demonstrates more of the tool's strengths in interactive visualization design.

Scatter Charts with Tableau Public

Scatter charts are best to show the relationship between two datasets, placed on the x- and y-axis, to reveal possible correlations. With Tableau Public, you can create an interactive scatter chart, where you can hover your cursor over points to view more details about the data. Organize your data in three columns, the same way as in "Scatter Charts with Google Sheets" on page 140: the first column for data labels, the second column for the x-axis, and the third column for the y-axis. Then you can create an interactive scatter chart as shown in Figure 6-32, which illustrates a strong relationship between household income and test scores (above or below the national average for 6th grade math and English) in Connecticut public school districts. To learn more about the data and related visualizations, see Sean Reardon et al. at the Stanford Education Data Archive (*https://oreil.ly/xCt37*), Motoko Rich et al. at *The New York Times* (*https://oreil.ly/rOhig*), Andrew Ba Tran at CT Mirror/TrendCT (*https://oreil.ly/9OuN0*), and this TrendCT GitHub repo (*https://oreil.ly/_5xyz*).

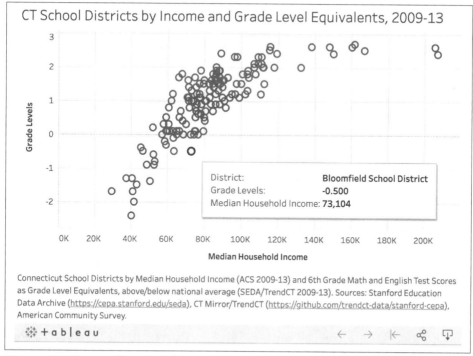

Figure 6-32. Scatter chart in Tableau Public: explore the interactive version (https://oreil.ly/2cWge). Data by CT Mirror/TrendCT and Stanford CEPA (https://oreil.ly/18Vgl).

To create your own scatter chart using this sample data in Tableau Public, follow the tutorial that follows.

Install Tableau Public and Connect Data

Follow these steps to install Tableau Public, launch it, and connect your data:

1. Download the CT Districts-Income-Grades sample data in Excel format (*https://oreil.ly/pYkFT*), or view and download the Google Sheets version (*https://oreil.ly/l2vDp*). The data file consists of three columns: district, median household income, and test-score levels.

2. Install and start up the free Tableau Public (*https://public.tableau.com*) desktop application for Mac or Windows. It may require several minutes to complete this process. Tableau Public's welcome page includes three sections: Connect, Open, and Discover.

3. Under Connect, you can choose to upload a Microsoft Excel file, choose "Text file" to upload a CSV file, or choose other options. To connect to a server, such as Google Sheets, click More... to connect to your account. After you successfully connect to your data source, you will see it under Connections in the Data Source tab. Under Sheets, you'll see two tables: *data* and *notes*.

4. Drag the *data* sheet into "Drag tables here" area. You will see the preview of the table under the drag-and-drop area. You have successfully connected one data source to Tableau Public, and you are ready to build your first chart.

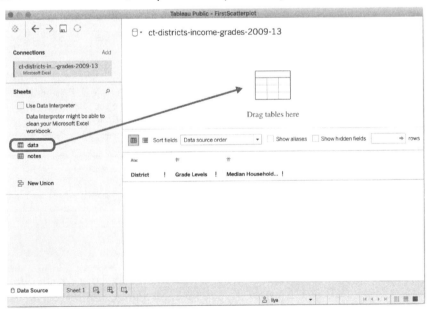

Create Scatter Chart in the Worksheet

Now let's create a scatter chart in the Tableau Public worksheet:

1. In the Data source screen, click on the orange Sheet 1 tab (in the lower-left corner) to go to your worksheet, where you will build the chart.

   Although it may feel overwhelming at first, the key is learning where to drag items from the Data pane (left) into the main worksheet. Tableau marks all data fields in blue (for discrete values, mostly text fields or numeric labels) or green (for continuous values, mostly numbers).

2. In your worksheet, drag the *Grade Levels* field into the *Rows* field above the charting area, which for now is just empty space. The following screenshot shows this dragging step and the following two steps. Tableau will apply a summation function to it, and you will see SUM(Grade Levels) appear in the *Rows* row, and a blue bar in the charting area. It makes little sense so far, so let's plot another data field.

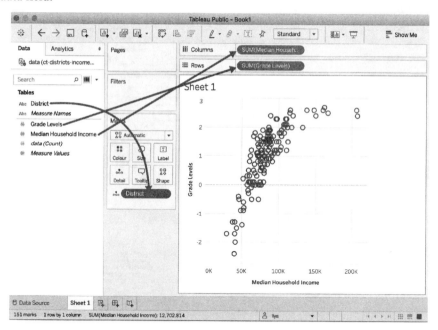

3. Drag Median Household Income to the *Columns* field, just above the *Rows* field. In general, choosing between Rows and Columns shelves can be challenging, but it is convenient to think of the *Columns* shelf as representing your x-axis and *Rows* as the y-axis. Once again, Tableau will apply the summation function, so you'll see SUM(Median Household Income) in the *Columns* shelf. The bar chart will automatically transform into a scatter chart with just one data point in the

upper-right corner, because the data for both is aggregated (remember the SUM function).

4. We want to tell Tableau to disaggregate the household and grade levels variables. In other words, we want to introduce an extra level of granularity, or *detail* to our visualization. To do so, drag the *District* dimension into the *Detail* shelf of the *Marks* card. Now a real scatter chart will appear in the charting area. If you hover over points, you will see all three values associated with these points.

Add Title and Caption, and Publish

Give your scatter chart a meaningful title by double-clicking on the default Sheet 1 title above the charting area. Add more information about the chart, such as source of the data, who built the visualization and when, and other details to add credibility to your work. You can do so inside a Caption, a text block that accompanies your Tableau chart. In the menu, go to Worksheet > Show Caption. Double-click the Caption block that appears, and edit the text. As a result, your final worksheet will look like the one shown in Figure 6-33.

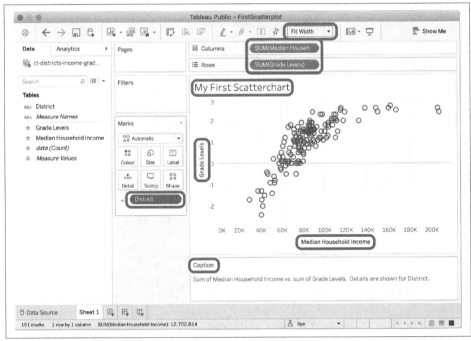

Figure 6-33. This scatter chart is ready to be published.

In the drop-down menu above the *Columns* shelf, change Standard to Fit Width to ensure your chart occupies 100% of available horizontal space.

1. To publish your interactive chart on the public web, go to File > "Save to Tableau Public As…" A window to sign in to your account will pop up. If you don't have an account, click "Create one now for free" at the bottom, and save the login details in your password manager.

2. After signing in, a window to set the workbook title will appear. Change the default *Book1* title to something meaningful, as this name will appear in the public web address for your published work. Click Save.

3. After saving your workbook on the public web, Tableau Public will open up a window in your default browser with the visualization. In the green banner above the chart, click Edit Details to edit the title or description. Under Toolbar Settings, find the checkbox to "Allow others to download or explore and copy this workbook and its data," and select the setting you wish. If you're publishing your visualization on the web, we also recommend that you keep this box checked so that others can download your data and see how you constructed it, to improve data accessibility for all.

Toolbar Settings ☑ Show view controls *Undo, Redo, Revert*

☑ Show author profile link

☑ Allow others to download or explore and copy this workbook and its data

Your entire portfolio of Tableau Public visualizations is online at `https://public.tableau.com/profile/USERNAME`, where your unique username is `USERNAME`.

See "Get the Embed Code or iframe Tag" on page 231 to insert the interactive version of your chart on a web page that you control.

Filtered Line Chart

Now that you've learned how to create a scatter chart in Tableau Public, let's move on to a new type of chart that highlights the tool's strengths. Instead of *static* charts, such as those found in print or PDFs, this book features *interactive* charts for their ability to display more data. You can also design interactive charts to show only the amount of data you desire. In other words, your interactive visualization can become a data-exploration tool that allows users to "dig" and find specific data points and patterns, without overwhelming them with too much information at once.

In this tutorial, we'll build an interactive filtered line chart with Tableau Public, to visualize how internet access has changed in different nations over time. Organize the data in three columns, as shown in Figure 6-34. The first column, *Country Name*, has the data labels that become the colored lines. The second column, *Year*, will appear on the horizontal x-axis. The third column, *Percent Internet Users*, has numeric values that appear on the vertical y-axis. Now you can create a filtered line chart with checkboxes, to show only selected lines on startup to avoid overwhelming users, while allowing them to toggle on other lines, and hover over each one for more details, as shown in Figure 6-35.

fx			
	A	B	C
1	CountryName	Year	PercentInternetUsers
839	Cameroon	2016	23.20297197
840	Cameroon	2017	23.20297197
841	Cameroon	2018	
842	Canada	1995	4.163525253
843	Canada	1996	6.76023965
844	Canada	1997	15.07235736
845	Canada	1998	24.8974003

Figure 6-34. In a filtered line chart, organize the data in three columns: data labels, year, and numeric values.

To create your own filtered line chart using this sample data in Tableau Public, follow this tutorial. We assume that you have already installed the free Tableau Public desktop application for Mac or Windows, and have become familiar with the tool by completing the tutorial "Scatter Charts with Tableau Public" on page 147, so the following steps are abbreviated.

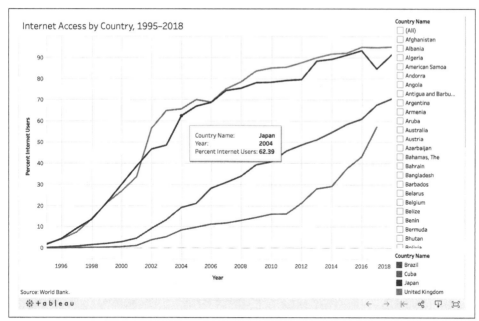

Figure 6-35. Filtered line chart: explore the interactive version (https://oreil.ly/W34xg). Data from World Bank (https://oreil.ly/POMyn).

Connect Data to Tableau Public

Follow these steps to open up the data and connect it to the application:

1. Download the World Bank Internet Users 1995–2018 sample data in Excel format (*https://oreil.ly/2sdhd*), or view and download the Google Sheets version (*https://oreil.ly/vh4fx*). The file consists of three columns: data labels, year, and numeric values.

2. Open Tableau Public, and under the Connect menu, you can upload your data as a Microsoft Excel file, choose "Text file" to upload a CSV file, or click More... to connect to a server and upload a Google Sheet from your account. After you successfully connect to your data source, you will see it under Connections in the Data Source tab. Under Sheets, you will see two tables: `data` and `notes`. Drag the `data` sheet into the "Drag tables here" area to preview it.

3. In the "Data source" screen, click on the orange Sheet 1 tab (in the lower-left corner) to go to your worksheet, where you will build the chart.

In your worksheet, your variables will be listed under Tables in the left-hand side. The original variables are displayed in normal font, the *generated* variables will be shown in *italics* (such as *Latitude* and *Longitude*, which Tableau guessed from the country names). Now you are ready to begin building your interactive chart.

Build and Publish a Filtered Line Chart

Follow these steps to create the visualization and share it online:

1. Drag the *Year* variable to the *Columns* shelf. This will place years along the x-axis.

2. Drag the *Percent Internet Users* variable to the *Rows* shelf to place them on the y-axis. The value in the shelf will change to SUM(Percent Internet Users). You should see a single line chart that sums up percentages for each year. That's completely incorrect, so let's fix it.

3. To "break" aggregation, drag and drop *Country Name* to the *Color* shelf of the *Marks* card. Tableau will warn you that the recommended number of colors should not exceed 20. Since we will be adding checkbox filtering, ignore this warning, and go ahead and press the "Add all members" button.

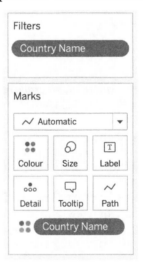

4. At first, everything will look like a spaghetti plate of lines and colors! To add filtering, drag *Country Name* to the Filters card. In the Filter window, make sure all countries are checked, and click OK.

5. In the Filters card, click the drop-down arrow of the Country Name symbol, then scroll down and select Show Filter.

6. You'll see a list of options with all checkboxes on the right side of the chart. Click (All) to add/remove all options, and select a few countries to see how the interactive filtering works. The checkboxes you select at this stage will appear "on" in the published map. You may notice that some countries from your "on" selection got assigned the same value. The good news is, Tableau lets you change colors of individual data points (in our case, countries). From the Marks card, click the *Color* shelf, and then Edit Colors... Double-click a country from the Select Data Item list to bring up a color picker window, pick your favorite color, and click OK. Although you can ensure that your preselected countries are painted in unique colors, there will be repetitions among other countries because your palette is limited to 20 colors. Unfortunately, there is little you can do to get around this.

7. Double-click on the Sheet 1 title (above the chart) and replace it with a more meaningful title, such as "Internet Access by Country, 1995–2018." In the menu, go to Worksheet > Show Caption to add a Caption block under the chart. Use this space to add the source of your data (World Bank), and perhaps credit yourself as the author of this visualization.

8. Change Standard to Fit Width in the drop-down menu above the *Columns* shelf.

9. You may notice that the x-axis (Year) starts with 1994 and ends with 2020, although our data is for 1995 through 2018. Double-click the x-axis, and change Range from Automatic to Fixed, with the Fixed start of *1995*, and the Fixed end of *2018*. Close the window and see that the empty space on the edges has disappeared.

10. Once your filtered line chart looks like this, you're ready to publish. Go to File > "Save to Tableau Public As…," and log into your account, or create one if you haven't yet done so. Follow the prompts to publish your chart on the public web, or see "Scatter Charts with Tableau Public" on page 147 for more details.

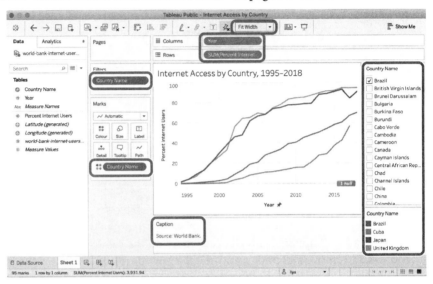

See "Get the Embed Code or iframe Tag" on page 231 to insert the interactive version of your chart on a web page that you control.

Summary

Congratulations on creating interactive charts that pull readers deeper into your story and encourage them to explore the underlying data! As you continue to create more, always match the chart type to your data format and the story you wish to emphasize. Also, design your charts based on the principles and aesthetic guidelines outlined near the top of this chapter. While anyone can click a few buttons to quickly create a chart nowadays, your audiences will greatly appreciate well-designed charts that thoughtfully call their attention to meaningful patterns in the data.

In this chapter, you learned how to create different types of interactive charts with Google Sheets, Datawrapper, and Tableau Public. For more advanced chart design with open source code, see Chapter 11, which gives you ever-more control over how you design and display your data, but also requires learning how to edit and host code templates with GitHub in Chapter 10.

Chapter 7 follows a similar format to introduce different map types, design principles, and hands-on tutorials to create interactive visualizations with spatial data. In Chapter 9, you'll learn how to embed interactive charts on your website.

Map Your Data

Maps draw your readers into data that includes a spatial dimension, while also developing a stronger sense of place. Seeing the relative distance between points on a map, or identifying geographic patterns in a *choropleth* map (where colored polygons represent data values), relays information to readers' eyes more effectively than text, tables, or charts. But creating meaningful maps that draw our attention to key insights in your data requires clear thinking about design choices.

In this chapter, we will examine principles of map design and distinguish between good and bad maps in "Map Design Principles" on page 160. You'll learn about rules that apply to all maps, and specific guidelines for creating choropleth maps. While many tools allow you to download maps as *static* images, our book also demonstrates how to construct *interactive* charts that invite readers to zoom in and explore the data in their web browsers. In Chapter 9, you'll learn how to embed interactive charts on your website.

Decisions about map types are based on two main factors: the format of your data, and the kind of story you wish to tell. Learn about different types of maps you can create in this book in Table 7-1. For example, point maps work best to show specific locations with colored markers to represent categories (such as hospitals), while choropleth maps are best suited to display relative values for regions (such as birth rates across US states). After selecting your map type, follow our tool recommendations and step-by-step tutorials that appear in the sections that follow. This chapter features *easy tools* with drag-and-drop menus, which you can find in "Point Map with Google My Maps" on page 177, "Symbol Point Map with Datawrapper" on page 185, "Choropleth Map with Tableau Public" on page 200, and "Current Map with Socrata Open Data" on page 207. The table also points you to *power tools* that give you more control to customize and host your visualizations, such as Leaflet code templates in

Chapter 12. These advanced tools require prior knowledge of how to edit and host code templates with GitHub in Chapter 10.

Table 7-1. Basic map types, best uses, and tutorials

Map	Best use and tutorials in this book
Point map with custom icons 	Best to show specific locations (such as addresses) with customized colored markers for categories, plus text and images in pop-up windows. • Easy tool: "Point Map with Google My Maps" on page 177 • Power tool: "Leaflet Maps with Google Sheets" on page 294
Symbol point map 	Best to show specific locations (such as cities), with variable-sized shapes or colors to represent data values (such as population growth). • Easy tool: "Symbol Point Map with Datawrapper" on page 185
Choropleth (colored polygon) map 	Best to show patterns across geographic areas (such as neighborhoods or nations) by coloring polygons to represent data values. • Easy tool: "Choropleth Map with Datawrapper" on page 191 or "Choropleth Map with Tableau Public" on page 200 • Power tools: "Leaflet Maps with Google Sheets" on page 294

Heat point map

Best to show clusters of points as colored hotspots to emphasize high frequency or density of cases.

- Power tool: "Leaflet Heatmap Points with CSV Data" on page 327

Story map

Best to show a point-by-point guided tour, with a scrolling narrative to display text, images, audio, video, and scanned map backgrounds.

- Power tool: "Leaflet Storymaps with Google Sheets" on page 308

Polyline map

Best to show routes (such as trails or transit), with colors for different categories.

- Easy tool: "Point Map with Google My Maps" on page 177
- Power tool: "Leaflet Maps with Google Sheets" on page 294

Customized point-polyline-polygon map

Best to show any combination of points, polylines, or polygons, with customized icons for categories, and colored regions to represent data values.

- Power tool: "Leaflet Maps with Google Sheets" on page 294

Searchable point map

Best to show specific locations for users to search by name or proximity, or filter by category, with optional list view.

- Power tool: "Leaflet Searchable Point Map" on page 329

Current map from open data repository

Best to show the most current information pulled directly from an open data repository such as Socrata and others.

- Easy tool: "Current Map with Socrata Open Data" on page 207
- Power tool: "Leaflet Maps with Open Data APIs" on page 331

Map Design Principles

Much of the data collected today includes a spatial component that can be mapped. Whether you look up a city address or take a photo of a tree in the forest, both can be geocoded as points on a map. We also can draw lines and shapes to illustrate geographical boundaries of neighborhoods or nations, and color them to represent different values, such as population and income.

However, just because data *can* be mapped doesn't always mean it *should* be mapped. Before creating a map, stop and ask yourself: *Does location really matter to your story?* Even when your data includes geographic information, sometimes a chart tells your story better than a map. For example, you can clearly show differences between geographic areas in a bar chart, trace how they rise and fall on different rates over time with a line chart, or compare two variables for each area in a scatter chart. Sometimes a simple table, or even text alone, communicates your point more effectively to your audience. Since creating a well-designed map requires time and energy, make sure it actually enhances your data story.

As you learned in Chapter 6, data visualization is not a science, but comes with a set of principles and best practices that serve as a foundation for creating true and meaningful maps. In this section, we'll identify a few rules about map design, but you may be surprised to learn that some rules are less rigid than others, and can be "broken" when necessary to emphasize a point, as long as you are honestly interpreting the data. To begin to understand the difference, let's start by establishing a common vocabulary about maps by breaking one down into its elements.

Deconstructing a Map

Our book features how to create *interactive* web maps, also called *tiled maps* or *slippy maps*, because users can zoom into and pan around to explore map data layers on top of a seamless set of basemap tiles. Basemaps that display aerial photo imagery are known as *raster* tiles, while those that display pictorial images of streets and buildings are tiles that are built from *vector* data. Raster map data is limited by the resolution of the original image, which gets fuzzier as we get closer. By contrast, you can zoom in very close to vector map data without diminishing its visual quality, as shown in Figure 7-1. You'll learn more about these concepts in the "Geospatial Data and GeoJSON" on page 336.

Figure 7-1. Raster map data from Esri World Imagery (on the left) and vector map data from OpenStreetMap (on the right) are both Ilya's childhood neighborhood in Mogilev, Belarus. Zooming into raster map data makes it fuzzier, while vector map data retains its sharpness.

Look at Figure 7-2 to learn about basic elements in the interactive maps you'll create in this chapter. The top layer usually displays some combination of *points, polylines,* and *polygons*. Points show specific places, such as the street address of a home or business, sometimes with a location marker, and each point is represented by a pair of latitude and longitude coordinates. For example, 40.69, -74.04 marks the location of the Statue of Liberty in New York City. Polylines are connected strings of points, such as roads or transportation networks, and we place the "poly-" prefix before "lines" to remind us that they may contain multiple branches. Polygons are collections of lines that create a closed shape, such as building footprints, census tracts, or state or national boundaries. Since points, polylines, and polygons fundamentally consist of latitude and longitude coordinates, all of them are vector data.

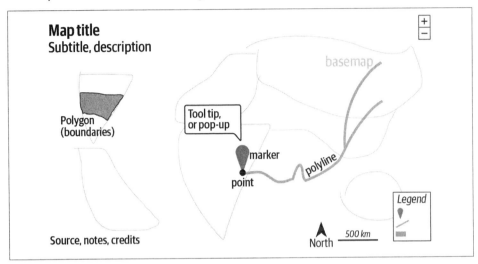

Figure 7-2. Key elements of an interactive map.

Interactive maps usually include *zoom controls* (+ and - buttons) to change the display of the basemap tiles and give the appearance of viewing the surface from different distances. Top-layer map data may display a hidden *tool tip* (when you hover the cursor over them) or a *pop-up* (when you click on them) that reveals additional information about its properties. Like a traditional static map, the *legend* identifies the meaning of symbols, shapes, and colors. Maps also may include a *north arrow* or *scale* to orient readers to direction and relative distance. Similar to a chart, a good map should include a title and brief description to provide context about what it shows, along with its data sources, clarifying notes, and credit to the individuals or organizations that helped to create it.

Clarify Point-Versus-Polygon Data

Before you start to create a map, make sure you understand your data format and what it represents. Avoid novice mistakes by pausing to ask these questions. First, *Can your data be mapped?* Sometimes the information we collect has no geographic component, or no consistent one, which makes it difficult or impossible to place on a map. If the answer is yes, then proceed to the second question: *Can the data be mapped as points or polygons?* These are the two most likely cases (which are sometimes confused), in contrast to the less common third option, polylines, which represent paths and routes.

To help you understand the difference, let's look at some examples. What type of data do you see listed here: points or polygons?

1. 36.48, –118.56 (latitude and longitude for Joshua Tree National Park, CA)
2. 2800 E Observatory Rd, Los Angeles, CA
3. Haight and Ashbury Street, San Francisco, CA
4. Balboa Park, San Diego, CA
5. Census tract 4087, Alameda County, CA
6. City of Los Angeles, CA
7. San Diego County, CA
8. State of California

In most cases, list items 1 through 4 represent *point* data because they refer to *specific locations* that can be displayed as point markers on a map. By contrast, numbers 5 through 8 generally represent *polygon* data because they refer to *geographic boundaries* that can be displayed as closed shapes on a map. See examples of both point and polygon maps in previous Table 7-1.

This point-versus-polygon distinction applies *most* of the time, but not always, with exceptions depending on your data story. First, it is possible, but not common, to represent all items 1 through 8 as *point* data on a map. For example, to tell a data story about population growth for California cities, it would make sense to create a symbol point map with different-sized circles to represent data for each city. To do this, your map tool would need to find the center point of the City of Los Angeles polygon boundary in order to place its population circle on a specific point on the map. A second way the point-versus-polygon distinction gets blurry is because some places we normally consider to be specific points *also* have polygon-shaped borders. For example, if you enter **Balboa Park, San Diego CA** into Google Maps, it will display the result as a map marker, which suggests it is point data. But Balboa Park also has a geographic boundary that covers 1.8 square miles (4.8 square kilometers). If you told a data story about how much land in San Diego was devoted to public space, it would make sense to create a choropleth map that displays Balboa Park as a polygon rather than a point. Third, it's also possible to transform points into polygon data with pivot tables, a topic we introduced in "Summarize Data with Pivot Tables" on page 33. For example, to tell a data story about the number of hospital beds in each California county, you could obtain point-level data about beds in each hospital, then pivot them to sum up the total number of beds in each county, and display these polygon-level results in a choropleth map. See a more detailed example in "Pivot Points into Polygon Data" on page 363.

In summary, clarify if your spatial data should represent points or polygons, since those two categories are sometimes confused. If you envision them as points, then create a point-style map; if polygons, then create a choropleth map. Those are the most common methods used by mapmakers, but there are plenty of exceptions, depending on your data story. You'll learn how to make a basic point map in "Point Map with Google My Maps" on page 177, and a symbol point map in "Symbol Point Map with Datawrapper" on page 185, then we'll demonstrate how to visualize polygon-level data in "Choropleth Map with Datawrapper" on page 191 and "Choropleth Map with Tableau Public" on page 200.

Map One Variable, Not Two

Newcomers to data visualization sometimes are so proud of placing one variable on a map that they figure two variables must be twice as good. This is usually not true. Here's the thought process that leads to this mistaken conclusion. Imagine you want to compare the relationship between income and education in eight counties of your state. First, you choose create a choropleth map of income, where darker blue areas represent areas with higher levels in the northwest corner, as shown in Figure 7-3 (a). Second, you decide to create a symbol point map, where larger circles represent a higher share of the population with a university degree, as shown in map (b). Both of those maps are fine, but they still do not highlight the relationship between income and education.

A common mistake is to place the symbol point layer on top of the choropleth map layer, as shown in map (c). This is where your map becomes overloaded. We generally recommend against displaying two variables with different symbologies on the same map, because it overloads the visualization and makes it very difficult for most readers to recognize patterns that help them to grasp your data story.

Instead, if the relationship between two variables is the most important aspect of your data story, create a scatter chart as shown in Figure 7-3 (d). Or, if geographic patterns matter for one of the variables, you could pair a choropleth map of that variable next to a scatter chart of both variables, by combining (a) and (d). Overall, remember that just because data *can* be mapped does not mean it *should* be mapped. Pause to reflect on whether location matters, because sometimes a chart tells your data story better than a map.

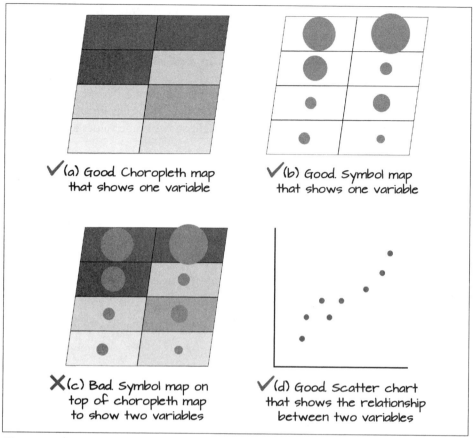

Figure 7-3. To compare two variables, such as income and education, avoid placing a symbol point map on top of a choropleth map. Instead, create a scatter chart, and consider pairing it with a choropleth map of one variable.

Choose Smaller Geographies for Choropleth Maps

Choropleth maps are best for showing geographic patterns across regions by coloring polygons to represent data values. Therefore, we generally recommend selecting *smaller* geographies to display more *granular* patterns, since larger geographies display aggregated data that may hide what's happening at lower levels. Geographers refer to this concept as the modifiable aerial unit problem (*https://oreil.ly/rxw2s*), which means that the way you slice up your data affects how we analyze its appearance on the map. Stacking together lots of small slices reveals more detail than one big slice.

For example, compare the two choropleth maps of typical home values in the Northeastern US, according to Zillow research data (*https://oreil.ly/HsLuZ*) for September 2020. Zillow defines typical values as a smoothed, seasonally adjusted measure of all single-family residences, condos, and co-ops in the 35th to 65th percentile range, similar to the median value at the 50th percentile, with some additional lower- and higher-value homes. Both choropleth maps use the same scale. The key difference is the size of the geographic units. In Figure 7-4, the map on the left shows home values at the larger state level, while the map on the right shows home values at the smaller county level.

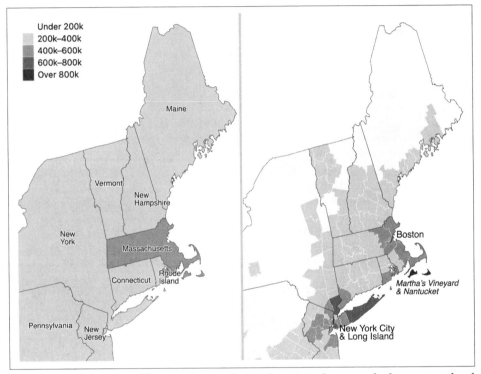

Figure 7-4. Zillow typical home values in September 2020 shown at the larger state level (left) versus the smaller county level (right).

Which map is best? Since both are truthful depictions of the data, the answer depends on the story you wish to tell. If you want to emphasize state-to-state differences, choose the first map because it clearly highlights how typical Massachusetts home prices are higher than those in surrounding Northeastern states. Or if you want to emphasize variation inside states, choose the second map, which demonstrates higher price levels in the New York City and Boston metropolitan regions, in comparison to more rural counties in those two states. If you're unsure, it's usually better to map smaller geographies, because it's possible to see both state-level and within-state variations at the same time, if the design includes appropriate labels and geographic outlines. But don't turn *smaller is better* into a rigid rule, since it doesn't work as you move farther down the scale. For example, if we created a third map to display every individual home sale in the Northeastern US, it would be *too detailed* to see meaningful patterns. Look for just the right level of geography to clearly tell your data story.

Design Choropleth Colors and Intervals

This section takes a deeper dive into map design principles for choropleth maps. Your choices about how to represent data with colors dramatically shapes its appearance, so it's very important to learn key concepts to ensure that your maps tell true and meaningful stories. Good choropleth maps make true and insightful geographic patterns clearly visible to readers, whether they are printed in black and white on paper or displayed in color on a computer screen. Furthermore, the best choropleth maps are designed to be interpreted correctly by people with colorblindness. For an excellent overview of visualization colors in general, see Lisa Charlotte Rost's "Your Friendly Guide to Colors in Data Visualization" and "How to Pick More Beautiful Colors for Your Data Visualizations," both on the Datawrapper blog.[1]

The best way to illustrate how color choices affect choropleth map design is with a wonderful online design assistant called ColorBrewer (*https://colorbrewer2.org*), created by Cynthia Brewer and Mark Harrower.[2] Unlike other tools in this book, you don't upload data directly into ColorBrewer to generate your visualization. Instead, you select the type of data you wish to display in your choropleth map, and Color-Brewer will assist you by recommending color palettes that work best with your data story. Then you can export those color codes into your preferred choropleth mapping tool, as shown in "Choropleth Map with Datawrapper" on page 191 and "Choropleth Map with Tableau Public" on page 200. See the ColorBrewer interface in Figure 7-5.

---

1 Rost, "Your Friendly Guide to Colors in Data Visualization," *https://oreil.ly/ndITD*; Rost, "How to Pick More Beautiful Colors for Your Data Visualizations," *https://oreil.ly/dRCBy*.

2 See also Cynthia A. Brewer, *Designing Better Maps: A Guide for GIS Users* (Esri Press, 2016).

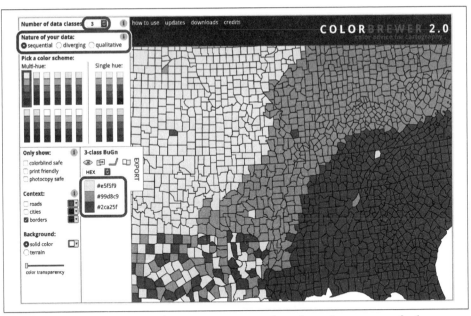

Figure 7-5. The ColorBrewer design assistant interface: data classes, type of color scheme, and recommended color codes.

In this section, we'll focus on two important decisions that ColorBrewer can assist you with when designing choropleth maps: choosing the type of color palette (sequential, divergent, or qualitative) and the intervals to group together similar-colored data points.

When you open ColorBrewer, the top row asks you to select the number of data classes (also known as intervals or steps) in the color range of your choropleth map. ColorBrewer can recommend distinct colors for up to 12 data classes, depending on the type of scheme you select. But for now, use the default setting of 3, and we'll return to this topic later when we discuss intervals in more detail later.

Choose Choropleth Palettes to Match Your Data

One of the most important decisions you'll make when designing a choropleth map is to select the type of palette. You're not simply choosing a color, but the *arrangement of colors* to help readers correctly interpret your information. The rule is straightforward: choose an appropriate color palette that matches your data format and the story you wish to tell.

ColorBrewer groups palettes into three types—sequential, diverging, and qualitative —as shown in Figure 7-6.

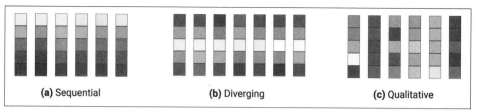

Figure 7-6. Sequential, diverging, and qualitative color palettes from ColorBrewer.

Sequential palettes

> Work best to show low-to-high numeric values. Examples include anything that can be placed in sequence on a scale, such as median income, amount of rainfall, or percent of the population who voted in the prior election. Sequential palettes can be single-hue (such as different shades of blue) or multihue (such as yellow-orange-red). Darker colors *usually* represent higher values, but not always.

Diverging palettes

> Work best to show numeric values above and below a standard level (such as zero, the average, or the median). They typically have two distinct hues to represent positive and negative directions, with darker colors at the extremes and a neutral color in the middle. Examples include income above or below the median level, rainfall above or below seasonal average, or percentage of voters above or below the norm.

Qualitative palettes

> Work best to show categorical data, rather than numeric scales. They typically feature unique colors that stand apart from one another to emphasize differences. Examples include different types of land use (residential, commercial, open space, and water) or categories such as a stoplight-colored warning system (green, yellow, and red).

To illustrate the difference between *sequential* and *diverging* numeric values, compare the two maps that display the same data on income per capita in the contiguous US states in 2018 in Figure 7-7. The sequential color palette shows five shades of blue to represent the low-to-high range of income levels, and it works best for a data story that emphasizes the highest income levels, shown by the darker blue colors along the Northeastern coast from Maryland to Massachusetts. By contrast, the diverging color palette shows dark orange for below-average states, dark purple for above-average states, and a neutral color in the middle, and it works best for a data story that emphasizes an economic division between lower-income Southern states and higher-income East Coast and West Coast states.

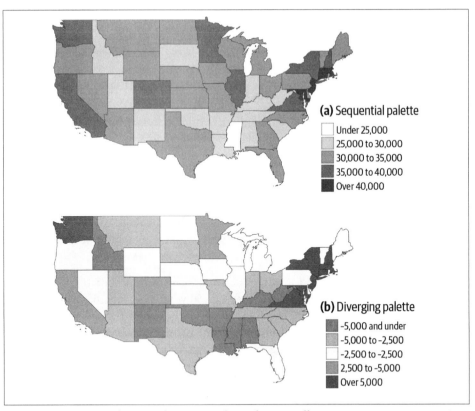

Figure 7-7. Sequential versus diverging color palettes to illustrate per capita income in US dollars in the contiguous states, from American Community Survey, 2018. Note that a diverging palette does not work well in black and white because it becomes difficult to distinguish shades moving away from the middle.

After you select data classes and a color palette, ColorBrewer displays alphanumeric codes that web browsers translate into colors. You can select hexadecimal codes (#ffffff is white), RGB codes (255,255,255 is white), or CMYK codes (0,0,0,0 is white), and export them in different formats, as shown in Figure 7-8, if your preferred map tool allows you to import color palettes.

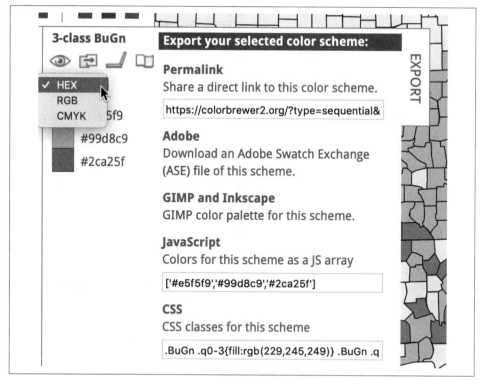

Figure 7-8. Click open the Export tab to display your color palette codes in various formats.

Choose Color Intervals to Group Choropleth Map Data

Another important design choice is color intervals, which determine how you group and display data on your choropleth map. This powerful set of decisions will dramatically shape how your map appears in readers' eyes, and the message conveyed by your data story. You will need to consider several options in this multistep decision-making process, and although there are few uniform design rules, we'll offer guidance and recommendations. Since options for selecting intervals vary across different mapping tools, we'll explain broad concepts in this section, with occasional screenshots from Datawrapper and Tableau Public, but will save the details for those specific tutorials later in the chapter.

Some mapping tools allow you to choose between two different *types of color intervals* to show movement up or down a data scale, as shown in Figure 7-9. *Steps* are clearly-marked color dividers, like a staircase, while *continuous* is a gradual change in color, like a ramp. Both go upward, but take you there in different ways.

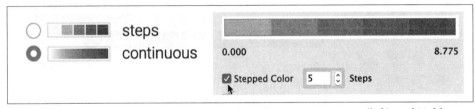

Figure 7-9. Steps versus continuous color intervals in Datawrapper (left) and Tableau Public (right).

If both options exist, which type of color interval is best: steps or continuous? There's no uniform map design rule about this, but consider these factors. On one hand, steps work best for data stories that show areas below or above a specific line or threshold, such as zones that will flood if the sea level rises by 1 meter. Also, since human eyes aren't always good at distinguishing between hues, steps can help readers quickly match colors from your map legend to your data. On the other hand, continuous works best for data stories that draw attention to subtle differences between neighboring areas, such as the wide range of values on an income scale. Read this Datawrapper Academy article on what to consider when creating choropleth maps (*https://oreil.ly/L08bj*). Overall, we advise you to make design choices that are both honest and insightful: tell the truth about the data and also draw attention to what matters in your data story.

If you choose *steps*, how many dividers should you use to slice up your data? Once again, there is no uniform rule, but reflect on these options and outcomes. Fewer steps creates a *coarse* map that highlights broad differences, while more steps creates a *granular* map that emphasizes geographic diversity between areas. However, simply adding more steps doesn't necessarily make a better map, because differences between steps become less visible to the human eye. Because the ColorBrewer design assistant was created specifically for steps (and does not show continuous options), we recommend experimenting by raising or lowering the *Number of data classes* (also known as steps) to visualize the appearance of different design choices, as shown in Figure 7-10. Make decisions with the best interests of your readers in mind, to represent your data in honest and insightful ways.

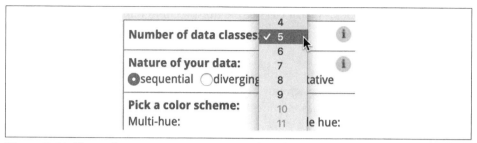

Figure 7-10. If you choose steps, experiment with ColorBrewer data classes and color palettes.

Some choropleth mapping tools also allow you to choose how to *interpolate* your data, meaning the method you use for grouping numbers to represent similar colors on your map. For example, Datawrapper displays two different sets of drop-down menus for interpolation options, depending on whether you chose steps or continuous, as shown in Figure 7-11.

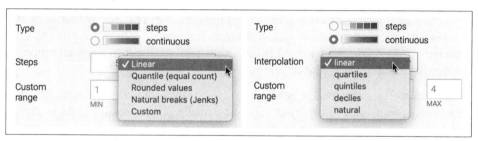

Figure 7-11. Interpolation options for steps (left) and continuous (right) in Datawrapper.

Before choosing how to interpolate, create a histogram chart in Google Sheets to gain a deeper understanding of how your data is distributed (see "Histograms" on page 121). Is your histogram evenly distributed with a symmetrical shape around the mean? Or is it skewed to one side, with one tail of outliers that's longer than the other? Compare the simplified histograms in Figure 7-12, which may influence your decision about how to interpolate, as described next.

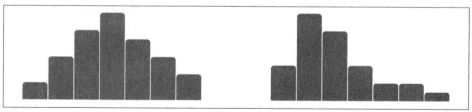

Figure 7-12. Histogram of evenly distributed data (on right) versus skewed data with a longer tail to one side (on left).

In this introductory book, we can classify the most common interpolation options in three basic categories:

Linear
> Places your data values in a straight line, from lowest to highest. This method works best when the data is evenly distributed, or if you wish to draw attention to the low and high extremes in your data, since it will stand out in light and dark colors.

Quantiles
> Divide your data values into groups of an equal number. More specifically, *quartiles*, *quintiles*, and *deciles* divide the values into 4, 5, or 10 groups of equal quantity. This method works best when the data is skewed to one side, because the regrouping allows you to draw attention to diversity inside the data, rather than the extremes. *Rounded values* are similar to quantiles, but the decimals are replaced with rounded numbers that look nicer to readers' eyes.

Natural breaks (Jenks)
> Offers a compromise between linear and quantile methods. They group data values that are close together, but maximizes differences with other groups. This method may work best with skewed data where you wish to draw attention to both internal diversity and extremes.

Which interpolation method is best? There are no uniform design rules, except that we advise *against* using *Custom* settings to manually place color intervals wherever you wish, since they are more likely to create misleading maps, as you'll learn in Chapter 14. Our best advice is to experiment with different interpolation methods, especially when working with skewed data, to better understand how these options shape the appearance of your choropleth maps and the data stories you tell with them.

Overall, Datawrapper Academy recommends (*https://oreil.ly/L08bj*) that you make color intervals choices to help readers "see all the differences in the data" by fully using all of the colors in your range, as shown in Figure 7-13. In other words, if your map displays only the lightest and darkest colors, you're not sufficiently using the middle portion of your color range to highlight geographic patterns and diversity within your data. To do so, you'll need to explore beyond the default map settings and test which options do the best job of telling an honest and insightful data story.

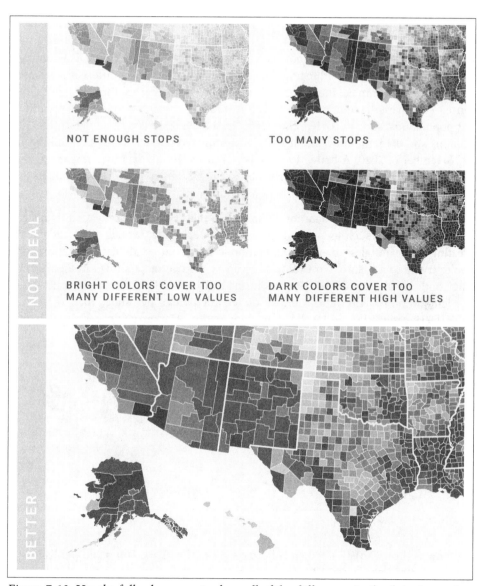

Figure 7-13. Use the full color range to show all of the differences in the data. Image by Datawrapper Academy (https://oreil.ly/L08bj), reprinted with permission.

Designing true and meaningful choropleth maps is challenging work. You'll improve your skills the same way we did, by reading widely, looking at different maps, and testing various ways to visualize your data. Become more aware of how your decisions about color intervals can dramatically alter how the data appears to readers. Most importantly, create maps that focus on telling your story and truthfully representing the data.

Normalize Choropleth Map Data

We introduced the concept of normalizing data in "Normalize Your Data" on page 90. Normalization means adjusting data that was collected using different scales into a common scale to make more appropriate comparisons. For example, it makes little sense to compare the total number of COVID cases between nations with very different populations, such as 9.61 million cases in the US (estimated population of 328.2 million) and 0.49 million cases in Belgium (estimated population of 11.5 million) as of November 6, 2020. A better strategy is to normalize the data by comparing cases per capita (such as 2,928 cases per 100,000 in the US versus 4,260 per 100,000 in Belgium) to adjust for the differences in population.

If you forget to normalize data for a choropleth map and display raw counts instead of relative values (such as percentages or rates per capita), you'll often end up re-creating a meaningless map of population centers, rather than the phenomenon you're trying to measure. For example, compare the two maps shown in Figure 7-14. They both are about COVID-19 cases in the continental US as of June 26, 2020. On the left, (a) shows the total number of recorded cases per state, then (b) shows COVID-19 cases adjusted by the state's population. Darker colors represent higher values. Do you notice any differences in spatial patterns?

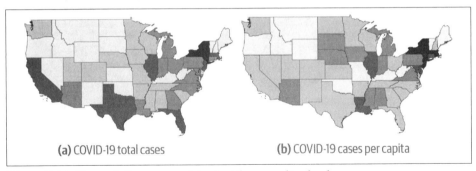

(a) COVID-19 total cases   (b) COVID-19 cases per capita

Figure 7-14. Choropleth maps work best with normalized values.

Both maps show COVID-19 data collected by *The New York Times* and published on GitHub (*https://oreil.ly/xvcXE*). In the map in (b), we normalized values by dividing the total number of cases by the population in each state, according to the 2018 US Census American Community Survey, the most recent data available on the day of writing. We didn't add legends or other important cartographic elements so that you can better focus on interpreting spatial patterns. In both cases, we used Jenks natural breaks for classification.

What are the worst-hit states according to the map showing total COVID-19 counts, Figure 7-14 (a)? If you're familiar with US geography, you can quickly tell that these are New York, New Jersey, Massachusetts, Florida, Illinois, Texas, and California. But five of these happen to be some of the most populous states in the US, so it makes sense that they will also have more COVID-19 cases.

Now, how about the map in Figure 7-14 (b)? You can see that New York and its neighbors, including New Jersey and Massachusetts, have by far the highest rates per capita (per person), which we saw in the first map. But you can also see that California, Texas, and Florida were impacted to a lesser extent than the map on the left suggests. So the map with per capita values is a much better illustration to the story about New York being the *first* epicenter of the COVID-19 crisis in the US.

At this point, you should have a better idea of key principles and best practices in map design. Now that we've covered key concepts for interactive maps in general, and choropleth maps in particular, we'll pivot to a series of hands-on tutorials with our recommended tools. In "Point Map with Google My Maps" on page 177, we'll create a point map with custom icons in Google My Maps to show information about specific locations with pop-up windows. In "Symbol Point Map with Datawrapper" on page 185, we'll build a symbol point map in Datawrapper that uses colored circles of varying sizes to represent population change for specific cities. Our final tutorials in this chapter will return to the topic of designing choropleth maps in "Choropleth Map with Datawrapper" on page 191 and "Choropleth Map with Tableau Public" on page 200 to compare these two tools.

Point Map with Google My Maps

Most people are already familiar with Google Maps (*https://www.google.com/maps*), the web mapping service that allows users to look up locations and directions around the world. In this section, you'll learn about Google My Maps (*https://oreil.ly/JzQgg*), a related tool that allows you to display groups of points on top of the Google Maps platform, which users can click on to reveal more data, including photos, websites, or directions. You can customize the colors and icons for your point markers, and all of the map layer content you create will reside in your Google Drive (*https://drive.google.com*), where you can edit and collaborate with others. Although Google My Maps has limited features, it's an easy-to-learn tool to build a basic interactive point map, along with simple polylines and polygons if desired. Finally, you can share a public link to your map or embed it on your website, a step that you'll learn more about in Chapter 9.

In this section, we'll construct a point map of museums and parks in North America with two different groups of styled markers and a custom photo icon. When users click on a marker, additional text, links, and images appear in the pop-up window, as shown in Figure 7-15.

Figure 7-15. Point map of parks and museums created with Google My Maps: explore the interactive version (https://oreil.ly/xY0HV).

To create your own interactive point map with custom icons, follow this tutorial:

1. Open the Parks and Museums data in Google Sheets (*https://oreil.ly/kgqRw*), which contains six popular locations in North America. Each row includes a *Group*, *Name*, *Address*, and *URL*. Log into your Google account and go to File > "Make a copy" to create a version you can edit in your Google Drive.

2. Navigate to Google My Maps (*https://oreil.ly/mLeh3*). In the upper-left corner, click the "Create a New Map" button. This will create an empty map with familiar Google Maps style.

3. Add a relevant title and description by clicking its current title, *Untitled map*, and typing in the new Map title and Description.

4. To add data to your map, click Import under the "Untitled layer" item.

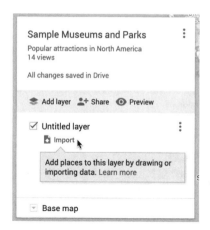

5. In the "Choose a file to import" screen, there are several ways to upload data. Choose Google Drive, since our sample data is already in that format, and select the Recent tab to locate the *Museums and Parks* file you saved to your Google Drive. Press Select.

Choose a file to import

↤	My Drive	Shared with me	**Recent**		

Name		Owner	Last modified ↓
Museums and Parks (go to File > Make a Copy)		me	11:09 AM

6. In the "Choose columns to position your placemarks" screen, select the *Address* column to place your point data on the map. Click Continue.

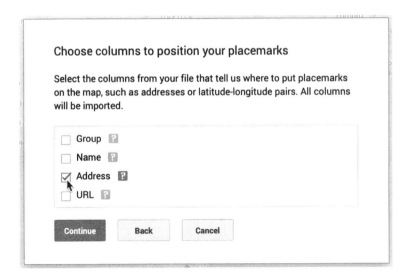

Choose columns to position your placemarks

Select the columns from your file that tell us where to put placemarks
on the map, such as addresses or latitude-longitude pairs. All columns
will be imported.

☐ Group
☐ Name
☑ Address
☐ URL

Continue   Back   Cancel

 You can select multiple boxes if your address is split across
several columns, such as *Address, City, State, Zip code*. Also, if
your point data is already geocoded, you can upload latitude
and longitude pairs, such as 41.76, -72.69.

7. In the "Choose a column to title your markers" window, select the *Name* column
   to title your point markers. Then click Finish.

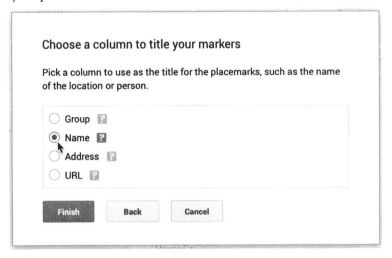

Choose a column to title your markers

Pick a column to use as the title for the placemarks, such as the name
of the location or person.

○ Group
⦿ Name
○ Address
○ URL

Finish   Back   Cancel

Google My Maps will automatically geocode your address data as we discussed in "Geocode Addresses in Google Sheets" on page 23, display them using its default blue markers, and center the map to fit all of the points.

8. Click the three-dot kebab menu next to the "Museums and Parks..." layer to Rename and shorten its name, since the full name of the file is imported by default.

9. Because our map contains two groups—museums and parks—let's create a custom color marker for each group to replace the default blue markers. Click on "Individual styles," and in the "Group places by" drop-down, change the value to "Style data by column: Group." This option is available because we intentionally created the *Group* column for museums and parks when setting up the sample data. Close this window by clicking X in the upper-right.

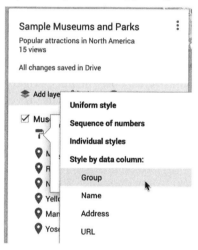

10. Under "Styled by Group," float your cursor over the Museum label to reveal the bucket styling symbol, and click it.

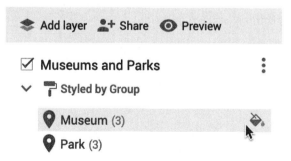

11. Assign a new color for Museums, and click "More icons" to find a more appropriate point marker symbol.

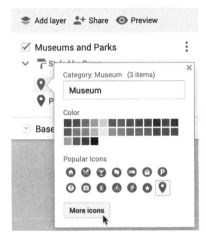

12. In the "Choose an icon" screen, use the upper-right Filter field to search for icon types by name, such as "museum." Repeat this process for "parks."

13. In the "Choose an icon" screen, you can click the lower-left "Custom icon" button to upload an image, which will be transformed into a thumbnail image icon. This custom icon was created from a Wikimedia image of the Washington Monument (*https://oreil.ly/QjQ1x*).

14. Click any map marker to edit its data, insert a photo to appear in its pop-up window, or add Google Map directions. This photo came from a Wikimedia image of the Metropolitan Museum of Art (*https://oreil.ly/5pAZe*). However, you must add photos or directions manually because these links cannot be preloaded into the data spreadsheet.

15. You can change the style of the basemap to one of nine different versions offered by Google. Choose high-contrast colors for basemap backgrounds and marker icons.

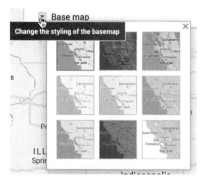

16. At the top of the map, see buttons to manually add more point markers, draw a line, add directions, or measure distance. However, Google My Maps has limited support for polylines and polygons, and you cannot easily create a choropleth map with colored boundaries that represent data values.

17. Click Preview to see how your map will appear to other people. When you finish editing your map, click Share underneath the map's title and description, and in the next screen, make sure "Enable link sharing" is activated, and copy the generated link. You can share the link with anyone, with or without a Google account. You also have the option to make your map publicly appear in web search results, if desired.

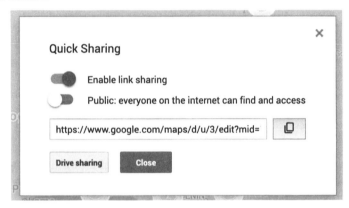

18. If you wish to embed your map as an iframe on a web page, click the three-button kebab menu to the right of the map title and select "Embed on my site." This will generate an HTML embed code, which we will explain in Chapter 9.

19. If you wish to edit your map in the future, there are two ways to access it when logged into your Google account. One is to open the Google My Maps platform to view all of your maps. A second way is to go to your Google Drive and search for your Google My Maps by keyword. When you create a Google My Map from data in a Google Sheet, we recommend that you keep the My Map and Sheet files together in the same folder in your Google Drive, to help you make edits more easily in the future.

		Name
▶ 🅰	My Drive	
		▣ Sample Museums and Parks 🔗
👥	Shared with me	
🕐	Recent	✝ Museums and Parks (go to File > Make...

Google My Maps is a good first tool to learn for making interactive maps, especially point maps with custom icons. You can design maps with multiple layers of points, polylines, and basic polygons, if desired. But the overall map design and features are limited to what the Google My Maps platform offers. Learn more at the Google My Maps support page (*https://oreil.ly/5T_at*).

In the next section, we'll explore how to use Datawrapper to create symbol point maps, where the size and color of each circle (or other shapes) represents data values for that specific point.

Symbol Point Map with Datawrapper

We first introduced you to the free and easy-to-learn Datawrapper tool in "Datawrapper Charts" on page 131. It also offers powerful features to create different types of maps, with professional-looking design elements. With Datawrapper, you can start to work right away in your browser, with no account required unless you wish to save and share your work online.

In this section, you'll learn how to create a symbol point map. Unlike the basic point map in "Point Map with Google My Maps" on page 177, a symbol point map shows data for specific locations through shapes of varying size or color. In Figure 7-16, a sample symbol map displays population change for three hundred major US cities as point locations with two variables: circle size (for 2019 population size) and circle color (for percent change since 2010). Remember that we use *point* data to create symbol maps, but *polygon* data to create choropleth maps, which you'll learn how to create in the following sections. In Chapter 9 we'll explain how to embed your interactive Datawrapper maps on the web.

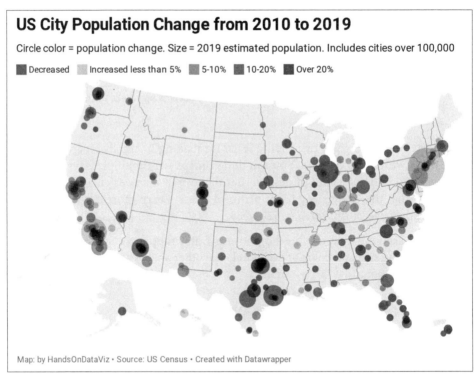

US City Population Change from 2010 to 2019

Circle color = population change. Size = 2019 estimated population. Includes cities over 100,000

■ Decreased   ■ Increased less than 5%   ■ 5-10%   ■ 10-20%   ■ Over 20%

Map: by HandsOnDataViz • Source: US Census • Created with Datawrapper

Figure 7-16. Symbol point map of US city population growth with Datawrapper: explore the interactive version (https://datawrapper.dwcdn.net/V0V9Y).

Datawrapper splits the process of creating a map into four steps: select map, add data, visualize, and publish and embed. To create your own symbol point map, follow this tutorial:

1. Open the US Cities Population Change 2010-2019 data in Google Sheets (*https:// oreil.ly/Qkrue*). Read the notes to understand its origin and some data issues. We downloaded city population data for 2010-2019 from the US Census (*https:// oreil.ly/qGMru*). But during this time period, some cities were newly incorporated or merged with outlying areas, which skews their population data over time. Note also that we included data for Washington, DC, (a major city not located in a US state) and for five major cities in Puerto Rico (not a state, but a US territory where residents are US citizens), so we'll select an appropriate map to include them below.

Good maps often require that messy data is cleaned up, as described in Chapter 4. In our spreadsheet we narrowed the original list down to about 300 cities with more than 100,000 residents in either 2010 or 2019. Also, since we're relying on Datawrapper to correctly identify *place names*, we combined *city* and *state* into one column to improve geocoding accuracy. Learn more about place name geocoding at the Datawrapper Academy (*https://oreil.ly/pxFEr*). Also, we created a new column named *Percent Change*, which we calculated this way: `(2019 -`
`2010) / 2010 × 100`.

2. In the Google Sheet, go to File > Download and select the CSV format to save the data to your local computer.

3. Open Datawrapper, click Start Creating, then New Map, and select "Symbol map."

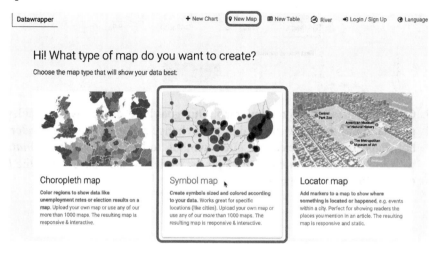

4. In the "Select your map" screen, search for USA > "States and Territories" to include Puerto Rico, rather than the USA > States option that appears closer to the top of the list. Proceed to the next screen.

5. In the "Add your data" screen, click "Import your dataset." In the next window, click the "Addresses and Place Names" button to inform Datawrapper that our information is organized this way. In the Import window, click to "Upload a CSV file," and select the file you downloaded previously.

6. In the "Match your columns" screen, select the *City-State* column to be "Matched as Address," then scroll down to click Next. In the next screen, click Go to see your geocoded data displayed on a map in the following screen.

Match your columns

Please select which column in your dataset contains "**Address**".

| MATCHED AS ADDRESS | MATCH AS ADDRESS | MATCH AS ADDRESS | MATCH AS ADDRESS |

City-State	Population2010	PopEstimate2019	PctChange2010-19
New York, New York	8175133	8336817	1.98
Los Angeles, California	3792621	3979576	4.93
Chicago, Illinois	2695598	2693976	-0.06
Houston, Texas	2099451	2320268	10.52
Phoenix, Arizona	1445632	1680992	16.28
Philadelphia, Pennsylvania	1526006	1584064	3.80
San Antonio, Texas	1327407	1547253	16.56
San Diego, California	1307402	1423851	8.91

☑ First row as caption

NEXT

7. Click Visualize to Refine your map. Our goal is to display two variables: 2019 population as the circle size and percent change as the circle color. Under "Symbol shape and size," select the circle symbol, to be sized by *Pop Estimate 2019*, with a maximum symbol size of 25 pixels. Under *Symbol colors*, select the *Percent Change 2010–2019* column.

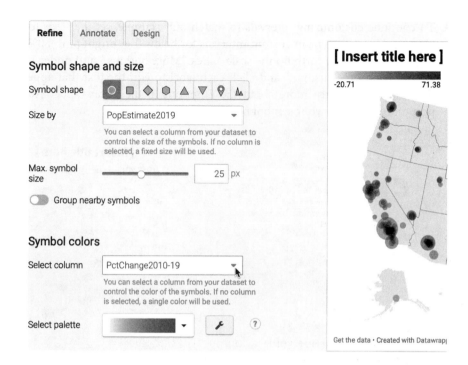

8. Optionally, to customize the color palette and intervals to match our example, click the wrench symbol next to the palette. Click "Import colors" and you can paste in the five hexadecimal codes listed here from ColorBrewer, as we described in "Design Choropleth Colors and Intervals" on page 167. The first code is dark pink, followed by a four-class sequential green: #d01c8b,#bae4b3,#74c476,#31a354,#006d2c.

9. To continue customizing intervals to match our example, set the steps to 5 and *Custom*. Manually type in custom intervals for below 0% (bright pink), 0% to 5% (light green), and so forth up the scale. Click "More options," and under Legend, change Labels to "custom," and click each label to edit the text that appears on the map menu. Learn more about these options in the Datawrapper Academy post on customizing your symbol map (*https://oreil.ly/0ajde*).

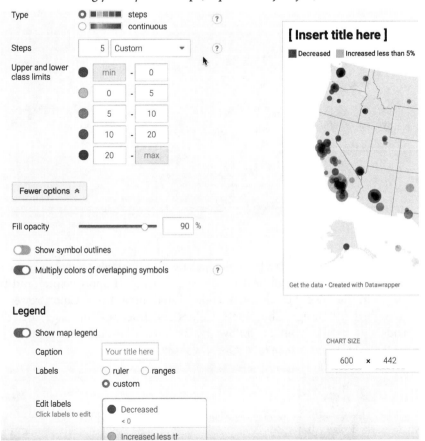

10. Under the *Visualize* screen, click the Annotate tab to insert a title, source notes, credits, and customize the tool tips as described by Datawrapper Academy (*https://oreil.ly/Um9B6*).

11. Click Proceed or advance to the Publish & Embed screen to share your work with others. If you logged into your free Datawrapper account, your work is automatically saved online in the My Charts menu in the top-right corner of the screen. Also, you can click the blue Publish button to generate the code to embed your interactive map on your website, as you'll learn about in Chapter 9. In addition, you can "add your chart to River" if you wish to share your work more widely by allowing other Datawrapper users to adapt and reuse it. Furthermore, scroll all the way down and click Download PNG to export a static image of your map. Additional exporting and publishing options require a paid Datawrapper account. Or, if you prefer not to create an account, you can enter your email to receive the embed code.

For assistance and additional options, see the Datawrapper Academy support pages on symbol maps (*https://oreil.ly/yTWkB*).

Now that you've learned how to create a symbol point map with Datawrapper, in the next section we'll build upon your skills with this tool to create a choropleth map.

Choropleth Map with Datawrapper

Let's pivot from point maps to polygon maps. Since you've already learned how to use Datawrapper to design charts (see "Datawrapper Charts" on page 131) and symbol maps (see Figure 7-16), let's use this tool to create a choropleth map, which looks like colored polygons. Choropleth maps are best for showing patterns across geographic areas by coloring polygons to represent data values. Datawrapper offers a wide collection of common geographical boundaries, including world regions, states and provinces, and also hexagons (cartograms), counties, congressional districts, and census tracts for the US.

In this section, you'll create a choropleth map of typical home values for US states in August 2020 according to the Zillow Home Value Index (*https://oreil.ly/HsLuZ*), as shown in Figure 7-17. The index reflects typical home values (meaning those in the 35th to 65th percentile range, around the median) for single-family residences, condos, and co-ops, and it's smoothed and seasonally adjusted.

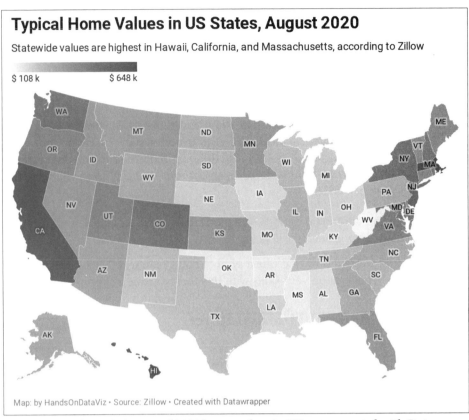

Typical Home Values in US States, August 2020

Statewide values are highest in Hawaii, California, and Massachusetts, according to Zillow

$ 108 k $ 648 k

Map: by HandsOnDataViz · Source: Zillow · Created with Datawrapper

Figure 7-17. Choropleth map of 2020 home values in US states created with Datawrapper: explore the interactive version (https://oreil.ly/B9XlT).

Datawrapper splits the process of creating a map into four steps: select map, add data, visualize, and publish and embed. To create your own choropleth map, follow this tutorial:

1. Open the Home Value Index data in Google Sheets (*https://oreil.ly/bFKT3*), which we downloaded from the Zillow research site (*https://oreil.ly/HsLuZ*). Read the notes to understand its origin and definitions.

   Good maps often require the cleaning up of messy data, as described in Chapter 4. In our spreadsheet, we removed all of the columns except two, August 2019 and August 2020, and we also inserted a *Percent Change* column, which we calculated this way: `(2020 - 2019) / 2019 × 100`. Also, we're fortunate that Datawrapper easily recognizes US state names and abbreviations.

2. In the Google Sheet, go to File > Download and select the CSV format to save the data to your local computer.

3. Open Datawrapper (*https://datawrapper.de*), click Start Creating, then click New Map, and select "Choropleth map." No login is required to create a map, but you should sign up for a free account to save your work and publish your map online.

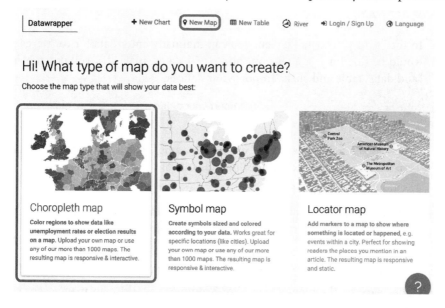

4. In the "Select your map" screen, choose your geographic boundaries. In this case, search and select USA > "States and Territories" to include data for Washington, DC, which is not a state, then click Proceed.

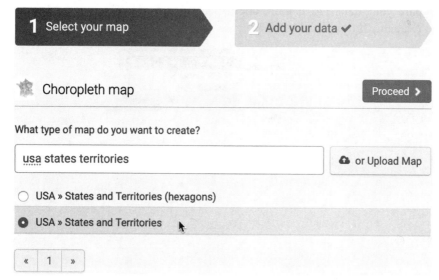

If Datawrapper doesn't list your preferred map outline, you can upload your own custom geography data in GeoJSON or TopoJSON format, which you'll learn more about in "Geospatial Data and GeoJSON" on page 336.

5. In the "Add your data" screen, you can manually enter data for each area, which would be fine for just a few, but not for 50 states. Instead, scroll down below the "add data" table and click "Import your dataset."

⊙ Import your dataset

Datawrapper will explain that when uploading data to the USA > "States and Territories map," your data must include one of the following columns:[3]

- Names, such as California.
- FIPS codes, the Federal Information Processing Standards numeric codes for US states and smaller geographies, where California is 06.
- ANSI codes, the American National Standards Institute alphabetical or numeric codes for US states and smaller geographies, where California is CA.

Codes vary by the type of map. For example, a world map may accept country names (which vary in spelling) or ISO three-letter codes (*https://oreil.ly/-9U-k*). To view all of the codes for your selected geography, go back one screen in Datawrapper and select the "Geo-Code" drop-down menu. If necessary, you could copy and paste names and their code equivalents into your spreadsheet to prepare your data. Learn more about place name geocoding at the Datawrapper Academy (*https://oreil.ly/pxFEr*).

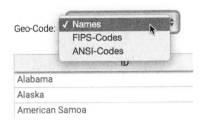

---

3 Learn more from the US Census Bureau about ANSI and FIPS codes (*https://oreil.ly/wZxzQ*).

6. Because our data includes columns for both Names and ANSI codes, go ahead and click Start Import.

7. On the "Import your dataset" screen, rather than paste your data, we recommend that you click "upload a CSV file" and select the file you downloaded in step 2.

8. In the "Match your columns" screen, click the column that matches up with ANSI codes. You may need to scroll down a bit to click the Next, then Continue.

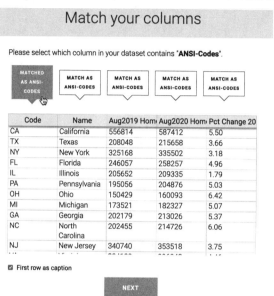

9. Proceed to the next screen, select the column of data values that you initially wish to map, and click "Matched as values." For this tutorial, select *Aug2020 Home Values*, scroll down to click Next, then Go, then Proceed. You'll be able to map other data values in a later step.

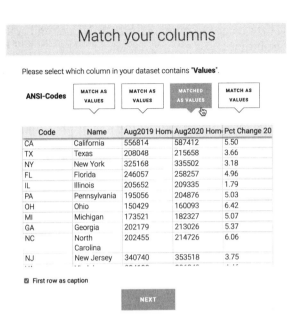

Match your columns

Please select which column in your dataset contains "**Values**".

ANSI-Codes	MATCH AS VALUES	MATCH AS VALUES	MATCHED AS VALUES	MATCH AS VALUES

Code	Name	Aug2019 Home	Aug2020 Home	Pct Change 20
CA	California	556814	587412	5.50
TX	Texas	208048	215658	3.66
NY	New York	325168	335502	3.18
FL	Florida	246057	258257	4.96
IL	Illinois	205652	209335	1.79
PA	Pennsylvania	195056	204876	5.03
OH	Ohio	150429	160093	6.42
MI	Michigan	173521	182327	5.07
GA	Georgia	202179	213026	5.37
NC	North Carolina	202455	214726	6.06
NJ	New Jersey	340740	353518	3.75

☑ First row as caption

NEXT

10. In the Visualize screen, under the Refine tab, click the wrench symbol next to the color palette to review the *default* map settings. Do not blindly accept the default map, but it's a good place to start and explore how factors shape its appearance.

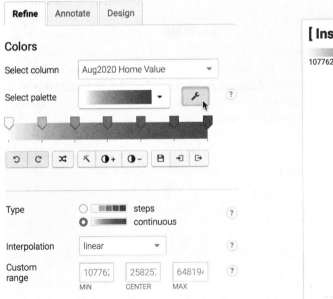

Let's review key concepts we first introduced in "Design Choropleth Colors and Intervals" on page 167. The default map shows a *continuous* green-to-blue color palette, with *linear* interpolation, which means the home values are distributed in a straight line up the scale. These colors and intervals work better for a data story that emphasizes the low and high extremes.

11. In the Refine tab, experiment with different types of interpolation to change how values are assigned to colors. For example, change from *linear* to *quartiles*, which groups the data into four groups of equal size. This map works better for a data story that emphasizes geographic diversity because we see more contrast between states in the middle range.

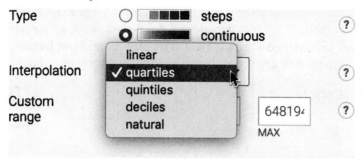

12. Experiment with other colors, intervals, and data columns. Change the palette from *sequential* to *diverging* colors, which displays a neutral color in the middle range and two dark colors at the extremes. Change from a *continuous* gradient to *steps*, and choose different numbers of dividers. Change the data column to *Pct Change 2019-20* to normalize the choropleth map data as discussed in "Normalize Choropleth Map Data" on page 176, since home values are so different across the country. For example, see the map of percent change in home value from 2019 to 2020, with a diverging red-to-blue palette, five steps, and rounded values here.

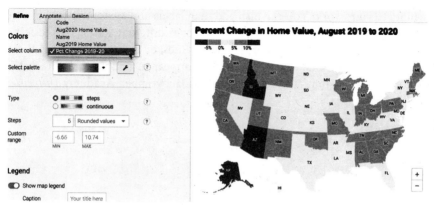

Which data columns, colors, and intervals make the best map? There's no easy answer, since there's more than one way to make a true and meaningful map. But keep two principles in mind. First, make sure that you honestly show the data, rather than hide or disguise it. Second, reflect on what kind of data story you believe is important to tell, since design choices emphasize different interpretations of the data. Review our guidance in "Design Choropleth Colors and Intervals" on page 167.

Let's move on to finalize the labels and styling of the map before we publish and share it with others:

13. Under the Refine tab, customize the legend format. For example, to convert long numbers (such as 107762) into abbreviated dollars ($ 108 k), we selected "custom format" and inserted the code **($ 0 a)**. Learn more about Datawrapper custom formats in their link to the numeral.js documentation (*https://oreil.ly/nFKBR*).

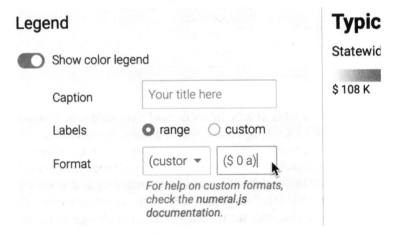

14. Under the Annotate tab, add a title, description, and source credits to add credibility to your work. You can also add map labels and customize tool tips that will display when readers hover their cursor over different states. The easiest way to edit tool tips is to click on blue column names, or format them using their drop-down menus, to make the proper codes appear in double curly brackets. Learn more about customizing tool tips from Datawrapper Academy (*https://oreil.ly/HV1MU*).

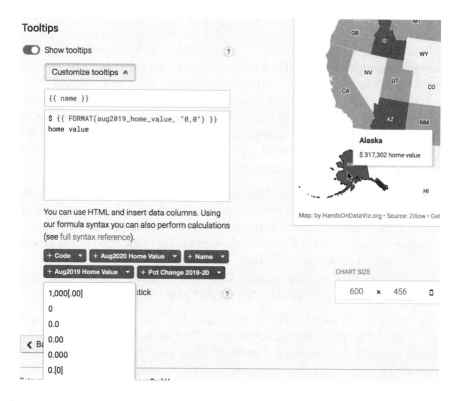

Tooltips

Show tooltips (?)

Customize tooltips ⌃

{{ name }}

$ {{ FORMAT(aug2019_home_value, "0,0") }}
home value

You can use HTML and insert data columns. Using
our formula syntax you can also perform calculations
(see full syntax reference).

+ Code ▾   + Aug2020 Home Value ▾   + Name ▾
+ Aug2019 Home Value ▾   + Pct Change 2019-20 ▾

1,000[.00]   stick   (?)
0
0.0
0.00
0.000
0.[0]

< Ba

Alaska
$ 317,302 home value

Map: by HandsOnDataViz.org • Source: Zillow • Get

CHART SIZE

600 × 456 □

15. Finally, click Proceed or advance to the Publish & Embed screen to share your
    work with others. Follow the prompts, or the more detailed Datawrapper tuto-
    rial, to obtain an embed code to your interactive map, and learn more about your
    next steps in Chapter 9.

Learn more about choropleth map design in this excellent series of
posts by the Datawrapper Academy (*https://oreil.ly/pU5zx*).

Now that you've learned how to create a choropleth map using one tool, Datawrapper, let's compare the process using a different tool, Tableau Public.

Choropleth Map with Tableau Public

We first introduced you to the free Tableau Public desktop application (for Mac or Windows) when building scattercharts and filtered line charts in Chapter 6. Now let's use the same tool to create an interactive choropleth map, and compare the process with the Datawrapper tool we described in the prior section. We're showing you how to create the same type of map with both tools to show you the difference. On one hand, Datawrapper gives you more control over interpolating data and shaping the appearance of color intervals in your choropleth map. On the other hand, some people prefer Tableau Public because they're already familiar with its interface.

Tableau Public can create many different types of maps for geographical place names or ISO codes it already recognizes, such as nations, states, counties, and airports. But Tableau Public cannot geocode street addresses by itself, so you'll need to obtain their latitude and longitude with another tool, such as those described in the geocode section of "Geocode Addresses in Google Sheets" on page 23. Furthermore, if you want to upload customized map boundaries, learn how to Create Tableau Maps from Spatial Files (*https://oreil.ly/J8mYF*) on the support page.

In this section, we'll create a choropleth map of healthcare spending per country as a percentage of their gross domestic product (GDP), as shown in Figure 7-18. Remember that choropleth maps work best when we normalize the data to show relative, rather than absolute, numbers (see "Normalize Choropleth Map Data" on page 176). Creating a map of total health spending per country wouldn't be very meaningful, as larger nations tend to have larger economies, so we'll base our map on the percentage of their economy that is spent on healthcare.

Before we start, you should obtain and install the free Tableau Public desktop application (*https://oreil.ly/kPcad*) if you don't have it yet. It is available for Mac or Windows. You'll need to enter an email address to download the application.

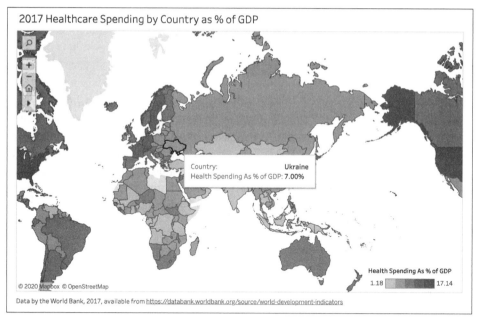

Figure 7-18 caption area (inside figure):

2017 Healthcare Spending by Country as % of GDP

Country: Ukraine
Health Spending As % of GDP: **7.00%**

Health Spending As % of GDP
1.18   17.14

© 2020 Mapbox © OpenStreetMap

Data by the World Bank, 2017, available from https://databank.worldbank.org/source/world-development-indicators

Figure 7-18. Choropleth map of healthcare spending with Tableau Public: explore the interactive version (https://oreil.ly/jIC2_). Data from the World Bank.

Let's look at the steps involved to create a choropleth from Figure 7-18 in detail:

1. Open the Healthcare Spending by Nation as Percent of GDP data in Google Sheets (*https://oreil.ly/3n7fl*), which we downloaded from the World Bank (*https://oreil.ly/IDsX3*). Examine the data and the notes.

   Good maps often require the cleaning up of messy data, as described in Chapter 4. In our spreadsheet, we removed rows for nations that did not report any data. Tableau Public recognizes many different types of geographic names (such as cities and nations), so we'll rely on the tool to deal with any spelling issues and properly place all of them on the map.

2. In the Google Sheet, go to File > Download and select CSV format to save the data to your local computer.

3. Launch Tableau Public. When you first open it, you'll see the Connect menu on the left-hand side that displays file formats you can upload. Choose the "Text file" format and upload the healthcare spending CSV data file you've just downloaded in the previous step.

Tableau lets you access data directly from Google Sheets that live in your Drive using Connect > "To a Server" option. So instead of downloading a CSV file in step 2, you could have made a copy of the sheet, and connected to it directly.

4. In the Data Source screen, inspect the dataset, which contains three columns: *Country Name*, *Country Code*, and *Health Spending As % of GDP*. Notice that a small globe appears at the top of the *Country Name* and *Country Code* columns, which shows that Tableau Public successfully recognized these as geographic data, rather than string or text data. Sometimes Tableau doesn't recognize location data automatically, so you need to manually change the data type. To do so, click the data type icon (e.g., globe or a green # for numeric values), and then choose Geographic Role > Country/Region.

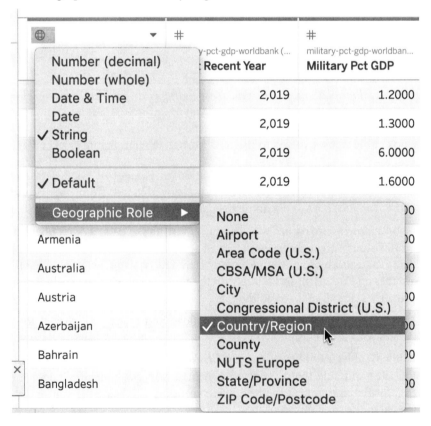

5. In the bottom-left corner, click the orange Sheet 1 button to create a worksheet with your first visualization.

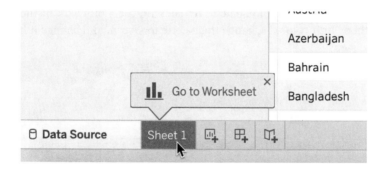

6. In *Sheet 1*, create your choropleth map using a two-step process. First, drag and drop the *Country Name* field into the middle of the worksheet (alternatively, to the Detail box of the Marks card) to create the map. The default view is the symbol map, which we need to replace with a polygon map. To add colored polygons, drag and drop the *Health Spending As % of GDP* field into the Color box of the Marks card to transform it into a choropleth map.

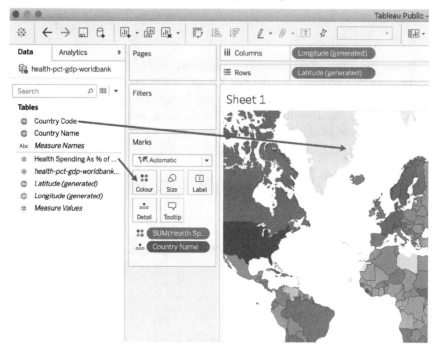

7. Tableau Public may hide the map legend behind the Show Me menu in the upper-right corner, so click the menu to shrink it and display your legend.

8. You can change the color palette by clicking the Color box of the Marks card, and then "Edit colors." Change the palette to Green, and change it from continuous to steps.

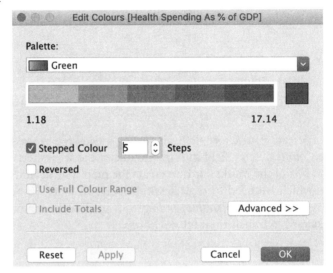

9. When you hover over countries, you'll notice a tool tip that tells you the name of the country and gives you the percent value. It's generally well-formatted as our initial data table had proper column headers. But we can make the tool tip even better. Click the Tooltip box of the Marks card and change the first instance of Country Name to just Country (don't change the grayed-out text inside < and > because these are variable names). Add a % sign at the end of the second row.

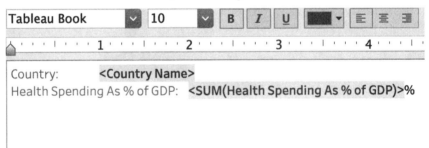

10. Let's make our map title more meaningful. Double-click the default *Sheet 1* name just above the map to bring up the Edit Title window, and change the name of your chart to *2017 Healthcare Spending by Country as % of GDP*.

11. At this point, the data is loaded and should be displayed correctly, so we're going to create the final layout that includes the map's title and credits, the legend, and is appropriate for sharing. At the bottom-left of the program, create a New Dashboard. Dashboards in Tableau are layouts that can contain visualizations from multiple sheets, as well as text boxes, images, and other elements, creating rich exploratory interfaces. In this tutorial, we'll stick to just a single sheet that contains our choropleth map.

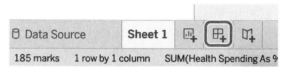

12. In your Dashboard 1 tab, change the size of the dashboard to Automatic so that the map is responsive and occupies 100% of the width on all devices. Drag and drop Sheet 1 to the "Drop sheets here" area. This will copy the map, the title, and the legend from Sheet 1.

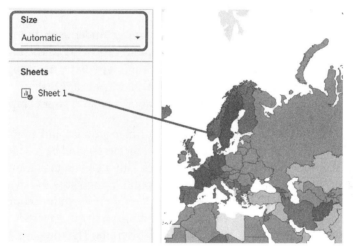

13. Right-click the upper part of the map legend, and select Floating. Now you're able to place your legend directly on top of the map to save space. Drag and drop it to one of the map's corners.

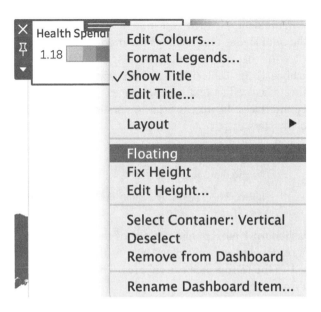

14. Finally, let's add a text block with data source underneath the map. From the Objects menu in the left-hand side, drag and drop *Text* to the lower half of the map. In the Edit Text window that appears, type **Data by the World Bank, 2017**, and click OK. Initially, the text area will occupy half the height of the screen, so resize it like you would resize any window on your computer.

And we're done! Make sure you position your map's center and zoom level because you want it to be visible by others. In this case, the best would be to have a world view because we're showing data for most countries, although you may want to zoom in to a specific continent. Once you are ready to publish and share the map, go to File > "Save to Tableau Public." In the pop-up window, log in to your account if requested. Give the map a title, such as Healthcare Spending, and click Save. See how to embed the map as an iframe in "Get the Embed Code or iframe Tag" on page 231.

Tableau may not be the best tool to create choropleth maps where you want to have full control of color breaks. By default, Tableau uses a linear color scheme that, as you learned earlier in the chapter, is prone to highlighting outliers, and there's no straightforward way to change the intervals to nonlinear methods, such as quantiles. If you're not happy with the way the linear scale represents your data, you can filter your data to remove outliers from the map (*https://oreil.ly/Quv4E*), see Andy Kriebel's VizWiz tutorial to use table calculations to group items into quantiles (*https://oreil.ly/WmAy5*), or revisit "Choropleth Map with Datawrapper" on page 191, which gives you more control over color intervals and interpolation.

In all of the prior tutorials, you created interactive maps using *static data*, meaning it came from a spreadsheet. In the next tutorial, you'll learn how to build a map using *continuously updated data* from a Socrata open data repository, which will always display the most current information.

Current Map with Socrata Open Data

A map built on the Socrata platform shows current data because it continuously pulls the most up-to-date information from an open data repository, which you learned about in "Open Data Repositories" on page 57. The advantage of creating visualizations directly on an open data platform is that your chart or map is directly linked to the source. Some government agencies frequently update selected open data repositories where current information matters, such as fire or police calls, property data, or public finances. Whenever an administrator revises the contents of an open data repository, your chart or map will automatically display the most current information. However, if the government agency stops updating the repository or switches to a different platform, your visualization will no longer show current information or it may break entirely.

Socrata (*https://oreil.ly/iAgJV*) is a company that provides an open data repository service that many government agencies use to make open data available to the public. It offers user-friendly ways to view, filter, and export data. In addition, the Socrata platform includes built-in support to create interactive charts and maps, which can be embedded in other websites (including your own). You can search for publicly available datasets on Socrata's Open Data Network (*https://oreil.ly/NsOGV*).

In this section, we'll build an interactive point map of fatal crashes involving cars in New York City, which continuously updates to display points over the past 365 days, as shown in Figure 7-19. Our interactive map pulls data from the Motor Vehicle Collisions—Crashes (*https://oreil.ly/bUthE*) public repository on New York City's Open-Data Portal, based on the Socrata platform. As long as government administrators continue to update this dataset on this platform, your map should always display the most recent data for the past 12 months.

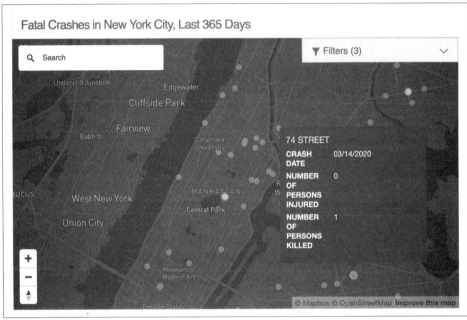

Figure 7-19. Map of fatal crashes in NYC during the past year, continuously updated from a Socrata open data repository. See the interactive version (https://oreil.ly/qadiO).

Anyone can create a map using public data hosted by Socrata, but you need to be a registered Socrata user to save and share your map. Only datasets that have a special location column can be mapped, which is different from traditional location columns (such as address or city) that you see in the dataset. Consider reaching out to dataset administrators if datasets you wish to map are missing geocoded locations.

To build your own continuously updated point map with this Socrata open data repository, follow this tutorial:

1. Register for your account on the NYC OpenData portal (*https://opendata.cityof newyork.us*) by clicking the Sign In button in the upper-right corner. Where it says, "Don't have an account yet? Sign Up," proceed to sign up. Follow the instructions, including confirming that you're not a robot, and accepting the License Agreement to create your free account. This account, including your username and password, are valid for the NYC OpenData portal, but *not* other websites that use Socrata.

2. Navigate to the Motor Vehicle Collisions—Crashes (*https://oreil.ly/bUthE*) dataset. In the menu on the right-hand side, choose Visualize > Launch New Visualization. This will open a Configure Visualization studio where you can create the map.

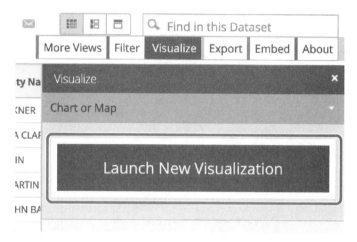

3. In the top menu, select Map (the globe icon between a scatter chart icon and a calendar) as the visualization type. In a few seconds, a basemap will appear, with Map Layers and Map Settings items in the side menu on the left.

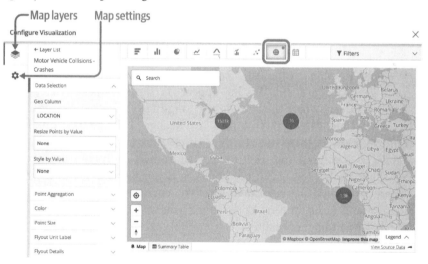

Socrata was able to determine which column contains geospatial value and automatically set the Geo Column value to "LOCATION" (see Layer List > Data Selection). By default, points are clustered together. That's why instead of individual crashes, you see bubbles with numbers, which represent how many points are clustered in that bubble. Clusters will change when you zoom in and out.

4. We need to limit our map to display only crashes with fatalities. In the upper-right corner, click Filters > "Add filter." The drop-down menu lists all columns (or fields) of the dataset, where you should choose "NUMBER OF PERSONS KILLED." In the newly appeared drop-down menu, choose "Is greater than," and set the value to 0. Alternatively, you can set this to "Is greater than or equal to," and set the value to 1.

5. We need to clean up the data. Zoom out and you'll notice that not all crashes were geocoded properly. Several appear on the imaginary Null Island in the Atlantic Ocean, where the latitude and longitude are both 0. You learned how to recognize and deal with bad data in "Recognize Bad Data" on page 61. To remove many of these incorrectly geocoded crashes, let's add another filter on *LATITUDE* column and set it to "Is greater than" with the value of 0. This way we show crashes located in the northern hemisphere, north of the Null Island, where New York City is located. After you correctly set both filters, the map will fly over and focus on New York City. If you wish, you can continue to clean up the data by adding more filters.

6. Instead of showing all recorded crashes since 2012, let's display crashes that happened over the past year, to be updated continuously. Add a third filter for *CRASH DATE* column, and set it to Relative Date > Custom > "Last 365 day(s)." You'll see a lot of points disappearing from the map because they don't fall in the selected dates range. You can now close the Filters window to free up screen space.

7. Let's ensure that crash locations appear as individual points and are never clustered together. Go to Map Settings > Clusters, and bring the "Stop Clustering at Zoom Level" slider to 1. You should now see individual crash locations at all zoom levels.

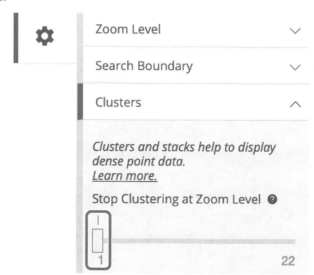

8. In the same accordion menu, change Basemap > Type from default Basic to Dark to give points maximum visibility and to give the map a more fashionable look. In General, set Title to *Fatal Crashes in New York City, Last 365 Days*, and hide the data table below the map by unchecking the "Show data table below visualization box." Under Map Controls, uncheck Show Locate Button because it's relevant only for those accessing the map from NYC. Under Legend Options, uncheck Show Legend. Feel free to experiment with other settings.

9. Finally, let's create meaningful tool tips for points. Return back to the Map Layers menu and choose our Motor Vehicle Collisions—Crashes point layer. To change what is shown in tool tips when you hover or click on points, navigate to Flyout Details, and set Flyout Title to "ON STREET NAME," adding "CRASH DATE," "NUMBER OF PERSONS INJURED," and "NUMBER OF PERSONS KILLED" as additional flyout values.

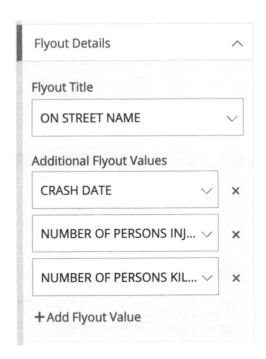

There are more more ways to modify the map that we won't demonstrate in this tutorial. For example, you could use "Resize Points by Value" functionality in the Data Selection menu to transform your point map into a symbol map, where larger circles represent larger numeric values (such as more people injured in a crash). You could also visualize textual categorical data, such as that stored in *CONTRIBUTING FACTOR VEHICLE 1* column of the dataset (with values such as passing too closely, driver inexperience, etc.), by applying "Style by Value" functionality to use different colors for different crash categories.

At this point, you should have a functional interactive point map that continuously updates to show fatal crashes in New York City over the past 365 days, and it should continue to work as long as administrators continue to update the database on this platform. Before you can share the map with others, you need to save it as a draft, and publish.

10. In the lower-right corner, click Save Draft. Give your map a name (which is different from the map's title that users will see), and hit Save. The gray ribbon at the top will tell you it's still a draft. When you are ready to make it public, go ahead and hit Publish…

Now you can embed the map on your website as an iframe. To do so, click Share in the upper-right side of your map, and copy the generated code from the

Embed Code text area. We will talk about embedding visualizations in detail in Chapter 9.

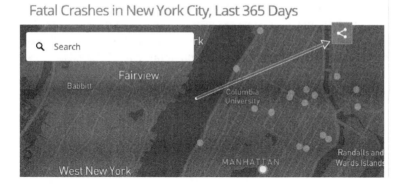

Fatal Crashes in New York City, Last 365 Days

iFrame Embed   JS Embed

Embed Code

```
<iframe src="https://data.cityofnewyork.us/dataset/Fatal-NYC-
Crashes/nx4u-jy9t/embed?width=800&height=600" width="800"
height="600" style="border:0; padding: 0; margin: 0;"></iframe>
```

Size

Large (800x600)   ∨

There are limitations to creating your chart or map on an open data repository platform. First, if the agency stops using the platform or changes the structure of the underlying data, your online map (or chart) may stop functioning. In fact, we had to rewrite this tutorial when it referred to a different Socrata platform that administrators stopped supporting. Second, you're limited to using datasets and geographic boundaries that exist on that platform. If these limitations concern you, a simple alternative is to export data from the open repository (which means that any "live" data would become "static"), and import it into your preferred data visualization tool, such as Datawrapper, Google Sheets, or Tableau. A second, more advanced alternative, is to learn to pull live data from Socrata using an API, as described in "Leaflet Maps with Open Data APIs" on page 331.

Summary

In this chapter, we reviewed map design principles and explored recommended tools and tutorials for telling different types of data stories. When creating maps, think carefully about whether you're working with point or polygon data, the two most common options. If the latter, remember that well-designed choropleth maps required normalized data and careful thought about color intervals.

We only scratched the surface and showed simple examples to help you quickly create some sample maps. See more advanced designs using Leaflet map code templates in Chapter 12, and learn how to find and transform geospatial data in Chapter 13.

CHAPTER 8

Table Your Data

You might be surprised that a data visualization book that emphasizes charts and maps also includes a chapter on creating tables. We don't normally think about data tables as a type of visualization. But depending on your data and the story you wish to tell about it, sometimes a table is the most appropriate way to present information, especially when it's an interactive table on the web. Tables make sense when readers want to look up a specific row of data that's highly relevant to them, such as their local community or an organization they belong to, which can be too hard to identify inside a large chart or map. Also, tables work best when readers wish to precisely compare individual values with one another, but not necessarily to the rest of the dataset. Finally, tables work better than charts when there's no broad visual pattern to emphasize, and work better than maps when there's no particular spatial pattern. Before you start designing a chart or map, consider whether it makes more sense to create a table instead. Sometimes the best visualization is simply a good table.

In this chapter, you'll learn about table design principles and how to use Datawrapper (*https://www.datawrapper.de*), a tool we introduced in Chapters 6 and 7, to create an interactive table with sparklines. Of course, if you need to quickly make a short table, then a static version usually makes sense, which you can create with a spreadsheet, as described in "Other Table-Making Tools" on page 225. This chapter focuses on interactive tables because they have many advantages over static tables, especially when you need to publish large amounts of tabular content online, rather than only in print. First, interactive tables allow readers to search by keyword for specific details that interest them, which is vital when you present long tables with lots of rows. Second, readers can sort interactive tables in ascending or descending order for any column, which enables them to quickly scan those near the top or bottom of a long list. Finally, you'll also learn how to insert *sparklines*, or tiny charts that visually summarize data trends in each row, and automatically place them inside your interactive table. Sparklines blend the best qualities of tables and charts by making it easier for readers to visually scan for trends while skimming down columns of your data table. In Chapter 9, you'll learn how to integrate your interactive table into your website.

Table Design Principles

Let's begin with some principles of good table design, similar to "Chart Design Principles" on page 103 and "Map Design Principles" on page 160. Jonathan Schwabish, an economist who specializes in creating policy-relevant data visualizations, offers advice on creating tables that communicate clearly with multiple audiences.[1] Here's a summary of several of his key points, an example of which appears in Figure 8-1:

- Make column headers stand out above the data.
- Use light shading to separate rows or columns.
- Left-align text and right-align numbers for easier reading.
- Avoid repetition by placing labels only in the first row.
- Group and sort data to highlight meaningful patterns.

Category	Food	Color	Calories per serving
Fruit	Banana	Yellow	105
	Apple	Red	95
	Blueberries	Blue	42
Vegetable	Kale	Green	34
	Carrot	Orange	26
	Eggplant	Purple	10

Figure 8-1. A sample table that illustrates selected design principles.

In addition, Schwabish and others recommend using color to highlight key items or outliers in your data, a topic we'll discuss in Chapter 15.

---

1 Jon Schwabish, "Thread Summarizing 'Ten Guidelines for Better Tables'" (Twitter, August 3, 2020), *https://oreil.ly/JCJpG*; Jonathan A. Schwabish, "Ten Guidelines for Better Tables," *Journal of Benefit-Cost Analysis* 11, no. 2: 151–78, accessed August 25, 2020, *https://doi.org/10.1017/bca.2020.11*; Jonathan Schwabish, *Better Data Visualizations: A Guide for Scholars, Researchers, and Wonks* (Columbia University Press, 2021).

When creating cross-tabulations to illustrate data correlations and possible causal relationships, statistician Joel Best offers two more design recommendations:[2]

- Place the independent variable (the suspected cause) at the top in the column headers and the dependent variable (the possible effect) on the side for each row.
- Calculate percentages from raw numbers in a vertical direction going downward, so that each value of the independent variable (the suspected cause) totals 100%.

Let's apply these design principles by constructing two different tables that calculate percentages, the bad way versus the better way, with data from the Pfizer coronavirus vaccine trial study results that were reported in November 2020. In this blind trial, 43,661 volunteers were randomly divided into two groups, about 21,830 each. One group received the vaccine and the other group received a placebo, so these were the independent variables (the suspected causal factors). Researchers watched closely and observed these dependent variables (the possible effects): 162 people in the placebo group became infected with the virus, compared to 8 people in the vaccine group.[3]

Table 8-1 calculates the percentages of this trial in the *wrong* direction (horizontally) and confuses the relationship between cause and effect, especially in the last row.

Table 8-1. Bad because it calculates percentages horizontally

	Vaccine	Placebo	Total
Infected	4.7% (8)	95.3% (162)	100% (170)
Not infected	50.2% (21,822)	49.8% (21,668)	100% (43,490)

Table 8-2 calculates percentages in the *correct* direction (vertically), which more clearly shows how the vaccine correlates with infection rates. Researchers determined this was a strong causal relationship and received approval to distribute the vaccine.

Table 8-2. Better because it calculates percentages vertically

	Vaccine	Placebo
Infected	0.04% (8)	0.74% (162)
Not infected	99.96% (21,822)	99.26% (21,668)
Total	100% (21,830)	100% (21,830)

---

2 Joel Best, *More Damned Lies and Statistics: How Numbers Confuse Public Issues* (Berkeley, CA: University of California Press, 2004), pp. 31–35.

3 Carl Zimmer, "2 Companies Say Their Vaccines Are 95% Effective. What Does That Mean?" *The New York Times: Health*, November 20, 2020, *https://oreil.ly/uhIwf*, Dashiell Young-Saver, "What Does 95% Effective Mean? Teaching the Math of Vaccine Efficacy" (*The New York Times Learning Network*, December 14, 2020), *https://oreil.ly/3bLMP*.

Overall, the core principles of table design reflect similar concepts we previously discussed in chart and map design. Organize your presentation of the data with the readers' eyes in mind, to focus their attention on the most important elements of your interpretation, to help them take away the key points. Do the visualization work for them, so that you don't have to rely on them to draw the same mental connections in their own minds? Do they remove any clutter or unnecessary repetition that stands in the way of these goals? Most importantly, do they tell true and meaningful stories about the data?

Now that you understand several key principles of table design, see how several are built directly into the Datawrapper tool featured in the next section.

Datawrapper Table with Sparklines

In this section, you'll learn how to create an interactive table with Datawrapper, the free online drag-and-drop visualization tool we previously introduced to create charts in "Chart Design Principles" on page 103 and maps in "Map Design Principles" on page 160. You can start creating in Datawrapper right away in your browser, even without an account, but signing up for a free one will help you to keep your visualizations organized. Remember that you'll probably still need a spreadsheet tool, such as Google Sheets, to compile and clean up data for large tables, but Datawrapper is the best tool to create and publish the interactive table online.

You'll also learn how to create sparklines, or tiny line charts that quickly summarize data trends. This chart type was refined by Edward Tufte, a Yale professor and data visualization pioneer, who described sparklines as "datawords...intense, simple, word-sized graphics."[4] While Tufte envisioned sparklines on a static sheet of paper or PDF document, you'll create them inside an interactive table, as shown in Figure 8-2. Readers can search by keyword, sort columns in ascending or descending order, and scroll through pages of sparklines to quickly identify data trends that would be difficult to spot in a traditional numbers-only table.

---

4 Edward R. Tufte, *Beautiful Evidence* (Graphics Press, 2006), pp. 46-63.

Life expectancy at birth by nation, 1960-2018

Page 1 of 11 >

Nation	Continent	Life expectancy 1960 – 2018	Difference
Afghanistan	Asia	32.4 — 64.5	32
Albania	Europe	62.3 — 78.5	16
Algeria	Africa	46.1 — 76.7	31
Angola	Africa	37.5 — 60.8	23
Antigua and Barbuda	North America	62 — 76.9	15
Argentina	South America	65.1 — 76.5	12
Armenia	Asia	66 — 74.9	9

Figure 8-2. Table with sparklines: explore the interactive version (https://oreil.ly/ Rdwy1).

In this tutorial, you'll create an interactive table with sparklines to visualize differences in life expectancy at birth from 1960 to 2018 for more than 195 nations around the world. Overall, life expectancy gradually rises in most nations, but a few display "dips" that stand out in the tiny line charts. For example, Cambodia and Vietnam both experienced a significant decrease in life expectancy, which corresponds with the deadly wars and refugee crises in both nations from the late 1960s to the mid-1970s. Sparklines help us to visually detect patterns like these, which anyone can investigate further by downloading the raw data through the link at the bottom of the interactive table.

While it's possible to present the same data in a filtered line chart as shown in "Filtered Line Chart" on page 152, it would be difficult for readers to spot differences when shown more than 180 lines at the same time. Likewise, it's also possible to present this data in a choropleth map as shown in "Choropleth Map with Datawrapper" on page 191, though it would be hard for readers to identify data for nations with smaller geographies compared to larger ones. In this particular case, when we want readers to be able to search, sort, or scroll through sparklines for all nations, the best visualization is a good table.

To simplify this tutorial, we downloaded life expectancy at birth from 1960 to 2018 by nation, in CSV format, from the World Bank (*https://oreil.ly/DJku8*), one of the open data repositories we listed in Chapter 3. In our spreadsheet, we cleaned up the data, such as removing nations with five or fewer years of data reported over a half-century, as described in the Notes tab in the Google Sheet. Using the VLOOKUP spreadsheet method from "Match Columns with VLOOKUP" on page 38, we merged in columns of two-letter nation codes and continents from Datawrapper (*https://oreil.ly/WYx2W*). We also created two new columns: one named *Life Expectancy 1960* (intentionally blank for the sparkline to come) and *Difference* (which calculates the difference between the earliest and the most recent year of data available, in most cases from 1960 to 2018). See the Notes tab in the Google Sheet for more details.

To create your own interactive table with sparklines, follow this tutorial, which we adapted from Datawrapper training materials (*https://oreil.ly/LbCo_*) and their gallery of examples (*https://oreil.ly/EeN-z*):

1. Open our cleaned-up World Bank data on life expectancy at birth, 1960 to 2018 in Google Sheets (*https://oreil.ly/LaW6D*).

2. Go to Datawrapper, click Start Creating, and select New Table in the top navigation. You're not required to sign in, but if you wish to save your work, we recommend that you create a free account.

3. In the first Upload Data tab, select Import Google Spreadsheet, paste in the web address of our cleaned-up Google Sheet, and click Proceed. Your Google Sheet must be *shared* so that others can view it.

4. Inspect the data in the "Check & Describe" tab. Make sure that the "First row as label" box is checked, then click Proceed.

5. In the Visualize screen, under Customize Table, check two additional boxes: Make Searchable (so that users can search for nations by keyword) and Stripe Table (to make lines more readable).

6. Let's use a special Datawrapper code to display tiny flags before each country's name. In the *Nation* column, each entry begins with a two-letter country code, surrounded by colons, followed by the country name, such as `:af: Afghanistan`. We created the *Nation* column according to "Combine Data into One Column" on page 75.

To learn more about flag icons, read the Datawrapper post on this topic (*https://oreil.ly/xsA8q*) and their list of country codes and flags on GitHub (*https://oreil.ly/ABTTc*).

7. In the Visualize screen, under "Customize columns," select the third line named *Nation*. Then scroll down and push the slider to "Replace country codes with flags."

8. Let's hide the first two columns, since they're no longer necessary to display. In the Visualize screen under "Customize columns," select the *Name* column, then scroll down and uncheck the boxes "Show on desktop and mobile." Repeat this step for the *Code* column. A "not visible" symbol (an eye with a slash through it) appears next to each customized column to remind us that we've hidden it.

9. Now let's color-code the *Continent* column to make it easier for readers to sort by category it in the interactive table. In the Visualize screen under Customize columns, select the *Continent* column, then scroll down and push the slider to select "Color cells based on categories." In the drop-down menu, select the column *Continent*, and click on the Background > "Customize background" button. Select each continent and assign them different colors.

To choose colors for the six continents, we used the Color-Brewer design tool as described in "Design Choropleth Colors and Intervals" on page 167, and selected a six-class qualitative scheme. Although this tool is designed primarily for choropleth maps, you can also use it to choose table and chart colors.

10. Now let's prepare our data to add sparklines, or tiny line charts, to visually represent change in the *Life expectancy 1960* column, which we intentionally left blank for this step. Before you begin, you must change this column from textual data (represented by the A symbol in the "Customize columns" window) to numerical data (represented by the # symbol). At the top of the screen, click on the "Check & Describe" arrow to go back a step. (Datawrapper will save your work.) Now click on the table header to edit the properties for *column E: Life Expectancy 1960*. On the left side, use the drop-down menu to change its properties from *auto (text)* to *Number*. Click Proceed to return to the Visualize window.

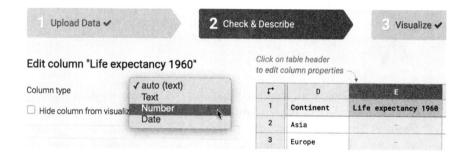

Edit column "Life expectancy 1960"

Column type

☐ Hide column from visualiz

✓ auto (text)
Text
Number
Date

Click on table header
to edit column properties

↱	D	E
1	Continent	Life expectancy 1960
2	Asia	-
3	Europe	-

11. To create the sparklines, in the Visualize screen under "Customize columns," select *all* of the columns from *Life expectancy 1960* down to *2018*. To select all at once, click on one column, then scroll down and shift-click on the next-to-last column. Then scroll down the page and click the "Show selected columns as tiny chart" button. These steps will create the sparklines in the column and automatically rename it *Life expectancy 1960–2018*.

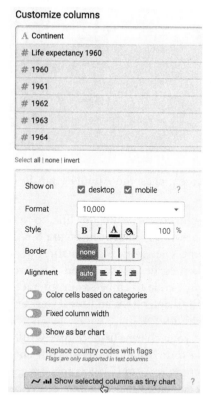

Customize columns

A Continent

Life expectancy 1960

1960

1961

1962

1963

1964

Select all | none | invert

Show on   ☑ desktop ☑ mobile   ?

Format   10,000   ▾

Style   **B** *I* A̲ 🎨   100 %

Border   none | | | ∥

Alignment   auto ☰ ☱ ☲

◯ Color cells based on categories

◯ Fixed column width

◯ Show as bar chart

◯ Replace country codes with flags
  Flags are only supported in text columns

〰 ▪▪ Show selected columns as tiny chart   ?

By design, we initially named this column *Life expectancy 1960* because when we selected several columns to create sparklines, the tool added *–2018* to the end of the new column name.

12. Let's add one more visual element: a bar chart to visually represent the *Difference* column in the table. In the Visualize screen under "Customize columns," select Difference. Then scroll down and push the slider to select "Show as bar chart." Also, select a different bar color, such as black, to distinguish it from the continent colors.

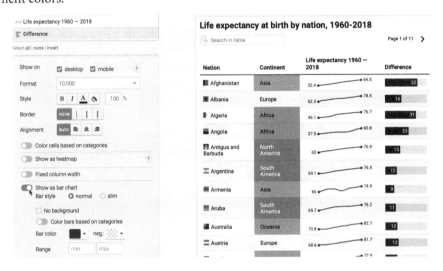

13. In the Visualize screen, click the Annotate tab to add a title, data source, and byline.

14. Click "Publish & Embed" to share the link to your interactive table (*https://oreil.ly/lw1Ot*), as previously shown in Figure 8-2. If you logged into your free Datawrapper account, your work is automatically saved online in the My Charts menu in the top-right corner of the screen. Also, you can click the blue Publish button to generate the code to embed your interactive chart on your website, as you'll learn about in Chapter 9. In addition, you can "add your chart to River" if you wish to share your work more widely by allowing other Datawrapper users to adapt and reuse your chart. Furthermore, scroll all the way down and click Download PNG to export a static image of your chart. Additional exporting and publishing options require a paid Datawrapper account. If you prefer not to create an account, you can enter your email to receive the embed code.

To learn more, we highly recommend the Datawrapper Academy support pages (*https://oreil.ly/q112s*), the extensive gallery of examples (*https://oreil.ly/EeN-z*), and well-designed training materials (*https://oreil.ly/LbCo_*).

Other Table-Making Tools

While Datawrapper is a good choice for creating interactive tables with long content and sparklines, there are many other tools for making less complex tables to publish in print or online.

To quickly make a short static table, look to your preferred spreadsheet tool. For example, in Google Sheets, you can lay out your table data and download it as a PDF document. Then use any image editor to convert the PDF to a PNG or JPG file and crop it to size, then insert the final version in a static document or a web page. Also, remember the spreadsheet pivot table feature you learned in "Summarize Data with Pivot Tables" on page 33 to create a more sophisticated cross-tabulation, and export it as an image to insert in a document or website.

In Datawrapper, you can also create a simple static table as a *Chart* type, and publish it to download the PNG version.

In Google Sheets, you can can also publish any of your tables online and embed them on a web page, as we'll discuss in Chapter 9, so that whenever you update your Google Sheet, the current data will automatically appear on the web page.

In Tableau Public, a tool we previously introduced in "Tableau Public Charts" on page 146 and "Choropleth Map with Tableau Public" on page 200, you can also create a high-light table, which automatically colors the backgrounds of cells to draw your eye to higher versus lower values.

Finally, if you're designing tables primarily for web pages, consider using the online Tables Generator tool (*https://oreil.ly/zM3e9*), which converts tabular content into HTML and other formats.

Summary

In this chapter, we reviewed principles about table design and how to create an interactive table with sparklines using Datawrapper, as well as other tools. In the next chapter, you'll learn how to embed interactive charts, maps, and tables on your website so that readers can explore your data and engage with your stories.

CHAPTER 9

Embed on the Web

So far you've learned how to create charts in Chapter 6, maps in Chapter 7, and tables in Chapter 8. Our book emphasizes the benefits of designing *interactive* visualizations that engage broad audiences on the internet by inviting them to interact with your data, investigate new patterns, download files if desired, and easily share your work on social media. In this chapter, you'll learn about a computer code tag called an *iframe*, which allows readers to actively explore your data on a different page. Like a picture frame, an iframe displays a live web page (such as your interactive data visualization) inside a second web page that you control (such as your personal or organizational website), as shown in Figure 9-1. When done correctly, the iframe makes your data visualization appear seamlessly on your web page, so that audiences can explore the content without needing to know that it's coming from a different host.

Several of the visualization tools you've learned so far, such as Google Sheets, Datawrapper, and Tableau Public, generate an *embed code* that contains an iframe to the online chart or map you've created on their platform. We'll demonstrate how to get the embed code or link from your visualization tool site and paste the code into a second website to seamlessly display your interactive content (see "Get the Embed Code or iframe Tag" on page 231 and "Paste Code or iframe to a Website" on page 238). No coding skills are required in this introductory book, but it certainly helps to be *code-curious*.

Your web page
With text & images

<iframe> that shows another web page, such as your data visualization hosted on another site

The rest of your web page

Figure 9-1. You can use an iframe to embed other web pages in your web page.

Static Image Versus Interactive iframe

First, let's clarify the difference between *static* and *interactive* visualizations. A static picture of a chart or map is a frozen image. Many visualization tools allow you to download static images of your charts or maps in JPG or PNG or PDF format. Static images are useful when that's all that you want to insert in a document, a presentation slide, or even a web page. Another option is to paste a static image, and add a link or custom shortlink with the web address to an interactive chart or map, and invite audiences to explore it online (see "Share Your Google Sheets" on page 20).

If you need to capture a static image of any web page on your computer, take a screenshot (*https://oreil.ly/UNbcf*) with these built-in commands:

Chromebook
Shift+Ctrl+F5 (the "show windows" button), then click and drag the crosshair cursor

Mac
Shift-Command-4, then click and drag the crosshair cursor to capture screenshot

Windows
Windows logo key+Shift+S to call up the Snip & Sketch tool

A related strategy is an animated GIF, which is a series of static images that captures motion on the screen. You can insert an animated GIF file on a web page to illustrate a short sequence of steps while using an interactive visualization, but audiences cannot interact with it, other than to play the animated loop over again. Paid software tools such as Snagit (*https://oreil.ly/39tW_*) allow you to create screenshots that include drop-down menus and cursors, animated GIFs, and more.

By contrast, *interactive* visualizations allow audiences to directly engage with your data story through their web browsers. Visitors usually can float their cursor over a chart to view tool tips or underlying information, zoom into a map and pan around, or search terms or sort columns in an interactive table. Interactive visualizations are usually hosted online, such as a chart or map tool platform, and are primarily designed to be viewed online, although in some cases it's possible for you to download and interact with them on your local computer.

Now let's turn to the central question: how can we make an interactive visualization, which resides on its online host (the primary site), appear seamlessly on a different website that we control (the secondary site)? While it's possible to insert a link on our secondary site to the charts or maps on the primary site, that's inconvenient for our audiences because it requires them to click away from the web page they were reading. A better solution is to insert an embed code that usually contains an iframe tag (*https://oreil.ly/tSF4K*), written in HTML, the code that displays content inside our web browsers. While you don't need any coding experience, you'll benefit in the long run by learning how to recognize the core features of an embed code and how it works.

In its simplest form, an iframe instructs the secondary site to display a web page address from the primary site, known as the source, as if it were a seamless picture frame on the wall of a room. The sample iframe code that follows begins with a start tag `<iframe ... >`, which contains the source `src='https://...'` with either single- or double-quotes around the primary site URL, then concludes with an end tag `</iframe>`:

```
<iframe src='https://datawrapper.dwcdn.net/LtRbj/'></iframe>
```

This sample iframe refers to an interactive US income inequality chart on the Datawrapper platform, which first appeared in the Introduction, as shown in Figure 9-2.

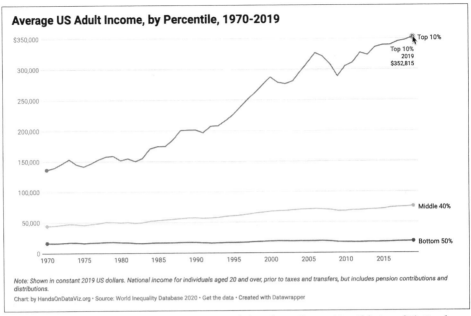

Figure 9-2. Explore the interactive version of this chart (https://oreil.ly/rqodT). In the US, income for the top 10% of earners has grown since the 1970s, but remained stagnant for the bottom 50%.

When you copy an embed code from some of the visualization tools featured in this book, their iframe tags may be *much longer* than the simple example provided. For example, an iframe tag might include other attributes, such as `width` or `height`, measured in pixels (`px`) or a percentage of its dimensions on the secondary site. Also, you may see other iframe tag attributes, such as `frameborder="0"` or `scroll ing="no"`, which create a seamless appearance between the iframe content and its surroundings. Finally, you may see *really long* embed codes that contain a dozen or more lines of code that even we don't fully understand. That's okay, because all of these are optional add-ons to improve the appearance of the iframe in the secondary site. The most essential ingredient of an embed code is the iframe and its three core parts: the iframe start tag, source web address, and end tag. When in doubt, look for those key ingredients.

Now that you have a clearer definition of an interactive visualization, embed codes, and iframe tags, in the next section, we'll learn how to copy the embed code from different visualization platforms.

Get the Embed Code or iframe Tag

In this section, you'll learn how to copy the embed code or iframe tag that is automatically generated when you publish a chart or map on different visualization platforms featured in this book. Remember that embed codes contain the essential iframe tag, along with other bits of code to display the chart or map from the primary site and make it appear seamlessly on the secondary site.

We'll break this down into three steps for each visualization platform. First, we'll demonstrate how to copy your embed code or iframe tag from Google Sheets, Datawrapper, Tableau Public, and other platforms listed. Second, we'll show you how to test the embed code or iframe tag in a wonderful assistant called the W3Schools TryIt iframe page (*https://oreil.ly/Nfmma*), shown in Figure 9-3. It's a great way to see what happens if you need to trim parts of the embed code before placing it in a web page, and test if it still works. Third, we'll point you to the next section to learn how to properly paste the embed code in your preferred website, including common platforms such as WordPress, Squarespace, Wix, and Weebly.

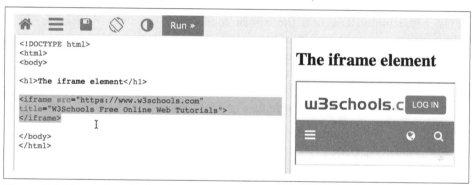

Figure 9-3. For each embed code in the following sections, paste it in place of the selected text of the W3Schools TryIt iframe page to test how it works.

From Google Sheets

After you create a Google Sheets chart as you did in "Google Sheets Charts" on page 113:

1. Click the three-dot kebab menu in the upper-right corner of the chart to publish it.

2. In the next screen, select the Embed tab and Interactive chart, and click Publish to share it online. Select and copy the embed code.

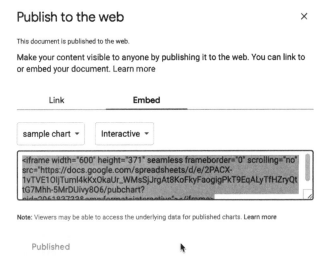

3. To better understand how the embed code works, open the W3Schools TryIt
   iframe page (*https://oreil.ly/2jb9p*). Select the current iframe tag, paste in your
   embed code to replace it, and press the green Run button. The result should be
   similar to the following, but instead will display your embed code and interactive
   visualization.

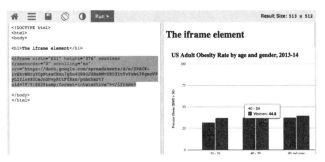

At first glance, the Google Sheets embed code may appear long, but it's actually a
straightforward iframe tag with a long source link. Look closely and you'll see
iframe settings such as `width` and `height` (measured here in pixels), and `seam
less` and `frameborder='0'` and `scrolling='no'` to improve its appearance.

4. Now jump to the paste code to "Paste Code or iframe to a Website" on page 238
   to learn how to properly insert your embed code into your preferred platform.

From Datawrapper

After you create a Datawrapper chart as you did in "Datawrapper Charts" on page 131, a map as you did in Chapter 7, and an interactive table as you did Chapter 8:

1. Proceed to the final screen and click Publish. This publishes the interactive version of your chart or map online. Further down on the same screen you can also export a static image, if desired.

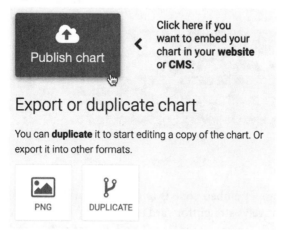

2. On the next screen, click "copy" to get the Datawrapper embed code. The default "responsive iframe" version of the embed code contains additional instructions to improve its appearance on both small and large device screens.

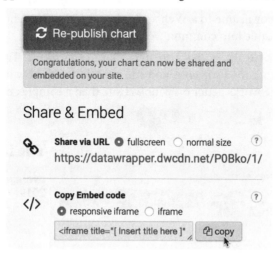

3. To better understand how the embed code works, open the W3Schools TryIt iframe page (*https://oreil.ly/N_CQT*). Select the current iframe tag, paste in your embed code to replace it, and press the green Run button. The result should be similar to the following, but instead will display your unique embed code and interactive visualization.

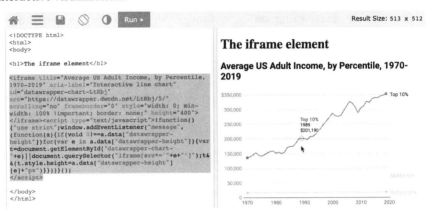

The Datawrapper embed code is *long*, but if you look closely, the first half contains a relatively straightforward iframe tag that includes familiar-looking attributes such as src, scrolling, and frameborder, and width and height inside a style tag. The second half of the embed code contains JavaScript instructions to make the iframe appear responsive depending on the size of the device screen.

4. Always try to paste the *full embed code* in your desired web platform. Jump to "Paste Code or iframe to a Website" on page 238 to learn how to properly insert your embed code into common websites.

If that doesn't work, go back to step 3 and experiment. Try to edit the embed code down to a *simple iframe*, and run it again to see how it looks. Sometimes a simple iframe works better on your website than a complex embed code.

The Datawrapper iframe tag source follows this general format: `https://datawrapper.dwcdn.net/abcdef/1/`, where the 1 refers to the first version of the chart or map you published. If you make edits and re-publish your visualization, Datawrapper will increase the last digit (to 2 and so forth), and *automatically redirect* older links to the *current version*, which keeps your work up to date for your audience.

From Tableau Public

After you create a Tableau Public chart in "Tableau Public Charts" on page 146 or map in "Choropleth Map with Tableau Public" on page 200:

1. Publish your worksheet, dashboard, or story online by selecting File > "Save to Tableau Public" in the desktop application menu.

2. In your online Tableau Public account profile page, click View to see the details of any of your published visualizations.

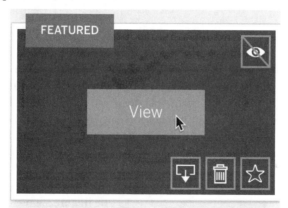

All of your published visualizations appear under your username account profile on the Tableau Public server (*https:// public.tableau.com*). If you don't recall your username, search the Tableau Public server for the first and last name that you entered when creating your online account.

3. When viewing details for a published visualization in your Tableau Public online account, scroll down and click on the Share symbol in the lower-right corner. Select and copy its embed code.

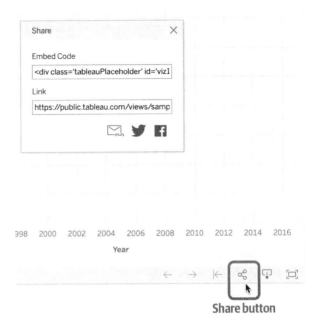

998 2000 2002 2004 2006 2008 2010 2012 2014 2016

Year

Share button

4. To better understand how the embed code works, open the W3Schools TryIt iframe page (*https://oreil.ly/N_CQT*). Select the current iframe tag, paste in your embed code to replace it, and press the green Run button. The result should be similar to the following, but instead will display your embed code and interactive visualization. Note how the Tableau Public embed code is so long that it doesn't fit in this image.

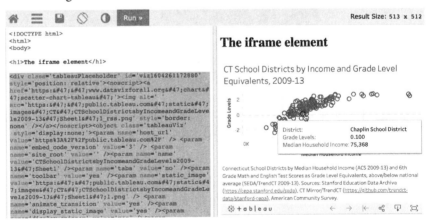

5. Always try to paste the full embed code in your desired web platform. Jump to "Paste Code or iframe to a Website" on page 238 to learn how to properly insert on different common websites.

If your web platform does not accept the full embed code for Tableau Public, the next strategy is to try to copy the Tableau Public link to your visualization and convert it into a *simpler iframe tag*, and see how it works in your website. Here's how to copy and convert it:

1. In your published visualization on your Tableau Public online account, scroll down and click the Share symbol in the lower-right corner. But this time, select and copy its link, not the embed code. A typical link looks similar to this one:

   ```
   https://public.tableau.com/views/
   CTSchoolDistrictsbyIncomeandGradeLevels2009-13/
   Sheet1?:language=en&:display_count=y&:origin=viz_share_link
   ```

2. Paste the link into the W3Schools TryIt iframe page (*https://oreil.ly/N_CQT*), and delete all of the code that appears *after* the question mark (?), so that it looks like this:

   ```
   https://public.tableau.com/views/
   CTSchoolDistrictsbyIncomeandGradeLevels2009-13/Sheet1?
   ```

3. At the end, after the question mark, attach this code snippet to replace what you deleted previously:

   ```
   :showVizHome=no&:embed=true
   ```

4. Now your edited link should look like this:

   ```
   https://public.tableau.com/views/
   CTSchoolDistrictsbyIncomeandGradeLevels2009-13/Sheet1?:showViz
   Home=no&:embed=true
   ```

5. Enclose your edit link inside an iframe source tag src= with quotes, to make it look similar to this:

   ```
   src="https://public.tableau.com/views/
   CTSchoolDistrictsbyIncomeandGradeLevels2009-13/Sheet1?:showViz
   Home=no&:embed=true"
   ```

6. Add iframe start and end tags, as well as attributes for width, height, frameborder="0", and scrolling="no", to make it look similar to this:

   ```
   <iframe
     src="https://public.tableau.com/views/CTSchoolDistricts\
   byIncomeandGradeLevels2009-13/Sheet1?:showVizHome=no&:embed=true"
     width="90%" height="500" frameborder="0" scrolling="no"></iframe>
   ```

Insert width="90%" rather than 100% to help readers scroll more easily down your web page by giving it a margin.

7. Press Run to see how it looks in the W3Schools TryIt iframe page. Sometimes a simple iframe works better on your website than a complex embed code.

Learn more about how to embed an iframe on the Tableau Public support page (*https://oreil.ly/ZaNJ5*).

Now that you have a better sense of how to copy embed codes, and edit them down to simpler iframes if needed, in the next section you'll learn how to paste them into common websites to share your interactive visualizations with wider audiences.

Paste Code or iframe to a Website

In the previous section, you learned how to copy the embed code or create an iframe for your interactive visualization that is hosted online by the primary site. For example, your live chart or map might be hosted on a Google Sheets, Datawrapper, or Tableau Public server. In this section, we'll demonstrate ways to properly paste the embed code or iframe to seamlessly display your interactive chart or map on a secondary website that you control, and we'll focus on common web-building platforms such as WordPress (WP), Squarespace, Wix, and Weebly. Even if your website runs on a different platform, the principles will likely be the same.

To WordPress.com Sites

If you own a free or personal or premium WordPress.com site, with a web address in the format *anyone.wordpress.com*, you *cannot* insert an embed code that contains an iframe or JavaScript due to security concerns, as described on their support page (*https://oreil.ly/iW_BP*). This means that if you wish to show data visualizations created from this book on a WordPress.com site, you have two options. First, with your free/personal/premium plan, you can still insert a static image of a chart or map and a link to its interactive site, but that's clearly not ideal. Second, WordPress.com suggests that you can update to their paid Business or eCommerce plan (*https://oreil.ly/JpwLF*), which supports embed codes that contain iframes or JavaScript, following instructions similar to the self-hosted WordPress sites described next.

To Self-Hosted WordPress Sites

Make sure you understand the difference (*https://oreil.ly/2DrOW*) between a WordPress.com site and a self-hosted WordPress site. The latter is sometimes called a WordPress.org site because anyone can freely download the software from that address and *host it on their own web server*, or more commonly, have access to a self-hosted WordPress server through their school or work, or by renting space on a vendor's web server. But the web address of a self-hosted WordPress site does *not* necessarily need to end in *.org*. It also could be *.com* or *.edu* or any other ending, so don't let that confuse you.

There are two ways to insert an embed code or iframe in a self-hosted WordPress site, but your success may depend on your WP version, your access level, and the complexity of the code. We'll show you both Method A (which is simpler, but not always reliable) and Method B (which requires a few more steps, but works more reliably). See which method works best for your self-hosted WordPress site.

Method A: simple, but not always reliable

Assume that you're using self-hosted WordPress version 5.0 or above with the newer block editor, and you have editor or administrator access to your site. (This method does not work reliably with author-level access or below.)

1. In your block editor, select a *custom HTML* block, and directly insert the embed code or the iframe.

2. Preview your WordPress page or post, and if your iframe appears, publish and view it in another browser to test how it appears to your readers.

Method B: more steps, but more reliable

Assume that you're using self-hosted WordPress, any version, with either the classic or block editor, and that you have author-level or above access to the site.

1. First, the site administrator must install and activate the iframe plug-in (*https://oreil.ly/2t8Rp*). This plug-in allows authors to embed iframe codes in a modified "shortcode" format surrounded by square brackets in this general format: [iframe...].

2. In the WordPress block editor, click to add a *Custom HTML* block (or in the classic editor, click the "text" tab to view the HTML code). Paste the embed code or iframe, which initially should appear similar to the "Method A: simple, but not always reliable" step 1 screen.

3. Initially, the code you pasted probably included HTML iframe tags at the start (<iframe...) and the end (...></iframe>). Modify the start tag by replacing the less-than symbol (<) with a square opening bracket ([). Modify the backend by erasing the greater-than symbol *and* the entire end tag (> </iframe>), and replacing both of them with one square closing bracket (]). Closely compare the two figures to see what these small code edits look like.

 For long embed codes from Datawrapper and Tableau Public, you may need to experiment with trimming them down to the most relevant portions of the iframe using the W3Schools TryIt iframe page (*https://oreil.ly/N_CQT*), as described in the prior section, then pasting it into the WordPress editor and modifying the frontend and backend with square brackets.

4. Preview your WordPress page or post, and if your iframe appears, publish and view it in another browser to test how it appears to your readers.

For Squarespace, Wix, Weebly, or Other Web-Building Sites

In other web-building sites, the process of pasting in your data visualization iframes or embed codes is similar to that on WordPress sites, but details will vary, depending on freemium versus paid subscription level and author-administrator status. Here are details for three of the most popular web-building services:

- See these Squarespace support pages about embed blocks (*https://oreil.ly/tAKLp*) and adding custom code to your site (*https://oreil.ly/-n9Nu*).

- See this Wix support page about using iframes to display content on your site (*https://oreil.ly/UJ58w*).

- See this Weebly support page about adding external content and widgets with embedded code (*https://oreil.ly/bbmwa*).

When working with long or complex embed codes, you may need to experiment with pasting and trimming down to the most relevant portion of the iframe in the W3Schools TryIt iframe page (*https://oreil.ly/N_CQT*), then pasting that portion into your web-builder platform.

Summary

In this chapter, you learned about iframes and embed codes, and how they seamlessly display your interactive data visualization from their home site onto a second website that you personally manage. This concept will be valuable in the next chapter, where you'll learn how to edit and host open source code templates on the GitHub platform, because you can also create iframes to make those charts and maps seamlessly appear on your own website.

PART III

Code Templates and Advanced Tools

CHAPTER 10

Edit and Host Code with GitHub

In Parts I and II, you created interactive charts and maps on free drag-and-drop tool platforms created by companies such as Google and Tableau. These platforms are great for beginners, but their preset tools limit your options for designing and customizing your visualizations, and they also require you to depend upon their web servers and terms of service to host your data and work products. If these companies change their tools or terms, you have little choice in the matter, other than deleting your account and switching services, which means that your online charts and maps would appear to audiences as dead links.

In Parts III and IV, get ready to make a big leap—and we'll help you through every step—by learning how to copy, edit, and host code templates. These templates are prewritten software instructions that allow you to upload your data, customize its appearance, and display your interactive charts and maps on a website that you control. No prior coding experience is required, but it helps if you're *code-curious* and willing to experiment with your computer.

Code templates are similar to cookbook recipes. Imagine you're in your kitchen, looking at our favorite recipe we've publicly shared to make brownies (yum!), which begins with these three steps: `Melt butter`, `Add sugar`, `Mix in cocoa`. Recipes are templates, meaning that you can follow them precisely or modify them to suit your tastes. Imagine that you copy our recipe (or "fork" it, as coders say) and insert a new step: `Add walnuts`. If you also publicly share your recipe, now there will be two versions of instructions, to suit both those who strongly prefer or dislike nuts in their brownies. (We do not take sides in this deeply polarizing dispute.)

Currently, the most popular cookbook among coders is GitHub (*https://github.com*), with more than 40 million users and more than 100 million recipes (or "code repositories" or "repos"). You can sign up for a free account and choose to make your repos private (like Grandma's secret recipes) or public (like the ones we share next). Since

GitHub was designed to be public, think twice before uploading any confidential or sensitive information that should not be shared with others. GitHub encourages sharing *open source code*, meaning the creator grants permission for others to freely distribute and modify it, based on the conditions of the type of license they have selected.

When you create a brand-new repo, GitHub invites you to Choose a License (*https:// choosealicense.com*). Two of the most popular open source software licenses are the MIT License (*https://oreil.ly/_5hiW*), which is very permissive, and the GNU General Public License version 3 (*https://oreil.ly/2smHI*), which mandates that any modifications be shared under the same license. The latter version is often described as a *copyleft* license that requires any derivatives of the original code to remain publicly accessible, in contrast to traditional *copyright* that favors private ownership. When you fork a copy of someone's open source code on GitHub, look at the type of license they've chosen (if any), keep it in your version, and respect its terms.

To be clear, the GitHub platform is also owned by a large company (Microsoft purchased it in 2018), and when using it to share or host code, you're also dependent on its tools and terms. The magic of code templates is that you can migrate and host your work anywhere on the web. You could move to a competing repository-hosting service such as GitLab (*https://gitlab.com*), or purchase your own domain name and server space through one of many web hosting services. Or you can choose a hybrid option, such as hosting your code on GitHub and choosing its custom domain option, to display it under a domain name that you've purchased from an internet service provider.

In "Copy, Edit, and Host a Simple Leaflet Map Template" we'll introduce basic steps to copy, edit, and host a simple Leaflet map code template on GitHub. When you publish any chart or map code template by hosting it on GitHub Pages, you can easily transform its online link into an iframe that you can embed on a secondary website, which we discussed in see "Convert GitHub Pages Link to iframe" on page 255. In "Create a New Repo and Upload Files on GitHub" on page 256, you'll learn how to create a new GitHub repo and upload code files.

This chapter introduces GitHub using its web browser interface, which works best for beginners. In "GitHub Desktop and Atom Text Editor to Code Efficiently" on page 261, you'll learn about intermediate-level tools, such as GitHub Desktop and Atom text editor, to work more efficiently with code repos on your personal computer.

If problems arise, turn to the Appendix: Fix Common Problems. All of us make mistakes and accidentally "break our code" from time to time, and it's a great way to learn how things work—and what to do when it doesn't work!

Copy, Edit, and Host a Simple Leaflet Map Template

Now that you understand how GitHub code repositories are like a public cookbook of recipes, which anyone can copy and modify, let's get into the kitchen and start baking! In this section, we'll introduce you to a very simple code template based on Leaflet (*https://leafletjs.com*), an open source code library for creating interactive maps that are popular in journalism, business, government, and higher education.

Many people choose Leaflet because the code is freely available to everyone, relatively easy to use, and has an active community of supporters who regularly update it. Unlike drag-and-drop tools that we previously covered in Chapter 7, working with our Leaflet templates requires you to copy and edit a few lines of code before hosting it on the web. While no prior coding experience is necessary, it's helpful to know that these code templates as based on the three core languages that communicate with browsers: HTML, Cascading Style Sheets (CSS), and JavaScript. Furthermore, we can edit these code templates using the GitHub web interface, which means you can do this on any type of computer (Mac, Windows, Chromebook, etc.) with any modern web browser.

Here's an overview of the key steps you'll learn about GitHub in this section:

- Make a copy of our simple Leaflet map code template
- Edit the map title, start position, background layer, and marker
- Host a live online version of your modified map code on the public web

Your goal is to create your own version of this simple interactive map, with your edits, as shown in Figure 10-1.

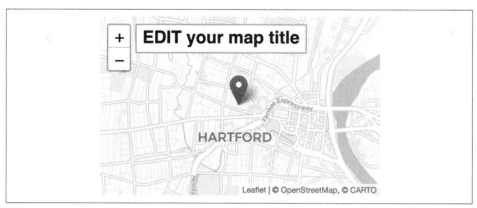

Figure 10-1. Create your own version of this simple interactive Leaflet map (https:// oreil.ly/I-eGl).

Follow these steps to create and edit your own version of this simple Leaflet map code template:

1. Create your own free account on GitHub. It may ask you to do a simple quiz to prove you're a human. If you don't see a confirmation message in your email, check your spam folder.

Choose a GitHub username that's relatively short, and one that you'll be happy seeing in the web address of charts and maps you'll publish online. `DrunkBrownieChef6789` may not be the wisest choice for a username, if `BrownieChef` is also available.

2. After you log into your GitHub account in your browser, go to our simple Leaflet map template (*https://oreil.ly/handsondataviz*).

3. Click the green "Use this template" button to make your own copy of our repo:

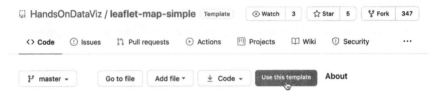

4. On the next screen, your account will appear as the owner. Name your copy of the repo *leaflet-map-simple*, the same as ours. Click the green "Create repository from template" button.

The upper-left corner of the next screen will say *USERNAME/leaflet-map-simple* generated from *HandsOnDataViz/leaflet-map-simple*, where *USERNAME* refers to your GitHub account username. This confirms that you copied our template into your GitHub account, and it contains only three files:

LICENSE
    Shows that we've selected the MIT License, which allows anyone to copy and modify the code as they wish

README.md
    Provides a simple description and link to the live demo, which we'll come back to later

index.html
    The key file in this particular template because it contains the map code

Create a new repository from leaflet-map-simple

The new repository will start with the same files and folders as HandsOnDataViz/leaflet-map-simple.

Owner *   **Repository name ***

| HandsOnDemo ▾ | / | leaflet-map-simple   ✓ |

Great repository names are short and memorable. Need inspiration? How about **ubiquitous-disco**?

Description (optional)

⦿   **Public**
     Anyone on the internet can see this repository. You choose who can commit.

○   **Private**
     You choose who can see and commit to this repository.

☐ **Include all branches**
     Copy all branches from HandsOnDataViz/leaflet-map-simple and not just `master`.

Create repository from template

 We set up our repo using GitHub's template feature to make it easier for users to create their own copies. If you're trying to copy someone else's GitHub repo and don't see a Template button, then click the Fork button, which makes a copy a different way. Here's the difference: Template allows you to make *multiple* copies of the same repo by giving them different names, while Fork allows you to create *only one copy* of a repo because it uses the same name as the original, and GitHub prevents you from creating two repos with the same name. If you need to create a second fork of a GitHub repo, go to "Create a New Repo and Upload Files on GitHub" on page 256.

5. Click on the *index.html* file to view the code. If this is the first time you're looking at computer code, it may feel overwhelming, but relax! We've inserted several "code comments" to explain what's happening. The first block tells web browsers which formatting to apply to the rest of the page of code. The second block instructs the browser to load the Leaflet (*https://leafletjs.com*) code library, the open source software that constructs the interactive map. The third block describes where the map and title should be positioned on the screen. The good news is that you don't need to touch any of those blocks of code, so leave them as-is. But you do want to modify a few lines.

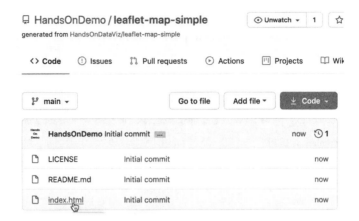

6. To edit the code, click on the pencil symbol in the upper-right corner ( ).

   Let's start by making one simple change to prove to everyone that you're now editing *your* map, by modifying the map title, which appears in the HTML division tag block around lines 21 to 23.

7. In the line `<div id="map-title">EDIT your map title</div>`, type your new map title in place of the words `EDIT your map title`. Be careful not to erase the HTML tags that appear on both ends inside the `< >` symbols.

8. To save your edit, scroll to the bottom of the page and click the green "Commit changes" button.

Commit changes

Update index.html

Add an optional extended description...

⦿ ⊸ Commit directly to the `master` branch.

○ ⑂ Create a **new branch** for this commit and start a pull request.

[Commit changes] [Cancel]

In the language of coders, we "commit" our changes in the same way that most people "save" a document, and later you'll see how GitHub tracks each code commit so that you can roll them back if needed. By default, GitHub inserts a short description of your commit as "Update index.html," and you have the option to customize that description when you start making lots of commits to keep track of your work. Also, GitHub commits your changes directly to the default branch of your code, which we'll explain later.

 If you wish to store your code on GitHub but need to scale up to a larger commercial-level web host, see freemium services such as Netlify (*https://www.netlify.com*). Netlify automatically detects any changes you push to your GitHub repository and deploys them to your online site.

Now let's publish your edited map to the public web to see how it looks in a web browser. GitHub not only stores open source code, but its built-in GitHub Pages (*https://pages.github.com*) feature allows you to host a live online version of your HTML-based code, which anyone with the web address can view in their browser. While GitHub Pages is free to use, there are some restrictions on usage, file size, and content (*https://oreil.ly/TYNNh*), and it's not intended for running an online business or commercial transactions. But one advantage of code templates is that you can host them on any web server you control. Since we're already using GitHub to store and edit our code template, it's easy to turn on GitHub Pages to host it online.

1. To access GitHub Pages, scroll to the top of your repo page and click Settings.

2. In the Settings screen, scroll way down to the GitHub Pages area. In the drop-down menu, change Source from None to Main, keep the default */(root)* option in the middle, and press Save. This step tells GitHub to publish a live version of your map on the public web, where anyone can access it in their browser, if they have the web address.

GitHub Pages

GitHub Pages is designed to host your personal, organization

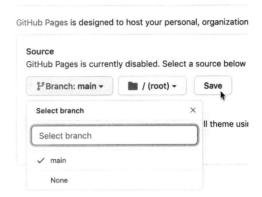

 In response to the Black Lives Matter movement in 2020, GitHub renamed its default branch (*https://oreil.ly/51Nx3*) from *master* to *main* to eliminate its master-slave metaphor.

3. Scroll down to Settings > GitHub Pages to see the web address where your live map has been published online, and right-click it to open in a new browser tab.

GitHub Pages

GitHub Pages is designed to host your personal, organization, or project pages from a GitHub repository.

Now you should have at least two tabs open in your browser. The first tab contains your GitHub repo, where you edit your code, with a web address in the following format. Replace *USERNAME* and *REPOSITORY* with your own:

```
https://github.com/USERNAME/REPOSITORY
```

The second tab contains your GitHub Pages live website, where your edited code appears online. GitHub Pages automatically generates a public web address in this format:

```
https://USERNAME.github.io/REPOSITORY
```

The live version of your code points to the *index.html* page by default, so it's not necessary to include it in the web address.

Remember how we advised you not to create your account with a username like DrunkBrownieChef6789? GitHub automatically places your username in the public web address.

Keep both tabs open so you can easily go back and forth between editing your code and viewing the live results online.

GitHub Pages usually displays your live map in less than 30 seconds, but may require several minutes in some cases. If you see no change after one minute, give your browser a "hard refresh" to bypass any saved content in your cache (*https://oreil.ly/i3-UE*) and re-download the entire web page from the server using one of these key combinations:

- Ctrl+F5 (most browsers for Windows or Linux)
- Command-Shift-R (Chrome or Firefox for Mac)
- Shift-Reload button toolbar (Safari for Mac)
- Ctrl+Shift+Backspace (on Chromebook)

Now let's edit your the GitHub repo so that the link points to *your* live map, instead of *our* live map:

1. Copy the web address of your live map from your second browser tab.

2. Go back to your first browser tab with your GitHub repo, and click on the repo title to return to its home page.

3. On your repo page, click to open the *README.md* file, and click the pencil again to edit it. Paste your live web link under the label *(replace with link to your site)* and scroll down to commit the change.

HandsOnDemo committed baf0cec 1 hour ago ✓   🕐 1 commits   ⑂ 1 branch   ◇ 0 tags

▢ LICENSE	Initial commit	1 hour ago
▢ README.md	Initial commit	1 hour ago
▢ index.html	Initial commit	1 hour ago

README.md   ✎

leaflet-map-simple

A simple Leaflet map template for new users to fork their own copy, edit, and host on GitHub Pages

Link to live map (replace with link to your site)

https://handsondataviz.github.io/leaflet-map-simple/

Now that you've successfully made simple edits and published your live map, let's make more edits to jazz it up and help you learn more about how Leaflet code works.

4. On your repo home page, click to open the *index.html* file, and click the pencil symbol to edit more code.

Wherever you see the EDIT code comment, this points out a line that you can easily modify. For example, look for the code block shown below that sets up the initial center point of the map and its zoom level. Insert a new latitude and longitude coordinate to set a new center point. To find coordinates, right-click on any point in Google Maps (*https://google.com/maps*) and select "What's here?" as described in "Geocode Addresses in Google Sheets" on page 23.

```
var map = L.map('map', {
    center: [41.77, -72.69], // EDIT coordinates to recenter map
    zoom: 12,  // EDIT from 1 (zoomed out) to 18 (zoomed in)
    scrollWheelZoom: false,
    tap: false
});
```

The next code block displays the basemap tile layer that serves as the map background. Our template uses a light map with all labels, publicly provided by CARTO, with credit to OpenStreetMap. One simple edit is to change light_all to dark_all, which will substitute a different CARTO basemap with inverted coloring. Or preview several other Leaflet basemap code options (*https://oreil.ly/sVVy5*) that you can copy and paste. Make sure to attribute the source, and also keep }).addTo(map); at the end of this code block, which displays the basemap:

```
L.tileLayer(
    'https://{s}.basemaps.cartocdn.com/light_all/{z}/{x}/{y}{r}.png', {
    attribution: '&copy; <a href="https://osm.org/copyright">\
OpenStreetMap</a> contributors, &copy;\
<a href="https://carto.com/attribution">CARTO</a>'
    }).addTo(map);
```

The last code block displays a single point marker on the map, colored blue by default in Leaflet, with a pop-up message when users click it. You can edit the marker coordinates, insert the pop-up text, or copy and paste the code block to create a second marker:

```
L.marker([41.77, -72.69]).addTo(map) // EDIT marker coordinates
.bindPopup("Insert pop-up text here"); // EDIT pop-up text message
```

 Be careful when editing your code. Accidentally removing or adding extra punctuation (such as quotation marks, commas, or semicolons) can stop your map from working. But breaking your code—and fixing it—can also be a great way to learn.

5. After making edits, remember to scroll down and press Commit to save changes. Then go to your browser tab with the live map, and do a hard refresh to view changes. Edits to your map normally will appear within 30 seconds, but remember that GitHub Pages sometimes requires longer to process code commits. If you have problems, see the Appendix.

Congratulations! If this is the first time that you've edited computer code and hosted it online, you can now call yourself a "coder." The process is similar to following and modifying a cookbook recipe, just like you also can call yourself a "chef" after baking your first batch of brownies! Although no one is likely to hire you as a full-time paid coder (or chef) at this early stage, you now understand several of the basic skills needed to copy, edit, and host code online, and you're ready to dive into the more advanced versions, such as Chart.js and Highcharts templates in Chapter 11 and Leaflet map templates in Chapter 12.

Convert GitHub Pages Link to iframe

In Chapter 9, we discussed the benefits of displaying interactive content from a primary site and making it appear seamlessly in a secondary site. You also learned how to convert very long Datawrapper and Tableau Public embed codes into shorter iframe tags when needed, so that you can embed them more easily on a secondary website.

The same concept applies to GitHub Pages. When you publish a code template for a chart or map (or any content) on GitHub Pages, it generates an online link that you can convert into an iframe tag, using the same principles as mentioned, to embed it on a secondary website. Follow these steps:

1. For any GitHub repository you have published online, go to its *Settings* page and scroll down to copy its GitHub Pages web address, which will appear in this general format:

   ```
   https://USERNAME.github.io/REPOSITORY
   ```

2. Convert it into an iframe by enclosing the link inside quotation marks as the source, and adding both start and end tags, in this general format:

   ```
   <iframe src="https://USERNAME.github.io/REPOSITORY"></iframe>
   ```

3. If desired, improve the iframe appearance on the secondary site by adding any of these optional attributes, such as `width` or `height` (measured in pixels by default, or percentages), or `frameborder="0"` or `scrolling="no"`, in this general format:

   ```
   <iframe src="https://USERNAME.github.io/REPOSITORY" width="100%"
   height="400" frameborder="0" scrolling="no"></iframe>
   ```

 Either single quote (') marks or double quote (") marks are acceptable in your iframe code, but be consistent and avoid accidentally pasting in curly quotes ("").

Now you are ready to paste your iframe into your preferred website ("Paste Code or iframe to a Website" on page 238), using methods described in Chapter 9, to display your interactive chart or map template from a published repository using GitHub Pages.

You should have a better sense of how to edit and host code repositories on GitHub. The next section describes how to enhance your GitHub skills by creating new repos and uploading your files. These are essential steps to create a second copy of a code template or to work with more advanced templates in the next two chapters.

Create a New Repo and Upload Files on GitHub

Now that you've made a copy of our GitHub template, the next step is to learn how to create a brand-new repo and upload files. These skills will be helpful for several scenarios. First, if you have to fork a repo, which GitHub allows you to do only one time, this method will allow you to create additional copies. Second, you'll need to upload some of your own files when creating data visualizations using Chart.js and Highcharts templates in Chapter 11 and Leaflet map templates in Chapter 12. Once again, we'll demonstrate how to do all of these steps in GitHub's beginner-level browser interface, but see "GitHub Desktop and Atom Text Editor to Code Efficiently" on page

261 for an intermediate-level interface that's more efficient for working with code templates.

In the previous section, you created a copy of our GitHub repo with the "Use this template" button, and we intentionally set up our repos with this newer feature because it allows the user to make *multiple* copies and assign each one a different name. Many other GitHub repos do not include a Template button, so to copy those you'll need to click the Fork button, which automatically generates a copy with the same repo name as the original. But what if you wish to fork someone's repo a second time? GitHub prevents you from creating a second fork to avoid violating one of its important rules: every repo in your account must have a unique name, to avoid overwriting and erasing your work.

How do you make a second fork of a GitHub repo if there's no "Use this template" button? Follow our recommended workaround that's summarized in the following three steps:

1. Download the existing GitHub repo to your local computer.

2. Create a brand-new GitHub repo with a new name.

3. Upload the existing code repo files to your brand-new repo.

Now let's get into more detail about this three-step workaround:

1. Click on the Code > Download ZIP drop-down menu button on any repo. Your browser will download a zipped compressed folder with the contents of the repo to your local computer, and it may ask you where you wish to save it. Decide on a location and click OK.

2. Navigate to the location on your computer where you saved the folder. Its file name should end with *.zip*, which means you need to double-click to "unzip" or decompress the folder (or for Windows users, right-click and select Extract All). After you unzip it, a new folder will appear named in this format, REPOSITORY-BRANCH, which refers to the repository name (such as *leaflet-map-simple*) and the

branch name (such as `main`), and it will contain the repo files. One of those files is named *index.html*, which you'll use in a few steps.

3. Go back to your GitHub account in your web browser, click on the plus (+) symbol in the upper-right corner of your account, and select "New repository."

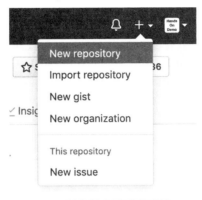

4. On the next screen, GitHub will ask you to enter a new repo name. Choose a short one, preferably all lowercase, and separate words with hyphens if needed. Let's name it *practice* because we'll delete it at the end of this tutorial.

Check the box to "Initialize this repository with a README" to simplify the next steps.

Also, select "Add a license" that matches the code you plan to upload, which in this case is MIT License. Other fields are optional. Click the green "Create repository" button at the bottom when done.

Create a new repository

A repository contains all project files, including the revision history. /
elsewhere? Import a repository.

Repository template
Start your repository with a template repository's contents.

[No template ▾]

Owner *   **Repository name** *

[🔲 HandsOnDemo ▾] / [practice   ✓]

Great repository names are short and memorable. Need inspiration?

Description (optional)

[   ]

◉ 🔲 **Public**
    Anyone on the internet can see this repository. You choose who car

○ 🔒 **Private**
    You choose who can see and commit to this repository.

Skip this step if you're importing an existing repository.

☑ **Initialize this repository with a README**
    This will let you immediately clone the repository to your computer.

[Add .gitignore: None ▾]   [Add a license: MIT License ▾]   ⓘ

[Create repository]

Your new repo will have a web address similar to *https://github.com/USERNAME/
practice*.

5. On your new repo home page, click the "Add file" > "Upload files" drop-down
   menu button, near the middle of the screen.

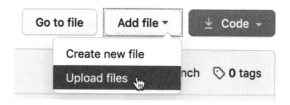

6. Inside the repo folder that you previously downloaded and unzipped on your local computer, drag-and-drop the *index.html* file to the upload screen of your GitHub repo in your browser. Do not upload *LICENSE* or *README.md* because your new repo already contains those two files. Scroll down to click the green Commit Changes button.

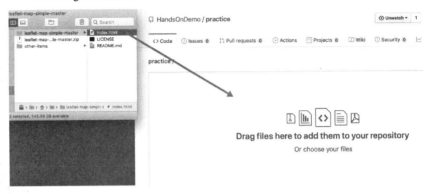

When the upload is complete, your repo should contain three files, now including a copy of the *index.html* code that you previously downloaded from the *leaflet-map-simple* template. This achieved our goal of working around GitHub's one-fork rule, by creating a new repo and manually uploading a second copy of the code.

Optionally, you could use GitHub Pages to publish a live version of the code online, and paste the links to the live version at the top of your repo and your README.md file, as described in "Copy, Edit, and Host a Simple Leaflet Map Template" on page 247.

7. Since this was only a practice repo, let's delete it from GitHub. In the repo screen of your browser, click the top-right Settings button, scroll all the way down to the Danger Zone, and click "Delete this repository." GitHub will ask you to type in your username and repo name to ensure that you really want to delete the repo, to prove you are not a drunken brownie chef.

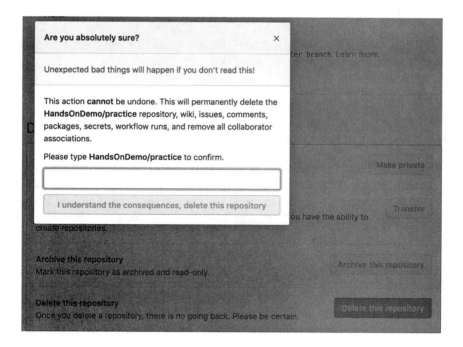

So far, you've learned how to copy, edit, and host code using the GitHub web interface, which is a great introduction for beginners. You're ready to move up to tools that will allow you to work more efficiently with GitHub, such as GitHub Desktop and Atom text editor, to quickly move entire repos to your local computer, edit the code, and move them back online.

GitHub Desktop and Atom Text Editor to Code Efficiently

Editing your code through the GitHub web interface is a good way to start, especially if you need to make only a few edits or upload a couple of files to your repo. But the web interface will feel very slow if you edit or upload multiple files in your repo. To speed up your work, we recommend that you download two free tools—GitHub Desktop (*https://desktop.github.com*) and Atom text editor (*https://atom.io*)—which run on Mac or Windows computers. When you connect your GitHub web account to GitHub Desktop, it allows you to "pull" the most recent version of the code to your local computer's hard drive, make and test your edits, and "push" your commits back to your GitHub web account. Atom text editor, which is also created by the makers of GitHub, allows you to view and edit code repos on your local computer more easily than the GitHub web interface. While there are many text editors for coders, Atom is designed to work well with GitHub Desktop.

Currently, neither GitHub Desktop nor Atom text editor are supported for Chromebooks, but Chrome's Web Store (*https://oreil.ly/5qRhP*) offers several text editors, such as Text and Caret, which offer some of the functionality described below.

Let's use GitHub Desktop to pull a copy of your *leaflet-map-simple* template to your local computer, make some edits in Atom text editor, and push your commits backup to GitHub:

1. Go to the GitHub web repo you wish to copy to your local computer. In your browser, navigate to *https://github.com/USERNAME/leaflet-map-simple*, using your GitHub username, to access the repo you created in "Copy, Edit, and Host a Simple Leaflet Map Template" on page 247. Click the Code > "Open with GitHub Desktop" drop-down menu button near the middle of your screen. The next screen will show a link to the GitHub Desktop web page, and you should download and install the application.

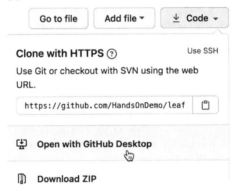

2. When you open GitHub Desktop for the first time, you'll need to connect it to the GitHub web account you previously created in this chapter. On the welcome screen, click the blue "Sign in to GitHub.com" button, and login with your GitHub username and password. On the next screen, GitHub will ask you to click the green "Authorize desktop" button to confirm that you wish to connect to your account.

Welcome to GitHub Desktop

GitHub Desktop is a seamless way to contribute to projects on GitHub and GitHub Enterprise Server. Sign in below to get started with your existing projects.

New to GitHub? **Create your free account.**

Sign in to GitHub.com [↗]

3. In the next setup screen, GitHub Desktop asks you to configure Git, the underlying software that runs GitHub. Confirm that it displays your username and click Continue.

Configure Git

This is used to identify the commits you create. Anyone will be able to see this information if you publish commits.

Name

HandsOnDemo

Email

66479711+HandsOnDemo@users.noreply.github.com

Continue   Cancel

4. On the Let's Get Started with GitHub Desktop screen, click Your Repositories on the right side to select your `leaflet-map-sample`, and further below, click the blue button to *Clone* it to your local computer.

Let's get started!

Add a repository to GitHub Desktop to start collaborating

Create a Tutorial Repository...

Clone a Repository from the Internet...

Create a New Repository on your Hard Drive...

Add an Existing Repository from your Hard Drive...

ProTip! You can drag & drop an existing repository folder here to add it to Desktop

Filter your repositories

Your Repositories

HandsOnDemo/leaflet-map-simple

Clone HandsOnDemo/leaflet-map-simple

5. When you clone a repo, GitHub Desktop asks you to select the Local Path, meaning the location where you wish to store a copy of your GitHub repo on your local computer. Before you click the Clone button, remember the path to this location, since you'll need to find it later.

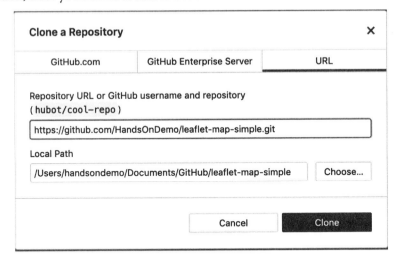

Clone a Repository   ✕

| GitHub.com | GitHub Enterprise Server | URL |

Repository URL or GitHub username and repository
(hubot/cool-repo)

https://github.com/HandsOnDemo/leaflet-map-simple.git

Local Path

/Users/handsondemo/Documents/GitHub/leaflet-map-simple   Choose...

Cancel   Clone

6. On the next screen, GitHub Desktop may ask, "How are you planning to use this fork?" Select the default entry "To contribute to the parent project," which means you plan to send your edits back to your GitHub web account, and click Continue.

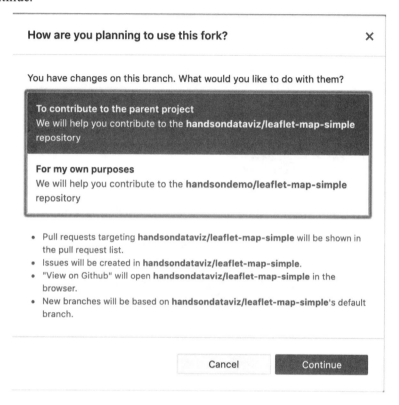

7. You now have copies of your GitHub repo in two places—in your GitHub web account and on your local computer. Your screen may look different, depending on whether you use Windows or Mac, and the Local Path you selected to store your files.

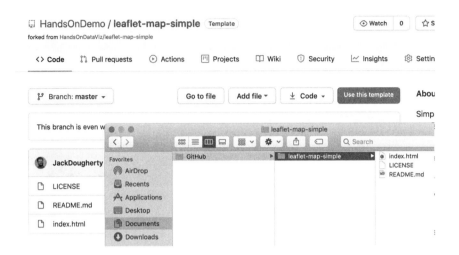

8. Before we can edit the code in your local computer, download and install the Atom text editor application (*https://atom.io*). Then go to your GitHub Desktop screen, confirm that the Current Repository is *leaflet-map-simple*, and click "Open in Atom."

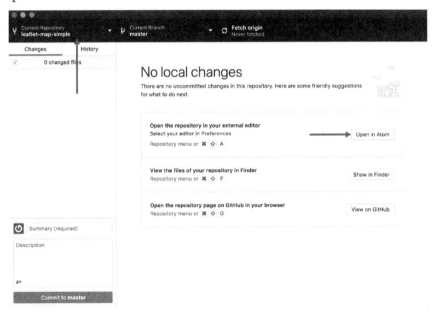

9. Because Atom text editor is integrated with GitHub Desktop, it opens up your entire repo as a "project," where you can click files in the left window to open as

---

new tabs to view and edit code. Open your *index.html* file and edit the title of your map, around line 22, then save your work.

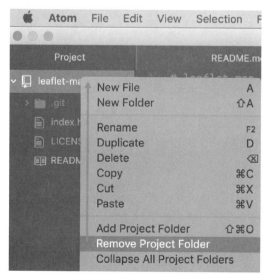

10. After saving your code edit, it's a good habit to clean up your Atom text editor workspace. Right-click on the current Project and select Remove Project Folder in the menu. Next time you open up Atom, you can right-click to Add Project Folder, and choose any GitHub repo that you have copied to your local computer.

Cross-Origin Resource Sharing

To fully view more complex code templates in your local browser, including some Chart.js or Highcharts templates in Chapter 11 or Leaflet templates in Chapter 12, you may need to temporarily relax same-origin policy restrictions (*https://oreil.ly/ wWbTA*), an internet security mechanism that limits how web pages access content from other domains. You can do so by managing your cross-origin resource sharing (CORS) settings (*https://oreil.ly/7g81U*).

Methods for doing this vary across operating systems and browsers. For example, to disable same-origin policy on Safari for Mac (*https://oreil.ly/iaalu*), go to Preferences > Advanced to enable the Developer menu, then in this new menu select Disable Cross-Origin Restrictions, as shown in Figure 10-2. After testing your code, restart Safari to reset the setting to its default safety position.

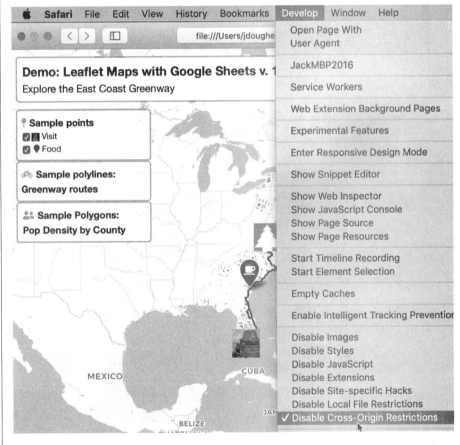

Figure 10-2. To view more complex code templates on your local computer with Safari, temporarily Disable Cross-Origin Restrictions.

There are also ways to run the Chrome browser without same-origin restrictions on various computers (*https://oreil.ly/KhSco*), as shown in Figure 10-3 and discussed on this popular Stack Overflow page (*https://oreil.ly/B_YcA*). If you temporarily disable this safety mechanism in your browser, be sure to re-enable it before browsing sites on the public web.

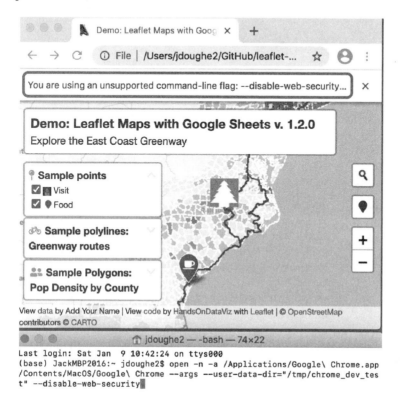

Figure 10-3. To view more complex code templates on your local computer with Chrome, use the Terminal application command-line (bottom window) to run a version without same-origin safety restrictions.

Now that you've edited the code for your map on your local computer, let's test how it looks before uploading it to GitHub:

11. Go to the location where you saved the repo on your local computer, right-click the *index.html* file, select Open With, and choose your preferred web browser.

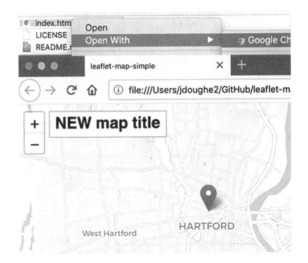

Because your browser is displaying only the *local computer* version of your code, the web address will begin with *file:///...* rather than *https://...*, as appears in your GitHub Pages online map. Also, if your code depends on online elements, those features may not function when viewing it locally. For this simple Leaflet map template, your updated map title should appear, allowing you to check its appearance before pushing your edits to the web.

Now let's transfer your edits from your local computer to your GitHub web account, which you previously connected when you set up GitHub Desktop.

12. Go to GitHub Desktop, confirm that your Current Repo is *leaflet-map-simple*, and you will see your code edits summarized on the screen. In this two-step process, first click the blue Commit button at the bottom of the page to save your edits to your local copy of your repo. (If you edit multiple files, GitHub Desktop will ask you to write a summary of your edit to help you keep track of your work.) Second, click the blue "Push origin" button to transfer those edits to the parent copy of your repo on your GitHub web account. Both steps are shown here.

Well done! You've successfully navigated a round-trip journey of code, from your GitHub account to your local computer, and back again to GitHub. Since you previously used the GitHub Pages settings to create an online version of your code, go see if your edited map title now appears on the public web. The web address you set up earlier follows this format *https://USERNAME.github.io/REPOSITORY*, substituting your GitHub username and repo name.

While you could have made the tiny code edit above in the GitHub web interface, hopefully you've begun to see many advantages of using GitHub Desktop and Atom text editor to edit code and push commits from your local computer. First, you can make more complex code modifications with Atom, which includes search, find-and-replace, and other features to work more efficiently. Second, when you copy the repo to your local computer, you can quickly drag-and-drop multiple files and subfolders for complex visualizations, such as data, geography, and images. Third, depending on the type of code, you may be able to test how it works locally with your browser, before uploading your commits to the public web.

 Atom has many built-in commands to help you edit code. One is View > Toggle Soft Wrap, which adjusts the right-hand margin to make long code strings visible. Another is Edit > Toggle Comments, which automatically detects the coding language and converts the selected text from executable code to nonexecuted code comments. A third command is Edit > Lines > Auto Indent, which cleans up code indentation to make it more readable. You can install many more Atom packages (*https://atom.io/packages*) from the Preferences menu.

GitHub also offers a powerful platform for collaborative projects. When two people work on a shared repository, one coworker can pull the most recent version of the code to their local computer using GitHub Desktop, then push their edits (also called commits) back to the online GitHub repo. The other coworker can pull and push from the same repo at the same time, though it's simpler if they work on different files or sections of code. Both can see the changes that the other person made by selecting the GitHub repo Code tab and selecting a specific commit, which can be viewed line by line in green (additions) or red (deletions), as shown in Figure 10-4.

```
21      <!-- Display the map and title with HTML         21      <!-- Display the map and title with HTML
        division tags  -->                                       division tags  -->
22  -   <div id="map-title">NEW map title</div>          22  +   <div id="map-title">EDIT map title</div>
23      <div id="map"></div>                             23      <div id="map"></div>
24                                                       24
```

Figure 10-4. View commits made by coworkers on a shared GitHub repo.

Although GitHub doesn't operate like Google Docs, which displays live edits, the platform has several advantages when working collaboratively with code. First, because GitHub tracks every commit, it allows you to go back and restore a very specific past version of the code if needed. Second, when GitHub repos are public, anyone can view your code and submit an issue to notify the owner about an idea or problem, or send a pull request of suggested code edits, which the owner can accept or reject. Third, GitHub allows you to create different branches of a repo to make edits, and then merge the branches back together if desired. Occasionally, if two collaborators attempt to push incompatible commits to the same repo, GitHub will warn about a Merge Conflict and ask you to resolve it to preserve everyone's work.

Many coders prefer to work on GitHub using its command-line interface (CLI), which means memorizing and typing specific commands directly into the Terminal application on Mac or Windows, but this is beyond the scope of this introductory book.

Summary

If this is the first time you've forked, edited, and hosted live code on the public web, welcome to the coding family! We hope you agree that GitHub is a powerful platform for engaging in this work and sharing with others. While beginners will appreciate the web interface, you'll find that the GitHub Desktop and Atom tools make it much easier to work with Chart.js and Highcharts code templates in Chapter 11 and the Leaflet map code templates in Chapter 12. Let's build on your brand-new coding skills to create more customized charts and maps in the next two chapters.

Chart.js and Highcharts Templates

In Chapter 6, we looked at powerful drag-and-drop tools, such as Google Sheets, Datawrapper, and Tableau Public to build interactive charts.

In this chapter, we'll look into creating interactive charts using two popular Java-Script libraries, Chart.js (*https://www.chartjs.org*) and Highcharts (*https://www.high charts.com*). Since we don't expect our readers to be proficient in JavaScript or any other programming language, we designed templates that you can copy to your own GitHub account, substitute data files, and publish them to the web without writing a single line of code. For those of you who are code-curious, we'll show how the Java-Script code in these templates can be customized.

Why would anyone prefer JavaScript to easy-to-use Datawrapper or Tableau, you may wonder? Well, a few reasons. Although JavaScript code may seem overwhelming and intimidating at first, it allows for greater customization in terms of colors, padding, interactivity, and data handling than most third-party tools can offer. In addition, you can never be sure that third-party apps will remain free, or at least have a free tier, forever, whereas open source tools are here to stay, free of charge, as long as someone maintains the code.

 Although both libraries are open source, Highcharts comes with a stricter license (*https://oreil.ly/YskDA*) that allows it to be used for free for noncommercial projects only, such as a personal, school, or nonprofit organization website. Keeping that in mind, we primarily focus on Chart.js, which is distributed under an MIT license that lets you use the library for commercial projects as well.

Table 11-1 lists all types of charts that we'll look at in this chapter. Both libraries include many more default chart types that you can explore in Chart.js Samples (*https://oreil.ly/UowOS*) and Highcharts Demos (*https://oreil.ly/Tp90B*). However, we strongly advise against using some chart types, such as three-dimensional ones, for reasons we discussed in the Chart Design Principles section of Chapter 7.

Table 11-1. Chart code templates, best uses, and tutorials

Chart	Best use and tutorials in this book
Bar or column chart 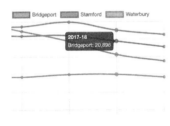	Best to compare categories side-by-side. If labels are long, use horizontal bars instead of vertical columns. Power tool: "Bar or Column Chart with Chart.js" on page 277
Error bars in a bar/column chart 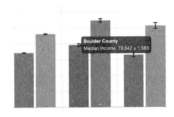	Best to show margin of error bars when comparing categories side-by-side. If labels are long, use horizontal bars instead of vertical columns. Power tool: "Error Bars with Chart.js" on page 280
Line chart 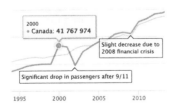	Best to show continuous data, such as change over time. Power tool: "Line Chart with Chart.js" on page 281 (see tutorial note to modify line chart into stacked area chart)
Annotated line chart	Best to add contextual notes inside chart of continuous data, such as change over time. Power tool: "Annotated Line Chart with Highcharts" on page 283

Scatter chart

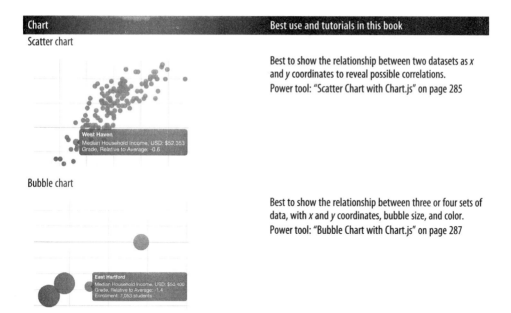

Best to show the relationship between two datasets as *x* and *y* coordinates to reveal possible correlations.
Power tool: "Scatter Chart with Chart.js" on page 285

Bubble chart

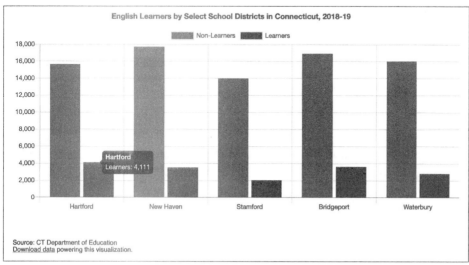

Best to show the relationship between three or four sets of data, with *x* and *y* coordinates, bubble size, and color.
Power tool: "Bubble Chart with Chart.js" on page 287

Bar or Column Chart with Chart.js

In this section, we'll show you how to create bar or column charts using Chart.js. We'll use a Chart.js code template that pulls data from a CSV file, as shown in Figure 11-1. This column chart shows how many students in five school districts in Connecticut were English-language learners in the 2018–2019 academic year.

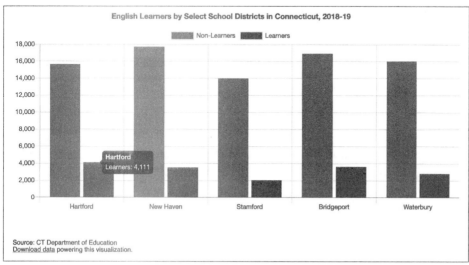

Figure 11-1. Bar chart with Chart.js: explore the interactive version (https://oreil.ly/7nTmu).

To create your own bar or column chart with CSV data using our Chart.js template:

1. Go to our GitHub repo (*https://oreil.ly/jVEKq*) that contains the code for the chart in Figure 11-1, log into your GitHub account, and click "Use this template" to create a copy that you can edit.

Template File Structure

If you don't remember how to use GitHub, we recommend you revisit Chapter 10. The repo contains three files that are directly related to the chart:

index.html
> Contains HTML (markdown) and CSS (stylesheets) that tell the browser how to style the document that contains the chart and what libraries to load.

script.js
> Contains the JavaScript code that reads data from the CSV file and constructs the interactive chart.

data.csv
> Is the comma-separated file that keeps all the data in the chart and can be edited in a text editor, or Google Sheets/Excel, etc.

The two remaining files are a *README.md* that describes the contents of the repo and *bar.png* that is an image that you can see in the README. All other GitHub templates in this chapter will be similarly structured.

---

2. Prepare your data in CSV format and upload into a *data.csv* file. Place labels that will appear along the axis in the first column, and each data series in its own column. Your CSV must contain at least two columns (labels and one data series). You can add as many data series columns as you wish.

```
| district  | nonlearner | learner |
| Hartford  | 15656      | 4111    |
| New Haven | 17730      | 3534    |
```

3. In *script.js*, customize the values of variables. Because you may not be familiar with JavaScript, let's take a look at the code snippet that describes a single variable in the file:

```
// `false` for vertical column chart, `true` for horizontal bar chart
var HORIZONTAL = false;
```

The first line starts with // and is a comment to help you understand what the variable in the next line is responsible for. It doesn't affect the code. As you can see, if the variable HORIZONTAL is set to false, the chart would have vertical bars (also known as columns). If set to true, the chart will contain horizontal bars. The second line contains the variable declaration itself. The equal sign (=) assigns the value that you see on the right (*false*) to the variable (var) called HORIZONTAL to the left. This line ends with the semicolon (;).

Here are some of the variables available for you to customize in *script.js*:

```
var TITLE = 'English Learners by Select School Districts in CT, 2018-19';

// `false` for vertical column chart, `true` for horizontal bar chart
var HORIZONTAL = false;

// `false` for individual bars, `true` for stacked bars
var STACKED = false;

// Which column defines 'bucket' names?
var LABELS = 'district';

// For each column representing a data series, define its name and color
var SERIES = [
  {
    column: 'nonlearner',
    name: 'Non-Learners',
    color: 'gray'
  },
  {
    column: 'learner',
    name: 'Learners',
    color: 'blue'
  }
];

// x-axis label and label in tool tip
var X_AXIS = 'School Districts';

// y-axis label, label in tool tip
var Y_AXIS = 'Number of Enrolled Students';

// `true` to show the grid, `false` to hide
var SHOW_GRID = true;

// `true` to show the legend, `false` to hide
var SHOW_LEGEND = true;
```

These basic variables should be enough to get you started. It's natural that you'll want to move the legend, edit the appearance of the tool tip, or change the colors of the grid lines. We recommend you look at the official Chart.js documentation (*https://oreil.ly/NuPQ2*) to get help with that.

Error Bars with Chart.js

If your data comes with uncertainty (margins of error), we recommend you show it in your visualizations with the use of error bars. The bar chart template shown in Figure 11-2 shows median and mean (average) income for different-sized geographies: the US state of Colorado, Boulder County, Boulder city, and a census tract in the city.

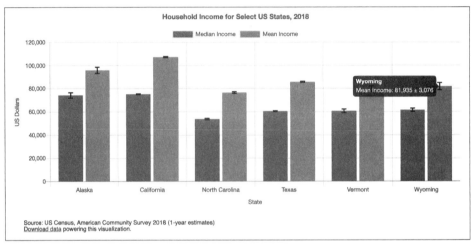

Figure 11-2. Interactive bar chart with error bars in Chart.js: explore the interactive version (https://oreil.ly/iJU3C).

To create your own bar or column chart with error bars, with data loaded from a CSV file, use our Chart.js template and follow these steps:

1. Go to our GitHub repo for this Chart.js template (*https://oreil.ly/93gqf*) that contains the code for the chart in Figure 11-2, log into your GitHub account, and click "Use this template" to create a copy that you can edit.

2. Prepare your data in CSV format and upload into a *data.csv* file. Place labels that will appear along the axis in the first column, and each data series in its own column (accompanied by a column with uncertainty values). Your CSV must contain at least three columns (labels and one data series with associated uncertainty values). You can add as many data series columns as you wish.

```
| geo            | median | median_moe | mean   | mean_moe |
| Colorado       | 68811  | 364        | 92520  | 416      |
| Boulder County | 78642  | 1583       | 109466 | 2061     |
| Boulder city   | 66117  | 2590       | 102803 | 3614     |
| Tract 121.02   | 73396  | 10696      | 120588 | 19322    |
```

3. In *script.js*, customize the values of variables shown in the following code snippet:

```
var TITLE = 'Household Income for Select US Geographies, 2018';

// `false` for vertical (column) chart, `true` for horizontal bar
var HORIZONTAL = false;

// `false` for individual bars, `true` for stacked bars
var STACKED = false;

// Which column defines "bucket" names?
var LABELS = 'geo';

// For each column representing a series, define its name and color
var SERIES = [
  {
    column: 'median',
    name: 'Median Income',
    color: 'gray',
    errorColumn: 'median_moe'
  },
  {
    column: 'mean',
    name: 'Mean Income',
    color: '#cc9999',
    errorColumn: 'mean_moe'
  }
];

// x-axis label and label in tool tip
var X_AXIS = 'Geography';

// y-axis label and label in tool tip
var Y_AXIS = 'US Dollars';

// `true` to show the grid, `false` to hide
var SHOW_GRID = true;

// `true` to show the legend, `false` to hide
var SHOW_LEGEND = true;
```

For more customization, see Chart.js documentation (*https://oreil.ly/NuPQ2*).

Line Chart with Chart.js

Line charts are often used to show temporal data, or change of values over time. The x-axis represents time intervals, and the y-axis represents observed values. Note that unlike column or bar charts, y-axes of line charts don't have to start at zero because we rely on the position and slope of the line to interpret its meaning. The line chart in Figure 11-3 shows the number of students in select school districts in Connecticut from 2012–2013 to 2018–2019 academic years. Each line has a distinct color, and the legend helps establish the color–district relations.

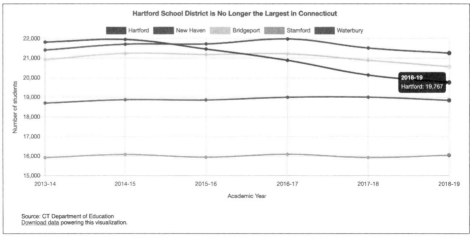

Figure 11-3. Interactive line chart with Chart.js: explore the interactive version (https://oreil.ly/8WCBp).

To create your own line chart with Chart.js, with data loaded from a CSV file, you can:

1. Go to our GitHub repo for the Chart.js template (*https://oreil.ly/Jjqps*) that contains the code of the line chart shown in Figure 11-3, log into your GitHub account, and click "Use this template" to create a copy that you can edit.

2. Prepare your data in CSV format and upload into a *data.csv* file. Place labels that will appear along the axis in the first column, and each data series in its own column. Your CSV must contain at least two columns (labels and one data series).

```
| year    | Hartford | New Haven | Bridgeport | Stamford | Waterbury |
| 2013-14 | 21820    | 21420     | 20929      | 15927    | 18706     |
| 2014-15 | 21953    | 21711     | 21244      | 16085    | 18878     |
| 2015-16 | 21463    | 21725     | 21191      | 15946    | 18862     |
| 2016-17 | 20891    | 21981     | 21222      | 16100    | 19001     |
| 2017-18 | 20142    | 21518     | 20896      | 15931    | 19007     |
| 2018-19 | 19767    | 21264     | 20572      | 16053    | 18847     |
```

You can add as many data series columns as you wish, but choose a reasonable number of lines because humans can distinguish only a limited number of colors. If you need to display multiple lines, consider using only one color to highlight the most significant line in your data story, and color others in gray, as you will learn in "Draw Attention to Meaning" on page 402.

3. In `script.js`, customize the values of variables shown in the following code snippet:

```
var TITLE = 'Hartford School District is No Longer Largest in CT';

// x-axis label and label in tool tip
var X_AXIS = 'Academic Year';

// y-axis label and label in tool tip
var Y_AXIS = 'Number of Students';

// Should y-axis start from 0? `true` or `false`
var BEGIN_AT_ZERO = false;

// `true` to show the grid, `false` to hide
var SHOW_GRID = true;

 // `true` to show the legend, `false` to hide
var SHOW_LEGEND = true;
```

To change a Chart.js line chart into a stacked area chart, see the Chart.js Stacked Area documentation (*https://oreil.ly/Z4KEP*). Make sure each `dataset` comes with a `fill: true` property, and also make sure that yAxes has its `stacked` property set to `true`.

Remember to look at the official Chart.js documentation (*https://oreil.ly/NuPQ2*) if you want to add more features. If something isn't working as desired, visit Stack Overflow (*https://oreil.ly/UNNvT*) to see if anyone had already solved your problem.

Annotated Line Chart with Highcharts

Although annotations are common elements of various type charts, they're especially important in line charts. Annotations help give historic context to the lines and explain sudden dips or raises in values. Figure 11-4 shows change in air passenger traffic for Australia and Canada between 1970 and 2018 (according to the World Bank). You can see that both countries experienced a dip in 2009, the year after the 2008 financial crisis, as suggested by the annotation.

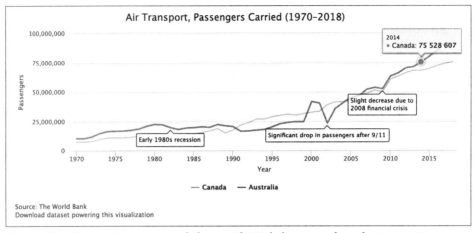

Figure 11-4. Interactive annotated chart with Highcharts: explore the interactive version (https://oreil.ly/_5Tqw).

Unfortunately, Chart.js is not great at showing annotations. This is why we are switching to Highcharts for this particular example. But don't worry—you'll see that the process is hardly different from the previous Chart.js examples.

To create your own annotated line chart with Highcharts, with data loaded from a CSV file, do the following:

1. Go to our GitHub repo (*https://oreil.ly/UGHCI*) that contains code for the chart shown in Figure 11-4, log into your GitHub account, and click "Use this template" to create a copy that you can edit.

2. Prepare your data in CSV format and upload into a *data.csv* file. Place labels that will appear along the axis in the first column, and each data series in its own column. Your CSV must contain at least three columns (labels, one data series, and notes). You can add as many data series columns as you wish, but you can only have one annotation (final column) per row.

   ```
   | Year | Canada   | Australia | Note                 |
   | 1980 | 22453000 | 13648800  |                      |
   | 1981 | 22097100 | 13219500  |                      |
   | 1982 | 19653800 | 13187900  | Early 1980s recession |
   ```

3. In script.js, customize the values of variables shown in this code snippet:

   ```
   var TITLE = 'Air Transport, Passengers Carried (1970-2018)';

   // Caption underneath the chart
   var CAPTION = 'Source: The World Bank';

   // x-axis label and label in tool tip
   var X_AXIS = 'Year';
   ```

```
// y-axis label and label in tool tip
var Y_AXIS = 'Passengers';

// Should y-axis start from 0? `true` or `false`
var BEGIN_AT_ZERO = true;

// `true` to show the legend, `false` to hide
var SHOW_LEGEND = true;
```

If you wish to further customize your chart, use the Highcharts API reference (*https://oreil.ly/KOL-6*) that lists all available features.

Scatter Chart with Chart.js

Now that you've seen Highcharts in action, let's get back to Chart.js and see how to build an interactive scatter chart. Remember that scatter charts (also *scatterplots*) are used to display data of two or more dimensions. Figure 11-5 shows the relationship between household income and test performance for school districts in Connecticut. Using x- and y-axes to show two dimensions, it's easy to see that test performance improves as household income goes up.

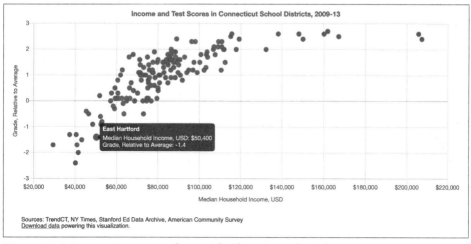

Figure 11-5. Interactive scatter chart with Chart.js: explore the interactive version (https://oreil.ly/hsSMY).

To create your own scatter plot with Chart.js, with data loaded from a CSV file, you can:

1. Go to our GitHub repo (*https://oreil.ly/wkbzV*) that contains the code for the chart shown in Figure 11-5, log into your GitHub account, and click "Use this template" to create a copy that you can edit.

2. Prepare your data in CSV format and upload into a *data.csv* file. The first two columns should contain *x* and *y* values, respectively, and the third column should contain the point name that will appear on mouse hover.

```
| income | grades | district |
| 88438  | 1.7    | Andover  |
| 45505  | -0.4   | Ansonia  |
| 75127  | 0.5    | Ashford  |
| 115571 | 2.6    | Avon     |
```

3. In *script.js*, customize the values of variables shown in the following code snippet:

```
var TITLE = 'Income and Test Scores in CT School Districts, 2009-13';

var POINT_X = 'income'; // column name for x values in data.csv
var POINT_X_PREFIX = '$'; // prefix for x values, e.g., '$'
var POINT_X_POSTFIX = ''; // postfix for x values, e.g., '%'

var POINT_Y = 'grades'; // column name for y values in data.csv
var POINT_Y_PREFIX = ''; // prefix for x values, e.g., 'USD '
var POINT_Y_POSTFIX = ''; // postfix for x values, e.g., ' kg'

var POINT_NAME = 'district'; // point names that appear in tool tip
var POINT_COLOR = 'rgba(0,0,255,0.7)'; // e.g., `black` or `#0A642C`
var POINT_RADIUS = 5; // radius of each data point

var X_AXIS = 'Median Household Income, USD'; // x-axis & tool tip label
var Y_AXIS = 'Grade, Relative to Average'; // y-axis & tool tip label

var SHOW_GRID = true; // `true` to show the grid, `false` to hide
```

A similarly good-looking interactive chart can be constructed in Highcharts (*https:// oreil.ly/WPS9_*), although it's up to you to undertake that challenge. In the meantime, remember to refer to the official Chart.js documentation (*https://oreil.ly/SDpzM*) if you want to further tweak your chart.

You may want to show an additional third variable, such as enrollment in each school district, in the same scatter chart. You can do so by resizing each dot so that larger school districts are marked with a larger circle, and smaller districts are shown using a smaller dot. Such use of size will result in a *bubble chart*, which we'll look at next.

Bubble Chart with Chart.js

Bubble charts are similar to scatter plots, but add one more variable (also known as dimension). The size of each point (marker) also represents a value.

The bubble chart in Figure 11-6 shows how median household income (x-axis) and test performance (y-axis) in six school districts in Connecticut are related. The size of the data point corresponds to the number of students enrolled in the school district: bigger circles represent larger school districts.

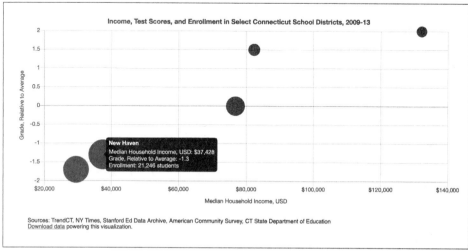

Figure 11-6. Interactive bubble chart with Chart.js: explore the interactive version (https://oreil.ly/Bk8Cr).

To create your own bubble chart with Chart.js, with data loaded from a CSV file, you can:

1. Go to our GitHub repo for this template (*https://oreil.ly/l5x-F*), log into your GitHub account, and click "Use this template" to create a copy that you can edit.

2. Prepare your data in CSV format and upload into a *data.csv* file. The first two columns should contain *x* and *y* values, respectively. The third column should contain bubble names that will appear on mouse hover. The final, fourth column, represents the size of your bubble:

```
| income | grades | district      | enrollment |
| 29430  | -1.7   | Hartford      | 21965      |
| 82322  | 1.5    | West Hartford | 10078      |
| 50400  | -1.4   | East Hartford | 7053       |
```

3. In script.js, customize the values of variables shown in this code snippet:

```
var TITLE = 'Income, Test Scores, and Enrollment in Select \
  Connecticut School Districts, 2009-13';

var POINT_X = 'income'; // column name for x values in data.csv
var POINT_X_PREFIX = '$'; // prefix for x values, e.g., '$'
var POINT_X_POSTFIX = ''; // postfix for x values, e.g., '%'

var POINT_Y = 'grades'; // column name for y values in data.csv
var POINT_Y_PREFIX = ''; // prefix for x values, e.g., 'USD '
var POINT_Y_POSTFIX = ''; // postfix for x values, e.g., ' kg'

var POINT_R = 'enrollment'; // column name for radius in data.csv
var POINT_R_DESCRIPTION = 'Enrollment'; // description of radius value
var POINT_R_PREFIX = ''; // prefix for radius values, e.g., 'USD '
var POINT_R_POSTFIX = ' students'; // postfix for radius values
var R_DENOMINATOR = 800;   // use this to scale the dot sizes, or set to 1
                           // if your dataset contains precise radius values

var POINT_NAME = 'district'; // point names that appear in tool tip
var POINT_COLOR = 'rgba(0,0,255,0.7)'; // e.g., `black` or `#0A642C`

var X_AXIS = 'Median Household Income, USD'; // x-axis & tool tip label
var Y_AXIS = 'Grade, Relative to Average'; // y-axis & tool tip label

var SHOW_GRID = true; // `true` to show the grid, `false` to hide
```

To display smaller data points that may be hidden behind larger
neighbors, use semitransparent circles with RGBa color codes. The
first three characters represent red, green, and blue, while the a
stands for alpha and represents the level of transparency on a scale
from 0.0 (fully transparent) to 1.0 (fully opaque). For example,
rgba(160, 0, 0, 0.5) creates a red color that is semitransparent.
Learn more by playing with RGBa color values at W3Schools
(*https://oreil.ly/Tx_f4*).

If you have more than three variables that you would like to show in your bubble
chart, you can use *color* and *glyphs* (instead of simple dots) to represent two extra
dimensions. For example, you may want to use blue to show only school districts in
Fairfield County (generally a richer part of CT) and gray to represent all other districts. You may want to use circles, squares, and triangles to represent results for
males, females, and nonbinary students. We won't be showing you how to achieve
this, but we can assure you that it can be done in 5 to 10 extra lines of code.

Chart.js is pretty limitless when it comes to customization, but remember not to
overwhelm the viewer and communicate only the data that is necessary to prove or
illustrate your idea.

Summary

In this chapter, we introduced Chart.js and Highcharts templates that can be used to construct rich and interactive charts that you can host in your own GitHub account, and showed you how to embed them anywhere on the web. You can use these templates as a base to kickstart your interactive visualizations. You can refer to Chart.js Samples (*https://oreil.ly/UowOS*) and Chart.js documentation (*https://oreil.ly/SDpzM*) for more information on Chart.js customization and troubleshooting. Highcharts Demos gallery (*https://oreil.ly/MuZDu*) shows plenty of charts along with the code that you can copy, and Highcharts API Reference (*https://oreil.ly/KOL-6*) lists all features available to refine your visualizations. Remember that you need to obtain a license (*https://shop.highsoft.com*) to use Highcharts in commercial projects.

In the next chapter, we'll introduce Leaflet.js map templates that were designed in a similar fashion to the chart templates we have just looked at. Leaflet is a leading open source JavaScript library for web mapping, and will let you create stunning interactive maps that live in your GitHub account and can be shared across the web.

CHAPTER 12

Leaflet Map Templates

In Chapter 7, we described several easy-to-learn drag-and-drop tools, such as Google My Maps and Datawrapper, to create several basic types of interactive maps. If you want to create more customized or advanced maps to stretch beyond the scope of those tool platforms, this chapter offers several code templates based on Leaflet (*https://leafletjs.com*), a powerful open source library for displaying interactive maps on desktop or mobile devices. We first introduced you to Leaflet when you learned how to edit and host code on GitHub in Chapter 10.

All of the Leaflet map templates in this chapter are summarized in Table 12-1. The first two templates are good for beginners, because they pull your map data from a linked Google Sheets table, and don't require any coding skills, but you need to follow some detailed GitHub instructions. The first template, "Leaflet Maps with Google Sheets" on page 294 is best for showing any combination of points, polylines, or polygons, with your choice of custom icons and colors, and the option to display a summary table of point data below your map. The second template, "Leaflet Storymaps with Google Sheets" on page 308, is best for guiding viewers through a point-by-point tour, with a scrolling narrative to display text, images, audio, video, or scanned map backgrounds. We specifically created both code templates for readers of this book, to fill a gap in maps offered on hosted platforms.

The remainder of the Leaflet templates are designed to improve your coding skills and apply them to more specialized cases. Even if you have no prior coding experience, but can follow instructions and are code-curious, start with "Leaflet Maps with CSV Data" on page 326 to learn the basics of pulling point data from a CSV file. Then move on to more advanced examples, such as "Leaflet Heatmap Points with CSV Data" on page 327, which shows point clusters as hotspots, "Leaflet Searchable Point Map" on page 329, which allows users to search and filter multiple locations, and "Leaflet Maps with Open Data APIs" on page 331, which continuously pulls the most current information directly from open repositories, a topic we introduced in "Open Data Repositories" on page 57 and raised again in "Current Map with Socrata Open Data" on page 207.

These Leaflet templates are written in the three most common coding languages on the web: HTML to structure content on a web page (typically in a file named *index.html*), CSS to shape how content appears on the page (either inside *index.html* or a separate file such as *style.css*), and JavaScript to create the interactive map using the open source Leaflet code library (either inside *index.html* or a separate file such as *script.js*). These Leaflet templates also include links to other online components, such as zoomable basemap tiles from various open access online providers (*https://oreil.ly/ A0npS*). Also, they pull in geospatial data, such as polygon boundaries from a *map.geojson* file, which you'll learn how create in Chapter 13.

If you're new to coding, creating Leaflet maps can be a great place to start and quickly see the results of what you've learned. To help solve problems that may arise, see how to fix common mistakes in the Appendix. Or to delve further into JavaScript, the language that Leaflet relies on, we strongly recommend Marijn Haverbeke's *Eloquent JavaScript*, available both in print and as an open source online book with an interactive coding sandbox to try out examples.[1]

Table 12-1. Map code templates, best uses, and tutorials

Map templates	Best use and tutorials in this book
Leaflet Maps with Google Sheets	
	Best to show interactive points, polygons, or polylines, using your choice of colors, styles, and icons, based on data loaded into your linked Google Sheet (or CSV file) and GitHub repository. Includes option to display a table of point map markers next to your map. Template with tutorial: "Leaflet Maps with Google Sheets" on page 294

---

1 Marijn Haverbeke, *Eloquent JavaScript: A Modern Introduction to Programming*, 3rd Edition, 2018, *https:// eloquentjavascript.net*.

Leaflet Storymaps with Google Sheets

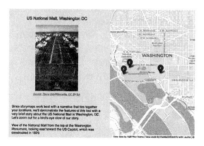

Best to show a point-by-point guided tour, with a scrolling narrative to display text, images, audio, video, and scanned map backgrounds loaded into your linked Google Sheet (or CSV file) and GitHub repository.
Template with tutorial: "Leaflet Storymaps with Google Sheets" on page 308

Leaflet Point Map with CSV Data

Learn how to code your own Leaflet point map that pulls data from a CSV file in your GitHub repo.
Template with tutorial: "Leaflet Maps with CSV Data" on page 326

Leaflet Heatmap Points with CSV Data

Best to show clusters of points as colored hotspots to emphasize high frequency or density of cases.
Template with tutorial: "Leaflet Heatmap Points with CSV Data" on page 327

Leaflet Searchable Point Map with CSV Data

Best to show multiple locations for users to search by name or proximity, or filter by category, with optional list view. Developed by Derek Eder (https://derekeder.com) from DataMade.
Template with tutorial: "Leaflet Searchable Point Map" on page 329

Leaflet Maps with Open Data APIs

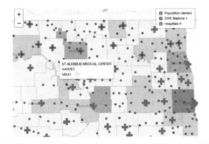

Learn how to code your own Leaflet map with an API that continuously pulls the most current information directly from an open-data repository, such as Socrata and others. Template with tutorial: "Leaflet Maps with Open Data APIs" on page 331

Leaflet Maps with Google Sheets

Sometimes you need to create a map that cannot be made easily with drag-and-drop tools because you need to customize its appearance or show some combination of point, polygon, or polyline data. One solution is to build your map based on our Leaflet Maps with Google Sheets code template, which allows you to display custom point icons, pick any choropleth color palettes, and stack different combinations of map data layers, as shown in Figure 12-1.

If you've explored prior chapters in this book, this template is a good template for newer users, because you enter your map data and settings in a linked Google Sheet, as shown in Figure 12-2, and upload images or geographic files into a folder in your GitHub repository. All of the data you enter can easily be exported and migrated to other platforms as visualization technology continues to evolve in the future, as we discussed in Chapter 1. Furthermore, the map design is responsive, meaning it automatically resizes to look good on small or large screens. Finally, the Leaflet Maps template is built on flexible open source software that's written primarily in JavaScript, a very common coding language for the web, so you can customize it further if you have skills or support from a developer.

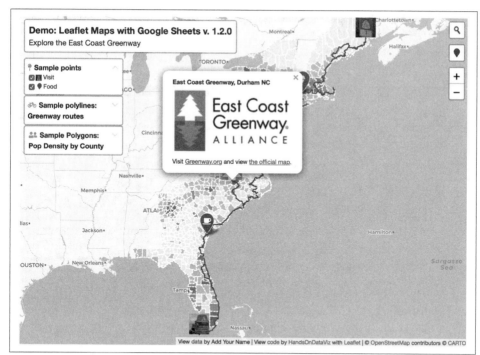

Figure 12-1. Explore the interactive Leaflet Maps with Google Sheets (https://oreil.ly/ CqHIw), which shows the East Coast Greenway—a walking–biking route that connects cities between Maine and Florida. More than one-third of the 3,000 mile route is on traffic-free trails as of 2021. To learn more, see the official Greenway map (https:// oreil.ly/SjHyc).

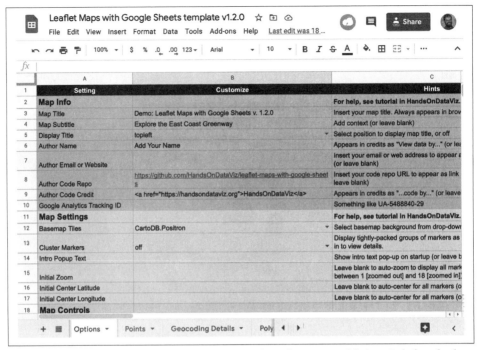

Figure 12-2. View the online Google Sheet template (https://oreil.ly/z4aG5) that feeds data into the Leaflet Maps demo above.

Tutorial Requirements and Overview

Before you begin, you must have a Google Drive account (*https://drive.google.com*) and know how to make a copy in Google Sheets (see "Make a Copy of a Google Sheet" on page 19). Also, you must have a GitHub account (*https://github.com*) and know how to edit and host code with GitHub (see Chapter 10). We omitted some screenshots that illustrate steps we previously covered, so if you get lost, go back to earlier chapters.

Since this tutorial involves multiple steps, we created this outline to provide a broad overview. In the first part, you'll create and publish your copies of two templates, one for GitHub and another for its linked Google Sheet:

- "A. Copy the GitHub template and publish your version with GitHub Pages"
- "B. File > Make a copy of Google Sheet template, share, and publish"
- "C. Paste your Google Sheet browser address in two places in your GitHub repo"
- "D. Update your Google Sheet Options and refresh your live map"

In the second part, you'll learn how to upload and display different types of map data, such as points, polygons, and polylines, and to edit colors, icons, and images, by entering data into the linked Google Sheet and uploading files to your GitHub repo.

- "E. Geocode locations and customize new markers in the Points tab"
- "F. Remove or display point, polygon, or polylines data and legends"

In the third part, you have two options to finalize your map before publicly sharing it with others:

- "G. Save each Google Sheets tab as a CSV file and upload to GitHub"
- "H. Get your own Google Sheets API Key to insert into the code"

If any problems arise, see the Appendix.

Now that you have a better sense of the big picture, let's get started with the first part of the tutorial.

A. Copy the GitHub template and publish your version with GitHub Pages

1. Open the GitHub code template (*https://oreil.ly/H4vKZ*) in a new tab.

2. In the upper-right corner of the code template, sign in to your free GitHub account.

3. In the upper-right corner, click the green "Use this template" button to make a copy of the repository in your GitHub account. On the next screen, name your repo *leaflet-maps-with-google-sheets* or choose a different meaningful name in all lowercase. Click the "Create repository from template" button.

   Your copy of the repo will follow this format:

   ```
   https://github.com/USERNAME/leaflet-maps-with-google-sheets
   ```

4. In your new copy of the code repo, click the upper-right Settings button and scroll way down to the GitHub Pages area. In the drop-down menu, change Source from None to Main, keep the default */(root)* setting, and press Save. This step tells GitHub to publish a live version of your map on the public web, where anyone can access it in their browser, if they have the web address.

GitHub Pages

GitHub Pages is designed to host your personal, organization

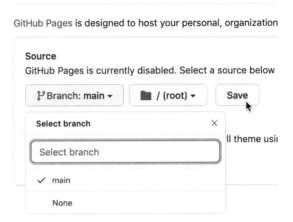

5. Scroll down to the GitHub Pages section again, and copy the link to your published website, which will appear in this format:

    https://USERNAME.github.io/leaflet-maps-with-google-sheets

6. Scroll up to the top, and click on your repo name to go back to its main page.

7. At the top level of your repo main page, click *README.md*, and click the pencil icon to edit this file.

8. Delete the link to *our* live site, and paste in the link to *your* published site. Scroll down to Commit your changes.

9. On your repo main page, right-click the link to open your live map in a new tab. Be patient. GitHub Pages normally will display your live map within 30 seconds, but sometimes it may require several minutes to appear.

B. File > Make a copy of Google Sheet template, share, and publish

1. Open the Google Sheets template (*https://oreil.ly/PZRev*) in a new tab.

2. Sign into your Google account, and select File > "Make a copy" to save your own version of this Google Sheet on your Google Drive.

3. Click the blue Share button, click "Change to anyone with the link," then click Done. This publicly shares your map data, which is required to make this template work.

4. Go to File > "Publish to the web," and click the green Publish button to publish the entire document so that the Leaflet code can read it. Then click the upper-right X symbol to close this window.

5. At the top of your browser, copy your Google Sheet address or URL (which usually ends in ...*XYZ/edit#gid=0*). Do *not* copy the "Published to the web" address (which usually ends in ...*XYZ/pubhtml*) because that link is slightly different and will not work in this template.

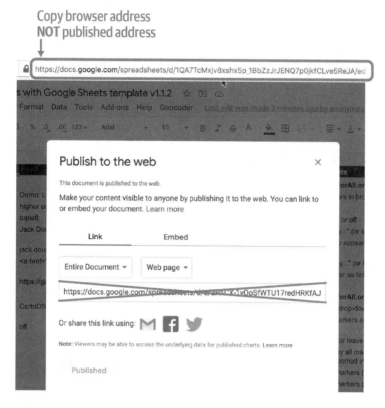

C. Paste your Google Sheet browser address in two places in your GitHub repo

Our next task is to link your published Google Sheet to your Leaflet code in GitHub, so that it can pull your data from the Sheet to display on the map:

1. At the top of your GitHub repo, click to open the file named *google-doc-url.js*, and click the pencil symbol to edit it.

2. Paste *your* Google Sheet address or URL (which usually ends in *...XYZ/ edit#gid=0*) to replace *our* existing URL. Be careful not to erase the single quotation marks or the semicolon at the end. Scroll down to Commit your changes. See separate instructions about the Google API key further below.

3. Also, let's paste your Google Sheet URL in second place to help you keep track of it. In your GitHub repo, click the *README.md* file to open it, click the pencil symbol to edit it, and paste *your* Google Sheet URL to replace *our* existing URL. Scroll down to Commit your changes.

Feel free to remove any other content from the README that you don't wish to keep.

D. Update your Google Sheet Options and refresh your live map

Now that your published Google Sheet is linked to your live map, go to the Options tab to update any of the following items:

- Map Title
- Map Subtitle
- Author Name
- Author Email or Website
- Author Code Repo

Open the browser tab that displays your live map and refresh the page to see your changes. If your changes don't appear within a few seconds, see the Appendix.

E. Geocode locations and customize new markers in the Points tab

Now we can start to add new content to your map. In the *Points* tab of your Google Sheet, you'll see column headers to organize and display interactive markers on your map. Replace the demonstration data with your own, but do *not* delete or rename the column headers because the Leaflet code looks for these specific names:

Group
> Create any labels to categorize groups of markers in your legend.

Marker icon
> Insert a Font Awesome free and solid icon name (*https://oreil.ly/Mz_5F*) such as `fa-ice-cream` or `fa-coffee`, or any Material Design icon name (*https://oreil.ly/ OUCGU*) such as `rowing` or `where_to_vote`. Or leave this blank for no icon inside the marker. Note that Font Awesome pro or brand icons do not work with this template. To create your own custom icon, see further below.

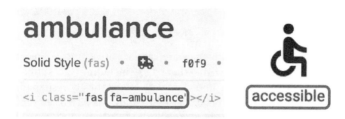

Marker color
> Insert any standard web color name such as `blue` or `darkblue`, or insert a web color code such as `#775307` or `rgba(200,100,0,0.5)`. See options at W3Schools Color Names (*https://oreil.ly/2dapU*).

Icon color
> Set the color of the icon inside the marker. The default is `white`, which looks good inside darker colored markers.

Custom size
> Leave blank, unless you are creating your own custom icon.

The next set of columns include items that appear when users click on point markers:

Name
> Add a title to display in the marker pop-up window.

Description

Add text to appear in the marker pop-up window. You may insert HTML tags to add line breaks (such as <br>) or to open external links in a new tab, such as:[2]

```
<a href='https://www.w3schools.com/' target='_blank'>Visit W3Schools</a>
```

Image

You have two options to display images. You can insert an external link to an image hosted by an online service (such as Flickr), as long as it begins with *https* (secure) and ends with either *.jpg* or *.png*. Or you can upload an image into the *media* subfolder in your GitHub repo, and enter the pathname in the Google Sheet in this format: *media/image.jpg* or *...png*.

 Media file pathnames are case-sensitive, and we recommend using *all lowercase characters*, including the suffix ending. Also, since the code template automatically resizes images to fit, we recommend that you *reduce the size* of any images to 600 × 400 pixels or smaller before uploading to make sure your map operates smoothly.

Location, latitude, longitude

These place your markers at points on the map. Although the code template requires only latitude and longitude, it's wise to paste an address or place name into the *Location* column as a reminder to correspond with the numerical coordinates. Use the Geocoding by SmartMonkey add-on from "Geocode Addresses in Google Sheets" on page 23 and select Add-ons > "Geocoding by SmartMonkey" > "Geocode details" to create a new sheet with sample data and display results for three new columns: *Latitude, Longitude,* and *Address found.* Paste in your own address data and repeat the previous step to geocode it, then copy and paste the results into your *Points* sheet.

---

2 Learn about HTML syntax at W3Schools (*https://oreil.ly/hQdr3*).

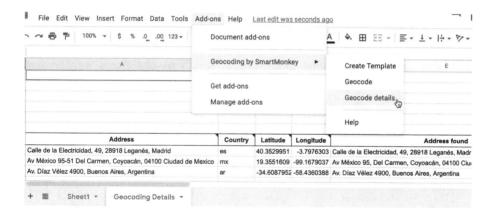

Optional table of viewable markers

Displays an interactive table at the bottom of your map. In the Options tab, set *Display Table* (cell B30) to *On*. You can also adjust the Table Height and modify the display of Table Columns by entering the column headers, separated with commas.

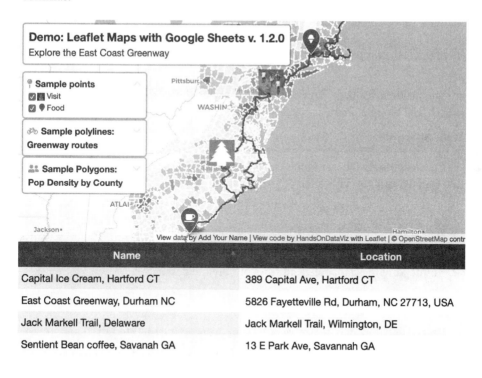

Name	Location
Capital Ice Cream, Hartford CT	389 Capital Ave, Hartford CT
East Coast Greenway, Durham NC	5826 Fayetteville Rd, Durham, NC 27713, USA
Jack Markell Trail, Delaware	Jack Markell Trail, Wilmington, DE
Sentient Bean coffee, Savanah GA	13 E Park Ave, Savannah GA

Optional custom markers

To create your own custom marker, such as a thumbnail photo icon, use any image editing tool to reduce a photo to a square of 64 × 64 pixels. Save it in PNG format and choose a filename using all lowercase characters with no spaces. Upload the image to the *media* folder in your GitHub repo as described previously. In the *Marker Icon* column, enter the file pathname in this format: *media/imagename-small.png*. In the *Custom Size* column, set the dimensions to 64x64 or similar, such as 40x40 if desired.

Group	Marker Icon	Marker Color	Icon Color	Custom
Visit	media/calais-64.jpg			40x40
Food	fa-ice-cream	green	white	
Visit	media/delaware-64.jpg			40x40
Visit	media/ecg-logo-64.png			40x40
Food	fa-coffee	green	white	
Visit	media/keywest-64.jpg			40x40

Open the browser tab that displays your live map and refresh the page to see your changes. If your changes don't appear within a few seconds, see the Appendix.

F. Remove or display point, polygon, or polylines data and legends

By default, the demo map displays three types of data—points, polygons, and polylines—and their legends. You can remove any of these from your map by modifying your linked Google Sheet.

To remove points:

1. In the Options tab, set *Point Legend Position* (cell B27) to Off to hide it.
2. In the Points tab, delete all rows of point data.

To remove polylines:

1. In the Options tab, set *Polyline Legend Position* (cell B36) to Off to hide it.
2. In the Polylines tab, delete all rows of polyline data.

To remove polygons:

1. In the Polygons tab, set *Polygon Legend Position* (cell B4) to Off to hide it.
2. Also in the Polygons tab, set *Polygon GeoJSON URL* (cell B6) to remove that data from your map.

3. In the next tab, Polygons1, use the tab drop-down menu to select Delete to remove the entire sheet.

You've already learned how to add more markers in the Points tab. If you wish to add new polygon or polyline data, you'll need to prepare those files in GeoJSON format using either "Draw and Edit with GeoJson.io" on page 341 or "Edit and Join with Mapshaper" on page 346.

After you've prepared your GeoJSON data, name the files using all lowercase characters and no spaces, and upload them into the *geojson* subfolder of your GitHub repo. Then update these settings in your linked Google Sheet.

To display polylines:

1. In the Options tab, make sure *Polyline Legend Position* (cell B36) is visible by selecting "topleft" or a similar position.

2. In the Polylines tab, enter the GeoJSON URL pathname to the file you uploaded to your GitHub repo, such as *geodata/polygons.geojson*. Then insert a Display Name, Description, and Color.

To display polygons:

1. In the Polygons tab, make sure *Polygon Legend Position* (cell B4) is visible by selecting "topleft" or a similar position.

2. In *Polygon GeoJSON URL* (cell B6), enter the pathname to the file you uploaded to your GitHub repo, such as *geodata/polygons.geojson*.

3. You can change the *Polygon Legend Title* (cell B3) and add an optional *Polygon Legend Icon* (cell B5).

4. Edit the Polygon Data and Color Settings sections to modify the labels and ranges to align with the properties of your GeoJSON file. In the *Property Range Color Palette*, you can automatically select a color scheme from the ColorBrewer tool we described in "Map Design Principles" on page 160, or manually insert colors of your choice in the cell below.

5. Read the *Hints* column in the *Polygons* sheet for tips on how to enter data.

6. If you wish to display multiple polygon layers, use the *Polygons* tab drop-down menu to Duplicate the sheet, and name additional sheets in this format: *Polygons1*, *Polygons2*, etc.

Now you're ready to finalize your map. If you wish to share your map link with the public, read the options here and choose either step G or step H.

We reserve the right to change *our* Google Sheets API key at any time, especially if other people overuse or abuse it. This means that you *must* finalize your map using either step G or H before sharing it publicly, because it will *stop working* if we change our key.

G. Save each Google Sheets tab as a CSV file and upload to GitHub

If you've finished entering most of your data into your Google Sheets, downloading them into separate CSV files and uploading those into your GitHub repo is the *best* long-term preservation strategy. This approach keeps your map and data together in the same GitHub repo and removes the risk that your map will break due to an interruption to Google services. Plus, you can still edit your map data. If this approach makes sense, follow these steps:

1. In your Google Sheets, go to each tab and select File > Download into CSV format, to create a separate file for each tab.

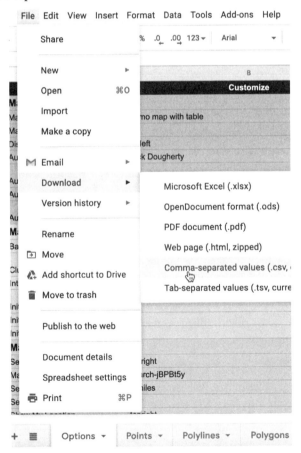

2. Shorten each filename as shown in the following list. The names must be exact. Only the first file (*Options.csv*) is required; the others are optional, depending on your data:

- *Options.csv*

- *Points.csv*

- *Polylines.csv*

- *Polygons.csv* (If additional files, name them: *Polygons1.csv*, *Polygons2.csv*, etc.)

- *Notes.csv* (or *.txt*) Recommended to keep any notes with your data, but not required.

3. In your GitHub repo, click the *csv* subfolder to open it, select "Add file" > "Upload files," and upload all of the CSV files above into this subfolder. The Leaflet template code checks here first for data, and if it finds CSV files with the names above, it will pull the map data directly from them, instead of your Google Sheets. *Remember* that from this point forward, any edits in your Google Sheet will *no longer appear automatically* in your map.

4. If you wish to edit your map after uploading your CSV files, you have two options. You can make small edits directly to your CSV files by opening them in the GitHub web interface. Or you can make larger edits in the Google Sheet, repeating the previous steps to download them in CSV format and upload them to replace your existing files on GitHub.

H. Get your own Google Sheets API Key to insert into the code

As an alternative to step G, if you wish to continue to store your map data in your Google Sheets that is published online, go to "Get Your Google Sheets API Key" on page 321, and insert it into the Leaflet map code as described, to avoid overusing our key. Google Sheets requires an API key to maintain reasonable usage limits (*https:// oreil.ly/3Wd-W*) on its service. You can get a free Google Sheets API key if you have a personal Google account, but *not* a Google Suite account provided by your school or business. If problems arise, see the Appendix.

Leaflet Storymaps with Google Sheets

The Leaflet Storymaps code template is designed to show a point-by-point guided tour, with a scrolling narrative to display text, images, audio, video, and scanned map backgrounds, as shown in Figure 12-3. You enter all of your map data into a linked Google Sheet (or CSV file) or upload it into a GitHub repository, as shown in Figure 12-4. In addition, the Leaflet Storymaps template allows you to customize the appearance of your data and add more layers, such as historical maps and geographic boundaries, which you'll learn how to prepare in Chapter 13. Furthermore, the story-map design is responsive, so that it appears top-to-bottom on smaller screens (where width is smaller than 768 pixels), and automatically switches to side-by-side on larger ones. Finally, the Leaflet template is built on flexible open source software that's written primarily in JavaScript, a very common coding language for the web, so you can customize it further if you have skills or support from a developer.

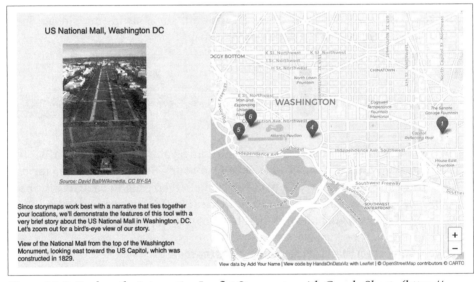

Figure 12-3. Explore the interactive Leaflet Storymaps with Google Sheets (https://oreil.ly/agGac). This demo version illustrates features of the code template while telling a brief story about the US National Mall in Washington, DC.

Chapter	Media Link	Media Credit	Media Credit Link	Description
US National Mall, Washington DC	https://upload.wikimedia.org/wikipedia/common s/thumb/a/a4/Mall-002.JPG/400px-Mall-002.JP G	Source: David Ball/Wikimedia, CC BY-SA	https://commons.wikimedi a.org/wiki/File:Mall-002.JP G	Since storymaps work best with a narr your locations, we'll demonstrate the fo a very brief story about the US Nation: DC. Let's zoom out for a bird's-eye vie story. View of the National Ma Washington Monument, looking east to which was constructed in 1829.
	media/google-sheet-screenshot.png	Screenshot of linked Google Sheet.		Right-click on the tiny "View data" link map to open the contents of the linked new tab. Each row is a chapter, which story, links to media, and data about e The Google Sheet also includes an "C settings for the overall map appearanc
Washington Monument	media/washington-monument-nps.png	Source: US National Park Service, public domain	https://www.nps.gov/nama /learn/photosmultimedia/p hotogallery.htm	You can upload JPG or PNG images ir of your GitHub repository and enter th the linked Google Sheet. The template images to fit the scrolling narrative, bu
Lincoln Memorial	https://live.staticflickr.com/3747/9114059928_b 5f4d56ce6_z.jpg	Source: Anthony Citrano/Flickr, Cr	https://flic.kr/p/eTnWuh	Also, you can link directly to photos in such as Flickr and Wikimedia. To add Share button, choose a small-to-medic embed code, and paste only the portic address that begins with "https://live.st ends in JPG or PNG. To add a Wikime small-to-medium size and copy its dire JPG or PNG. Always credit your imag∈ Lincoln Memorial was constructed at t! Mall in 1922.
				You can display multiple images for or a series of rows in the Google Sheet. I Location information only in the first ro leave those fields blank for the other r∈

+ ▤ Chapters ▾   Options ▾   Notes ▾   Geocoding Details ▾

Figure 12-4. View the online Google Sheet template (https://oreil.ly/Sabon) that feeds data into the Leaflet Storymaps demo above.

We created Leaflet Storymaps with Google Sheets to fill a gap that was not addressed by other tools. To be clear, other storymap platforms are easier for beginners to start using right away, such as the free and open source Knight Lab StoryMap platform (*https://oreil.ly/Gtzyj*), and also the subscriber-only, proprietary ArcGIS StoryMaps platform (*https://oreil.ly/fhIb1*), successor to the older Esri Story Maps platform (*https://oreil.ly/K0ped*). We don't recommend either of them because both lack *data portability*, meaning that you can't easily export any data or images you enter, something we cautioned you to watch out for when we discussed how to choose tools wisely in Chapter 1. By contrast, all of the data you enter into the Leaflet Storymaps-linked Google Sheet and GitHub repo can easily be migrated to other platforms, as visualization technology evolves in the future.

Explore the Gallery of Leaflet Storymaps with Google Sheets in Table 12-2 to see what other people created with this template.

Table 12-2. Gallery of Leaflet Storymaps with Google Sheets

Synagogue Map, Past and Present (*https://oreil.ly/bE8X1*) by Elizabeth Rose, Jewish Historical Society of Greater Hartford

Mapping the Upper Missouri (*https://oreil.ly/tp89f*) by Jen Andrella

Kensington Remembers (*https://oreil.ly/7_Ngd*) by Gordon Coonfield, Erica Hayes, James Parente, David Uspal, Cheyenne Zaremba

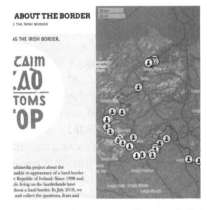

We Need to Talk about the Border (*https://oreil.ly/laVcY*) by Elisabeth Blanchet and Laurent Gontier

Tutorial Requirements and Overview

Before you begin, you must have a Google Drive account (*https://drive.google.com*) and know how to make a copy in Google Sheets, as described in "Make a Copy of a Google Sheet" on page 19. Also, you must have a GitHub account (*https://github.com*) and know how to edit and host code with GitHub, as described in Chapter 10. We omitted some screenshots below that illustrate steps we previously covered, so if you get lost, go back to those chapters.

You'll notice that this tutorial outline is similar to the one in the previous section, but the links in the first part are different, and several steps in the second part are new.

This tutorial involves multiple steps, so we created this outline to provide a broad overview. In the first part, you'll create and publish your copies of two templates, one for GitHub and another for its linked Google Sheet:

- "A. Copy the GitHub template and publish your version with GitHub Pages"
- "B. File > Make a copy of Google Sheet template, share, and publish"
- "C. Paste your Google Sheet browser address in two places in your GitHub repo"
- "D. Update your Google Sheet Options and refresh your live map"

In the second part, you'll learn how to geocode and customize point data in the linked Google Sheet, upload images and other map data to your GitHub repo, and add scanned background map layers if desired:

- "E. Add text, media, markers, and geocode locations in the Chapters tab"
- "F. Optional: Add historical map image or GeoJSON overlays"

In the third part, you have two options to finalize your map before publicly sharing with others:

- "G. Save each Google Sheets tab as a CSV file and upload to GitHub"
- "H. Get your own Google Sheets API Key to insert into the code"

If any problems arise, see the Appendix.

Now that you have a better sense of the big picture, let's get started with the first part of the tutorial.

A. Copy the GitHub template and publish your version with GitHub Pages

1. Open the GitHub code template (*https://oreil.ly/ZWoxB*) in a new tab.
2. In the upper-right corner of the code template, sign in to your free GitHub account.
3. In the upper-right corner, click the green "Use this template" button to make a copy of the repository in your GitHub account. On the next screen, name your repo *leaflet-storymaps-with-google-sheets* or choose a different meaningful name in all lowercase. Click the "Create repository from template" button.

Your copy of the repo will follow this format:

```
https://github.com/USERNAME/leaflet-storymaps-with-google-sheets
```

4. In your new copy of the code repo, click the upper-right Settings button and scroll way down to the GitHub Pages area. In the drop-down menu, change Source from None to Main, keep the default /(root) setting, and press Save. This step prompts GitHub to publish a live version of your map on the public web, where anyone can access it in their browser if they have the web address.

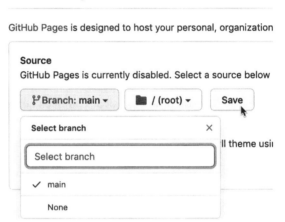

5. Scroll down to the GitHub Pages section again, and copy the link to your published website, which will appear in this format:

```
https://USERNAME.github.io/leaflet-maps-with-google-sheets
```

6. Scroll up to the top, and click on your repo name to go back to its main page.

7. At the top level of your repo main page, click on README.md, and click the pencil icon to edit this file.

8. Delete the link to *our* live site, and paste in the link to *your* published site. Scroll down to Commit your changes.

9. On your repo main page, right-click the link to open your live map in a new tab. Be patient. GitHub Pages normally will display your live map within 30 seconds, but sometimes it may require several minutes to appear.

B. File > Make a copy of Google Sheet template, share, and publish

1. Open the Google Sheets template (*https://oreil.ly/PZRev*) in a new tab.

2. Sign into your Google account, and select File > "Make a copy" to save your own version of this Google Sheet on your Google Drive.

3. Click the blue Share button, click "Change to anyone with the link," then Done. This publicly shares your map data, which is required to make this template work.

4. Go to File > "Publish to the web," and click the green Publish button to publish the entire document so that the Leaflet code can read it. Then click the upper-right X symbol to close this window.

5. At the top of your browser, copy your Google Sheet address or URL (which usually ends in ...*XYZ/edit#gid=0*). Do *not* copy the "Published to the web" address (which usually ends in ...*XYZ/pubhtml*) because that link is slightly different and won't work in this template.

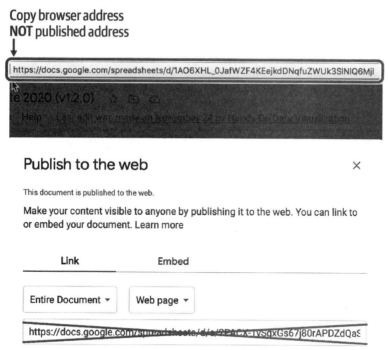

C. Paste your Google Sheet browser address in two places in your GitHub repo

Our next task is to link your published Google Sheet to your Leaflet code in GitHub, so that it can pull your data from the Sheet to display on the map:

1. At the top of your GitHub repo, click to open the file named *google-doc-url.js*, and click the pencil symbol to edit it.

2. Paste *your* Google Sheet address or URL (which usually ends in *…XYZ/edit#gid=0*) to replace *our* existing URL. Be careful not to erase the single quotation marks or the semicolon at the end. Scroll down to Commit your changes. See separate instructions about the Google API key further below.

3. Also, let's paste your Google Sheet URL in a second place to help you keep track of it. In your GitHub repo, click the *README.md* file to open it, click the pencil symbol to edit it, and paste *your* Google Sheet URL to replace *our* existing URL. Scroll down to Commit your changes.

Feel free to remove any other content from the README that you don't wish to keep.

D. Update your Google Sheet Options and refresh your live map

Now that your published Google Sheet is linked to your live map, go to the Options tab to update any of these items:

- Storymap Title
- Storymap Subtitle with code for downward arrow:

<small>Scroll down <i class='fa fa-chevron-down'></i></small>

- Author Name
- Author Email or Website
- Author GitHub Repo Link

Open the browser tab that displays your live map and refresh the page to see your changes. If your changes don't appear within a few seconds, see the Appendix.

E. Add text, media, markers, and geocode locations in the Chapters tab

We can now start to add new content to your map. In the Chapters tab of your Google Sheet, you'll see column headers to organize and display interactive markers on your map. Replace the demonstration data with your own, but do *not* delete or rename the column headers because the Leaflet code looks for these specific names:

Chapter
> The title appearing at the top of each section in the scrolling narrative.

Media link
> You have several options to display either an image, audio, or video in each chapter. For images, you can insert an external link to an online service (such as Flickr), as long as it begins with *https* (secure) and ends with either *.jpg* or *.png*. You can also insert a YouTube video link. Or you can upload an image file into the *media* subfolder in your GitHub repo, and enter the pathname in the Google Sheet in this format: *media/your-file-name.jpg* or *...png*. Similarly, you can upload an audio file in .mp3 (recommended) or *.ogg* or *.wav* format.

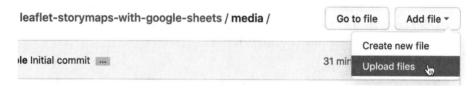

 Media file pathnames are case-sensitive, and we recommend using *all lowercase characters*, including the suffix ending. Also, since the code template automatically resizes images to fit, we recommend that you *reduce the size* of any images to 600 × 400 pixels or smaller before uploading to make sure your storymap loads faster.

Media credit
> To display text about the origin of the media, such as "Source..."

Media credit link
> Add a direct link to the source information in the Media Credit text above.

Description

Designed to display approximately a paragraph or less of text for the Chapter. You may insert HTML tags to add line breaks (such as <br>) or to open external links in a new tab, such as:[3]

```
<a href='https://www.w3schools.com/' target='_blank'>Visit W3Schools</a>
```

Zoom

Leaflet's default zoom levels are between 0 (world view) and 18 (individual buildings), and most free basemap tiles, such as those provided by Stamen or CartoDB are available for each level in this range. There exist more detailed basemaps that allow you to use higher values. Experiment with zoom levels to get the best view for your story, and remember that given the same zoom level, larger screens will show larger areas compared to smaller screens, such as smartphones.

Marker

Select either Numbered (the default), Plain, or Hidden. The latter works best when assigning several chapters to one location (to avoid stacking markers on top of each other) or when zooming out for a broader view (without highlighting one specific location).

Marker color

Insert any standard web color name such as `blue` or `darkblue`, or insert a web color code such as `#775307` or `rgba(200,100,0,0.5)`. See options at W3Schools Color Names (*https://oreil.ly/2dapU*).

Location, latitude, longitude

These place your markers at points on the map. Although the code template requires only latitude and longitude, it's wise to paste an address or place name into the *Location* column as a reminder to correspond with the numerical coordinates. Use the Geocoding by SmartMonkey add-on from "Geocode Addresses in Google Sheets" on page 23 and select Add-ons > "Geocoding by SmartMonkey" > "Geocode details" to create a new sheet with sample data and display results for three new columns: *Latitude, Longitude*, and *Address found*. Paste in your own address data and repeat the previous step to geocode it, then copy and paste the results into your *Points* sheet.

---

3 Learn about HTML syntax at W3Schools (*https://oreil.ly/hQdr3*).

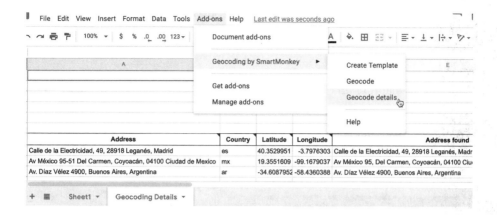

You can display multiple images for one location by creating a series of rows, but list only the Chapter and Location information in the first row of the series, and leave it blank for the others.

Open the browser tab that displays your live map and refresh the page to see your changes. If your changes do not appear within a few seconds, see the Appendix.

F. Optional: Add historical map image or GeoJSON overlays

The code template allows you to enrich your story by placing two different types of layers on top of the background map: georeferenced map images (such as a historical map) and GeoJSON geodata (such as a pathway, boundary lines, or a color-coded choropleth map). You can add both types of layers to specific chapters or the entire story. Also, you can adjust the transparency level to reveal or hide the present-day background map. To prepare both types of layers, you will need to jump ahead to Chapter 13, but here we'll explain the steps to insert them in your storymap template.

To add a historical map overlay to one or more storymap chapters, it must be *georeferenced* (also called georectified), which means to digitally align the static map image with a more precise present-day interactive map. If you have a high-quality static image of a historical map, use the Map Warper tool, as described in "Georeference with Map Warper" on page 360, to align several known points with those on a present-day interactive map. Map Warper transforms the static map image into interactive map tiles, and publicly hosts them online with a link in Google/Open-StreetMap format, similar to *https://mapwarper.net/maps/tile/14781/{z}/{x}/{y}.png*. Or you can search for historical maps that have already been georeferenced and transformed into tiles (and volunteer for crowdsourcing efforts to align maps) on platforms such as Map Warper (*https://mapwarper.net*) and the New York Public Library Map Warper (*http://maps.nypl.org/warper*). Although map tile links are *not* viewable in a normal browser, they can be displayed by the Leaflet Storymaps code. Enter the tile link and your desired transparency level into the Overlay columns in the Chapters tab of your Google Sheet template, as shown in Figure 12-5:

Overlay
> Enter a map tile link in Google/OpenStreetMap format, similar to the previous sample.

Overlay transparency
> Enter a number from 0 (transparent) to 1 (opaque). The default is 0.7.

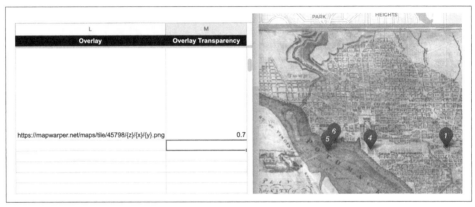

Figure 12-5. Enter a map tile link and transparency level into the Google Sheet template (on left) to display it in one or more storymap chapters (on right).

To add a visible path, geographic boundaries, or a filled choropleth map to your story, consider adding a GeoJSON data layer to one or more chapters. Read about GeoJSON and geospatial data formats in "Geospatial Data and GeoJSON" on page 336, where you can also learn how to find existing GeoJSON boundary files (see "Find GeoJSON Boundary Files" on page 340), draw or edit your own geodata with the Geo-Json.io tool (see "Draw and Edit with GeoJson.io" on page 341) or Mapshaper tool (see "Edit and Join with Mapshaper" on page 346). We recommend that you name your Geo-JSON files in lowercase characters with no spaces. Upload the file to your GitHub repository by opening the geojson folder and selecting "Add file" > "Upload files." In your Google Sheet template, enter the pathname in the *GeoJSON Overlay* column in this format: *geojson/your-file-name.geojson*, as shown in Figure 12-6.

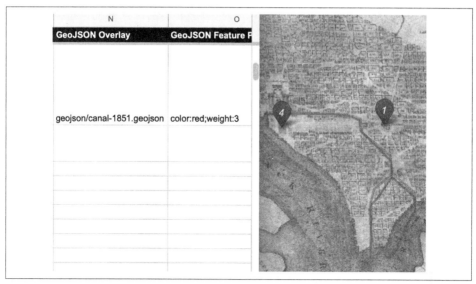

Figure 12-6. Enter the pathname in the GeoJSON Overlay column (on left) to display it in one or more storymap chapters (on right).

When you create or edit GeoJSON data with a tool like GeoJson.io (see "Draw and Edit with GeoJson.io" on page 341), you can directly edit its feature properties. If you wish to display the same properties that you assigned to your GeoJSON file in your storymap, we recommend naming them as follows:

- weight (width of line or polygon border; storymap template default is 1px)
- color (of line or polygon border; default is gray)
- opacity (of line or polygon border; default is 0.5)
- fillColor (of polygon; default is white)
- fillOpacity (of polygon; default is 0.7)

Or you can enter properties and CSS codes in the *GeoJSON Feature Properties* template column, in this format, separated by semicolons, with no quotation marks required: `weight:3; color:red; opacity:1; fillColor:orange; fillOpacity: 0.9`. You can assign colors with standard names, hex codes, or RGBa values as described in the W3Schools Colors Picker (*https://oreil.ly/KbeOR*).

Inside the template you'll discover more ways to customize your storymap, such as:

- Insert logo (see Options tab in Google Sheets)
- Insert Google Analytics tracking ID (see Options tab in Google Sheets)
- Adjust title size and font (go to *css/styles.css* file in GitHub)
- Insert a horizontal divider in Chapter text (copy and paste this text into Description field in Google Sheets, and avoid changing single quote marks into curly apostrophes):

```
<span style='display:block;width:100%;height:1px;background-color:
         silver; margin: 20px 0;'></span>
```

Now you're ready to finalize your map. If you wish to share your map link with the public, read the options here and choose either step G or step H.

 We reserve the right to change *our* Google Sheets API key at any time, especially if other people overuse or abuse it. This means that you *must* finalize your map using either step G or H before sharing it publicly because it will *stop working* if we change our key.

G. Save each Google Sheets tab as a CSV file and upload to GitHub

If you have finished entering most of your data into your Google Sheets, downloading it into separate CSV files and uploading those into your GitHub repo is the *best* long-term preservation strategy. This approach keeps your map and data together in the same GitHub repo, and removes the risk that your map will break due to an interruption to Google services. Plus, you can still edit your map data. If this approach makes sense, follow these steps:

1. In your Google Sheets, go to each tab and select File > Download into CSV format, to create a separate file for each tab.
2. Shorten each filename as shown. The names must be exact. The first two files are required, and others are optional:
   - *Chapters.csv*
   - *Options.csv*
   - *Notes.csv* (or *.txt*) Recommended to keep any notes with your data, but not required.
3. In your GitHub repo, click the *csv* subfolder to open it, select "Add file" > "Upload files," and upload all of the CSV files listed into this subfolder. The Leaflet template code checks here first for data, and if it finds CSV files with these names, it will pull the map data directly from them, instead of your Google

Sheets. Remember that from this point forward, any edits in your Google Sheet will *no longer appear automatically* in your map.

4. If you wish to edit your map after uploading your CSV files, you have two options. You can make small edits directly to your CSV files by opening them in the GitHub web interface, or you can make larger edits in the Google Sheet, repeating the previous steps to download them in CSV format and upload them to replace your existing files on GitHub.

H. Get your own Google Sheets API Key to insert into the code

As an alternative to step G, if you wish to continue to store your map data in your Google Sheets that is published online, go to "Get Your Google Sheets API Key" on page 321, and insert it into the Leaflet map code as described, to avoid overusing our key. Google Sheets requires an API key to maintain reasonable usage limits (*https:// oreil.ly/3Wd-W*) on its service. You can get a free Google Sheets API key if you have a personal Google account, but *not* a Google Suite account provided by your school or business. If problems arise, see the Appendix.

Get Your Google Sheets API Key

After you've created your own version of Leaflet Maps with Google Sheets or Leaflet Storymaps with Google Sheets (see "Leaflet Maps with Google Sheets" on page 294 and "Leaflet Storymaps with Google Sheets" on page 308), there are two ways to finalize your map, as described previously: either save your Google Sheet tabs in CSV format or get your own Google Sheets API key and paste it into your Leaflet code on GitHub. You'll learn about the latter method in this section.

As of January 2021, Google Sheets version 4 requires an API key to allow code to read your data to maintain reasonable limits on use of its services. For Google Sheets, the limit is five hundred requests per hundred seconds per project, and one hundred requests per hundred seconds per user. There's no daily usage limit.

Before you begin:

- You need a personal Google account, *not* a Google Suite account issued by your school or business.

- This tutorial presumes that you have already completed "Leaflet Maps with Google Sheets" on page 294 or "Leaflet Storymaps with Google Sheets" on page 308 and wish to finalize your map.

- If you already created a Google Sheets API key for one template, you can also use that key for another template.

 Your screen instructions may vary from those that follow.

You can get your own free Google Sheets API key by taking the following steps. Overall, you'll create and name your Google Cloud project, enable the Google Sheets API to allow a computer to read data from your Google Sheet, copy your new API key, and paste it into the Leaflet code in place of our key:

1. Go to the Google Developers Console (*https://oreil.ly/69spv*) and log in to your Google account. Google may ask you to identify your country and agree to its terms of service.

2. Click "Create a Project" on the opening screen. Alternatively, go to the upper-left drop-down menu to "Select a project" > "New project."

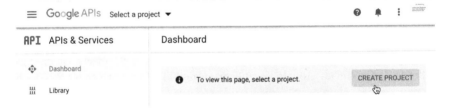

3. In the next screen, give your new project a meaningful short name to remind you of its purpose, such as *handsondataviz*. You do not need to create an organization or parent folder. Then click Create.

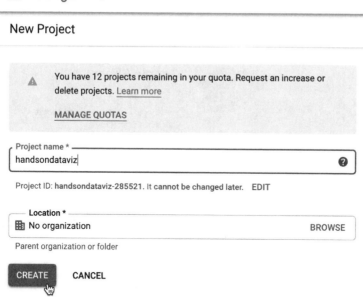

4. In the next screen, press "Enable APIs and Services" at the top of the menu. Make sure that your new project name appears near the top.

5. In the next screen, type **Google Sheets** into the search bar, and select this result.

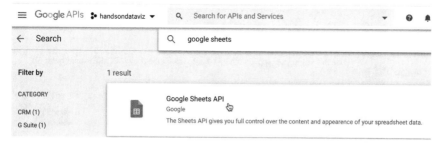

6. In the next screen, select Enable to turn on the Google Sheets API for your project.

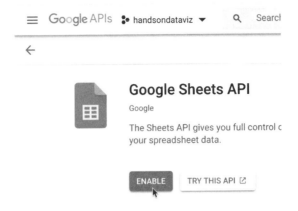

Google Sheets API

Google

The Sheets API gives you full control c
your spreadsheet data.

ENABLE   TRY THIS API ☑

7. In the left sidebar menu, click Credentials, then click "Create Credentials" and select "API key."

8. In the next screen, the console will generate your API key. Copy it, then press Restrict Key.

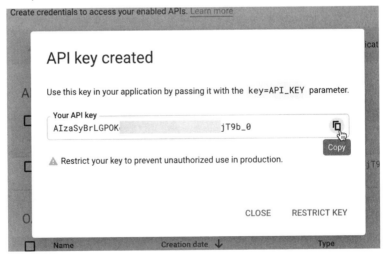

9. In the new window, under "API restrictions," choose the "Restrict key" radio button. In the drop-down menu that appears, choose Google Sheets API, then click Save.

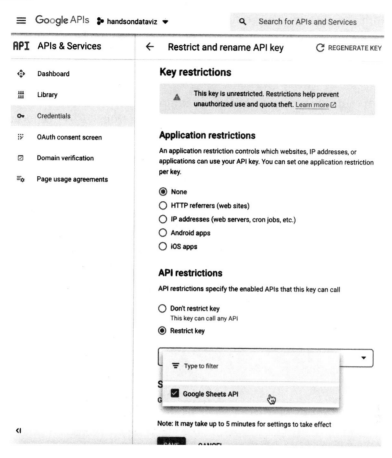

10. In your Leaflet map code on your GitHub repo, open the *google-doc-url.js* file, click the pencil symbol to edit it, and paste in *your* Google Sheets API key to replace *our* key. Be careful not to erase the single quote marks or the semicolon. Scroll down to Commit your changes.

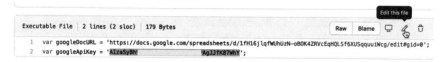

You might receive a notification from GitHub stating that you have an exposed API key, but don't worry. This key can be used only with Google Sheets, you received it for free, and you didn't attach any billing information to it, so Google cannot charge you for its use.

Now that you've learned how to create a Google Sheets API key to use with Leaflet Maps with Google Sheets or Leaflet Storymaps with Google Sheets, in the next sections you'll learn more about other types of Leaflet map templates.

Leaflet Maps with CSV Data

This open source template is designed to improve your coding skills by demonstrating how to create a Leaflet point map that pulls data from a CSV file located in your GitHub repo. While you can make the same type of map on other platforms, such as Google My Maps as described in "Point Map with Google My Maps" on page 177, you'll learn more about how the Leaflet code library works by doing it yourself.

Figure 12-7 shows a simple point map of some colleges and universities in Connecticut. Instead of individually creating markers in JavaScript using Leaflet's L.marker() function, the point data is stored in a local CSV file (*data.csv*) that's easy to modify in any text editor or spreadsheet. Each time the map is loaded by the browser, point data from the CSV file is read and markers are generated "on the fly."

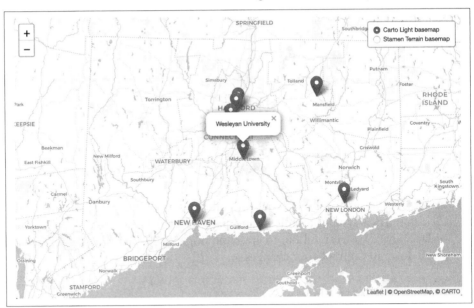

Figure 12-7. Explore the interactive Leaflet point map with CSV data (https://oreil.ly/ouz0b).

You can adapt this template to create your own point map by following these instructions:

1. Visit the GitHub repo (*https://oreil.ly/_n_Zm*) that stores the code for this template. Make sure you're logged in, and press "Use this template button" to create a copy of this repository in your own GitHub account.

2. Put your point data inside *data.csv*. The only relevant columns that will be read by the template are *Latitude*, *Longitude*, and *Title*. The first two determine the location of the marker, and the last one is displayed in a pop-up. The order of columns doesn't matter. There can be other columns in the dataset, but they will be ignored.

   Your data can look like the following:

   ```
   Title,Latitude,Longitude
   Trinity College,41.745167,-72.69263
   Wesleyan University,41.55709,-72.65691
   ```

3. Depending on the geography of your points, you'll want to change the default position of the map when it's first loaded. In *index.html*, find the <script> tag, and edit the following chunk of code:

   ```
   var map = L.map('map', {
     center: [41.57, -72.69], // Default latitude and longitude on start
     zoom: 9,  // Between 1 & 18; decrease to zoom out, increase to zoom in
     scrollWheelZoom: false
   });
   ```

We used default Leaflet markers for code simplicity, but you may want to use custom icons instead. The following code snippet can give you an idea of how to set it up in your GitHub repository, where you insert your unique pathname to your icon in place of the sample.

```
var marker = L.marker([row.Latitude, row.Longitude], {
  opacity: 1,
  // Customize your icon
  icon: L.icon({
    iconUrl: 'path/to/your/icon.png',
    iconSize: [40, 60]
  })
}).bindPopup(row.Title);
```

To learn more, see this helpful Leaflet documentation example about custom icons (*https://oreil.ly/pHCHn*).

Leaflet Heatmap Points with CSV Data

Heatmaps turn individual points into hotspots or clusters, allowing viewers to explore spatial distributions of events, such as areas of high and low population density or incidents of crime. Figure 12-8 shows an interactive heatmap of bike theft locations in London between January and July 2020. The underlying data are coordinate locations for each reported bike theft, which the `Leaflet.heat` (*https://oreil.ly/lmwPQ*) plug-in transforms into areas of various densities. Red shows areas of highest density, or areas where bike theft happened most often. When you zoom in, areas are recalculated into more distinct clusters.

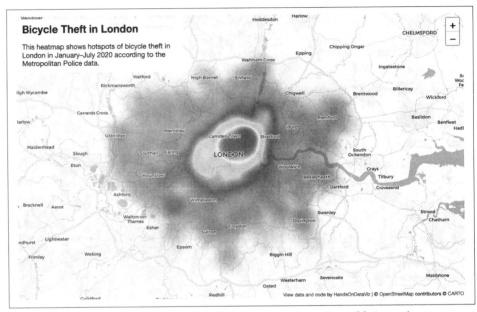

Figure 12-8. Explore the interactive Leaflet Heatmap (https://oreil.ly/r-nwt).

You can adapt the code we used for this London heatmap to create your own:

1. Visit the GitHub repository with our code (*https://oreil.ly/rSLAf*), make sure you're logged in, and click the "Use this template" to make a personal copy of this repo.

2. Modify the map's title and description inside *index.html*.

3. Place your point coordinates data inside *data.csv*. Do *not* insert any column headers. Instead of the traditional order, you must write them in *latitude,longitude* (or y,x) order, one pair per line, with no spaces, like this:

   ```
   51.506585,-0.139387
   51.505467,-0.14655
   51.507758,-0.141284
   ```

4. Depending on your data density, you might want to tweak *radius* and *blur* parameters inside the `<script>` tag of *index.html*:

   ```
   var heat = L.heatLayer(data, {
     radius: 25,
   ```

```
    blur: 15,
  })
```

5. Edit the following chunk of code to set your map's default position and zoom level:

```
var map = L.map('map', {
  center: [51.5, -0.1], // Initial map center
  zoom: 10, // Initial zoom level
})
```

If for some reason you cannot see clusters, make sure your point data is represented in latitude,longitude order, not the other way around. If you have few points, try increasing the value of radius property of L.heatLayer.

Leaflet Searchable Point Map

A searchable point map works best for showing multiple locations, where users can search by name or proximity to a location, or filter by category, with an optional list view. Figure 12-9 shows a powerful Leaflet template of a searchable and filterable point map, which draws from a CSV data file developed by Derek Eder (*https://dere keder.com*) from DataMade in Chicago. This map allows you to show points of interest, filter them by using "Search by name" functionality, and show them as a list instead of points on a map. In addition, the About page gives you plenty of space to describe the purpose and content of your map.

Figure 12-9. Explore the interactive Searchable Map template (https://oreil.ly/wFqyk).

This template uses Leaflet.js in combination with Google Maps API to perform address search.

To begin using the template for your own project, visit the template's GitHub page (*https://oreil.ly/XAaSO*), and fork it so that you get your own copy (Chapter 10 to remind yourself about forks).

Step 1: Prepare Your Data

This template will work with data in CSV (see "Download to CSV or ODS Format" on page 17) and GeoJSON (see "Geospatial Data and GeoJSON" on page 336) formats. If you have an Excel file, save it in CSV format with any spreadsheet tool. The CSV file must have a latitude column and longitude column and all rows must be geocoded. If you have only street-address or location data, learn how to geocode it in "Geocode Addresses in Google Sheets" on page 23.

Step 2: Download and Edit This Template

1. Download or clone this project and fire up your text editor of choice. Open up */js/map.js* and set your map options in the `SearchableMapLib.initialize` function:

   `map_centroid`
   The latitude/longitude (lat/long) you want your map to center on.

   `filePath`
   Path to your map data file. This file needs to be in CSV or GeoJSON format and placed in the *data* folder. This file's first line must be the header, and it must have a latitude column and longitude column.

   `fileType`
   Set if you are loading in a *csv* or *geojson* file.

2. Edit the templates in the *templates* folder for how you want your data displayed. These templates use embedded JavaScript templating (EJS), which allows the display of your variables with HTML, as well as conditional logic. Read more in the EJS documentation (*https://ejs.co/#docs*).

   /templates/hover.ejs
   Template for when you hover over a dot on the map.

   /templates/popup.ejs
   Template for when a dot on the map is clicked.

/templates/table-row.ejs
> Template for each row in the list view.

3. Remove the custom filters and add your own.

index.html
> Custom HTML for filters starts around line 112.

/js/searchable_map_lib.js
> Logic for custom filters starts around line 265.

Step 3: Publish Your Map

1. Before you publish, you'll need to get a free Google Maps API key (*https://oreil.ly/Hi8gd*), which is similar but different from "Get Your Google Sheets API Key" on page 321. Replace the Google Maps API key on this line of *index.html* with yours:

```
<script type="text/javascript"
src="https://maps.google.com/maps/api/js?libraries=places&
key=[YOUR KEY HERE]"></script>
```

2. Upload this map and all the supporting files and folders to your site. This map requires no backend code, so any host will work, such as GitHub Pages, as described in Chapter 10, Netlify (*https://netlify.com*), or your own web server.

Leaflet Maps with Open Data APIs

Learn how to code your own Leaflet map with an API that continuously pulls the most current information directly from an open data repository, similar to the Socrata Open Data map you learned about in "Current Map with Socrata Open Data" on page 207. Leaflet maps can pull and display data from various open data repositories using APIs. Figure 12-10 shows an interactive map of North Dakota counties, colored by population density, with hospitals and emergency medical service (EMS) locations.

This map template pulls data from three different open repository sources:

- Hospital information is pulled directly from the Medicare.org Socrata database (*https://data.medicare.gov*).

- County boundaries and population density are pulled from the North Dakota GIS (*https://www.gis.nd.gov*) ArcGIS server.

- EMS stations are fetched from the Homeland Infrastructure Foundation-Level Data (*https://oreil.ly/XWwD6*) ArcGIS server.

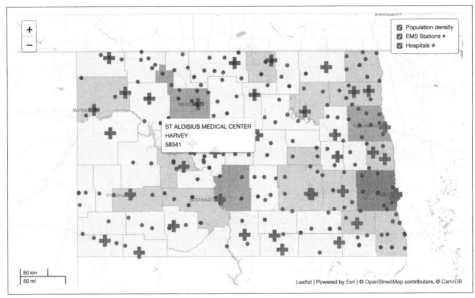

Figure 12-10. Explore the interactive Leaflet Map with Open Data (https://oreil.ly/ ZT8Ow).

You can enable Leaflet to pull data from ArcGIS servers using a free `esri-leaflet` (*https://oreil.ly/Ia-VB*) plug-in. Data from Socrata can be pulled using jQuery's `$.getJSON()` function, and then passed to Leaflet directly using `L.geoJSON()` function.

To adapt this template for your own project:

1. Visit the GitHub repository (*https://oreil.ly/Ir0XH*) that contains the code for the map in Figure 12-10, and press the "Use this template" button to copy the repo to your own GitHub account.

2. All data is pulled from the code inside the `<script>` tag of *index.html*. To pull data from Socrata or another JSON/GeoJSON endpoint, modify the following code snippet with the appropriate URL and icon:

```
/*
  From Medicare's Socrata database, add general hospitals in North Dakota
  using simple filtering on the `state` column, and a GeoJSON endpoint.
  Each point is a custom .png icon with a tool tip containing hospital's name,
  city, and zip code.
*/
$.getJSON("https://data.medicare.gov/resource/xubh-q36u.geojson?state=ND",

  function(data) {

    var hospitals = L.geoJSON(data, {
```

```
    pointToLayer: function(feature, latlng) {
      return L.marker(latlng, {
        icon: L.icon({
          iconUrl: 'images/hospital.png',
          iconSize: [24, 24],
          iconAnchor: [12, 12],
          opacity: 0.5
        })
      }).bindTooltip(
        feature.properties.hospital_name
          + '<br>' + feature.properties.city
          + '<br>' + feature.properties.zip_code
      )
    }
  }).addTo(map)

}

)
```

The following code snippet uses the `esri-leaflet` plug-in to pull polygon data from an ArcGIS server, and creates a choropleth layer based on population density (stored in `POP10_SQMI` variable of each feature, or polygon):

```
var counties = L.esri.featureLayer({
  url:'https://ndgishub.nd.gov/arcgis/rest/services\
/All_GovtBoundaries/MapServer/20',
  style: function(feature) {
    return {
      fillOpacity: 0.5,
      weight: 0.5,
      color: 'silver',
      fillColor: getDensityColor(feature.properties.POP10_SQMI)
    }
  }
}).addTo(map)
```

Here, the `getDensityColor()` function returns a color for a given value based on pre-defined thresholds. In the North Dakota example, population density of more than one hundred people per square mile is assigned the darkest shade of red, while the density of five and fewer is shown with the lightest:

```
var getDensityColor = function(d) {
  return d > 100  ? '#7a0177' :
         d > 50   ? '#c51b8a' :
         d > 20   ? '#f768a1' :
         d > 5    ? '#fbb4b9' :
                    '#feebe2'
}
```

While it's convenient to pull data directly from the source databases, remember that those resources are out of your control (unless you administer them, of course). Data changes often come unannounced. For example, if the dataset owner decides to rename the population density field from POP10_SQMI to Pop10_sqmi, your map will stop showing values correctly. Datasets may get moved to a different domain name or get deleted entirely, so it's wise to have a backup file saved locally.

If you're more concerned about the long-term functioning of your map as opposed to displaying the most up-to-date version of the dataset, you may consider serving your data from local GeoJSON files instead (but ensure first that the data license permits it).

Summary

In this chapter, we introduced Leaflet map templates for common map problems, such as telling stories about places using scrollable interface, showing point data from databases like Socrata, and creating heatmaps to visualize areas of high-event density.

You can use these templates as a base to kickstart your own mapping projects. Leaflet.js is well-documented (*https://oreil.ly/ZjP2J*), and we recommend looking at their tutorials (*https://oreil.ly/pPRJR*) for more inspiration.

In the next chapter, we'll talk about geospatial data and introduce several tools that can convert, create, and edit geospatial files.

CHAPTER 13

Transform Your Map Data

In Chapter 7, we introduced basic concepts about interactive web maps, which are made up of different data layers. When users explore an interactive map, they usually click on the upper layer, which often displays some combination of points, polylines, and polygons on top of a seamless set of basemap tiles that are built from raster or vector data. Whether you create maps with drag-and-drop tools, such as Datawrapper (see "Choropleth Map with Datawrapper" on page 191), or customize Leaflet map code templates (see Chapter 12), you may need to transform data to work with one of these types of map layers.

In this chapter, we'll delve further into geospatial data and its different formats, such as GeoJSON, the open-standard format most commonly used in this book (see "Geospatial Data and GeoJSON" on page 336). You'll learn how to find and extract geographic boundary files in this format from the crowdsourced OpenStreetMap platform in "Find GeoJSON Boundary Files" on page 340. We'll show how to convert or create your own top-level map layer data using the GeoJson.io tool in "Draw and Edit with GeoJson.io" on page 341, and how to edit these layers with spreadsheet data using the Mapshaper tool in "Edit and Join with Mapshaper" on page 346. You'll also learn how to georeference a high-quality static map image and transform it into interactive map tiles using the Map Warper tool in "Georeference with Map Warper" on page 360. All of these free, web-based geodata tools are easy to learn, and in many cases they replace the need for more costly or complex geographic information systems, such as the proprietary ArcGIS and the open source QGIS desktop applications.

We'll conclude in "Bulk Geocode with US Census" on page 361 and "Pivot Points into Polygon Data" on page 363 with strategies to bulk geocode large batches of address data and to pivot points into polygon data, which enables you to display this information in choropleth maps. By the end of this chapter, you should feel much more confident in navigating the somewhat overwhelming world of geospatial data.

Let's start with a general overview of geospatial data, and introduce you to various file formats to ensure that you're ready to create, use, and share map data.

Geospatial Data and GeoJSON

Let's talk about the basics of geospatial data to help you to better understand the map layers that you'll create and edit later in this chapter. The first thing to know about geospatial data is that it consists of two components: *location* and *attribute*. When you use Google Maps to search for a restaurant, you see a red marker on the screen that points to its location in latitude and longitude coordinates, such as 41.7620891, -72.6856295. Attributes include additional information such as the restaurant name, its human-friendly street address, and guest review comments. All of these attributes add value to your location data.

Second, geospatial data can be *raster* or *vector*, a concept we previously introduced in "Map Design Principles" on page 160. In digital maps, raster data often appears as satellite and aerial images, and the quality depends on the resolution of the camera that captured them. If a satellite camera has a 1-meter resolution, its images display the different colors it captured as a grid of cells, which measure 1 meter on each side. Each of these cells appears as a color-coded pixel on our computer screens. If you zoom in too close to a raster image, it may appear fuzzy or pixelated due to the resolution limitations of the original image, as shown in Figure 13-1.

By contrast, vector data often appears in digital maps as pictorial images of buildings, rivers, and regions. Vector maps can be created by humans or algorithms when they draw points, polylines, and polygons from raster satellite or aerial images, from devices such as GPS trackers that record runs or hikes, or from other sources. For example, much of OpenStreetMap (*https://oreil.ly/LC190*) has been built by volunteers who trace outlines of objects from satellite images, and anyone can sign up to help expand this crowdsourced map of the world. Unlike raster maps, vector maps remain sharply focused at any zoom level because every point and line is represented by latitude and longitude coordinates, which can be expressed with precise decimals. In addition, while raster data is generally limited to one value per cell (such as color for traditional satellite images or height above sea level for digital elevation models), vector data can contain multiple attributes about each object (such as its name, street address, and comments). Moreover, vector map files tend to be smaller in size than raster ones, which is important when we create and upload maps to share and display online.

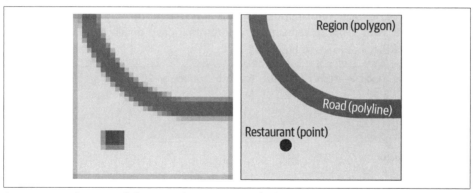

Figure 13-1. Geospatial data can be a raster grid of cells (on the left) or a vector collection of points, polylines, and polygons (on the right).

Because we focus on vector data in several sections of this chapter, let's take a look at some of its most common file formats, starting with GeoJSON, the format that works best with our recommended tools.

GeoJSON

GeoJSON (*https://geojson.org*) is a popular map data format, based on an open standard created in 2016, with file extensions *.geojson* or *.json*. The following code snippet represents a single point in GeoJSON format, with latitude of 41.76 and longitude of −72.67, and a name attribute (also known as a property) whose value is Hartford:

```
{
  "type": "Feature",
  "geometry": {
    "type": "Point",
    "coordinates": [-72.67, 41.76]
  },
  "properties": {
    "name": "Hartford"
  }
}
```

In addition to Point feature type shown above, other GeoJSON types can be Line String (also known as lines or polylines) or Polygon, both of which are represented as arrays of points. The simplicity and readability of GeoJSON allows you to edit it even in the most simple text editor, such as the Atom text editor described in "GitHub Desktop and Atom Text Editor to Code Efficiently" on page 261.

We strongly recommend that you create and edit map data in GeoJSON format, which is supported by the map tools we recommend in this book (such as Datawrapper and Leaflet) and dozens of others. Storing and sharing your geospatial data in GeoJSON ensures that others will be able to use the file without installing bulky or expensive geographical information systems (GIS) desktop applications. Another benefit is that your GitHub repository will automatically display a map preview of any GeoJSON file, as shown in Figure 13-2.

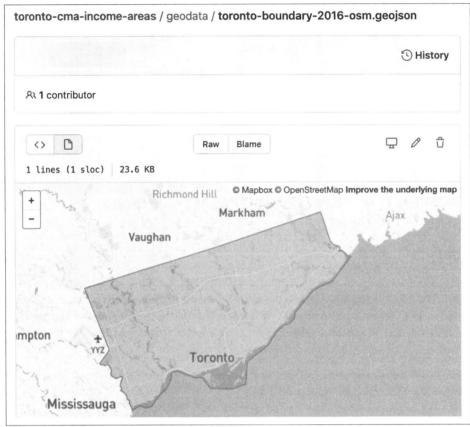

Figure 13-2. GitHub repositories automatically show a map preview for GeoJSON files.

 In GeoJSON format, coordinates are ordered in *longitude–latitude* format, the same as *x* and *y* coordinates in mathematics. But this is the opposite of Google Maps and some other web map tools, which place coordinate values in *latitude–longitude* format. For example, *Hartford, Connecticut* is located at (–72.67, 41.76) according to GeoJSON, but at (41.76, –72.67) in Google Maps. Neither notation is right or wrong. Just make sure you know which one you are dealing with. Tom MacWright created a great summary table showing lat/long order of different geospatial formats and technologies (*https://oreil.ly/XRRjf*).

Now that you've been introduced to the GeoJSON geospatial file format, let's compare it with some other formats.

Shapefiles

The shapefile format was created in the 1990s by Esri, the company that develops ArcGIS software. Shapefiles typically appear in a folder of files with extensions such as *.shp*, *.shx*, and *.dbf*, and the folder may be compressed into a *.zip* file.

Government agencies commonly distribute map data in shapefile format. However, the standard tools for editing shapefiles—ArcGIS and its free and open source cousin, QGIS—are not as easy to learn as other tools in this book. For this reason, we recommend converting shapefiles into GeoJSON files if possible, and you can do this with the Mapshaper tool, discussed in "Edit and Join with Mapshaper" on page 346.

GPS Exchange Format

If you ever recorded your run or bike ride with a GPS device, chances are you ended up with a *.gpx* file. GPS Exchange Format (GPX) is an open standard and is based on XML markup language. Like GeoJSON, you can inspect the contents of a GPX file in any simple text editor. Most likely, you'll see a collection of timestamps and latitude/ longitude coordinates that the GPS device recorded at that particular time. You can convert GPX to GeoJSON format with the GeoJson.io tool, discussed in "Draw and Edit with GeoJson.io" on page 341.

Keyhole Markup Language

The Keyhole Markup Language (KML) format rose in popularity during the late 2000s, when it was developed for Google Earth (*https://www.google.com/earth*), a free and user-friendly tool to view and edit two- and three-dimensional geographic data. KML files were also used with maps powered by Google Fusion Tables, but that tool was dropped by Google in late 2019 (*https://killedbygoogle.com*). You can convert your KML file into GeoJSON format with the GeoJson.io tool described in "Draw and Edit with GeoJson.io" on page 341.

Sometimes *.kml* files are distributed in a compressed *.kmz* format. To learn how to transform them, see "Convert Compressed KMZ to KML" on page 358.

MapInfo TAB

The proprietary TAB format is created and supported by MapInfo, Esri's competitor, and is designed to work well with MapInfo Pro GIS software. Similar to Esri's shapefiles, MapInfo TAB files usually appear in a folder with extensions that end with *.tab*, *.dat*, *.ind*, and some other files. Unfortunately, you'll most likely need MapInfo Pro, QGIS, or ArcGIS to convert these to Shapefile or GeoJSON format.

We've mentioned only a handful of the most common geospatial file formats, and there's a myriad of lesser-known formats (*https://oreil.ly/KT0AO*). Remember that GeoJSON is one of the best, most universal formats for your *vector* data, and we strongly recommend that you store and share your point, polyline, and polygon data in this format. In the next section, we'll describe how to find GeoJSON boundary files for many locations around the globe.

Find GeoJSON Boundary Files

You may be searching for geographic boundary files in GeoJSON format to create a customized map. For example, both the Datawrapper tool described in "Choropleth Map with Datawrapper" on page 191 and the Leaflet map code templates described in Chapter 12 allow you to upload your own GeoJSON files. Since GeoJSON is an open data standard, you may find these files in several open data repositories listed in "Open Data Repositories" on page 57.

Another way to find and download GeoJSON files is the clever Gimme Geodata tool (*https://oreil.ly/1xM5b*), developed by Hans Hack, which provides quick access to multiple layers of OpenStreetMap (*https://openstreetmap.org*) boundary files. When you open the tool, search for a location and click a specific point on the map. The tool displays the names and outlines of different geographic boundaries around that point that have been uploaded into OpenStreetMap, which you can select and download in GeoJSON format. For example, when you search and click on Toronto Centre, the tool displays several neighborhood-level boundaries, the Old Toronto city boundary, the present-day Toronto city boundary, and regional and provincial boundaries, as shown in Figure 13-3. Read more details about each layer to evaluate their accuracy, then select any layer to download in GeoJSON format. The tool also includes an editor (the scissors symbol) to remove water areas from the boundary file (such as deleting Lake Ontario from Toronto). When using any type of data that you downloaded from OpenStreetMap, always credit the source in your final product like this: © OpenStreetMap contributors.[1]

---

[1] Learn more about OpenStreetMap copyright and licensing policy (*https://oreil.ly/5eSzl*).

Figure 13-3. Use the Gimme Geodata tool to select a point and download surrounding geographic boundaries from OpenStreetMap.

You know how to find geodata now, so let's look at free online tools to create, convert, edit, and join GeoJSON files with other types of data.

Draw and Edit with GeoJson.io

GeoJson.io (*https://geojson.io*) is a popular open source web tool to convert, edit, and create GeoJSON files. The tool was originally developed by Tom MacWright (*https://oreil.ly/KyP2E*) in 2013 and quickly became a go-to tool for geospatial practitioners.

In this tutorial, we'll show you how to convert existing KML, GPX, TopoJSON, and even CSV files with latitude/longitude data into GeoJSON files. We'll also explore how to edit attribute data, add new features to GeoJSON files, and create new geodata from scratch by tracing satellite imagery.

Convert KML, GPX, and Other Formats into GeoJSON

Navigate to the GeoJson.io tool. You will see a map on the left, and a Table/JSON attribute view area on the right. At the start, it represents an empty feature collection. Remember that features are points, polylines, and polygons.

Drag and drop your geospatial data file into the map area on the left. Alternatively, you can also import a file from Open > File menu. If you don't have a geospatial file, download the Toronto neighborhoods sample file in KML format (*https://oreil.ly/dv4nC*) to your computer, and upload it to the GeoJson.io tool. This simplified sample KML file was created from the Toronto Open Data portal (*https://oreil.ly/yIQvY*).

If GeoJson.io can recognize and import your geodata file, you'll see a green pop-up message in the upper-left corner indicating how many features were imported. For example, Figure 13-4 shows us that 140 features were imported from the sample Toronto neighborhoods KML file, and these polygons appear in the top of the map view.

> If GeoJson.io cannot import your file, you'll see a red pop-up saying it "Could not detect file type." Instead, try to convert your file into GeoJSON format using the Mapshaper tool, as described in "Edit and Join with Mapshaper" on page 346.

Figure 13-4. GeoJson.io successfully imported the Toronto neighborhoods sample KML file.

To download a converted GeoJSON file to your computer, go to Save > GeoJSON.

The GeoJson.io tool will automatically name your downloaded file as *map.geojson*, so rename it to avoid confusion.

Create GeoJSON from a CSV File

GeoJson.io can transform a CSV spreadsheet with *latitude* (or *lat*) and *longitude* (or *lon*) columns into a GeoJSON file of point features. Each row in the spreadsheet becomes its own point, and all columns other than *lat* and *lon* become *attributes* (or *properties*) of point features. For this exercise, you can download the Toronto locations sample CSV file (*https://oreil.ly/tVKJE*) to your computer, which contains three rows of data as shown in Figure 13-5.

	A	B	C	D
1	name	lat	lon	link
2	CN Tower	43.6425956	-79.38712307	http://www.cntower.ca/
3	Toronto Pearson International Airport	43.6777176	-79.6270137	http://www.torontopearson.com/
4	Royal Ontario Museum	43.667679	-79.394809	http://www.rom.on.ca/en
5				

Figure 13-5. A CSV spreadsheet with lat/lon columns can be transformed into a Geo-JSON with point features.

1. Select New to clear data from the prior exercise in the GeoJson.io tool, then drag-and-drop the Toronto locations CSV file you downloaded into the map area of the tool. A green pop-up will notify you that three features were successfully imported.

If you add new data to existing data in GeoJson.io, it will combine them into one file, which can be useful for certain tasks.

2. Click on a marker to see a pop-up with point properties. If you used the Toronto locations sample file, you'll see *name* and *link* features, in addition to the tool's default *marker-color*, *marker-size*, and *marker-symbol* fields. Note that you can edit and delete properties in the Map view.

3. Click the *Table* tab to the right of the map to view all of the data at once, rather than individual marker pop-ups. You can edit and delete properties in the Table view, as well as the JSON code view.

4. If you edited your map data, go to Save > GeoJSON to download the file to your computer, which will automatically be named *map.geojson*, so rename it to avoid confusion. You can also log into GeoJson.io with your GitHub account and save it directly to your repository.

Create New GeoJSON Data with Drawing Tools

GeoJson.io lets you create geospatial files from scratch by using simple drawing tools to place points, polylines, or polygons on the map. These are useful when you have no original file to work with. Let's create some new data:

1. Click New to clear data from the prior exercise in the GeoJson.io tool.

2. In the lower-left corner, switch from Mapbox (vector tiles) to Satellite (raster data).

3. In the upper-right corner of the map, use the Search tool to find an area of interest. For this exercise, we'll trace the geography around an athletic field in Toronto.

4. In the toolbar, you have a choice of four drawing tools: a polyline (which is a series of points connected by lines, but not closed like a polygon), a polygon, a rectangle (which is just an instance of a polygon), and a point marker.

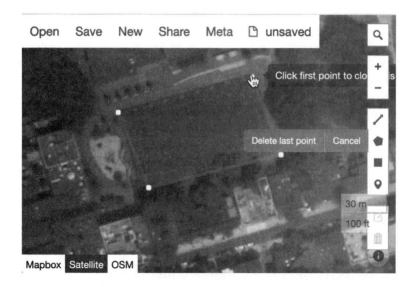

5. Select the "Draw a marker" button, and click anywhere on the map to place it. You'll see a gray marker that is now part of your map. You can modify its properties or delete it in the interactive pop-up.

6. Select the "Draw a polyline" button and click on multiple locations in the map to see connected lines appearing. Polylines are generally used for roads and paths. To finish and create a feature, click again on the final point.

7. Select the "Draw a polygon" button, which is similar to drawing a polyline, except that you need to complete the feature by making your final point at the same location as your initial point. Polygons are used to define boundaries, including small and large geographical areas.

8. Use the "Edit layers" tool (above Delete) to move a marker to a better position or adjust the shapes of your features.

9. After you have created features and their physical boundaries, add meaningful attribution data. Use the interactive pop-ups or the Table view to give objects names and other properties. When finished, save the GeoJSON file to your computer.

You can also use drawing tools to edit existing GeoJSON files. For example, if you created a GeoJSON from a CSV file, you might decide to move some markers with "Edit layers" instead of modifying their latitude and longitude values. Or you might decide to make polygons more precise by tracing around satellite imagery.

In the next section, we will introduce Mapshaper, another free online tool to convert and modify geospatial files.

Edit and Join with Mapshaper

Like GeoJson.io, Mapshaper (*https://mapshaper.org*) is a free, open source editor that can convert geospatial files, edit attribute data, filter and dissolve features, simplify boundaries to make files smaller, and much more. Mapshaper's edit and join commands are much more powerful than the GeoJson.io tool. Unlike GeoJson.io, Mapshaper doesn't have drawing tools, so you won't be able to create geospatial files from scratch.

Mapshaper is developed and maintained by Matthew Bloch on GitHub (*https://oreil.ly/hYTwc*). This easy-to-learn web tool has replaced *many* of our map preparation tasks that previously required expensive and hard-to-learn ArcGIS software, or its free but still-challenging-to-learn cousin QGIS. Even advanced GIS users may discover that Mapshaper can be a quick alternative for some common but time-consuming tasks.

Import, Convert, and Export Map Boundary Files

You can use Mapshaper to convert between geospatial file formats. Unlike GeoJson.io, Mapshaper also allows you to upload Esri Shapefiles, so you can easily convert them into the web-friendly GeoJSON format. In the following steps, we'll convert a geospatial file by importing it to Mapshaper, and then exporting it as a different file type:

1. Navigate to Mapshaper.org. The start page has two large drag-and-drop zones that you can use to import your file. The smaller area at the bottom, "Quick import," uses default import settings and is a good way to begin.

2. Drag and drop your geospatial file to the "Quick import" area. For this exercise, you can download our US states Shapefiles in *.zip* format (*https://oreil.ly/p_AwT*), which is a compressed archive that contains four Shapefiles.

 If you want to import a folder of Shapefiles, you need to either select all files inside that folder and drop them all together to the import area, or upload all of them inside a compressed *.zip* archive.

3. Each imported file becomes a layer and is accessible from the drop-down menu in the top-middle of the browser window. There, you can see how many features each layer has, toggle their visibility, or delete them.

4. To export, go to Export in the upper-right corner, and select a desired file format. The choice of export formats is shown here. Currently, available formats are Shapefile, GeoJSON, TopoJSON (similar to GeoJSON, but with topographical

data), JSON records, CSV, or SVG (Scalable Vector Graphics, for web and print). If you export more than one layer at a time, Mapshaper will archive them first, and you will download an *output.zip* that contains all exported layers.

 Mapshaper doesn't work with KML or KMZ files, but you can use GeoJson.io to first convert them into GeoJSON format, then upload to Mapshaper (see "Geospatial Data and GeoJSON" on page 336).

Edit Data for Specific Polygons

You can edit attribute data of individual polygons (as well as points and lines) in Mapshaper:

1. Import the file whose polygon attributes you want to edit.

2. Under the cursor tool, select "edit attributes."

3. Click on the polygon you want to edit. A pop-up will appear in the upper-left corner listing all attributes and values of the polygon.

4. Click on any value (underlined, in blue) and edit it.

5. When you're finished, export your geospatial file by clicking Export and choosing the desired file format.

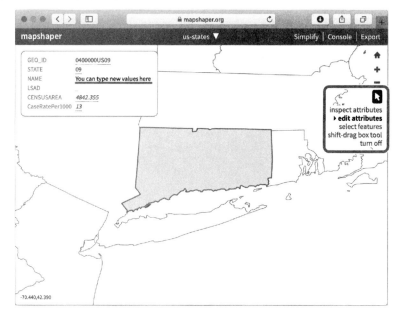

Rename Data Fields

Mapshaper's most powerful tools are available through the Console button at the top, which opens a window where you can type commands for common map editing tasks.

Sometimes map features (such as points, polylines, and polygons) contain *attributes* (data fields or columns) with long or confusing names. In the Mapshaper *Console*, you can easily change field names by entering the rename command in this generic format:

```
-rename-fields NewName=OldName
```

First, select the "inspect features" arrow in **Mapshaper** and float your cursor over map features to view their field names, then click open the *Console* windows, as shown in Figure 13-6. In this example, to change the longer field name (STATE_TITLE) to a shorter one (name), enter this command into the console:

```
-rename-fields name=STATE_TITLE
```

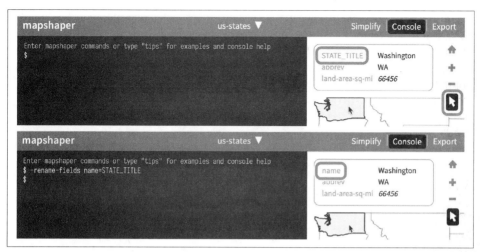

Figure 13-6. Select the "inspect features" arrow to view field names, and rename them using the -rename-fields *command in the console.*

Remove Unwanted Data Fields

Sometimes map features contain unwanted attributes that you want to remove, which you can easily do with the -filter-fields command in the Mapshaper console.

For example, this command removes all fields except *town*:

```
-filter-fields town
```

If you want to leave more than one field, separate them with a comma, but without spaces, like this:

```
-filter-fields town,state
```

If you leave a space after a comma, you will get a *Command expects a single value* error.

Simplify Map Boundaries to Reduce File Size

When you find GeoJSON maps on the web, they may contain detailed boundaries (especially around coastlines) that increase the file size, which may slow down the performance of your online web maps. Since you don't always need highly-detailed boundaries for data visualization projects with zoomed-out geographies, consider using Mapshaper to simplify your map boundaries. The result will be less precise, but load faster in users' browsers.

To understand how to simplify map boundaries, consider two maps of the contiguous US states (also known as *the lower 48*, the term Ilya learned in 2018 while traveling in Alaska), as shown in Figure 13-7. Map (a) is more detailed and is about 230 kilobytes, but map (b) is only 37 kilobytes, or six times smaller! However, be careful not to simplify boundaries so much that you remove important features.

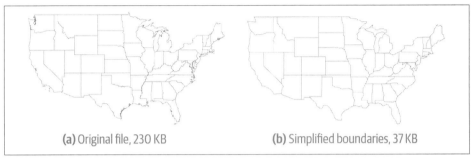

(a) Original file, 230 KB   (b) Simplified boundaries, 37 KB

Figure 13-7. Consider simplifying geometries with Mapshaper to make your web maps faster.

 When you upload a geographic file to Mapshaper, you may need to change its projection to align with your visualization tools or related geodata. Open the console and type `-proj webmercator` (or `-proj EPSG:3857`) to change the projection to Web Mercator, the format commonly used by Google Maps and other web mapping tools.

To simplify map boundaries in Mapshaper, follow these steps:

1. Import your geodata file to Mapshaper. You can use the sample contiguous US states in GeoJSON format (*https://oreil.ly/KFTSF*).

2. Click the Simplify button in the upper-right corner. The Simplification menu will appear, where you can choose one of three methods. We recommend checking "prevent shape removal," and leaving the default "Visvalingam / weighted area." Click Apply.

3. You will see a slider with 100% appear on top, replacing the layer selection dropdown. Move the slider to the right and see the map simplify its shape as you go. Stop when you think the map looks appropriate (when the shapes are still recognizable).

■ 2 line intersections ⊗
Repair

-103.40,52.63

4. In the upper-left corner, Mapshaper may suggest repairing line intersections. Click Repair.

5. You can now export your file using the Export feature.

Dissolve Internal Polygons to Create an Outline Map

A common map editing task is to create an outline map by removing the internal boundaries. For example, you can dissolve state boundaries of the US map in the previous exercise to get the outline of the country, as shown in Figure 13-8.

Click Console, which opens a window to type in commands. Enter the `dissolve` command exactly as shown, then press Return or Enter:

```
-dissolve
```

You'll see that internal boundaries became lighter in color, and that's Mapshaper's way of saying they no longer exist. You can now export your outline shape.

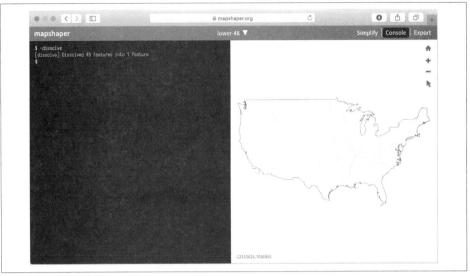

Figure 13-8. Mapshaper lets you dissolve boundaries to create an outline shape.

Clip a Map to Match an Outline Layer

Another common map editing task is to "clip" out a smaller portion of a larger map to obtain only the area you need. For example, the State of Connecticut consists of eight counties, which in turn are divided into a total of 169 towns. Imagine that you're given a boundary file of all 169 towns (*https://oreil.ly/N7O7f*) and the outline of Hartford county (*https://oreil.ly/gVLOK*). You need to clip the original towns map to include only those towns that fall within a specific portion of Connecticut: Hartford County.

Mapshaper allows you to do just that using one simple -clip command:

1. Import two boundary files into Mapshaper. One is the larger one that's being clipped (if you use sample files, *ct-towns*), and one is the desired final shape (*hartfordcounty-outline*). The latter is what ArcGIS calls the *clip feature*.

2. Make sure your active layer is set to the map you're clipping (*ct-towns*).

3. In the *Console*, type **-clip** followed by the name of your clip layer, like this:

   ```
   -clip hartfordcounty-outline
   ```

4. You should see that your active layer got clipped. Sometimes you end up with tiny slivers of clipped areas that remain alongside the borders. If that's the case, use a related command to remove them, like this:

   ```
   -clip hartfordcounty-outline -filter-slivers
   ```

5. Your Mapshaper state should look like the one pictured here. You can now save the file on your computer using the Export button.

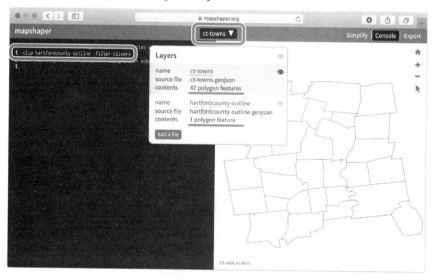

Join Spreadsheet Data With Polygon Map

Combining spreadsheet data with geographical boundaries is a common task in data visualization. In this exercise, you'll download this Connecticut town boundaries map in GeoJSON format (*https://oreil.ly/N7O7f*), and this Connecticut town population data in CSV format (*https://oreil.ly/gVLOK*), and join the two of them to build a choropleth map.

Mapshaper provides a powerful -join command to connect these files. Remember that you need some common keys in both datasets (such as *town name*, *state*, or *country*) to join the two files. Without a common field, Mapshaper has no way of knowing which numbers belong to which polygons.

1. Import both the GeoJSON file and the CSV file you downloaded before into Mapshaper using its Quick import box.

2. Make sure both files appear in the drop-down list of layers. Your CSV data will appear to resemble a table. Use the Cursor > "inspect features" tool to make sure the data is imported correctly. If you use the sample Connecticut data, note that the *ct-towns* layer has *name* attribute with the name of the town, and *ct-towns-popdensity* has town names in the *town* column.

3. Make your geospatial layer (*ct-towns*) the active layer.

4. Open the Console and enter the -join command, like this:

```
-join ct-towns-popdensity keys=name,town
```

In this command, ct-towns-popdensity is the CSV layer you're merging with, and keys are the attributes that contain values to join by. For our sample data, these would be town names that are stored in name attribute of the map file and town column of the CSV file.

5. You'll see a message in the console notifying you if the join command was performed successfully or if Mapshaper encountered any errors.

6. Use the Cursor > "inspect features" tool to make sure you see CSV columns as fields of your polygons.

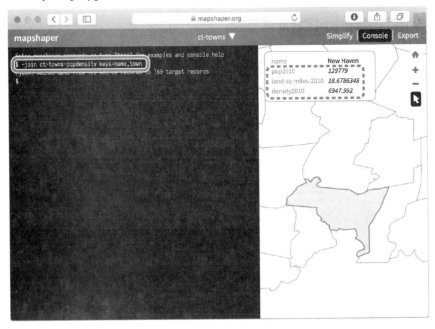

7. You can now save the file to your computer by clicking Export.

To avoid confusion, consider using the -rename-fields command on your CSV data that contains key values to match the key attribute name of your map. In our example, first you would -rename-fields name=town to your CSV file. Renaming this CSV field to name avoids confusion in the second step because your join command would end with keys=name,name.

Count Points in Polygons with Mapshaper

Mapshaper lets you count points in polygons and record that number in polygon attributes using the -join command:

1. Download two sample GeoJSON files to your computer: the points that you want to aggregate, such as hospital points in the US (*https://oreil.ly/Rjm3H*), and polygon boundaries, such as US state boundaries (*https://oreil.ly/i3yg5*). Import both into Mapshaper.

2. Make sure you choose "polygons" (not points) for the active layer by selecting that option from the drop-down menu.

3. In the Console, do a -join command using a count() function, like this:

   ```
   -join hospitals-points calc='hospitals = count()' fields=
   ```

   This command tells Mapshaper to count points inside the *hospitals–points* layer and record them as the *hospitals* attribute of the polygons. The fields= part tells Mapshaper to not copy any fields from the points, because in our case we're performing many-to-one matching, meaning many hospitals per state.

4. Use the Cursor > "inspect features" tool to make sure polygons obtained a new field with the recorded count of points.

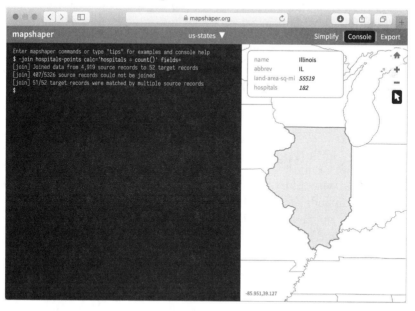

5. Save the new file using the Export button and choose the desired output format. In the next section we'll talk about what happens to objects that don't join.

More About Joins

In the previous section, you didn't need to specify *keys* to join locations between two geographical layers: points and polygons. But if one of the files you wish to join is a CSV dataset, you need *keys*.

If you don't have a CSV dataset that matches the columns in your boundary map data, you can easily create one. Upload the boundary map to Mapshaper, and export in CSV format. Open the downloaded CSV file in any spreadsheet tool. To match data columns in the CSV spreadsheet, use the VLOOKUP function (see "Match Columns with VLOOKUP" on page 38).

In real life, you'll rarely have perfect files with one-to-one matches, so you might want to have more information about which features didn't get matched so that you can fix your data. Mapshaper helps you keep track of data that's not properly joined or matched. For example, if the polygon map contains 169 features (one for each town in Connecticut), but the CSV table contains only 168 rows of data, Mapshaper will join all of those with matching keys, then display this message:

```
[join] Joined data from 168 source records to 168 target records
[join] 1/169 target records received no data
[join] 1/169 source records could not be joined
```

For more details on which values weren't joined, add `unjoined unmatched -info` flags to your join command, like this:

```
-join ct-towns-popdensity keys=name,town unjoined unmatched -info
```

The `unjoined` flag saves a copy of each unjoined record from the source table into another layer named *unjoined*. The `unmatched` flag saves a copy of each unmatched record from the target table to a new layer named *unmatched*. Finally, the `-info` flag outputs some additional information about the joining procedure to the console.

Merge Selected Polygons with Join and Dissolve Commands

In Mapshaper, you can merge selected polygons into larger clusters using `-join` and `-dissolve` commands. Imagine that you're employed by the CT Department of Public Health, and your task is to divide 169 towns into 20 public health districts (*https://oreil.ly/MaAnS*) and produce a new geospatial file.

You should begin by creating a *crosswalk* of towns and their health districts, which means some way of matching two sets of data, such as zip codes and towns where they are located. In our case, the crosswalk can be as simple as a two-column CSV list of a town and its district, each on a new line. Because your boss didn't give you a list of towns in a spreadsheet format, but instead a GeoJSON file with town boundaries, let's extract a list of towns from it:

1. Import *ct-towns.geojson* (*https://oreil.ly/N7O7f*) to Mapshaper using Quick import box.

2. Use the Cursor > "inspect features" tool to see that each polygon has a *name* attribute with the name of the town.

3. Save attribute data as a CSV file using the Export button. Open the file in any spreadsheet tool. You will see that your data is a one-column file with a *name* column that lists 169 towns.

4. In your spreadsheet, create a second column titled *merged* and copy and paste values from the first *name* column. At this point, your spreadsheet contains two columns with the same values.

5. Pick a few towns, such as West Hartford and Bloomfield, and assign *Bloomfield-West Hartford* to their *merged* column. You can stop here and move to the next step, or keep assigning district names to a few other neighboring towns.

	A	B	C
1	name	merged	
2	Bloomfield	Bloomfield-West Hartford	
3	West Hartford	Bloomfield-West Hartford	
4	Bethel	Bethel	
5	Bridgeport	Bridgeport	
6	Brookfield	Brookfield	
7	Danbury	Danbury	
8	Darien	Darien	
9	Easton	Easton	
10	Fairfield	Fairfield	
11	Greenwich	Greenwich	

6. Save this new spreadsheet file as *ct-towns-merged.csv*, and drag and drop it to Mapshaper on top of your *ct-towns* layer. Click Import.

7. In Mapshaper, this new CSV layer, named *ct-towns-merged*, will appear as a series of table cells. From the drop-down menu, select *ct-towns* to get back to your map.

8. Now you're ready to merge certain towns into districts according to your uploaded CSV file. Open the *Console*, and type `-join ct-towns-merged keys=name,name` to join the CSV layer with the boundaries layer that you see on the screen. Then type `-dissolve merged` to dissolve polygons of towns according to the *merged* column of the CSV file.

In our example, only Bloomfield and West Hartford are dissolved into a combined Bloomfield-West Hartford regional health district, with the shared boundary line between those towns becoming grayed out. All of the other poly-gons remain the same. Here's the final result.

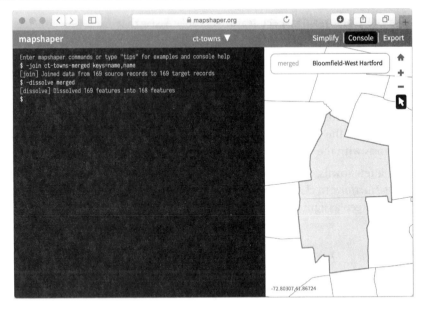

You can inspect attribute data of polygons using Cursor > "inspect features" tool, and save the resulting file using the Export button.

Overall, Mapshaper is a powerful geodata editing tool with many more commands that are worth exploring. Some of these include changing projections, filtering features using JavaScript expressions, assigning colors to polygons based on values, and many more. Explore the Mapshaper Wiki on GitHub (*https://oreil.ly/MATMD*) to learn more commands and see more examples.

Convert Compressed KMZ to KML

In the previous two sections, we demonstrated how to use the GeoJson.io tool and the Mapshaper tool to convert geospatial files from one format to another. However, not all file types can be converted with these tools. This section shows a specific example of a commonly requested conversion between *.kmz* and *.kml* formats, using the free Google Earth Pro desktop application. KMZ is a compressed version of a KML file, a native format of Google Earth:

1. Download and install the Google Earth Pro (*https://oreil.ly/ivIRH*) desktop application for Mac, Windows, or Linux.

2. Double-click on any *.kmz* file to open it in Google Earth Pro. Alternatively, open Google Earth Pro first, and go to File > Open and choose your KMZ file.

3. Right-click (or control-click) on the KMZ layer under the Places menu, and select Save Place As…

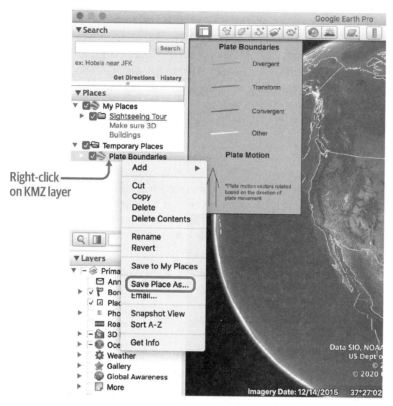

4. In the drop-down menu of "Save file…" window, choose KML format.

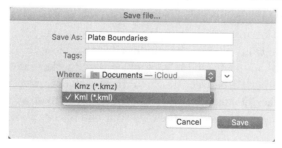

Alternatively, you can use any zip utility to extract a KML file from KMZ, because KMZ is simply a *zipped* version of a KML file.

Georeference with Map Warper

Map Warper (*https://mapwarper.net*), an open source tool created and hosted by Tim Waters, allows users to upload and georeference (also called georectify) a scanned map image. This means to precisely align the static map image on top of a present-day interactive map. As a result of this process, older map images often appear warped when updated for the digital age. After your map image is georeferenced and hosted on this site, a special link allows you to place this raster data as an overlay on an interactive map, such as in "Leaflet Storymaps with Google Sheets" on page 308. Anyone can create a free account to upload and georeference a map on the developer's public Map Warper site. See also how the tool is used by organizations such as the New York Public Library's digital maps collection (*http://maps.nypl.org*).

 While Map Warper is a wonderful open source platform, the service may be unstable. A July 2020 update states: "Ran out of disk space. Maps older than two years will need re-warping to work. Downtime will happen again." We recommend that users be mindful of the platform's limitations, but also consider donating funds to the developer to continue this open source project.

Follow this abbreviated tutorial to create a georeferenced overlay map, based on a more detailed version by digital librarians Erica Hayes and Mia Partlow (*https://oreil.ly/-YZdn*):[2]

1. Create a free account on Map Warper.

2. Upload a high-quality image or scan of a map that has not yet been georeferenced, such as an image of a paper historical map, and enter metadata for others to find it. Follow guidelines about fair-use copyright or works in the public domain.

3. After you upload the image, click on the Rectify tab in the Map Warper interface, and practice moving the map around.

4. Click to add a control point in the historic map window, then click to add a matching control point in the modern map window to align the two images. Good control points are stable locations or landmarks that haven't changed during the time period between the two maps. For example, major cities, railroad tracks, or road intersections might be a good way to align maps from the early 1900s to today, depending on the map scale and historical context.

---

2 Erica Hayes and Mia Partlow, "Tutorial: Georeferencing and Displaying Historical Maps Using Map Warper and StoryMapJS" (Open Science Framework; OSF, November 20, 2020), *https://doi.org/10.17605/OSF.IO/7QD56*.

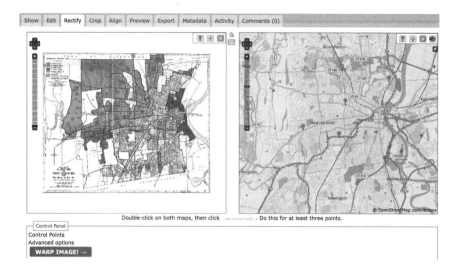

Double-click on both maps, then click [Add Control Point] . Do this for at least three points.

Control Panel
Control Points
Advanced options
WARP IMAGE! →

5. Add at least four or five control points to match the two maps and spread them out. When you are satisfied, click the Warp Image button at the bottom of the page. Map Warper transforms the static map image into a set of georeferenced map tiles, which now appear as a layer on top of the modern map.

6. Click the Export tab, and under Map Services, copy the Tiles URL that appears in Google/OpenStreetMap format, similar to this:

```
https://mapwarper.net/maps/tile/14781/{z}/{x}/{y}.png
```

7. You can copy and paste this special Tiles URL into the Leaflet Storymaps with Google Sheets template as described in "Leaflet Storymaps with Google Sheets" on page 308 or other web map tools or code templates that display overlay maps in this format. But it won't work if you paste it into a regular web browser.

You can search for historical maps that have already been georeferenced and transformed into tiles, or contribute to crowdsourcing efforts to align maps, on platforms such as Map Warper (*https://mapwarper.net*) and the New York Public Library Map Warper (*http://maps.nypl.org/warper*).

Bulk Geocode with US Census

In "Geocode Addresses in Google Sheets" on page 23, you learned how to geocode addresses with a Google Sheets add-on called Geocoding by SmartMonkey (*https:// oreil.ly/XBCSE*). Geocoding converts street addresses to latitude–longitude coordinates (such as *300 Summit St, Hartford CT, USA* to *41.75,-72.69*) that can be placed on maps. While the Geocoding by SmartMonkey add-on for Google Sheets works well for medium-sized batches of addresses, sometimes you need a faster geocoding service for larger jobs.

One of the fastest ways to geocode up to 10,000 US addresses at a time is to use the US Census Geocoder (*https://oreil.ly/XY1_1*). First, create a CSV file with five columns. Your file must *not* contain a header row, and needs to be formatted in the following way:

```
| 1 | 300 Summit St | Hartford | CT | 06106 |
| 2 | 1012 Broad St | Hartford | CT | 06106 |
```

- Column 1: Unique IDs for each address, such as 1, 2, 3, etc. While it does not necessarily have to start at 1 or be in consecutive order, this is easiest. To quickly create a column of consecutive numbers in most spreadsheets, enter 1, select the bottom-right corner of the cell, hold down the Option or Control key, and drag your mouse downward.

- Column 2: Street address.

- Column 3: City.

- Column 4: State.

- Column 5: Zip Code.

Although some of your data, such as zip codes or states, may be missing and the geocoder may still be able to recognize and geocode the location, unique IDs are absolutely necessary to include for each row (address).

 If your original data combines address, city, state, and zip into one cell, then see "Split Data into Separate Columns" on page 72. If your street addresses contain apartment numbers, you can leave them in.

Second, upload your CSV file to the US Census Geocoder address batch form (*https://oreil.ly/yHdH9*). Select "Find Locations Using…" > Address Batch, then choose your file to upload. Select *Public_AR_Current* as the benchmark, and click Get Results.

 In left-side menu, you can switch from Find Locations to Find Geographies if you wish to obtain additional information, such as the GeoID for each address. The US Census assigns a unique 15-digit GeoID to every place, and a sample (such as 090035245022001) consists of the state (09), followed by the county (003), the census tract (524502, or more conventional 5245.02), the census block group (2), and finally, the census block (001).

After a few moments, the tool will return a file named *GeocodeResults.csv* with geocoded results. It usually takes longer for larger files. Save it, and inspect it in your favorite spreadsheet tool. The resulting file is an eight-column CSV file with the original ID and address, match type (exact, nonexact, tie, or no match), and latitude-longitude coordinates. A *tie* means there are multiple possible results for your address. To see all possible matches of an address that received a *tie*, use One Line or Address tools in the left-side menu and search for that address.

 If you see some unmatched addresses, use the filtering functionality of your spreadsheet to filter for unmatched addresses, then manually correct them, save as a separate CSV file, and re-upload. You can use the US Census Geocoder as many times as you want, as long as a single file doesn't exceed 10,000 records.

To learn more about this service, read the Overview and Documentation section of the US Census Geocoder (*https://oreil.ly/Vio89*).

If for some reason you cannot geocode address-level data and you need to produce some mapping output, you can use pivot tables to get counts of points for specific areas, such as towns or states. In the next section, we will look at hospital addresses in the US and how we can count them by state using pivot tables.

Pivot Points into Polygon Data

If you deal with geographical data, you may find yourself in a situation where you have a list of addresses that need to be counted (*aggregated*) by area and displayed as a polygon map. In this case, a simple pivot table in a spreadsheet can solve the problem.

 A special case of a polygon map is a *choropleth* map, which represents polygons that are colored in a particular way to represent underlying values. A lot of polygon maps end up being *choropleth* maps.

Let's take a look at a list of all hospitals (*https://oreil.ly/2ZWWd*) that are registered with the Medicare program in the US, made available by The Centers for Medicare and Medicaid Services. The dataset has information on each hospital's name, location (nicely divided into address, city, state, and zip code columns), a phone number, and some other indicators, such as mortality and patient experience.

Imagine you're asked to create a choropleth map of total number of hospitals by US state. Instead of showing individual hospitals as points, you want darker shades of blue to represent states with more hospitals (see Figure 13-9).

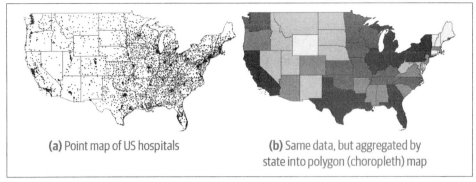

(a) Point map of US hospitals

(b) Same data, but aggregated by
state into polygon (choropleth) map

Figure 13-9. You can count addresses by state (or other areas) to produce polygon, or choropleth, maps instead of point maps.

First, save the database to your local machine by clicking the "Download this dataset" button to the right of the table (see Figure 13-10).

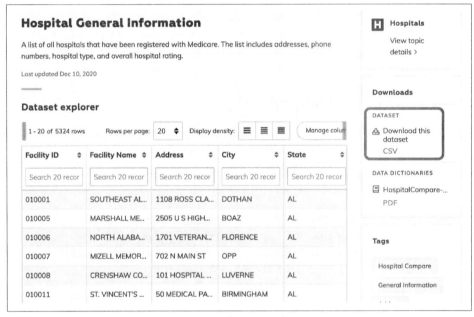

Figure 13-10. In Socrata, you can export the entire dataset as a CSV.

Next, open the file in your favorite spreadsheet tool. If you use Google Sheets, use File > Import > Upload to import CSV data. Make sure your address columns are present, and move on to creating a pivot table (in Google Sheets, go to Data > "Pivot table," make sure the entire data range is selected, and click Create). In the pivot table, set Rows to *State*, because we want to get counts by state. Next, set pivot table's Values to

State—or really any other column that has no missing values—and choose "Summarize by: COUNTA." Voilà!

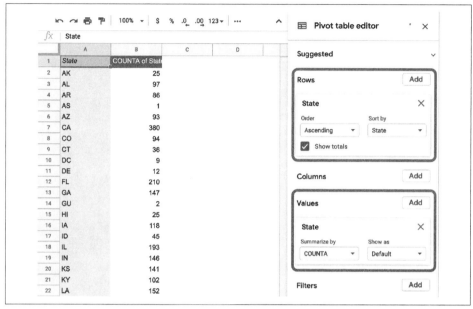

Figure 13-11. Use pivot tables in any spreadsheet software to count addresses per area (such as state, county, of zip code).

Your aggregated dataset is ready, so save it as a CSV. If you use Google Sheets, go to File > Download > "Comma-separated values (.csv, current sheet)." You can now merge this dataset with your polygons manually using editing capabilities of GeoJson.io, or merge it all in one go using powerful Mapshaper.

Summary

In this chapter, we delved into geospatial data and the GeoJSON format. You also learned how to use various open source tools to find geodata, convert and create vector data, and edit and join these layers with spreadsheet data. You also warped historical raster map images by georeferencing them onto modern maps. Finally, you acquired some additional strategies to bulk geocode large batches of US addresses, and to pivot point-level data into polygons for use in choropleth maps.

In the next chapter, we'll discuss how to detect lies and reduce bias in charts and maps, so that you become a more critical consumer of visualizations as well as a better data storyteller.

PART IV

Telling True, Meaningful Stories

CHAPTER 14

Detect Lies and Reduce Bias

The goal of data visualization is to encode information into images that capture true and insightful stories. But we've warned you to watch out for people who lie with visualizations. Looking back at income inequality examples in the Introduction, we intentionally manipulated charts in Figures I-1 and I-2 and maps in Figures I-3 and I-4 to demonstrate how the same data can be rearranged to paint very different pictures of reality. Does that mean all data visualizations are equally valid? Definitely not. On closer examination, we declared that the second of the two charts about US income inequality was *misleading* because it intentionally used an inappropriate scale to hide the truth. We also confided that the two world maps were *equally truthful*, even though the US appeared in a darker color (signaling a higher level of inequality) than the other.

How can two different visualizations be equally right? Our response may conflict with those who prefer to call their work *data science*, a label that suggests an objective world with only one right answer. Instead, we argue that data visualization is best understood as an *interpretative skill* that still depends on evidence, but in which more than one portrayal of reality may be valid. As you recall, our field has only a few definitive rules about how *not* to visualize data, which we introduced in "Chart Design Principles" on page 103 and "Map Design Principles" on page 160. Rather than a binary world, we argue that visualizations fall into three categories: wrong, misleading, and truthful.

Visualizations are *wrong* if they misstate the evidence or violate one of these rigid design rules. For examples of the latter, if a bar or column chart begins at a number other than zero, it's wrong because those types of charts represent values through *length* or *height*, which readers cannot determine if the baseline has been truncated. Similarly, if the slices of a pie chart add up to more than 100%, it's wrong because readers cannot accurately interpret the chart, which also incorrectly presents data.

Visualizations are *misleading* if they technically follow the design rules, but unreasonably hide or twist the appearance of relevant data. We acknowledge that *unreasonably* can be subjective, but we'll review several examples in this chapter, such as using inappropriate scales, or warping the aspect ratio. Inserting this category between *wrong* and *truthful* underscores how charts and maps can accurately display data and adhere to design rules, yet misdirect us from the truth, just as magicians know how to misdirect their audience while performing sleight of hand tricks.

Visualizations are *truthful* if they show accurate data and follow the design rules. Still, there's a wide spectrum of quality within this category. When looking at two visualizations that are equally valid, sometimes we say that one is *better* than the other because it illuminates a meaningful data pattern that we didn't yet recognize. Or we may say that one is better because it portrays these patterns more beautifully, or with less ink on the page and greater simplicity, than the other. In any case, let's agree that we're aiming for truthful visualizations, with a preference for the better side of the quality spectrum.

In this chapter, you'll learn to sort out differences between the three categories. The best way to improve your lie-detector skills is through hands-on tutorials in the art of data deception, "How to Lie with Charts" on page 371 and "How to Lie with Maps" on page 382. As the saying goes, it takes a thief to catch a thief. Learning *how to lie* not only makes it harder for people to mislead you, but also educates you more deeply about the ethical decisions we make when designing visualizations that *tell the truth*, while recognizing there's more than one path to that destination. Finally, we'll discuss how to recognize and reduce four general categories of data bias—sampling, cognitive, algorithmic, and intergroup—as well as spatial biases ("Recognize and Reduce Data Bias" on page 388 and "Recognize and Reduce Spatial Bias" on page 392) that are more specific to working with maps. While we may not be able to stop bias entirely, you'll learn how to identify it in the works by other people and strategies to reduce its presence in your own visualizations.[1]

---

1 The "how to lie" tutorials were inspired by several excellent works in data visualization: Cairo, *The Truthful Art*, 2016; Cairo, *How Charts Lie*, 2019; Darrell Huff, *How to Lie with Statistics* (W.W. Norton & Company, 1954); Mark Monmonier, *How to Lie with Maps*, 3rd edition (University of Chicago Press, 2018); Nathan Yau, "How to Spot Visualization Lies" (FlowingData, February 9, 2017), *https://oreil.ly/o9PLq*; NASA Jet Propulsion Laboratory (JPL), "Educator Guide: Graphing Global Temperature Trends," 2017, *https://oreil.ly/Gw-6z*.

How to Lie with Charts

In this section, you'll learn how to avoid being fooled by misleading charts, and also how to make your own charts more honest, by intentionally manipulating the same data to tell opposing stories. First, you'll *exaggerate* small differences in a column chart to make them seem larger. Second, you'll *diminish* the rate of growth in a line chart to make it appear more gradual. Together, these tutorials will teach you to watch out for key details when reading other people's charts, such as the vertical axis and aspect ratio. Paradoxically, by demonstrating *how to lie*, our goal is to teach you to *tell the truth* and to think more carefully about the ethics of designing your data stories.

Exaggerate Change in Charts

First we'll examine data about the economy, a topic that politicians often twist to portray more favorably for their perspective. The gross domestic product (GDP) measures the market value of the final goods and services produced in a nation, which many economists consider to be the primary indicator of economic health.[2] We downloaded US GDP data from the US Federal Reserve open data repository (*https://oreil.ly/0n9E1*), which is measured in billions of dollars. It is published quarterly, with seasonal adjustments to allow for better comparisons across industries that vary during the year, such as summertime farming and tourism versus winter-time holiday shopping. Your task is to create a deceptive column chart that *exaggerates* small differences to make them appear larger in the reader's eye.

1. Open the US GDP mid-2019 data in Google Sheets (*https://oreil.ly/3chLY*), and go to File > "Make a copy" to create a copy that you can edit in your own Google Drive. We'll create charts in Google Sheets, but you can also download the data to use in a different chart tool if you prefer.

2. Examine the data and read the notes. To simplify this example, we show only two figures: the US GDP for the second quarter (April through June 2019) and the third quarter (July through September 2019). The second quarter was about $21.5 trillion, and the third quarter was slightly higher, at $21.7 trillion. In other words, the quarterly GDP rose by just under 1%, which we calculated this way: (21747 - 21540)/21540 = 0.0096 = 0.96%.

3. Create a Google Sheets column chart in the same sheet using the *default* settings, although we never blindly accept them as the best representation of the truth. In the *data* sheet, select the two columns, and go to Insert > Chart, as you learned

---

2 Note that not everyone agrees because GDP doesn't count unpaid household labor such as caring for one's children, nor does it consider the distribution of wealth across a nation's population.

when we introduced charts with Google Sheets in "Google Sheets Charts" on page 113. The tool should recognize your data and automatically produce a column chart, as shown in the left side here.

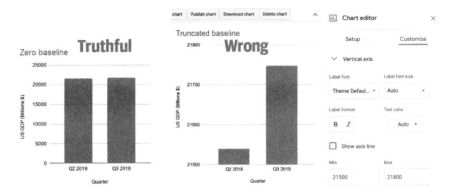

In this default view, with the zero baseline for the vertical axis, the difference between $21.5 and $21.7 trillion looks relatively small to the reader.

4. *Truncate the vertical axis to exaggerate differences.* Instead of a zero baseline, let's manipulate the scale to make the 1% change in GDP look larger. Click on the three-dot kebab menu to open the "Chart editor" and select the Customize tab. Scroll down to the vertical axis settings, and reduce the scale by changing the minimum from 0 (the zero baseline) to 21,500, and also change the maximum to 21,800, as shown in the right side of the preceding image.

Although the data remains the same, the small difference between the two columns in the chart now appears much larger in our eyes. Only people who read charts closely will notice this trick. The political candidate who's campaigning on rising economic growth will thank you!

As you can see, the truncated baseline chart is *wrong* because you've violated one of the cardinal rules about chart design in "Chart Design Principles" on page 103. Column (and bar) charts *must* start at the zero baseline because they represent value using *height* (and *length*). Readers cannot determine if a column is twice as high as another column unless both begin at the zero baseline. By contrast, the default chart with the zero baseline is truthful. Let's move on to a different example where the rules aren't as clear.

Diminish Change in Charts

Next we'll examine data about climate change, one of the most pressing issues we face on our planet, yet deniers continue to resist reality, and some of them twist the facts. In this tutorial, we'll examine global temperature data from 1880 to the present, downloaded from US National Aeronautics and Space Administration (NASA) (*https://oreil.ly/1kASv*). It shows that the mean global temperature has risen about 1° Celsius (or about 2° Fahrenheit) during the past 50 years, and this warming has already begun to cause glacial melt and rising sea levels. Your task is to create *misleading* line charts that *diminish* the appearance of rising global temperature change in the reader's eye:[3]

1. Open the global temperature change 1880–2019 data in Google Sheets (*https://oreil.ly/D-AK1*), and go to File > "Make a copy" to create a version you can edit in your own Google Drive.

2. Examine the data and read the notes. Temperature change refers to the mean global land–ocean surface temperature in degrees Celsius, estimated from many samples around the earth, relative to the temperature in 1951–1980, about 14°C (or 57°F). In other words, the 0.98 value for 2019 means that global temperatures were about 1°C above normal that year. Scientists define the 1951–1980 period as "normal" based on standards from NASA and the US National Weather Service; adults who grew up during that time can remember this "normal." While there are other ways to measure temperature change, this data from NASA's Goddard Institute for Space Studies (NASA/GISS) is generally consistent with data compiled by other scientists at the Climatic Research Unit (*https://oreil.ly/_dXSb*) and the National Oceanic and Atmospheric Administration (*https://oreil.ly/TxZkD*).

3. Create a Google Sheets line chart by selecting the two columns in the *data* sheet, then Insert > Chart. The tool should recognize your time-series data and produce a *default* line chart, though we never blindly accept it as the best representation of the truth. Click on the three-dot kebab menu to open the "Chart editor" and select the Customize tab. Add a better title and vertical axis label using the notes to clarify the source and how temperature change is measured.

---

3 The tutorial on misleading climate change data was inspired by a high school classroom activity created by the NASA Jet Propulsion Laboratory (JPL), as well as Alberto Cairo's analysis of charts by climate change deniers. NASA JPL; Cairo, *How Charts Lie*, 2019, pp. 65–67, 135–141.

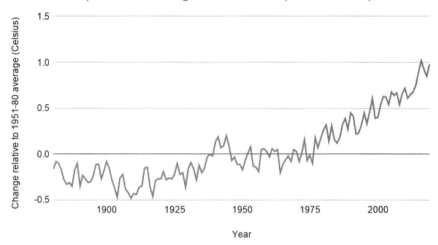

Now let's create three more charts using the same data but different methods, and discuss why they are *not wrong* from a technical perspective, but nevertheless *very misleading*.

Lengthen the vertical axis to flatten the line

We'll use the same method as shown in previous section, but change the axes in the opposite direction. In the Google Sheets Chart editor, customize the vertical axis by changing the minimum value to –5 and the maximum to 5, as shown in Figure 14-1. By increasing the length of the vertical scale, you flattened our perception of the rising line, and canceled our climate emergency—but not really.

What makes this flattened line chart *misleading* rather than *wrong*? In the first half of the tutorial, when you reduced the vertical axis of the US GDP chart, you violated the zero-baseline rule, because column and bar charts *must* begin at zero because they require readers to judge *height* and *length*, as described in "Chart Design Principles" on page 103. You may be surprised to learn that the zero-baseline rule does *not* apply to line charts. Visualization expert Albert Cairo reminds us that line charts represent values in the *position* and *angle* of the line. Readers interpret the meaning of line charts by their shape, rather than their height, so the baseline is irrelevant. Therefore, flattening the line chart for temperature change may mislead readers, but it's technically not wrong, as long as it's labeled correctly.[4]

---

4 Cairo, *How Charts Lie*, 2019, p. 61.

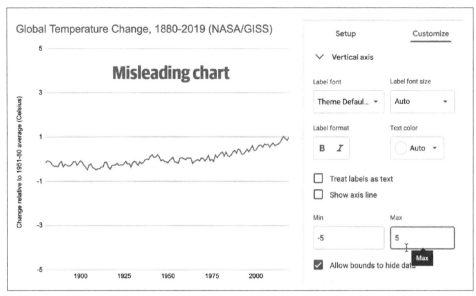

Figure 14-1. Misleading chart with a lengthened vertical axis.

Widen the chart to warp its aspect ratio

In your Google Sheet, click the chart and drag the sides to make it very short and wide, as shown in Figure 14-2. Image measurements are listed in width by height, and we calculate the aspect ratio as width divided by height. Since the default chart is 600 × 370 pixels, its aspect ratio is about 1.6 to 1. But the stretched-out chart is 1090 × 191 pixels, and its ratio is about 5.7 to 1. By increasing the aspect ratio, you have flattened our perception of the rising line, and canceled our climate crisis once again—but not really.

What makes this warped line chart *misleading* rather than *wrong*? Once again, since changing the aspect ratio of a line chart doesn't violate a clearly defined rule of data visualization, it's not technically wrong, as long as it's accurately labeled. But it's definitely misleading. Cairo states that we should design charts with an aspect ratio that "neither exaggerates nor minimizes change." What specifically does he suggest? Cairo recommends, yet clearly states this "isn't a universal rule of chart design," that the percent change expressed in a chart should roughly match its aspect ratio. For example, if a chart represents a 33% increase, which is the same as 33/100 or one-third, he recommends an aspect ratio of 3:1 (because the fraction is flipped by placing width before height), or in other words, a line chart that is three times wider than its height.[5]

---

5 Cairo, *How Charts Lie*, 2019, p. 69.

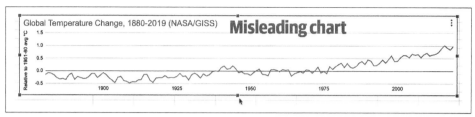

Figure 14-2. Misleading chart with a stretched aspect ratio.

 Some experts advise that aspect ratios for line charts should follow the *banking to 45 degrees* principle, which states that the average orientation of line segments should be equal to an angle of 45°, upward or downward, to distinguish individual segments. But this requires statistical software to calculate slopes for all of the lines, and still isn't a *rule* that fits all cases. Read "Aspect Ratio and Banking to 45 Degrees," a good overview by Robert Kosara.[6]

Cairo does *not* propose his aspect ratio recommendation as a universal rule because he recognizes how it fails with very small or very large values. For example, if we apply Cairo's recommendation to our global temperature change chart, the difference between the lowest and highest values (–0.5° to 1°C) represents a 300% increase. In this case, we calculate the percent change using the lowest value of –0.5°C, rather than the initial value of 0°C, because dividing by zero is not defined, so `(1°C - (-0.5°C)) / |-0.5°C| = 3 = 300%`. Following Cairo's general recommendation, a 300% increase suggests a 1:3 aspect ratio, or a line chart three times taller than its width, as shown in Figure 14-3. While this very tall chart is technically correct, it's *misleading* because it *exaggerates change*, which is contrary to Cairo's main message. The aspect ratio recommendation becomes ridiculous when we divide by numbers that are very close to zero.

---

6 Robert Kosara, "Aspect Ratio and Banking to 45 Degrees" (Eagereyes, June 3, 2013), *https://oreil.ly/0KNUb*.

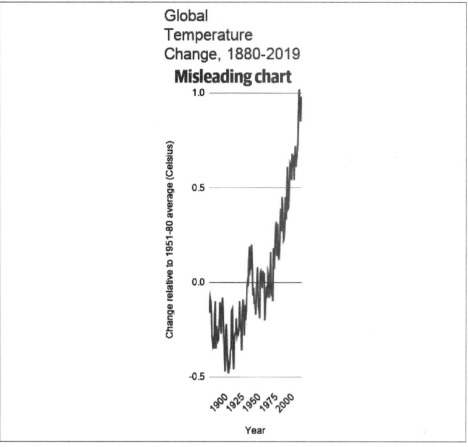

Figure 14-3. Rules of thumb do not always work. Cairo's recommendation to use 1:3 aspect ratio to represent 300% change results in a misleading chart in this particular example.

Cairo acknowledges that his aspect ratio recommendation can result in *misleading charts* in the opposite way that *diminish change*. For example, instead of *global temperature change*, which increased from 0°C to 1°C, imagine a chart that displays *global temperature*, which increased from about 13°C to 14°C (or about 55°F to 57°F) over time. Even though a 1°C difference in average global temperature may not *feel* very significant to our bodies, it has dramatic consequences for the Earth. We can calculate the percent change as: (14°C - 13°C) / 13°C = 0.08 = 8% increase, or about one-twelfth. This translates into a 12:1 aspect ratio, or a line chart that is 12 times wider than it is tall, as shown in Figure 14-4. Cairo warns that this significant global temperature increase looks "deceptively small," so he cautions against using his aspect ratio recommendation in all cases.[7]

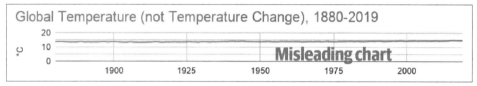

Figure 14-4. *Once again, rules of thumb do not always work. Cairo's recommendation for an 8% increase results in a 12:1 aspect ratio that produces a misleading chart in this particular example.*

Where does all of this leave us? If you feel confused, that's because data visualization has *no universal rule about aspect ratios*. What should you do? First, never blindly accept the default chart. Second, explore how different aspect ratios affect the chart's appearance. Finally, even Cairo argues that you should use your own judgment rather than follow his recommendation in every situation, because there's no single rule about aspect ratio that fits all circumstances. Make a choice that honestly interprets the data and clearly tells a story to your reader.

Add more data and a dual vertical axis

Another common way to mislead is to add more data, such as a second data series that corresponds to a second vertical axis on the right side of a line chart. While it's technically possible to construct a dual-axis chart, we strongly advise against them because they can be easily manipulated to mislead readers. Let's illustrate how with an example that combines two prior datasets—global temperature change and US GDP—in one dual-axis chart. In the Google Sheet, go to the *temp+GDP* sheet, where you will see temperature change plus a new column: US GDP in billions of dollars from 1929 to 2019, downloaded from the US Federal Reserve (*https://oreil.ly/LJcut*). To simplify this example, we deleted pre-1929 temperature data to match it up more neatly with available GDP data.

---

7 Cairo, *How Charts Lie*, 2019, p. 70.

1. Select all three columns and Insert > Chart to produce a default line chart with two data series: temperature (in blue) and US GDP (in red).

2. In the "Chart editor," select Customize and scroll down to Series. Change the drop-down menu from "Apply to all series" to US GDP. Just below that, in the Format area, change the Axis menu from "Left axis" to "Right axis," which creates another vertical axis on the right side of the chart, connected only to the US GDP data.

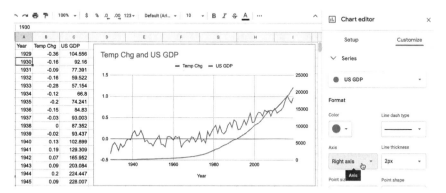

3. In the "Chart editor" > Customize tab, scroll down and you'll now see separate controls for "Vertical axis" (the left side, for temperature change only), and a brand-new menu for the "Right axis" (for US GDP only).

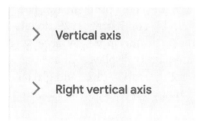

4. Finish your chart by adjusting "Vertical axis" for temperature change, but with even more exaggeration than you did in "Lengthen the vertical axis to flatten the line" on page 374. This time, change the minimum value to 0 (to match the right-axis baseline for US GDP) and the maximum to 10 to flatten the temperature line further. Add a title, source, and labels to make it look more authoritative.

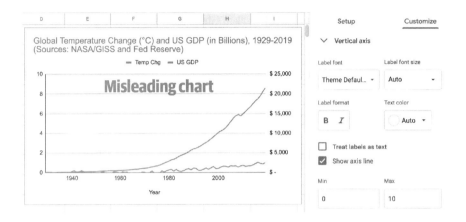

What makes this dual-axis chart *misleading* rather than *wrong*? Once again, since it doesn't violate a clearly defined visualization design rule, the chart isn't wrong. But many visualization experts strongly advise against dual-axis charts because they confuse most readers, don't clearly show relationships between two variables, and sometimes lead to mischief. Although both axes begin at zero in step 4, the left-side temperature scale has a top level of 10°C, which is unreasonable because the temperature line rises only 1°C. Therefore, by lowering our perception of the temperature line in comparison to the steadily rising GDP line, you've misled us into ignoring the consequences of climate change while we enjoy a long-term economic boom! Two additional issues also make this chart problematic. The GDP data is *not* adjusted for inflation, so it misleads us by comparing 1929 dollars to 2019 dollars, a topic we warned about in Chapter 5. Furthermore, by accepting default colors assigned by Google Sheets, the climate data is displayed in a "cool" blue, which sends our brain the opposite message of rising temperatures and glacial melt. In sum, this chart misleads in three ways: an unreasonable vertical axis, noncomparable data, and color choice.

What's a better alternative to a dual-axis line chart? If your goal is to visualize the relationship between two variables—global temperature and US GDP—then display them in a scatter chart, as we introduced in "Scatter and Bubble Charts" on page 139. We can make a more meaningful comparison by plotting US real GDP (*https:// oreil.ly/Q_Ijd*), which has been adjusted into constant 2012 dollars, and entered alongside global temperature change in this Google Sheet (*https://oreil.ly/0wTID*). We created a *connected scatter chart* that displays a line through all of the points to represent time by following this Datawrapper Academy tutorial (*https://oreil.ly/ KBcy3*), as shown in Figure 14-5. Overall, the growth of the US economy is strongly associated with rising global temperature change from 1929 to the present. Furthermore, it's harder to mislead readers with a scatter chart because the axes are designed to display the full range of data, and our reading of the strength of the relationship is not tied to the aspect ratio.

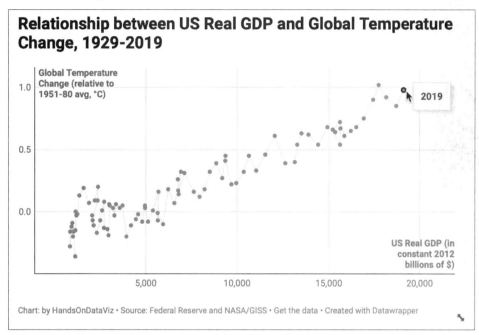

Figure 14-5. Connected scatter chart of the relationship between US real GDP and global temperature change from 1929 to 2019: explore the interactive version (https://oreil.ly/NrxXD).

To sum up, in this tutorial we created several charts about global temperature change. None of them were technically wrong, only some were truthful, and most were unreasonably manipulated to fool readers by hiding or disguising important patterns in the data. We demonstrated several ways that charts can be designed to deceive readers, but didn't exhaust all of the options. For example, see additional readings on ways to create three-dimensional charts and to tilt the reader's perspective below the baseline, which causes readers to misjudge the relative height of column or line charts.[8]

You may feel frustrated that data visualization lacks clearly defined design rules for many cases, like we're accustomed to reading in our math, science, or grammar textbooks. Instead, remember that the important visualization rule is a *three-step process*: never blindly accept the default, explore how different designs affect the appearance

---

8 Cairo, *How Charts Lie*, 2019, p. 58.

of your interpretation, and use your best judgment to tell true and meaningful data stories.

You've learned how to lie with charts and in the next section, you'll build on these skills to lie with maps.

How to Lie with Maps

One of the best ways to learn how to detect lies is to intentionally manipulate a map, and tell two (or more) opposing stories with the same data. You'll learn what to watch out for when viewing other people's maps, and to think more carefully about the ethical issues when you design your own. We'll focus our attention on choropleth maps that use shading or color to represent values in geographic areas because they can be a source of considerable mischief. This exercise was inspired by geographer Mark Monmonier's classic book of the same name, *How to Lie with Maps*, originally published in 1991, now in its third edition.[9]

Before we get started, review "Map Design Principles" on page 160 to avoid common mistakes when designing choropleth maps. For example, in most cases you should avoid mapping raw counts (such as the total number of people with a disease) and instead show relative rates (such as the percentage of people with a disease), because a raw count map would generally show that most people live in urban rather than rural areas. Also, this section assumes that you're already familiar with the steps in "Choropleth Map with Datawrapper" on page 191.

Let's return to the two maps in the Introduction, where we presented two different interpretations of world income inequality. In particular, Figure I-3 colored the US in medium blue, which suggested its level of inequality was similar to other nations, while Figure I-4 made the US stand out in dark blue at the highest tier of inequality. We argued that both were *truthful* interpretations. You'll understand the concepts more clearly by following this hands-on tutorial to re-create both maps, plus one more.

Examine Data and Upload to Datawrapper

First, let's examine the data and upload it to Datawrapper to start making our choropleth maps:

1. Open the world income top 1% data in Google Sheets (*https://oreil.ly/dbpr9*), and go to File > "Make a copy" to create a version that you can edit in your own Google Drive.

---

9 Monmonier, *How to Lie with Maps*, 3rd edition, 2018.

2. Examine the data and read the notes. Overall, this data offers one way to make international comparisons about income distribution by showing "how big a slice of the pie" is held by the richest 1% in each nation. Each row lists a nation and its three-letter code, along with the percent share of pretax national income held by the top 1% of the population and the most recent year when this data was collected by the World Inequality Database. For example, in Brazil, the top 1% of the population held 28.3% of the nation's income in 2015, while in the US, the top 1% held 20.5% in 2018.

 To be clear, social scientists have developed many other ways to compare the distribution of income or wealth across nations, but this topic is beyond the scope of this book. In this tutorial we capture this complex concept using one easy-to-understand variable: percent share of pretax national income held by the top 1% of the population in each nation.

3. Because we cannot directly import this Google Sheet into our Datawrapper mapping tool, go to File > Download to export the first tab in CSV format to your computer.

4. Open the Datawrapper visualization tool (*https://datawrapper.de*) in your browser and upload your CSV map data. Select New Map, select "Choropleth map," and select World, then Proceed. In the "Add your data screen," scroll down below the table and select the "Import your dataset" button, then the Start Import button, then "click here to upload a CSV file," and upload the CSV file you created in the previous step. Click to confirm that the first column is *Matched as ISO code*, click Continue, click to confirm that the *Percent Share* column is *Matched as Values*, then click Go and Proceed to visualize your map.

5. In the Visualize screen, in the Colors section of the Refine tab "Select palette," click the wrench symbol to open up the color settings. Let's skip past the light-green-to-blue color palette, which you can modify later, and let's focus on settings for color ranges.

Modify the Map Color Ranges

While we never blindly accept the default visualization, it's a good place to begin. The default map displays a *continuous* type of range with a *linear* interpolation of data values. The map places all of the values in a straight line, from the minimum of 5% to the maximum of 31%, and assigns each value to a color along the gradient, as shown in Figure 14-6. Notice that the US (20.5%) blends in with a medium blue color, just above the midpoint in this range.

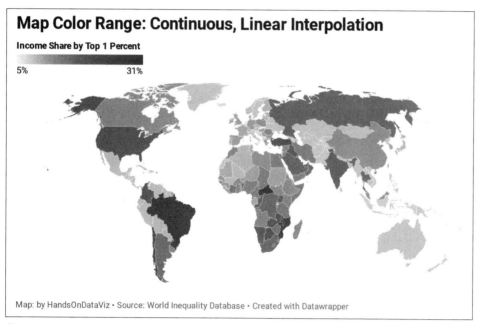

Map Color Range: Continuous, Linear Interpolation

Income Share by Top 1 Percent

5%   31%

Map: by HandsOnDataViz • Source: World Inequality Database • Created with Datawrapper

Figure 14-6. Income inequality map with continuous range and linear interpolation: explore the interactive version (https://oreil.ly/EMfwQ).

Create a second map with the same data but different settings. Change the Type setting to steps, and adjust to three steps, using "Natural breaks (Jenks)" interpolation, as shown in Figure 14-7. This means that the map now places all of the values in three ascending groups. Natural breaks offers a compromise between using colors to highlight the outliers and diversity inside the range. Notice that the US (still 20.5%) now stands out in a dark blue color at the top one-third of this range (19% or above).

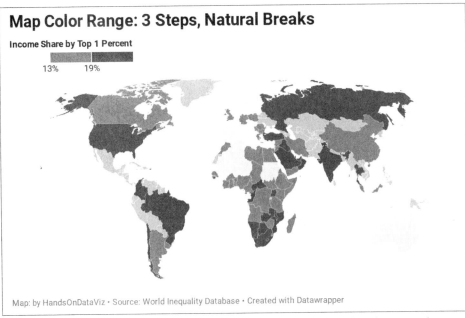

Map Color Range: 3 Steps, Natural Breaks

Income Share by Top 1 Percent

13%   19%

Map: by HandsOnDataViz • Source: World Inequality Database • Created with Datawrapper

Figure 14-7. Income inequality map with three steps and natural breaks interpolation: explore the interactive version (https://oreil.ly/asCkV).

The first map portrays US income inequality as similar to most nations, while the second map places the US at the higher end of the color scale. Which map is misleading? Which one is truthful? If you prefer clear and definitive rules in map design, this answer may frustrate you. Although the two maps generate very different impressions, both maps present accurate data that's clearly labeled, based on reasonable and truthful interpretations of the data.

To understand what's happening behind the scenes with your choropleth map, visualization expert Alberto Cairo recommends creating a histogram to better understand the data distribution. Go back to the data in the Google Sheet (*https://oreil.ly/ Nt9ZG*) and create a histogram, as we described in "Histograms" on page 121, to view the frequency of nations when sorted by percent share into "buckets," as shown in Figure 14-8. While most nations are clumped around the median, this is not a normal distribution curve, because a handful are outliers near the 30% mark. In the first map, which used continuous type and linear interpolation, the US appeared closer to the median and blended in with a medium blue. By contrast, the second map used three steps and natural breaks, which meant that the US appeared in the top range and stood out in dark blue.

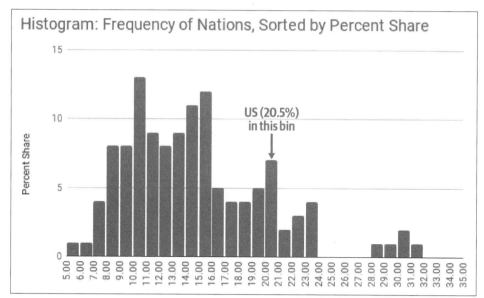

Figure 14-8. *Histogram of income inequality map data.*

So how *should* we make decisions when designing choropleth maps? Similar to the chart section, there are few universal rules, but several wise recommendations. First and foremost, always look for *better* ways to use map color ranges to show true and meaningful differences in the data, rather than hiding them out of sight. Datawrapper Academy recommends finding "a compromise between honesty and usefulness" when creating choropleth maps (*https://oreil.ly/aHIcZ*).

In other words, tell the truth when displaying evidence *and* use design choices to emphasize an interpretation that calls our attention to what's most important in the data story. For example, a *linear* interpolation works best to emphasize extreme lows and highs, while *quantiles* or other nonlinear groupings reveal more geographic diversity in the middle ranges. Datawrapper Academy also recommends using a *con-tinuous* color palette to show nuances in the data (*https://oreil.ly/Bu_gx*), unless your data story has a compelling reason to display discrete *steps* to emphasize regions above or below certain thresholds. For steps, increasing the *number of steps* will display more contrast in your map, but too many steps can give the mistaken impression that light- and dark-colored regions are very different, though their numbers may vary only slightly. Whatever you decide, avoid the temptation to manually adjust a map's settings to manipulate its appearance to fit a preconceived point of view.

In short, show us a story and tell the truth. You may need to create several maps with different settings to decide which one is the best compromise.

Now that you have a clearer idea of how to lie with charts and maps, let's examine a related topic: recognizing and reducing data bias.

Recognize and Reduce Data Bias

We define bias as unfairly favoring one view over another. When working with data and designing visualizations, it's important to be aware of different types of bias so you can recognize them as potential factors that may influence your perception and reduce their presence in your own work. The first step toward reducing bias is to correctly identify various types, which at first glance may appear hidden, so that we can call them out. In this section, we'll discuss four categories of bias that anyone who works with data needs to recognize: sampling biases, cognitive biases, algorithmic biases, and intergroup biases.

Sampling biases occur when we believe our data has been selected fairly, but some behind-the-scenes process has influenced its composition and skews the results. We previously warned you about several types in "Beware of Biased Comparisons" on page 93. One type to avoid is *selection bias*, which means that the sample selected for your study differs systematically from the larger population, such as when you randomly measure the height of people who happen to be leaving the gym after basketball practice. A second type to avoid is *nonresponse bias*, which happens when certain subgroups of a population are less likely to respond to a survey, leading to less representative results. We also cautioned you about a third type, *self-selection bias*, where participants who apply or volunteer for a program must be evaluated carefully to avoid comparisons with nonparticipants, who may not share the same motivations. Always question your data, as described in "Question Your Data" on page 64, before you attempt to make meaningful comparisons. If you suspect that a sampling issue may have snuck into the data collection process, either do not use the data, or clearly describe your concerns in your visualization notes and companion text to call out potential biases.

Cognitive biases refer to a category of human behaviors that skew how we interpret data. One example is *confirmation bias*, which refers to the tendency to accept only claims that fit our preconceived notions of how the world works. Counter this by actively searching for alternative interpretations and considering contradictory findings with open eyes. A second example is *pattern bias*, which describes how people tend to see meaningful relationships in data even when numbers were randomly selected. Fight against this by reminding readers (and yourself) that data is noisy, and our brains are wired to see patterns even where none exist. See additional resources on statistical analysis mentioned in Chapter 5 to learn about appropriate tests to determine whether apparent patterns in your data exist at odds greater than chance. A third example is *framing bias*, which refers to negative or positive labels or conceptual categories that affect how we interpret information. On the power of labels, British statistician David Spiegelhalter notes that US hospitals tend to report *mortality rates*, while UK hospitals report *survival* rates. When weighing the risks of a surgical procedure for member of your family, a 5% mortality rate seems worse than a 95%

survival rate, even though they're identical. Furthermore, Spiegelhalter observes that when we supplement rates with raw counts, it further increases our impression of risks. For example, if we told you a surgical procedure had a 5% mortality rate *and* that 20 out of 400 patients died, that outcome seems worse because we begin to imagine real people's lives, not just abstract percentages.[10] Counter framing bias by being aware of its potential effect on our minds and calling it out.

Algorithmic biases occur when computer systems routinely favor certain outcomes over others, often by reinforcing privileges held by dominant social groups. Several cases have recently gained public attention. For example, algorithms have contributed to racial bias in the US court system. The Northpointe software company (now named Equivant) developed an algorithm to predict the risk of recidivism among defendants, which judges used when deciding on prison sentences or probation. But ProPublica investigative journalists found that the algorithm wrongly predicted Black defendants to be repeat offenders at almost twice the rate as White defendants, even when controlling for the types of prior crimes they committed.[11] Algorithms also have added to gender bias in the financial services industry. When Apple and Goldman Sachs partnered to offer a new type of credit card, several customers noticed that the software formula to evaluate applications sometimes offered men 10 to 20 times the amount of credit as women, even if they were married, owned the same assets, and had similar credit scores.[12] In both cases, companies denied the charges of algorithmic bias but refused to reveal the decision-making process within their software formulas, which they argued was proprietary. As a result, we need to be vigilant about the misuse of data.

Intergroup biases refer to multiple ways that people privilege or discriminate by social categories, such as race, gender, class, and sexuality. Clearly, intergroup biases have a long history that predate the digital era. But in the wake of the Black Lives Matter movement, some authors have called attention to ways that intergroup bias pervades the field of data visualization and have advocated for ways to counter its impact. For example, Jonathan Schwabish and Alice Feng describe how they applied a racial equity lens to revise the Urban Institute's Data Visualization Style Guide.[13] Schwabish and Feng recommend ordering group labels to focus on the data story, rather than

---

10 David Spiegelhalter, *The Art of Statistics: Learning from Data* (Penguin UK, 2019), pp. 22–5

11 Julia Angwin et al., "Machine Bias" (ProPublica, May 23, 2016), *https://oreil.ly/3Q6Em*.

12 Neil Vigdor, "Apple Card Investigated After Gender Discrimination Complaints" (Published 2019), *The New York Times: Business*, November 10, 2019, *https://oreil.ly/gs5lb*.

13 Jonathan Schwabish and Alice Feng, "Applying Racial Equity Awareness in Data Visualization," preprint (Open Science Framework, August 27, 2020), *https://doi.org/10.31219/osf.io/x8tbw*. See also this web post summary of the paper, Jonathan Schwabish and Alice Feng, "Applying Racial Equity Awareness in Data Visualization" (Medium), accessed October 16, 2020, *https://oreil.ly/uMoi6*, and Urban Institute, "Urban Institute Data Visualization Style Guide," 2020, *https://oreil.ly/_GRS2*.

listing White and Men at the top by default. They also call on us to proactively acknowledge missing groups in our data by calling attention to those often omitted, such as nonbinary and transgender people, in US federal datasets, rather than ignoring their absence. Furthermore, when choosing color palettes to represent people in charts and maps, the authors remind us to avoid stereotypical colors and to avoid color-grouping Black, Latino, and Asian people as polar opposites of White people.

Schwabish and Feng offer several excellent recommendations to improve racial equity in data visualization, though some of their more provocative proposals are likely to generate more discussion and debate. For example, they contrast different ways to portray COVID-19 pandemic data (*https://oreil.ly/uMoi6*) and recommend that we stop placing disaggregated racial and ethnic data on the same chart because it promotes a "deficit-based perspective" that judges lower-performing groups by the standards of higher-performing ones, as shown in Figure 14-9.

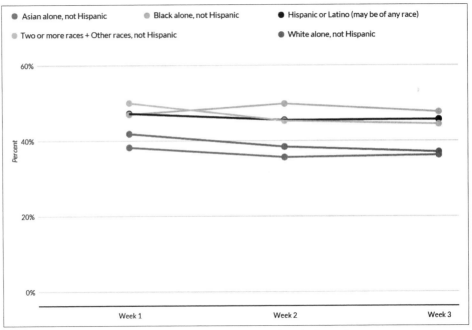

Figure 14-9. To avoid a deficit-based perspective, Schwabish and Feng argue against combining racial and ethnic data on the same chart. Image by Urban Institute (https://oreil.ly/uMoi6), reprinted with permission.

Instead, Schwabish and Feng suggest that we plot racial and ethnic data in separate but adjacent charts, each with its own reference to state or national averages and confidence intervals, as shown in Figure 14-10.

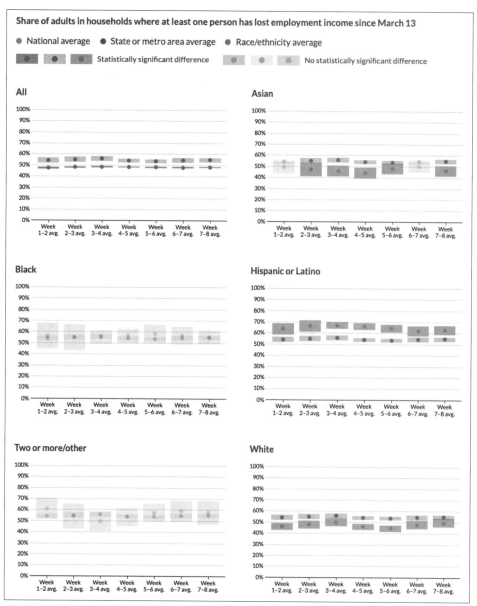

Figure 14-10. Schwabish and Feng recommend placing racial and ethnic data in separate charts, with state or national averages as a comparison point. Image by Urban Institute (https://oreil.ly/uMoi6), reprinted with permission.

Comparing both sets of charts lead us to wonder about the broad question: whose interests are best served by data visualizations? On one hand, if dominant groups use racial disparities in charts to *blame the victim*, then it makes sense to stop feeding racist stereotypes of group behavior and cease comparing different groups on the same chart. On the other hand, if racial disparities are caused by *structural obstacles* to quality jobs, housing, and healthcare, then do separate six-panel visualizations make it harder for readers to recognize and challenge the roots of systemic racism? Schwabish and Feng raise an important perspective, but do not persuade us that separating racial and ethnic data necessarily promotes equity and justice. Nevertheless, we agree on the need to continually reflect on and reduce bias in data visualization, while also considering the broader context around how people in our unjust world interpret our charts and maps, to strengthen our continuing search for better ways to tell true and meaningful data stories.

All of us who create data visualizations should strive to recognize and reduce these general categories of data bias: sampling, cognitive, algorithmic, and intergroup. In the next section, we'll focus on different types of spatial bias that are particular to working with map data.

Recognize and Reduce Spatial Bias

In addition to recognizing and reducing data biases in general, we also need to watch out for spatial biases that negatively influence how we create and interpret maps. In this section, we'll identify four types of spatial biases: map area, projection, disputed territory, and exclusion. We'll also suggest specific ways to try to counter these biases when creating visualizations.

Map area bias refers to the tendency for our eyes to focus primarily on larger regions on a map and less on smaller ones. A classic example arises every four years with choropleth maps of US presidential elections, which draw our attention to the geographic area of US states rather than their population or number of electoral votes, as shown in Figure 14-11. Conventional maps exaggerate the political influence of rural states with larger geographic areas (such as spacious Wyoming with less than 600,000 people) and diminish the role of urban states with small areas (such as tiny Rhode Island with more than 1,000,000 people). Although Wyoming covers 80 times more area than Rhode Island, it casts only three electoral votes in US presidential races, while Rhode Island has four electoral votes. But when looking at conventional maps, most readers cannot easily make this distinction because our eyes are drawn to states with larger geographic areas, not population.

Projection bias is a related issue about how maps portray geographic areas. Over time, mapmakers have developed different projection systems to display a three-dimensional globe on a two-dimensional surface. Mercator, one of the most common projection systems, inflates the size of many European and North American countries and diminishes the relative size (and importance) of Central African and Central American countries that lie closer to the equator. See the Engaging Data site (*https://oreil.ly/9Dhrm*) and How Map Projections Lie by Maps Mania (*https://oreil.ly/7JoL6*)

for interactive visualizations about Mercator projection map bias and comparisons to other systems. As Google maps and similar online services grew in popularity over the past 15 years, their default projection system, known as Web Mercator (*https:// oreil.ly/ikEBh*), became ubiquitous on the web, further cementing distorted geography in our minds. (In 2018, Google Maps allowed desktop users who zoomed out to enable its 3D Globe view instead of Web Mercator, but this may not be the default setting and may need to be switched on.)

One way to address both map area and projection bias in national or global maps is to replace conventional map outlines with *cartograms*, which are also called hexagon maps or population squares on some platforms. Cartograms display the size of geographic regions by their relative importance, which in this case is population, but it could also be based on the size of the economy or other factors, depending on the data story. One advantage is that cartograms can focus our attention more evenly on the most relevant aspect of our data story, such as electoral votes, as shown in Figure 14-11. One drawback is that cartograms require readers to recognize abstract shapes in place of familiar boundaries, since these population-based visualizations do not align perfectly with conventional Mercator geography-based land maps. See also Lisa Charlotte Rost's post in Datawrapper Academy on how to visualize US elections results (*https://oreil.ly/5hFYO*).

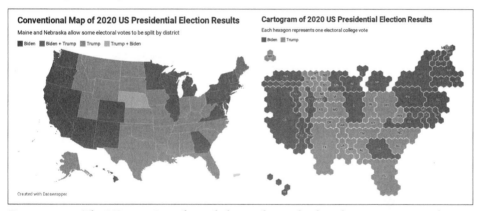

Figure 14-11. The US 2020 Presidential electoral vote displayed in a conventional US map (left) versus a cartogram (right), both created with Datawrapper.

 To re-create the cartogram map in Figure 14-11 in Datawrapper, select the file named USA > "Electoral College (hexagon)" because it allows users to split up electoral votes by district in Maine and Nebraska.

In "How to Lie with Maps" on page 382, we created choropleth maps of world inequality data in Datawrapper. To convert one from a conventional world map to a population square map, go to My Charts and select and right-click the map to make a duplicate. (You may instead choose to create a new map, in which case, follow the steps in the previous section.) Then go to the "Select your map" screen and type **squares** to see all of those available types (including world population squares). Similarly, type **hexagons** to see all of the cartograms available (including US states). Select your preferred map, and proceed to visualize the data in the same way as other Datawrapper choropleth maps, as shown in Figure 14-12.

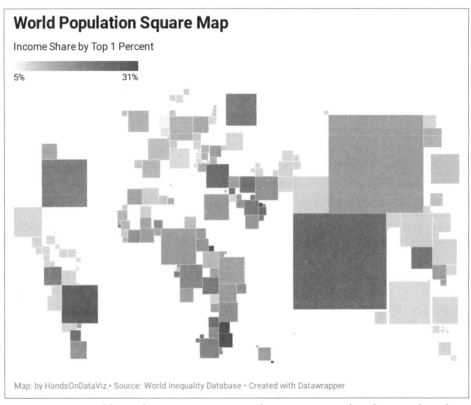

World Population Square Map

Income Share by Top 1 Percent

5%   31%

Map: by HandsOnDataViz • Source: World Inequality Database • Created with Datawrapper

Figure 14-12. World population square map with income inequality data: explore the interactive version (https://oreil.ly/o-TsA).

Disputed territory bias refers to how web map providers sometimes display different views of the world, depending on the location where you access them. For example, Russia sparked a geopolitical dispute when it forcibly seized the Crimean Peninsula away from Ukraine in 2014. Since Google desired to continue making profits in Russia, it created two versions of its border with Ukraine on its Google Maps platform. When viewed from a Russian IP address, Google Maps shows a solid-line border to signify that the territory is controlled by Russia. When viewed from anywhere else in the world, Google Maps shows a dotted-line border that represents a disputed territory. Although Google claims to "remain neutral on geopolitical disputes," according to the *Washington Post*, the corporation clearly took a side by displaying a solid border for Russian viewers.[14] Google and several other web map providers have taken similar actions regarding the contested border between India and Pakistan, the waterway between Iran and Saudi Arabia, and the sea between Japan and South Korea.

While ordinary people can recognize disputed territory bias in Google Maps and other proprietary services, it's difficult for us to directly challenge their decisions or pressure them to revise their basemaps. But we can draw on other strategies to reduce these biases. For example, contributors to OpenStreetMap, the crowdsourced global map, have actively discussed different approaches (*https://oreil.ly/uEllx*) to recognize disputed territories on their platform (*https://oreil.ly/OXyzs*). Furthermore, we can use data visualization tools to draw different boundaries on top of proprietary map layers. As one example, the Native Land map (*https://native-land.ca*), created by a nonprofit organization based in Canada, displays outlines of territories and languages of indigenous people on present-day maps to publicly remind us of colonialist policies and forcible displacement. One way to challenge the monolithic Google Maps platform is to create and publicize alternatives.

Map exclusion bias refers to ways that we fail to represent people or land through the act of omission. Sometimes these actions are taken by Google and other proprietary map providers, and sometimes we make them through our everyday decisions while creating maps. Take a close look at maps you recently made and ask yourself if they truly represent what their titles claim to show. For example, if you've created a US map with state-level data, how did you address the District of Columbia? The nation's capital is not counted as a state, nor does it have a voting representative in the US Congress. But DC has more than 700,000 residents (more than Wyoming or Vermont), and Amendment XXIII to the US Constitution grants it electoral votes as if it were a state (though it can never have more than the least populous state). Similarly, how did your US maps represent Puerto Rico, a territory with more than three million residents who are US citizens, but have no vote in Congress or for the Presidency? What about other US territories whose residents are also US citizens, such as American Samoa, Guam, the Northern Mariana Islands, and the US Virgin Islands? When data exists for these places, do your maps make them visible—or do they vanish? If the latter, then you need to consider if your act of omission is also a type of intergroup bias, given that the majority of residents in DC and these territories are Black, Latino, and Pacific Islanders.

---

14 Greg Bensinger, "Google Redraws the Borders on Maps Depending on Who's Looking," Washington Post, February 14, 2020, *https://oreil.ly/agLUY*.

To be clear, some data visualization tools make it very difficult to include people and places that have traditionally been excluded from our maps. But sometimes the problem lies within us, or the default settings of our tools and our decisions about whether to try to change them. Take another look at your favorite map tool and closely examine the geographic outlines that appear when you choose to map data for the "United States." If you feed in data that includes DC and US territories—but the map only displays the 50 recognized states—then this omission will erase the existence of four million US citizens from your map. Look beyond the default settings to determine if your tool offers more inclusive options. For example, Datawrapper recently improved how its *USA > States and Territories* map options display both symbol point and choropleth map data, as seen in Figure 14-13. For other regions that do not yet appear in Datawrapper's options, you can create and upload your own map boundary file in GeoJSON format, as described in "Geospatial Data and GeoJSON" on page 336. Or, if your tool forces you to omit part of your data story, then call out this bias by describing its absence in the map notes or the companion text. Our mission in data visualization is to tell true and meaningful stories, so include people and places that belong on the map, rather than ignoring their existence.

Figure 14-13. Datawrapper recently improved how it displays DC and noncontiguous places in its USA > States and Territories option for both symbol and choropleth maps.

Summary

In this chapter, you learned how to distinguish between wrong, misleading, and truthful visualizations, and strengthened your lie-detector skills to understand the importance of being honest when telling your own data stories. You also learned how to recognize ways to reduce four categories of data bias in general, and spatial bias in particular.

The next chapter will bring together all of the concepts from different parts of the book to emphasize the importance of storytelling in our data visualizations.

CHAPTER 15

Tell and Show Your Data Story

For our concluding chapter, we'll draw on knowledge and skills you've developed while reading this book and offer some final recommendations for creating true and meaningful data stories. Here we emphasize *storytelling*. The goal of data visualization is not simply to make pictures about numbers, but also to craft a truthful narrative that convinces readers how and why your interpretation matters.

Writers have a saying—"show, don't tell"—which means to let readers experience a story through the actions and feelings of its characters, rather than narration by the author. We take a different stance, as shown in our chapter title: *tell and show* your data story. Make a regular habit of these three steps: tell your audience what you found that's interesting in the data, show them the visual evidence to support your argument, and remind us why it matters. In three words: *tell, show, why.* Whatever you do, avoid the bad habit of showing lots of pictures and leaving it up to the audience to guess what it all means. We rely on you, the storyteller, to guide us on a journey through the data and highlight what aspects deserve our attention. Describe the forest, not every tree, but point out a few special trees as examples to help us understand how different parts of the forest stand out.

In this chapter, you'll learn how to build visualizations into the narrative of the storyboard that we started in Part I. You'll try out ways to draw attention to what's most meaningful in your data through text and color in "Draw Attention to Meaning" on page 402. You will also learn how to acknowledge sources and uncertainty in "Acknowledge Sources and Uncertainty" on page 405. Finally, we'll discuss decisions you'll need to make about the format of your data story, with continual emphasis on sharing interactive visualizations rather than static images in "Decide on Your Data Story Format" on page 406.[1]

Build a Narrative on a Storyboard

Let's return to the exercise from "Start Sketching Your Data Story" on page 1. We encouraged you to scribble words and sketch pictures on sheets of paper to lay out at least four initial elements of your story:

1. Identify the *problem* that motivates your project.
2. Reframe the problem into a researchable *question*.
3. Describe your plan to *find* data to answer the question.
4. Dream up one or more *visualizations* you might create using imaginary data.

Spread out these sheets like a *storyboard* to define the sequence of your narrative, as shown in Figure 15-1. Imagine them as preliminary slides for your presentation, or paragraphs and pictures for your written report or web page, for how you will explain the process to your audience. If you prefer to construct your storyboard digitally, another option is to convert blocks of text and images from your sheets into a Google Slides presentation (*https://oreil.ly/memZB*) or a draft Google Doc (*https://oreil.ly/V2amE*), or your preferred tools for telling the data story. Of course, it's perfectly normal to update the sheets you created at the beginning of your project to reflect changes in your thinking. For example, you may have refined your research question, found new sources during your search, and of course, turned your imagined visualizations into actual tables, charts, or maps with real data.

---

1 Our inspiration for this chapter is drawn from excellent books by visualization experts Cole Nussbaumer Knaflic and Alberto Cairo: Nussbaumer Knaflic, *Storytelling with Data: A Data Visualization Guide for Business Professionals*, (Hoboken, New Jersey: Wiley, 2015); Nussbaumer Knaflic, *Storytelling with Data: Let's Practice!* (John Wiley & Sons, 2019); Cairo, *The Truthful Art*, 2016; Cairo, *How Charts Lie*, 2019.

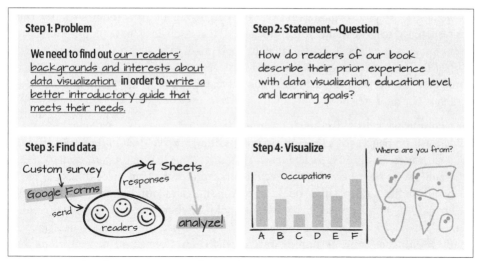

Figure 15-1. Sketch out your story idea on four pages: problem, question, find data, visualize.

Let's enrich your storyboard by adding content about what you discovered while searching, cleaning, analyzing, and visualizing your data. Select only your most meaningful tables, charts, or maps. Print them out on separate sheets of paper, or download static images or capture screenshots to place them in your draft slides or document (see "Static Image Versus Interactive iframe" on page 228). Leave room for you to write at the top and bottom of each table, chart, or map to tell your data story.

The next step is to *summarize* the most important message the data reveals, and write it as a one-sentence summary at the top of each page that contains a table, chart, or map. Verbalize what your eyes see as the most insightful finding for your most important visualizations. Become our guide, and focus our attention on the data forest, rather than individual trees. Two sentences are acceptable, but one succinct sentence is better. If your prose becomes too wordy, try writing the first sentence in "headline" style and the second as a more descriptive follow-up. Despite the old saying that a picture is worth a thousand words, data visualizations do *not* speak for themselves. Your job is to interpret their meaning for your audience. One of the best ways to translate charts or maps into words is to describe exactly what captures your eye as the designer and communicate this to your reader, who is seeing it for the first time and relying on your guidance. In every case, you need to decide on the ideal mix of words and images.

At the bottom of each visualization, tell us *why it matters*, and build up to how audiences should rethink or react. A good way to discuss the significance of your data story is to focus on how this new information *changes us*. When you discovered interesting patterns in your data visualization, how did it make you feel about the problem you (or your organization) were trying to solve? How did your answers to the research question make you think about the issue in a new or different way? Overall, does your data story inspire you or others to take action in some way? Once again, think about these questions from the perspective of your audience, and find words that capture how the data story should change our mindset, alter our habits, or influence our next steps.

For example, we started to sketch our own data storyboard in "Start Sketching Your Data Story" on page 1 to define our problem statement: *We need to find out our readers' backgrounds and interests about data visualization, to write a better introductory guide that meets their needs.* We collected data from more than three thousand readers of an earlier draft of this book who responded to our online survey (*https:// oreil.ly/GXTUT*) and agreed that we would publicly share the survey results (*https:// oreil.ly/SOuTl*), as we discussed in Chapter 2. We cleaned up the data as described in Chapter 4 because some responses were partially empty or contained locations that couldn't be accurately geocoded. Then we looked for meaningful comparisons, as described in Chapter 5, and visualized our most interesting results in two ways. We created a scatter chart in Chapter 6 and a point map in Chapter 7.

Now, we'll follow our own advice by writing short summaries at the top of each visualization, and explaining why it matters at the bottom.

What did we discover in our reader survey about the earlier draft of this book? How did we respond to the key data findings? First, more than 70% of readers who responded live outside of North America. Most notably, 35% reside in Asia, 20% in Europe, 6% each in Africa and South America, and 3% in Oceania, as shown in the left side of Figure 15-2. Our first draft of the book mostly included examples from Hartford, Connecticut, where we both worked. While we knew that our book had a global audience, we were surprised to see how many readers—among those who responded to the survey—live outside of the US. To be more inclusive and expand our international audience, we revised the book to add more sample charts and maps from other regions around the world.

Second, we learned that readers who responded to our survey have relatively high levels of education, but limited data visualization experience. In particular, 89% reported completing the equivalent of a college degree (16 or more years of schooling), and 64% of these rated themselves as data visualization beginners (either 1 or 2 on the 5-point experiential scale), as shown in the right side of Figure 15-2. In our earlier draft of the book, our primary audience was college undergraduates, and we were uncertain about the reading and background levels of other readers. Based on the survey responses, we revised the manuscript to add deeper concepts about data visualization, because we believe most of our readers can grasp them, yet we continue to write at an introductory level that assumes no prior knowledge beyond a secondary school or early college education. Now we can add these new sheets to our storyboard.

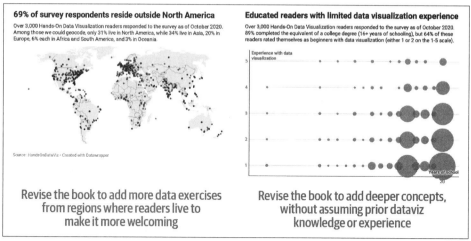

Figure 15-2. *Verbalize meaningful insights at the top of each visualization, and tell why it matters at the bottom, then insert them into your storyboard.*

Let's pivot back to your storyboard. Insert your new data visualization sheets (or slides, or blocks of text and images) into the pages you've already assembled. As you complete your work, your layout might look something like this:

- Problem statement
- Research question
- How you found data
- Tell first data insight—show evidence—why it matters
- Tell second data insight—show evidence—why it matters

…and so forth toward your summary conclusion.

As the storyteller, it's your job to organize your data narrative in a way that makes sense *to your audience*, who most likely will be viewing all of this content for the first time. While there's no one way to tell a story, consider this advice to avoid making rookie mistakes:

- Tell us the problem and question *before* you offer an answer because our brains expect to hear them in that order.
- Summarize each insight *before* you show us the supporting evidence because, once again, reversing the normal sequence makes it harder for us to follow your argument.

- Make sure that your research question and key insights are *aligned* with one another because your audience will be confused if you ask one question, but answer a different one. It's perfectly normal to tweak or fully revise the wording of your research question after you've dug deep into the data because sometimes you don't really know what you're looking for until you've discovered it.

Now you should have a clearer sense of how a storyboard helps you to bring together narrative and data. In the next section, you'll learn how to refine your visualizations by using text and color to draw attention to what is most important.

Draw Attention to Meaning

When finalizing your visualizations, add finishing touches to draw attention to the most meaningful aspects of the data. In addition to writing text to accompany your charts and maps, you can also add annotations and use colors *inside* some types of visualizations to point out what's most significant in your data story. Let's demonstrate how to use these features to transform your visualization in Datawrapper, a tool we first introduced in "Datawrapper Charts" on page 131.

One of the environmental challenges we face today is the ever-growing production of plastics. While these inexpensive and lightweight materials offer many quality-of-life benefits, we often deposit them in mismanaged waste streams that cause them to enter our rivers and oceans. To understand the growth of plastics, we consulted Our World In Data (*https://oreil.ly/Mjd-4*), and you can view the annual global production data from 1950-2015 in Google Sheets format (*https://oreil.ly/G7s85*).[2]

First, let's upload the data in a single-column format to Datawrapper. By default, the tool transforms this time-series data into a line chart, as shown in Figure 15-3, which shows how global plastic production has increased over time:

```
| year | plastics |
| 1950 |        2 |
| 1951 |        2 |
...
```

---

2 This example was inspired by the Datawrapper Academy article on pro tips (*https://oreil.ly/gR37W*).

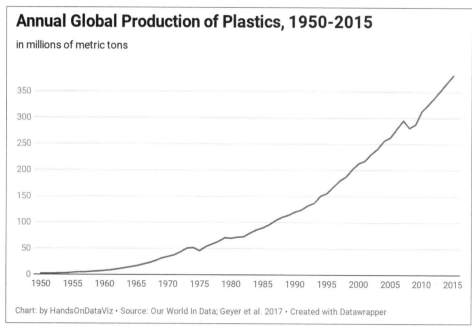

Annual Global Production of Plastics, 1950-2015

in millions of metric tons

Chart: by HandsOnDataViz • Source: Our World In Data; Geyer et al. 2017 • Created with Datawrapper

Figure 15-3. The default line chart for historical plastic production in Datawrapper.

Figure 15-3 does not yet focus on the bigger story: the total amount of plastics manufactured in global history. More than 60% of all of the plastics ever manufactured in
the world have been made since 2000, or the last 15 years of this chart, according to
our analysis of the data. Let's highlight this broader point by editing the chart and
building on skills you learned in prior chapters. First, divide the data into two columns, *before 2000* and *since 2000*, which allows you to apply different colors to each
data series. Insert the same data for year 2000 in both columns to make the new chart
look continuous:

```
| year | before 2000 | since 2000 |
| 1999 |         202 |            |
| 2000 |         213 |        213 |
| 2001 |             |        218 |
...
```

Second, change the chart type from the default *line chart* to an *area chart* to fill the
space under the curve to draw attention to the total amount of plastics manufactured
over time. Third, in the Refine tab, since you do *not* want a stacked area chart,
uncheck the *stack areas* box. Assign a dark blue color to draw more attention to the
post-2000 data series, and a gray color to diminish the appearance of the pre-2000
data series, as shown in Figure 15-4.

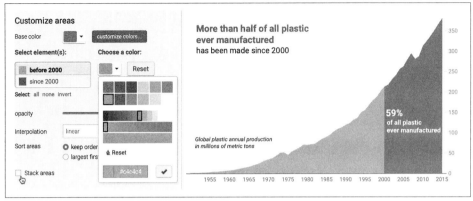

Figure 15-4. After dividing the data into two columns and switching to an area chart, uncheck the stacked areas box in the Refine tab.

Finally, hide the old title and replace it by adding annotations, as you learned in "Annotated Charts" on page 132. Place annotations inside the area chart, using colored text, to emphasize the new interpretation and place it where readers will look, as shown in Figure 15-5. Overall, redesigning your chart helps you communicate a more meaningful data story that global plastic production is increasing *and* our world has manufactured more than half of our historical total in just the past 15 years.

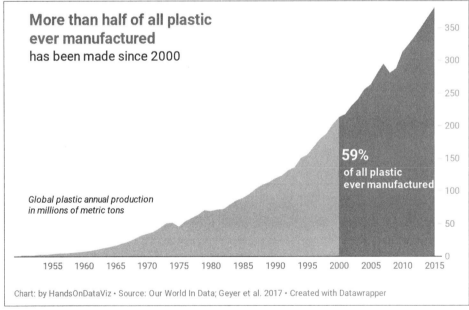

Figure 15-5. Explore the interactive version of the new area chart (https://oreil.ly/ 9YRSu), which uses color and annotations to draw attention to post-2000 global plastic production.

Now that you have a clearer idea about why and how to draw your audience's attention to the most meaningful aspects of your data story, we'll build on those skills in the next section about acknowledging sources and ambiguous data.

Acknowledge Sources and Uncertainty

Since our goal is to tell data stories that are meaningful and true, we also advise you to build credibility into your work, which you can do in several ways.

First, always represent data truthfully. Don't hide or obscure relevant evidence, and avoid visualization methods that might mislead your audience, as we discussed in Chapter 14 on detecting lies and reducing bias. We place our trust in you to fairly interpret the meaning of the data. Warn us if we're in danger of reading too much into the data or misinterpreting it by seeing something that isn't really there.

Second, credit and source your data origins, as we described in "Source Your Data" on page 59. Some of the visualization tools and templates featured in this book make it easy to display links to online sources, so use that feature whenever feasible. When it's not, write these important details into the text that accompanies your tables, charts, and maps. Also, let audiences know who created the visualization, and credit collaborators and other people who assisted in your work.

Third, save and show that your data works at different stages of the process. Save notes and copies of the data as you download, clean, or transform it; and document the important decisions you make along the way. One simple method is to save different versions of your data in separate spreadsheet tabs, as shown in Chapter 2. For more complex projects, consider sharing your data and documenting your methods in a public GitHub repository, as shown in Chapter 10. If someone questions your work, wants to replicate it, or if you need to refresh it with an updated dataset, you'll be grateful to have notes that allow you to trace it backward.

Finally, acknowledge the limitations of your data and disclose any uncertainty. Your work becomes more credible when you admit what you do *not* know, or that you are willing to consider alternative interpretations. Some of our recommended chart tools in Chapter 6 and chart code templates in Chapter 11 allow you to insert error bars to show the confidence level in the data, so use those when appropriate. Furthermore, the two-column method shown in the prior section also works to visually distinguish between observed versus project data with solid versus dashed lines, as shown in the Google Sheets Chart editor in Figure 15-6.

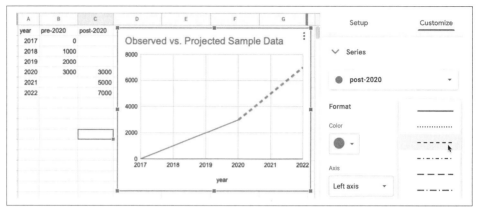

Figure 15-6. Split one data column into two columns to contrast observed data (solid line) versus projected data (dashed line).

Now that we've reviewed ways to build credibility in your work, let's move on to decisions you'll need to make about telling your data story in different formats.

Decide on Your Data Story Format

Most data visualization books and workshops presume that you will deliver your final product on a sheet of paper to people sitting around a board room, or perhaps in a PDF document sent via email or posted online. Those *static* formats are fine, but don't fully reflect the wide range of ways to share your story with broader audiences in the digital age. Moreover, as we write these words during the COVID-19 pandemic, when sitting around an indoor table is not an option, we need to find more creative formats to communicate our data stories.

Given that our book has emphasized the benefits of creating interactive visualizations, which invite audiences to engage with your data by floating their cursor over the charts and maps, we also encourage you to consider more interactive formats for your stories, such as:

- Websites that combine textual narrative and interactive visualizations using iframes

- Online presentation slides that link to live visualizations

- Video that combines live or voiceover narration with interactive visualization screencast

- A data walk format (*https://oreil.ly/zK0CR*), where community stakeholders move around and discuss connections between their lived experiences and the data stories

Of course, different storytelling methods require you to tailor content to fit the format. Furthermore, not every format requires interactive visualizations, nor are they always the most appropriate choice. While the details are beyond the scope of this book, we encourage you not to fall into traditional mindsets, but instead to think differently about ways to tell true and meaningful data stories.

Summary

This concluding chapter brought together broad concepts and pragmatic skills from the book to reinforce how data visualization is driven by truthful and meaningful *storytelling*. While we love to make pictures about numbers, our broader mission is to create narratives that convince our audiences how and why our data interpretations matter. You learned different strategies to achieve this goal, such as building storyboards, drawing attention to meaningful data with text and color, acknowledging sources and uncertainty, and thinking creatively about storytelling formats that fit our audiences.

We hope this book has helped you to better understand how to work with data and create better visualizations that tell true and meaningful stories. One of our goals is to introduce you to the wide array of free and powerful tools available to expand your knowledge and help you complete your data projects. If you found this book helpful, we'd be delighted to see data projects that you wish to share with us on social media. Feel free to share with us other introductory-level tools or methods that we didn't mention in this book.

Fix Common Problems

When creating data visualizations with online tools, public datasets, and code templates, it's not uncommon to encounter some occasional problems that prevent them from working as expected. We understand that finding the source of a problem can feel frustrating. But figuring out why it broke—and how to fix it—can be a great way to learn what's happening behind the scenes.

Reach out to others for advice on solving problems, and make it easier for them to help you. Clearly describe your issue, mention your computer operating system and/or browser version, and consider including a screenshot (*https://oreil.ly/FHe8L*) using these built-in commands:

Chromebook
Shift+Ctrl+F5 (the "show windows" button), then click and drag the crosshair cursor.

Mac
Shift-Command-4, then click and drag the crosshair cursor.

Windows
Windows logo key+Shift+S to call up the "Snip & Sketch" tool.

Review the following sections to diagnose the type of problem you're facing, and see our recommended solutions for the most common issues we've seen. Remember that some of the thorniest problems may be caused by two or more separate issues:

- "Tool or Platform Problems" on page 410
- "Try a Different Browser" on page 411
- "Diagnose with Developer Tools" on page 412
- "Mac or Chromebook Problems" on page 413

- "Watch Out for Bad Data" on page 414
- "Common iframe Errors" on page 415
- "Fix Your Code on GitHub" on page 417

Tool or Platform Problems

If you have a problem with one of our recommended digital tools, and have not found the answer in this book, go to the tool's support page (listed in alphabetical order):

- Airtable relational database support (*https://support.airtable.com*)
- Atom text editor documentation (*https://atom.io/docs*)
- Chart.js code library documentation (*https://www.chartjs.org*)
- Datawrapper Academy support (*https://academy.datawrapper.de*)
- GeoJson.io geodata editor (see the Help menu) (*https://geojson.io*)
- GitHub.com and GitHub Desktop documentation (*https://docs.github.com*)
- Google My Maps support (*https://support.google.com/mymaps*)
- Google Sheets support (*https://support.google.com/docs*)
- Highcharts code library (demo and support) (*https://www.highcharts.com*)
- Leaflet map code library (tutorials and documentation) (*https://leafletjs.com*)
- LibreOffice Calc support (*https://help.libreoffice.org*)
- Mapshaper geodata editor (documentation wiki) (*https://oreil.ly/ZVgcF*)
- Map Warper georectifier help (*https://mapwarper.net/help*) and see note about limited disk space (*https://mapwarper.net*)
- OpenRefine data cleaner (documentation) (*https://openrefine.org*)
- Tabula PDF table extractor (how to) (*https://tabula.technology*)
- Tableau Public resources page (*https://public.tableau.com/en-us/s/resources*)

Of course, if you encounter a problem when using an online tool or web platform, always check your internet connection. On rare occasions, online tools and platforms may be offline for all users. To clarify if an online service is down for everyone, and not just you, check for outage reports on sites such as:

- Downdetector.com (*https://downdetector.com*)
- Down for Everyone or Just Me? (*https://downforeveryoneorjustme.com*)

Also, some online services operate their own status pages:

- GitHub Status (*https://www.githubstatus.com*)
- Google Workspace Status (*https://www.google.com/appsstatus*)

Finally, note that rare outages by large providers, such as the problems Amazon Web Services faced in November 2020, can affect other online tool platforms.[1]

Try a Different Browser

Many problems we encounter with online tools and code templates turn out to be caused by our browser, not the tool or template itself. The *most important advice* we offer in this appendix is to *always try a different browser* to diagnose your problems. If you normally do all of your work in your favorite browser—such as Chrome, Firefox, Microsoft Edge, or Safari for Mac only—download a second browser for testing purposes. But please stop using the defunct Internet Explorer or Edge Legacy browsers, since Microsoft announced in 2020 (*https://oreil.ly/xSgsa*) that neither will be supported in the future.

In fact, you should *always* test your data visualization products in a second browser, where you are *not* logged in to an online account for the tool or service that created it, to check how it appears to regular users. On our computers, we installed a second browser, specifically for testing, and changed the settings to *Never Remember browsing history* so that it acts like a first-time user whenever we open it.

If you encounter any issues when using your favorite browser with digital tools or web services, give it a "hard refresh" to bypass any saved content in your cache (*https://oreil.ly/6WQZY*) and re-download the entire web page from the server, using one of these key combinations:

Windows or Linux browsers
    Ctrl+F5

Chromebook
    Shift+Ctrl+R

Chrome or Firefox for Mac
    Command-Shift-R

Safari for Mac
    Option-Command-R

---

1 Jay Green, "Amazon Web Services outage hobbles businesses," *The Washington Post*, Business, November 25, 2020. *https://oreil.ly/PTmQ6*.

Diagnose with Developer Tools

We recommend learning how to use your browser to diagnose other types of issues, such as those discussed in "Common iframe Errors" on page 415 and "Fix Your Code on GitHub" on page 417. Most browsers contain *developer tools* that allow you to view the source code of a web page and spot any errors that it flags. Even if you're not a software developer, learning how to open your browser's developer tools allows you to peek under the hood and make a more informed guess about what's not working. To open developer tools in various browsers:

- In Chrome, go to View > Developer > Developer Tools.
- In Firefox, go to Tools > Web Developer > Toggle Tools.
- In Microsoft Edge, go to "Settings and more (...)" icon > More Tools > Developer Tools.
- In Safari for Mac, first go to Safari > Preferences > Advanced > "Show Develop menu in menu bar," then go to Develop > Show JavaScript Console.

When you open the browser's developer tools, it displays a *console* window that shows error messages that may help to diagnose problems, particularly with code templates. For example, in "Copy, Edit, and Host a Simple Leaflet Map Template" on page 247, you learned how to edit the simple Leaflet map template in GitHub. If you accidentally make a mistake, such as deleting the comma between the latitude and longitude coordinates for map center, your code will "break" and display an empty gray box in your screen. If you turn on the browser developer tools, as shown in Figure A-1, the console will display several errors, including one that points you to a problem beginning in the *index.html* file on line 29. While the error does not specifically state that a comma is missing in line 30, it's still the best clue to alert you to a problem in that vicinity of the code. This is just one way to use the developer tools, so why not explore other features and how they differ across browsers?

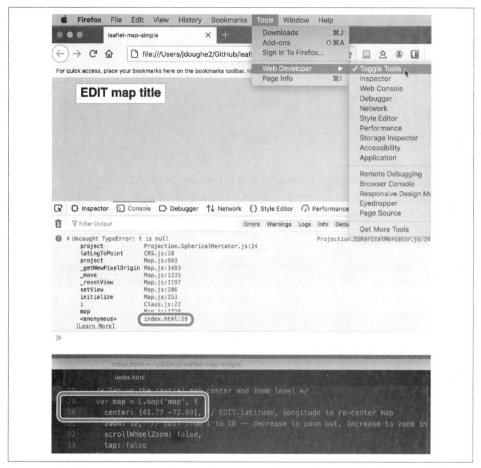

Figure A-1. When you open a browser's developer tools, the console window will display errors it flags in the web page's code. In this example, a "broken" map appears as a gray box (top), and the console shows an error in line 29 of the index.html file (middle), which offers a clue about a missing comma between the latitude and longitude coordinates in line 30 (bottom).

Mac or Chromebook Problems

If you are using a Mac, make sure your settings make visible the filename extensions, meaning the abbreviated file format that appears after the period at the end of a filename, such as *data.csv* or *map.geojson*. The Mac operating system hides these extensions by default, and several tools in this book will not work properly if they're not visible. Make them visible on a Mac by going to Finder > Preferences > Advanced, and check the box to "Show all filename extensions":

If you're using a Chromebook, beware that it may be difficult or impossible to install and run some of the recommended tools in this book. Tools that are *not* currently supported for Chromebook include most downloadable desktop applications, such as: Atom, GitHub Desktop, LibreOffice Calc, OpenRefine data cleaner, Tableau Public, and Tabula PDF table extractor. But Chromebooks can still operate most of the tools that run through the Chrome browser, such as: Google Sheets, Google My Maps, Datawrapper, the GitHub.com web interface, and several others. Also, if you wish to edit code templates on a Chromebook, see the open source Caret text editor for Chrome (*https://oreil.ly/CNhwB*) by Thomas Wilburn.

Watch Out for Bad Data

Sometimes a problem with a data visualization tool or service is caused by bad data. Revisit "Recognize Bad Data" on page 61 and different ways to clean data in Chapter 4. In addition, avoid common mistakes that will introduce errors into your data files, especially when working with Chart.js and Highcharts code templates in Chapter 11 and Leaflet map code templates in Chapter 12.

First, avoid typing blank spaces into spreadsheet entries—especially column headers. Although blank spaces may seem innocent, they may confuse digital tools and code templates that expect to find column headers spelled precisely as promised, without extra spaces:

	A	B	C
1	name	pop2019	land-area-sq-mi
2	Alabama	48*8979	50645
3	Alaska	728422	570641

Second, avoid blank rows in data files. For example, when using code templates such as Leaflet Maps with Google Sheets or Leaflet Storymaps with Google Sheets, your online map will break if you leave a blank row in the Google Sheets:

	A	B	C	D	E
	Group	**Marker Icon**	**Marker Color**	**Icon Color**	**Custom Size**
1					
2	Visit	media/calais-64.jpg			40x40
3	Food	fa-ice-cream	green	white	
4					
5	Visit	media/ecg-logo-64.png			40x40
6	Food	fa-coffee	green	white	
7	Visit	media/keywest-64.jpg			40x40

On a related note, in both of the Leaflet code templates described previously, media file pathnames are case-sensitive. In other words, *media/filename.jpg* is not the same as *media/filename.JPG*. Therefore, we recommend using *all lowercase characters*, including the extensions.

Finally, when working with Leaflet code templates that call GeoJSON data files, as described in Chapter 12, watch out for null (empty) field errors in your geodata. In the browser console diagnostic window described in the previous section, these may show a NaN (meaning "not a number") error message similar to this:

```
Uncaught Error: Invalid LatLng object: (NaN, NaN)
```

To resolve a NaN error in the browser console, use the GeoJson.io tool in "Draw and Edit with GeoJson.io" on page 341 to closely inspect your geodata for null fields.

Common iframe Errors

If you followed the steps in Chapter 9, but the contents of your iframe still don't appear in your browser, check for these common problems:

- Items listed in your iframe (such as the URL, width, or height) should be enclosed inside straight single quotes (') or double quotation marks ("). Choose either type, but be consistent.

- Always use *straight* quote marks, and avoid entering *curly quotes* (aka smart quotes or slanted quotes). This sometimes happens accidentally when pasting code from a word processor. Avoid curly quotes such as the opening single quote ('), the closing single quote ('), the opening double quote ("), and the closing double quote (").

- Always use `https` (the extra "s" means "secure"), not `http` in iframes. Some web browsers will block content if it mixes *https* and *http* resources. All of the code templates in this book require *https*.

Use the W3Schools TryIt iframe page (*https://oreil.ly/5T1hg*) to test your iframe embed codes, especially when you need to edit them, since it's a great way to check for mistaken punctuation. Figure A-2 shows three common problems in a simple iframe: a curly double quote (after `src=`), use of `http` instead of `https`, and mixture of double quotes and single quotes. All of these problems are corrected in Figure A-3, which causes the iframe to appear as expected.

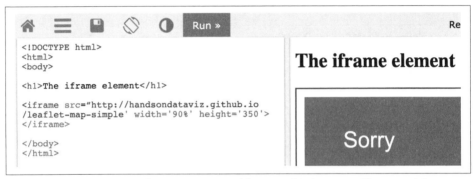

Figure A-2. Can you spot three common problems in this incorrect iframe code?

Figure A-3. All three problems are corrected here, which causes the iframe to appear as expected.

Fix Your Code on GitHub

As we discussed in Chapter 10, working with open source code templates gives you more control over how your data visualization appears and where it's hosted online. It also means that when your code breaks, you're responsible for fixing it or finding a qualified person to help you fix it, perhaps for a fee. If you encounter problems with fixing your code or hosting it on the free GitHub platform, review the relevant chapter(s) in this book and watch out for the following common problems:

- Be careful when editing your code. A single typo—such as a missing comma, semicolon, quotation mark, or parenthesis—can break your visualization. We understand how frustrated you may feel when this happens because it's also happened to us, so take a short break and come back to your screen a bit later, with fresh eyes to help you find the problem.

- Be patient. GitHub Pages normally will process edits to your visualization within 30 seconds, but sometimes it may require several minutes. Give your browser a "hard refresh" to bypass any saved content in your cache (*https://oreil.ly/ 6WQZY*) and re-download the entire web page from the server, using one of the following key combinations:

  — Ctrl+F5 (most Windows or Linux browsers)

  — Shift+Ctrl+R (Chromebook)

  — Command-Shift-R (Chrome or Firefox for Mac)

  — Option-Command-R (Safari for Mac)

- Always test the link to your published visualization in a *different* browser. Sometimes problems are actually caused by a glitch in the browser, not the code itself.

- On occasion, the GitHub platform may experience an outage or report known problems with building GitHub Pages from your code. Check the GitHub Status site (*https://status.github.com*).

When working with Chart.js and Highcharts code templates in Chapter 11 and Leaflet map code templates in Chapter 12, be cautious about making edits, especially to the structure of the data file. For example, in the Leaflet Maps with Google Sheets code template, don't change the names at the top of each column unless you know what you're doing, because the code template looks for these exact names to process your data:

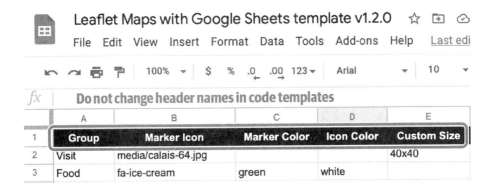

Remember that you can edit and test code templates more efficiently on your *local* computer, rather than upload every change to view on GitHub online. Use the GitHub Desktop and Atom tools as described in "GitHub Desktop and Atom Text Editor to Code Efficiently" on page 261. To fully view more complex Chart.js, Highcharts, or Leaflet code templates on your *local* computer, you may need to temporarily manage your CORS internet security settings in your browser, as shown in Figures 10-2 and 10-3.

Over time, code templates require maintenance to ensure that they will continue to work as technology evolves. For example, the code templates featured in this book all have *code dependencies*, which means they rely on other code or online services to operate. These dependencies include online code libraries that create charts and maps, such as Chart.js, Highcharts, Leaflet, and others. Also, map code templates depend on online map tiles from providers such as CARTO, Stamen, and OpenStreetMap. *If one of your online code dependencies is no longer operating*, your code template will probably stop working.

To check if your code template has an issue with one of its online code dependencies, go back to the original GitHub repository where you made your copy. Check to see if the current online demo chart or map is properly functioning. If yes, then check to see if the original GitHub repo has had recent code updates that may solve your problem. Some code updates are simple and can be typed directly into your repo through the GitHub web interface. Other code updates are more complex, so review how to pull code from a repo to your local computer using tools such as GitHub Desktop in "GitHub Desktop and Atom Text Editor to Code Efficiently" on page 261.

If the original GitHub repo from which you copied the code template has a non-functional online demo version, contact the open source software developer; the best way to do this is to create an *Issue* on their GitHub repository. There's no guarantee that open source software developers will continue to maintain their code project into the future. But one benefit of open source code is that anyone can create a new fork copy and maintain it themselves, or with collaborators in the open source coding community.

Finally, if you didn't find the answer to your problem here, consider other places to pose your question. Some of our recommended tools support pages include links to community help forums, where users can post questions and sometimes receive helpful answers from other users. Also, the Stack Exchange network (*https://stackex change.com*) brings together over 170 online communities where experts answer questions on specific topics, such as Web Applications Stack Exchange (*https://webapps.stackexchange.com*) for online tools such as Google Sheets and Stack Overflow (*https://stackoverflow.com*) for software coding. When posting a question on any of these public forums, be sure to follow their guidelines, clearly describe your problem, and mention the type of computer operating system and/or browser version you're using.

Index

excluding people or land from maps, 395

Decennial Census, 58
FIPS codes, 194
Geocoder for bulk geocoding, 361
    documentation link, 363
interactive historical map of racial change,
    65
levels of data available, 49
nonresponse bias, 94
race and ethnicity category shifts, 65
removing town label after place names, 69
site for accessing data, 58
US Cities population change, 186
US Census Geocoder for bulk geocoding, 361
    documentation link, 363
US Federal Election Commission database, 55
US Federal Reserve open data repository, 371
US government Data.gov, 58
US maps and excluded peoples, 395
US National Aeronautics and Space Adminis-
    tration (NASA) link, 373
US Overseas Loans and Grants dataset cleanup,
    79-86
University of Rochester Open Data listings, 59
uploading files as Google Sheets files, 21
Urban Institute Data Visualization Guide, 389

V

variables
    bubble charts for three variables, 287
        more than three variables, 288
    confounding, 90
    correlations between, 89
    independent and dependent, 89
        table design, 217
    maps
        one variable, not two, 164
        two variable solutions, 164
vector data
    basemaps, 161
    GeoJSON format, 337, 340
        (see also GeoJSON)
    geospatial data, 336
    OpenStreetMap data, 336
    points, polylines, polygons, 162
visualizations (see data visualizations)
    truthfulness categories, 369
        (see also truth)

visually impaired readers, 8
VLOOKUP function in spreadsheets, 38
    CSV joined with map polygon data, 356

W

W3Schools site
    HTML tags and syntax, 302
    semitransparent colors, 288
    TryIt iframe page, 231, 416
    web color codes and names, 301
Waters, Tim, 360
web embedding (see embedding in web page)
web hosting, 251
    (see also GitHub)
Web Mercator projection, 350
    projection bias, 393
web page–based tables, tool to create, 225
Weebly site embedding, 241
West, Jevin D., 94
Wheelan, Charles, 87
Wilburn, Thomas, 414
Williams, Serena, 52
Wix site embedding, 241
WordPress site embedding, 238-241
World Bank Open Data, 59
    life expectancy table with sparklines,
        218-225
World Inequality Database, 59, 383

X

xlsx data format, 17

Y

Yau, Nathan, 370

Z

z-scores, 93
zero-baseline rule for charts, 106
    exaggerating change in charts, 372
    line charts, 106, 374
Zillow research data, 166
    Zillow Home Value Index, 191
zip codes as plain text, 75
zoom controls on interactive maps, 162
Zuboff, Shoshana, 53

About the Authors

Jack Dougherty is a professor of educational studies at Trinity College in Hartford, Connecticut. He teaches a data visualization course where students partner with community organizations to help them tell their stories online with interactive charts and maps. Trained as a historian, Jack learned data visualization to share evidence more widely about cities, suburbs, and schools over time for his *On The Line* (*https://ontheline.trincoll.edu*) book. Visit his website (*https://jackdougherty.org*) or follow him on Twitter (*https://twitter.com/doughertyjack*).

Ilya Ilyankou is a civic technologist at the Connecticut Data Collaborative, where he creates web-based tools to explain and explore public data. At Trinity College he completed his bachelor's degree with a double major in computer science and studio arts, and is currently pursuing a master's degree in geographical information science (GIS) at the University of Leeds (UK). Ilya also heads Picturedigits (*https://picturedigits.com*), a design and technology lab that assists clients in analyzing and visualizing data. Follow him on Twitter (*https://twitter.com/ilyankou*) or on GitHub (*https://github.com/ilyankou*).

Colophon

The bird on the cover of *Hands-On Data Visualization* is a hoatzin (*Ophisthocomus hoazin*), and if you thought it looked simultaneously chicken-, hawk-, and cuckoo-like, you're in good company. Researchers have struggled to map the hoatzin's taxonomy, recently giving it its own order, *Ophisthocomus*, acknowledging that it is fairly unique. These birds are found in the Amazon River basin, where they have probably been for more than 20 million years.

Hoatzins have bright blue faces, red eyes, stubby bills, and unkempt orange crests on their disproportionately small heads. These birds grow to about 25 inches long and weigh about 2 pounds. As chicks, hoatzins retain a vestige of the dinosaurs: clawed wings. The claws disappear by adulthood, when they no longer need to climb back up to a nest if they fall out. Hoatzins eat only leaves, which necessitates an unusual digestive tract for a bird. Like cows, hoatzins have multichambered stomachs and burp as their meals break down, earning them the nickname "stinkbird."

Despite its other-wordly appearance, the hoatzin species is still with us today. The population is in decline, but not yet designated threatened. Many of the animals on O'Reilly's covers are endangered; all of them are important to the world.

The cover illustration is by Karen Montgomery, based on a black and white engraving from *Cassell's Natural History*. The cover fonts are Gilroy Semibold and Guardian Sans. The text font is Adobe Minion Pro; the heading font is Adobe Myriad Condensed; and the code font is Dalton Maag's Ubuntu Mono.

O'REILLY®

There's much more where this came from.

Experience books, videos, live online training courses, and more from O'Reilly and our 200+ partners—all in one place.

Learn more at oreilly.com/online-learning